THE SHAMEFUL PEACE

THE
SHAMEFUL
PEACE

HOW FRENCH ARTISTS AND INTELLECTUALS
SURVIVED THE NAZI OCCUPATION

FREDERIC SPOTTS

YALE UNIVERSITY PRESS
NEW HAVEN AND LONDON

For information about this and other Yale University Press publications, please contact:
U.S. Office: sales.press@yale.edu   www.yalebooks.com
Europe Office: sales@yaleup.co.uk   www.yaleup.co.uk

Set in Minion by IDSUK (DataConnection) Ltd.
Printed in Great Britain by TJ International Ltd, Padstow, Cornwall.

Library of Congress Cataloging-in-Publication Data

Spotts, Frederic.
    The shameful peace: how French artists and intellectuals survived the Nazi
occupation/Frederic Spotts.
        p. cm.
    Includes bibliographical references and index.
    ISBN 978–0–300–13290–8 (cloth: alk. paper)
    1.   France—History—German occupation, 1940–1945. 2.   France—Intellectual
life—20th century. 3.   War and civilization—France—History—20th century.
4.   World War, 1939–1945—Art and the war. 5.   World War, 1939–1945—Literature
and the war.   I. Title.
    DC397.S7 2008
    940.53'1—dc22
                                                                                    2008027968
A catalogue record for this book is available from the British Library.
10 9 8 7 6 5 4 3 2 1

But these are deeds which should not pass away,
  And names that must not wither, though the earth
Forgets her empires with a just decay,
  The enslavers and the enslaved, their death and birth. . . .

Byron, *Childe Harold's Pilgrimage*

CONTENTS

CHAPTER 1

THE JUDGEMENT OF PARIS

In Agatha Christie's 1933 mystery, *Lord Edgware Dies*, the murderer inadvertently unmasks herself at a smart luncheon party by commenting on another guest's reference to the Judgement of Paris. 'Paris? Why, Paris doesn't cut any ice nowadays,' she exclaimed. 'It's London and New York that count.' It was a painful moment. Around the table frowns were frowned and gasps were gasped. The hostess began to talk violently about Russian opera; the Duke of Merton's lips were tightly drawn.

In thinking of Paris as a place rather than a mythical person – confusing the Parisian avant-garde with the Greek epic – the culprit had exposed herself as a philistine impostor. Even her misunderstanding was based on a misapprehension. Paris in the Thirties continued to be, as it had been for a century or more, the centre of Western art and culture. Within a few years, however, her remark could have been regarded as apt and her cover would not have been blown.

That is to say, the French military debacle in 1940 marked a decisive moment in cultural history. In the wake of the German triumph, artistic life lay shattered. By the end of the decade several centuries of French ascendance in European culture had been broken and with it several millennia of European domination of Western culture. Not that modern French culture was richer than its German or British counterparts. But Berlin and Vienna were German, London was English. Paris was international. Artists from everywhere in the world looked on it as a talisman that could transform their dreams into reality. Given France's historic role, what happened to artists and the arts is therefore an essential part both of the history of the Occupation and, it is not too dramatic to claim, of Western civilization in the twentieth century.

The defeat and Occupation still remain, after all these years, a controversial and embarrassing topic in France. 'The shameful peace', Jean Cocteau called it. That is why, even more than the Germans, the French have found it difficult in the aftermath of the war to sort out what had happened to them and why. The 'dark years', as they came to be known, long lay buried in an unmarked grave. French history somehow skipped from 1939 to 1945. Beginning around the end of the 1960s, however, the collective denial gradually dissipated. By the end of the century those years are said to have become the most thoroughly investigated period of French history. Even so, the Occupation yielded its secrets only slowly and partially. The story remains complex and confusing, without a satisfying conclusion. Biography is still sanitized; history continues to be rewritten; silence prevails over candour. 'The true France was not at Vichy, the true France never collaborated.' So spake President Sarkozy as late as May 2008, on the anniversary of the end of the Second World War. But though the myths continue to be officially perpetuated, everyone in France knows they are false. Consequently there remains what de Gaulle once referred to as 'a dull pain in the depths of our national consciousness'.

For all that has been written about the subject, for all the continuing unease and for all the importance of the issues involved, if you want to know how artists and intellectuals survived, worked and adapted, or if you want to have some idea of what cultural life was like and what policies were followed by German and Vichy authorities, you will have difficulty finding answers. Diaries, memoirs and biographies of cultural figures abound. There are detailed studies about one or another of the arts. But amid all the vast bibliography of those years, there is no single book offering some idea of what daily life was like for individuals across the range of arts and letters.

Culture makes academic historians nervous. They like to deal with documents and quantifiable data. They think of the arts as entertainment, not as a quintessential part of the fabric of a nation, central to its sense of identity. 'Great nations write their autobiographies in three manuscripts,' Ruskin observed, 'the book of their deeds, the book of their words and the book of their art.' Most scholars study the first – the seemingly more macho topics of politics and economics. In the 766 pages of his 1954 *Histoire de Vichy*, the first comprehensive treatment of the Occupation, Robert Aron devoted at most three hundred words to cultural matters. Nearly forty years later there appeared *Le Régime de Vichy et les Français*, edited by Jean-Pierre Azéma and François Bédarida, comprising papers delivered at a colloquium of seventy-two scholars. In the course of this tome's 788 pages is to be found nary a word about artistic life and not so much as a passing reference to a single cultural figure. To be sure, Philippe Burrin and Julian Jackson address the topic – incisively but briefly – in their histories of the Occupation. But that's it.

This gaping omission betrays a blindness to several cardinal truths about the Occupation. Paramount among these is that the French nation's greatest psychological need in the wake of the ignominious debacle was to regain a sense of self-respect – the very *honneur* and *gloire* that de Gaulle invoked in his broadcasts from London – and that the French cultural heritage was all there was to provide it. 'France was not defeated on the artistic front', Louis Hautecoeur, head of the Beaux-Arts, declared in that desperate summer of 1940. 'Our architecture, our painting, our sculpture, our music continue to arouse admiration.' Pep-talk language, no doubt, but it points to the further truth that it was the arts – literature, theatre, film, art exhibitions, concerts, recitals and opera – more than anything else that helped the French to retain some sense of dignity and to get through the daily miseries of occupation. To ignore cultural life is also to overlook the fact that in the arts the French had a weapon – their only weapon – to continue the war. And fight on they did – however valiantly, however ridiculously at times – to protect their civilization from the Invader. Defending the cultural patrimony was, moreover, the one instance where Vichy adamantly resisted the Invader instead of collaborating.

Failure to understand the importance of culture in a nation's life was not a mistake Hitler made. Culture was not peripheral but central to his Occupation policy. In the arts he saw a narcotic to be used to pacify the French and make them amenable to collaboration while he was busy with his war in the Soviet Union. So he not only allowed but actively encouraged a rich artistic life. Indeed, he once boasted in a letter to Pétain that no victor in history had ever treated a defeated nation so leniently. But he had a further aim. Hitler's racial theories compelled him to assert German cultural supremacy over the French and in that way to challenge their self-confidence and to weaken their sense of national identity. Within a few months of the armistice he therefore launched a second blitzkrieg – this time artistic – with the intention of making Germany as supreme culturally as it was militarily.

In this larger struggle, individual cultural figures were almost bystanders. Living in their own world, artists are notorious for being so absorbed in their work that they can write, paint, sing, act or compose with a degree of indifference to external circumstances that ordinary mortals find difficult to understand. Picasso went on working in the face of unsettling visits by German military officers; Matisse ventured into a new phase of his work despite having German troops quartered in his villa in Vence; Utrillo painted one of his sunniest works in the summer of 1940; Messiaen composed his *Quartet for the End of Time* while captive in a prison camp in Silesia, and Milhaud his Second Quartet in July 1940 on board a boat in the mid-Atlantic. At the same time there were other artists who socialized with the Enemy and in some cases toured Germany as Hitler's guests as though unaware that the two countries were still at war. To what extent should artists and intellectuals be held politically responsible for their actions? This was the most controversial question facing the courts in the legal purge following the Liberation.

After the war the German ambassador in Paris during the Occupation made the astonishing claim that 'it would be extremely difficult to name any notable French artist who had not supported collaboration'. Collaboration. No other word in the Occupation vocabulary is so controversial or so ambiguous. Seen at the time as a matter of black and white, it was soon evident that there were various types, gradations and motivations and that collaboration with Vichy was quite different from collaboration with the Germans. In a much-quoted essay, Stanley Hoffmann drew the crucial distinction between those who collaborated involuntarily – administrators who stayed in their jobs to keep a town, factory or institution running – and those who did so voluntarily, either in a sincere belief in a united fascist Europe or out of sincere personal opportunism.

But in the case of cultural figures, what was collaboration? Was it accepting German hospitality to visit or perform in Germany, attending a reception hosted by a German official or even just seeking German approval to publish a book, perform a play or exhibit a painting? And what was resistance – fleeing the country, refusing to publish, to exhibit or to perform? Or was it just the opposite – staying to fling French culture into the face of the Occupier? Deciding how to react posed excruciating moral and political choices. Jean-Paul Sartre was blunt. 'Everything we did was equivocal. We never quite knew whether we were doing right or wrong. A subtle poison corrupted even our best actions.'

The behaviour of artists and intellectuals was a matter of considerable significance in a society where they enjoyed the prestige commanded today by sports heroes and pop stars. In the wake of the collapse in 1940 some of them were denounced by the collaborationist press as *fauteurs de défaite* – perpetrators of the defeat – and condemned more severely than the political or military leaders of the Third Republic. After the Liberation, certain others were the first, even before leading Vichy officials and German Occupation authorities, to be arrested and put on trial and in some cases executed. These trials, as Julian Jackson has noted, were as sensational as those of Pétain and Laval themselves. It is therefore perhaps not surprising that, as he further pointed out, they were punished more for who they were than for what they had done.

Who were they and what had they done? This book offers a glimpse into the life of a number of artistic and intellectual figures – villains, heroes and *attentistes* – who lived through those dark times. It might be objected that such a limited selection of examples gives a limited and disjointed picture of those years. Indeed it does, for the good reason that the Occupation was a disjointed affair, allowing few reliable generalizations. There were forty million French at the time and forty million stories of living through those years.

Before letting them speak for themselves, it is necessary to understand the extraordinary situation in which they lived – an entire population in a state of shock, a fragmented nation under an occupation directed from Berlin and a vague counter-revolution wafting from Vichy. During the first two years or so of the Occupation, collaborators – or *collabos* as they were derisively called by the French – looked to the future with hope of a new France in a united fascist Europe. Opponents lived in the very real fear that the Occupation would last a century. Then, after Stalingrad and the Allied landings in North Africa, those who had lived in hope now looked to the future with fear while the fearful saw reason to hope.

CHAPTER 2

GOOD-BYE TO ALL THAT

'I felt the German advance like a personal threat', Simone de Beauvoir wrote in her diary on 9 June 1940, two days after German forces breached the last French defences before Paris. 'I had only one thought, not to be caught like a rat in occupied Paris.' A friend suggested suicide as a way out, but she rejected it on the grounds that one did not do that sort of thing. But on hearing 'for certain' that the Germans would be in Paris in two days, she said she suffered a kind of nervous breakdown. 'It was for me the most frightful time of the war.' Although still somehow clinging to the bizarre rumour that American 'doughboys' were on their way back to France, she packed her suitcases and joined the mass flight at dawn the following day. On reaching the Loire valley that evening, she went into a hotel where the owner was euphorically proclaiming that the Russians and British had just landed in Hamburg. At a café the following morning, however, a woman sitting by a radio told her amid sobs that all was lost.

Literally millions of others shared de Beauvoir's desperation as panic swept through the population of northern France in the face of the German onslaught. Whole towns simply emptied themselves. Paris lost two-thirds of its population, including almost all its leading cultural figures. This was the famous 'exodus' in which as many as ten million people – fully one-quarter of the country's population – fled, creating a human flood in conditions of indescribable chaos and suffering. Recording what he saw from the air as a reconnaissance pilot, the writer Antoine de Saint-Exupéry said it appeared that a whole part of France was being smothered under a pall of smoke. 'Roads completely blocked, fires everywhere, supplies scattered helter-skelter, villages devastated, everything a shambles – a total shambles.' Everyone was running, but no one knew where to go. 'It looked as though a gigantic ant hill in the north had been kicked open and all the ants were running away.'

But no one described the chaos as vividly – and with as much masochistic relish – as the fascist cultural critic Lucien Rebatet in his 1942 bestseller, *Les Décombres* (The Debris).

Every aspect of this incredible panic was revealed in the fleeing cars which were filled, almost to the point of breaking their axles, with the most disparate collection of stuff, screaming females, males in shirt sleeves, dripping with sweat, eyes bulging, purple necks, reduced within an hour to the condition of Neolithic brutes, young virgins with their blouses completely open, mothers-in-law half-dead from shock and fatigue, little doggies in their own filth, piles of furs, quilts, boxes of jewellery, containers of camembert, fetish-dolls. . . .

So ran just a part of one sentence, the whole of which revealed both the horror of the scene and the author's pleasure in the suffering of others. Someone else also regarded the disaster with a joyous sang-froid. 'Curious by nature and, if I dare say so, by vocation, I was terribly happy to participate in an adventure that only occurs, I should imagine, every three or four centuries.' This was the comment of the novelist-physician Louis-Ferdinand Céline. He had commandeered an ambulance and, with his wife, his beloved cat Bébert, a stray grandmother and two newborn babes not his own, joined the fleeing millions on the same day as de Beauvoir.

The mass flight was one horror that no one had imagined beforehand. In the course of the 1930s there had been a growing fear that modern warfare would not be restricted to the battlefield – or, rather, that the battlefield would be everywhere. For a time le Tout-Paris – Everybody-Who-Is-Anybody-Socially-in-Paris – was terrified of a lethal gas attack. An impregnable armada of planes would swoop down and drown the population in a sea of poison gas, causing instant annihilation. But it was straightforward aerial bombing that came to be most dreaded, especially after the Luftwaffe in 1937 demolished the little Basque market town of Guernica – an act of destruction memorialized in one of the most celebrated art works of the century. The painter, like many others, was now convinced that cities would be prime targets in any conflict. 'Stop fooling yourself. Don't you know that there is a danger that German planes will fly over Paris tonight?' Picasso asked his close friend Jaime Sabartés on the eve of the war. So anxious was he that he fled in the middle of the night to Royan, a small port on the mid-Atlantic coast. His friend-rival Matisse happened to be in Paris and remained there. 'I'll just stay here like a demoralized dog, waiting for the blow to fall without budging,' he wrote to a friend.

Once war was declared on 3 September, however, Matisse decided to leave and eventually wandered back to his home in Nice. With his bad vision, James

Joyce found it almost impossible to get around in the blackouts, and since his wife, Nora, was frightened of being bombed, the Joyces decamped to a country village near Vichy and later went on to Switzerland. Gertrude Stein and Alice B. Toklas rushed to Bilignin near the Swiss border, taking along only two paintings from their large collection, Cézanne's portrait of his wife and Picasso's famous portrait of Stein. The artists Yves Tanguy, Man Ray and Piet Mondrian headed for New York while Jean Hélion returned from America to France to serve in the army. On a vastly larger scale, a portion of the population bordering on Germany was moved to the south of France. The whole of the University of Strasbourg, which had made contingency plans as early as 1934, was transferred to Clermont-Ferrand and the Polytechnic Academy to Toulouse. National Radio sent its entire instrumental and choral as well as its technical and administrative personnel, along with their families, to Brittany and installed them in Rennes.

But these migrations were exceptional. During the eight months of phoney war following Hitler's invasion of Poland, the vast majority of the French seemed afflicted with acute mental paralysis. So grievously had they suffered in the Great War, so exhausted were they afterwards, that going through another conflict was unthinkable. Anything, *anything* was felt to be better than a further bloodletting. The mood was articulated – trumpeted – by leading writers of the time, most of whom had been badly wounded on the front. 'What is the worst that can happen if Germany invades France?' novelist Jean Giono asked. 'Become German? For my part I prefer to be a living German to being a dead Frenchman.' And after all, as he said on another occasion, 'What is Hitler if not a poet in action?' Henri Jeanson, journalist-playwright, felt similarly about war. Both men paid for their views – which the government considered defeatist and disloyal – by being sent to jail. Pierre Drieu la Rochelle, Céline and Roger Martin du Gard, among others, wrote anti-war novels. Jean Giraudoux wrote anti-war plays. Jean Renoir produced his famous pacifist film *La Grande Illusion.*

And so in stark contrast to the burning German desire for revenge, the rampant pacifism in French artistic and intellectual circles had evolved during the interwar period into a desire to remain on friendly terms with Germany at any cost. Take, for instance, Giraudoux's highly successful 1928 play *Siegfried.* It was a great success precisely because its appeal for good relations between the two nations mirrored the widespread mood in French society. Far from altering this, Hitler's coming to power added to Germany's allure. Drieu, who had gone on a lecture tour of the country in 1932, was enticed to return the following year to witness the new Reich. In 1935 he went back again and this time was dazzled by the Nuremberg Party Rally. All too symptomatic of the mood on the eve of war was the chief character in Raymond Queneau's 1939 novel *Un Rude Hiver* (*A Hard Winter*), who seethed with despair at the thought of a democratic France run by Freemasons and Jews. The only solution appeared to him to be 'a German protectorate over France'.

The tragedy was that when the Weimar Republic became the Third Reich all too many French intellectuals were slow and sometimes unable to recognize that this was not simply a change of government but the transformation of a democratic Germany into a totalitarian Germany. The Nazis exploited this confusion to the hilt and equated criticism of the Third Reich with warmongering. It is not difficult to see how, in their hostility to Nazi Germany, Jews and other German refugees appeared to fit into this equation. Few there were when the conflict came in 1939 – whether intellectuals, politicians or men-on-the-street – who shared Paul Valéry's view that 'This is the most virtuous war we have ever been in'. The general public – partly pacifist, partly numb, partly confident in an army of three million men and an impregnable Maginot Line, but above all fatalistic – did its best to ignore a war that in fact scarcely seemed to be a war. 'Where's the war?' Camus asked in his *Carnets*.

Except for those living adjacent to Germany, life went on remarkably unchanged. Unlike in London, where places of entertainment were closed and trenches were dug in parks, in Paris theatres, concerts, cabarets, cinemas, horse races and restaurants carried on in their usual way. On the Left Bank the talk among the literati shifted from Drieu's controversial new novel, *Gilles*, to the likely winner of the most prestigious literary award, the Prix Goncourt. At the Café de Flore, de Beauvoir could be found whiling away the hours left over after teaching at her lycée. She read novels, wrote letters, studied Hegel at the Bibliothèque Nationale, occasionally went to the opera and regularly attended Charles Munch's concerts at the Conservatory. 'I feel relaxed and vague', she wrote at the time, perfectly summing up the popular mood. 'I am waiting, I don't know for what. They say everyone is waiting.'

She waited alone, since her lover, Jean-Paul Sartre, like all but the older cultural figures, was in uniform. Among writers, Saint-Exupéry was a pilot in air reconnaissance, André Malraux joined a tank unit, Sartre was in the weather service, Jean Anouilh was secretary to a commander, André Maurois served as a liaison officer with the British army, Louis Aragon was in a motorized division, Robert Brasillach was posted to a military headquarters near the front, André Breton worked in a medical unit. Logically enough, painters such as Jean Hélion were assigned to camouflage units while Henri Cartier-Bresson and Jean Renoir were in the army's film and photo service. Of the theatre and film world, Jean Gabin was in the navy, Fernandel was in the army in Marseille, Jean Marais went into the air force and Jean-Louis Barrault served in a camouflage unit. Like conscripts in every army, they waited numbly for something to happen.

Having plenty of time – if not enemies – to kill, these artist-soldiers read, wrote and boasted about women and booze. They also slept. One of de

Beauvoir's literary friends told her he was so bored he once slept for sixty hours straight. 'Even on the front line,' he told her, 'this war seems to be a phantom war, with not so much as the shadow of a German in sight.' Eventually boredom from inaction became so acute that Sartre noted in his *War Diaries*, 'If things go on this way, without any fighting, we will have a revolution and it will start with the army.' But France being France, the artists among them were allowed time off to pursue their art. The young, then unknown poet Pierre Seghers was given permission by his superiors to bring out a poetry review of his own inspiration to which Aragon was allowed time to contribute. Among actors, Gabin was given leave by the navy to finish a film. Hélion received permission to go to Paris to sell a painting to Peggy Guggenheim. On the Maginot Line a music-loving general organized a symphony orchestra.

Even the government's official propagandist found it difficult to take the war seriously, despite being hired by the government to convince the largely passive French people to do just that. It takes a crude huckster without intellectual integrity to manufacture effective propaganda. The last person suitable for the job is a playwright of sophisticated comedies, who also happens to be a gentle pacifist in favour of Franco-German cooperation. And it was the last person who got the job. Housed in a luxurious hotel, Jean Giraudoux took up his work as commissioner of information and filled his agency with has-beens from the military and diplomacy along with professors and journalists. Their chaotic operations were something out of Evelyn Waugh's comic wartime novel *Put Out More Flags*, which satirized similar goings-on across the Channel. Giraudoux and his team spent most of their time producing propaganda slogans to be pasted on walls around France – 'We will win because we are stronger', 'Time is working to our advantage' and similar inanities which were met with derision.

'If the 1914 war was Cubist, the 1939 war was Surrealist.' Perhaps nothing could have illustrated Vlaminck's aperçu more vividly than an event in Paris on 25 May. At the very moment the Belgian army was capitulating, Dunkirk was being encircled and mobs of refugees were fleeing south, in Paris music lovers were calmly filling the opera house to capacity for the premiere of Darius Milhaud's new work, *Médée*. 'The music struck me as quite lovely and the overall performance as remarkable', de Beauvoir blandly commented. 'For several hours I forgot the world.' Scarcely two weeks later German troops were marching down the Champs-Élysées.

The fall of Paris after a battle of only thirty-five days was one of the most shocking events of the Second World War. The City of Light – celebrated in songs, poetry, films, novels, plays and musicals, beloved of millions including millions who had never been there – incarnated not just France but modern

Western culture. To seize this precious object, to take it from its people, to subject it to harsh foreign rule, was worse than mere occupation. Not as terrible as the Sack of Rome in 411 or the Fall of Constantinople in 1453, perhaps, but the Wehrmacht's capture of Paris was an unspeakable profanation, a desecration, a sacrilege. *Un sentiment de viol* – a feeling of being raped – was a widespread reaction. With swastika flags everywhere, Wehrmacht soldiers marching around and *Bekanntmachungen* posted on the walls, there was not just a visible deprivation of independence, but also a stripping away of the very Frenchness of France.

And to deprive this city of its freedom was to destroy the most notable expression of that freedom – the arts. 'The laboratory of the twentieth century has been shut down.' That is how, in an often-quoted sentence, the New York art critic Harold Rosenberg mourned the fall of the city. 'Up to the day of the occupation, Paris had been the Holy Place of our time. The only one', he wrote in the *Partisan Review* that summer.

What was it about Paris? To some extent it was its unique French quality. Not just its parks and the Seine with its banks and bridges and the imposing buildings and vistas, but also its little shops and narrow streets, its cafés and bistros, its *bouquinistes*, its open-end buses and even its *pissoirs*. At the same time it was just the opposite. The grand paradox is that the Paris art world was not very Parisian, or even particularly French. That was why foreigners felt welcome there. For over a century artists from everywhere had come and encountered novel ideas, learned new ways of looking at the world, been inspired, excited and transformed. They found a place where painters and composers were esteemed, where poets and writers were admired. Twentieth-century Paris was to culture what nineteenth-century England had been to industry. Paris had fostered Impressionism and Post-Impressionism, Cubism, Fauvism and Symbolism as well as Dadaism, Futurism, Purism, Realism and Vorticism, not to mention Existentialism, Neo-Plasticism, Orphism, Pointillism, Simultanism, Surrealism and Transhylism. It enjoyed what seemed to be a predestined superiority, taking for granted that the best art was made in Paris and would go on being made there for evermore. An essential element of the cultural excitement and allure of Paris was not just the sheer density of achievement but also a sense of shared energy. However intangible, this creative effervescence captivated artists and intellectuals. It was what lured them there and why they stayed. It was what distinguished Paris from London, Berlin, Rome and Vienna.

The American writer Robert McAlmon said he could name 250 Americans connected with the arts living in Montparnasse alone during the 1920s. Other exiles included Man Ray, Alexander Calder, Ezra Pound, Ernest Hemingway, Kay Boyle, Sherwood Anderson, Sylvia Beach, Malcolm Cowley, F. Scott

Fitzgerald, Gertrude Stein, Henry Miller, Peggy Guggenheim, Djuna Barnes, e.e. cummings, Virgil Thomson, Janet Flanner and John Dos Passos.

These were among the countless others from around Europe – such as the Belgians Maurice de Vlaminck, René Magritte and Georges Simenon; the Dutch Mondrian; the English Ford Madox Ford, Mina Loy, Edward Gordon Craig, Nancy Cunard and Wyndham Lewis; the Irish James Joyce and Samuel Beckett; the Germans Ernst Lehmbruch, Max Ernst, Walter Benjamin and Arno Breker; the Italians Umberto Boccioni, Amedeo Modigliani, Giorgio de Chirico and Gino Severini; the Romanians Constantin Brancusi, Victor Brauner, Eugène Ionesco and Tristan Tzara; the Russians Igor Stravinsky, Sergei Prokofiev, Alexander Archipenko, Sergei Diaghilev, Wassily Kandinsky, Vladimir Nabokov and Marc Chagall; the Swiss Le Corbusier and Alberto Giacometti; and the Spaniards Picasso, Joan Miró, Salvador Dalí, Luis Buñuel and Juan Gris. Here was a unique historical phenomenon, a genuine 'cultural International'. It is why the judgement of Paris counted in the art world everywhere.

That was the world the Wehrmacht irreparably shattered in 1940. By the time of the armistice on 23 June artists and intellectuals had been scattered to every corner of the country and beyond. Never in history had there been a cultural migration like it. Ploughing through their names and the places to which they made their way is tedious, but only so is it possible even to begin to grasp the extent of the calamity.

By the time of the German breakthrough, foreign artists had either left – Nabokov sailed in May on the *Champlain*, the last boat to New York – or were scrambling to get out. Some were stuck in France. These were the 'enemy aliens' who had been interned at the outset of the war – Arthur Koestler in the notorious camp at Vernet, Walter Benjamin at one outside Nevers and Max Ernst in one near Nîmes. Among the best-known painters, Picasso was in Royan; Duchamp and Dalí were also on the Atlantic coast, further south. Matisse eventually made his way to St Jean de Luz, from where he took a taxi to his home in Nice; Chagall fled to the remote village of Gordes in Provence, Kandinsky to a small town in the Pyrenees, not far from Braque and Derain. Magritte reached Carcassonne, Léger wandered via Bordeaux to Marseille, while Rouault and Soutine were in the opposite corner of the country, in the northeast. Sonia and Robert Delaunay along with Pierre Bonnard escaped to the Riviera, André Masson landed in the Auvergne. Hans Arp – Alsatian by birth but after the armistice a citizen of the Grossdeutsche Reich – went to Grasse. Among sculptors, Aristide Maillol remained in his atelier in the Pyrenees while Jacques Lipchitz fled to Toulouse. Picabia was en route into France from Switzerland while Miró was on his way out, to Majorca.

Writers, actors, musicians and other cultural figures were equally dispersed. Jean-Louis Barrault, who ended up in Quercy, might have been speaking for all of them when he said, 'In the course of a month, I have toured all France. I now feel as though I am made of the earth of France.' Among noted writers, Roger Martin du Gard found himself in Nice, Paul Claudel in Algiers and André Breton in a town near Bordeaux. Jean Cocteau was in Perpignan, where he was soon joined by his companion, Jean Marais. Colette installed herself with her daughter in Corrèze; the writer-publisher Jean Galtier-Boissière was nearby in the Creuse. Jean Guéhenno got as far as Clermont. Georges Simenon remained in his house near La Rochelle. Céline ended up nearby, complaining with typical Célinese sarcasm, 'However fast you went, whatever you tried to do to catch up with the French Army – this road and that, zigs and zags, non-stop as if in a racing car, always ahead of us – it was never possible to go as fast as the retreating French Army.' Pierre Drieu la Rochelle was in the Dordogne, André Gide on the Riviera and Henri de Montherlant in Marseille, where he was already in trouble with the police following an indiscretion with a baker's apprentice. Simone de Beauvoir eventually found her way to friends near Angers. Among poets, Louis Aragon, after being evacuated from Dunkirk, re-entered France at Brest and ended up in the Dordogne. Paul Éluard was in the Tarn while Saint-Jean Perse made his way to England and eventually the United States. Raymond Aron escaped to London.

Playwright Sacha Guitry went to Dax, where the philosopher Henri Bergson had also wandered. On leaving Paris, Jean Gabin drifted to Toulouse and there managed to squeeze onto a train to Nice. In the meantime his ex-lover Michèle Morgan made it to Cannes. Among well-known composers, Arthur Honegger remained in Paris, Milhaud was in Aix-en-Provence, Poulenc near Cahors in the Dordogne, while Messiaen was en route to a prison camp in Silesia. The head of the Paris Opera, Jacques Rouché, and much of his staff made their way to Cahors, planning to broadcast from nearby Toulouse. Pablo Casals fled to Prades. The soprano Germaine Lubin was with friends in Auvergne. The pianist Alfred Cortot followed the government to Bordeaux and then to Vichy. Such writers as Malraux, Sartre, Anouilh, Henri Jeanson, Robert Desnos, Fernand Braudel, Emmanuel Mounier and Robert Brasillach along with such painters as Jean Hélion and André Fougeron as well as the photographer Henri Cartier-Bresson were all made prisoners of war.

Of the few cultural figures who remained in Paris, most were of an older generation. One of these was the septuagenarian Paul Léautaud, eminent theatre critic, essayist and much-loved misanthrope. An eccentric's eccentric, it would have taken more than the Wehrmacht to dislodge him and his thirty cats from their little house in the Parisian suburb of Fontenay-aux-Roses. Deeply Germanophile and even more deeply conservative, he was troubled neither by the collapse of the Third Republic nor by the presence of German troops. He found the abandoned city a delight, and his diary describes his wanderings around the streets. 'Empty: that is exactly the word. . . . And the silence!' So taken with it all was he that he again commented on the scene and his mood two years later, 'I do not know what word or words I used to portray my impression. Probably: astonishing, fascinating, extraordinary.' Another who remained was the octogenarian Edward Gordon Craig, too old and impoverished to be bothered to leave. Fleeing was the best thing he never did. By an amazing coincidence, German officials accidentally discovered that the vast archive relating to his work as a dramaturge was stored in Paris and bought it for Hitler at an astronomical price.

Not everyone who remained was a senior citizen. When the Germans arrived at 12 rue de l'Odéon they found Sylvia Beach and her Shakespeare and Company bookshop open for business as usual. Since she was American the Germans at first ignored her. Late in 1941, however, a Wehrmacht officer appeared and said he wished to buy the copy of *Finnegans Wake* on display in the window. She insisted it was her only copy and she wanted to keep it. Since there is little point in being a conqueror if you cannot plunder, he threatened to confiscate the whole shop in order to get his book. But no descendant of nine Calvinist divines could be bullied by a cretinous Kraut. In the twinkling of an eye Beach made the shop disappear. In the course of an afternoon she concealed the entire stock of books in an upstairs apartment, removed the bookshelves and other fixtures, and even had the name of the shop painted over. Whether her German ever returned, she never knew. However, as she later wrote, 'Eventually, they did come to fetch the proprietor of Shakespeare and Company.' She was interned for six months and after being released went into hiding. Another person who remained was the thirty-five-year-old head of the Paris Opera Ballet, Serge Lifar. A collaborator of the first hour – indeed, the first minute – he was one of countless opportunists who welcomed the Occupation. No sooner had the Wehrmacht arrived than he began scheming to take over as director of the Opera. Arthur Honegger also refused to flee. He had been far too busy composing – among other works his Second Symphony – to be bothered to take flight. Chanteuses like Edith Piaf, Mistinguett and Suzy Solidor stayed and in no time were singing to Wehrmacht officers. The pianist Lucienne Delforge remained, to play Liszt for them.

The first question facing cultural figures that summer was whether to flee the country. Some had absolutely no doubt about the answer. They were the fifty thousand Germans who had escaped to France after Hitler came to power and for them – as for other foreign refugees – the answer could not have been simpler. At the outbreak of the war they had been arrested and interned in camps where conditions were so appalling that their only hope of physical

survival was to get out. Now, as anti-Nazis, they also faced the urgency of political survival since clause 19 of the armistice agreement required the French to
'surrender on demand' anyone German authorities requested. Private American
organizations, in particular the Emergency Rescue Committee, did their best to
help. The director of the Committee's operations, Varian Fry, arrived in
Marseille in August 1940 with $3,000 strapped to one of his legs and a list of two
hundred endangered intellectuals and artists. By the time Vichy authorities
expelled him and later closed the Committee's offices at the end of 1941, nearly
two thousand people had been legally expatriated or illegally smuggled out –
among them, Heinrich and Golo Mann, Franz Werfel, Lion Feuchtwanger,
Hannah Arendt, Arthur Koestler and Max Ernst. Alma Mahler trudged over a
mountain into Spain with a suitcase containing the holograph scores of her
husband's works, the original manuscript of Bruckner's Third Symphony and
the text of the latest novel of her latest husband, Franz Werfel. As Victor Serge,
the hapless idealistic revolutionary, novelist and refugee himself, commented, 'If
it had not been for Varian Fry, a goodly number of refugees would have had no
reasonable course open to them but to jump into the sea.'

French artists and intellectuals faced a different situation – and their
responses are still a matter of controversy. Understandably, the exodus, sudden
defeat and Occupation left them staggering. Like everyone else they had no
idea how long the Occupation would last and what sort of life they faced,
personally and professionally. In a country partly occupied and partly unoccupied, still at war but sworn to collaboration with the former enemy, how
much personal freedom would be allowed? What did professional integrity
dictate? Would it be possible to practise one's art in exile? Would it be possible
in France? Was it patriotic to stay? Was it patriotic to leave? Was Matisse right
when he asked, 'If everyone of any value leaves France, what remains of
France?' Were Picasso's defenders right in arguing that his decision to stay was
'an act of courage' that 'gave hope to those who would have ended up
doubting their chances of survival'. Or what of Stefan Zweig's comment, 'I
could only mistrust a European artist who would still be capable of concentrating on his personal work'? Perhaps no one expressed the choice more
bleakly than Camus, when he wrote a few days after the armistice, 'Life in
France is hell for the mind now. . . . What we are going to experience now is
unbearable to think of, and I am sure that for a free man, there is no future,
apart from exile and useless revolt. Now the only moral value is courage.' By
rejecting exile, those who stayed in effect opted to be prisoners. Put another
way, they exchanged overt freedom for inner exile or in some cases collaboration. They believed it was necessary to work in familiar surroundings and that
their work was more important than the circumambient ideological environment of Occupation. Many were *attentistes*, those who decided to wait and

see, to hedge their bets, to remain uncommitted either to resistance or to collaboration.

If staying was a personal and professional gamble, leaving was even more so. Settling in the United States – going to Quebec or Latin America crossed hardly anyone's mind – was far from easy. There were the cultural barriers of language and a different way of life. It was necessary somehow to come up with money, obtain both exit and entry visas, find a sponsor, locate a place to live and get some kind of work. And while Vichy authorities were generally willing to let artists out, American consular officials were generally unwilling to let them in. Even if these problems were solved, simply booking a boat passage could be maddeningly difficult.

Many had no trouble deciding. Within days of the defeat Julien Green, Jules Romains, Fernand Léger, Salvador Dalí and Darius Milhaud prepared to leave. As a Marxist, Léger saw no future for himself in France. The Milhauds had lived in Aix-en-Provence for more than a century, but Darius was Jewish and, unlike most other French Jews at the time, intended to take no chances. Despite myriad difficulties, he made it with his wife and son through Spain to Lisbon and in early July sailed for New York – on the same boat as Green and Romains. After the Liberation, when correspondence could be re-established, Poulenc wrote, 'You can imagine what we lived through for four years. What would have become of you if you had stayed with us! Thank God you foresaw this. The number of deportees, of executions is, sad to say, incalculable.'

Such eminent figures as Picasso, Matisse, Malraux, Gide, Lipchitz, Chagall and Masson refused offers by the Emergency Rescue Committee and others to help them get out. Most went through agonies, weighing the pros and cons. Some weeks after the armistice André Breton and his wife decided to leave. 'We have come to the conclusion that our place is where you currently are and where circumstances have willed that the greatest effervescence of ideas should be taking place', Breton wrote to a friend in New York. But then he was assailed with second thoughts, describing himself as 'rather unpleasantly suspended between New York and Paris'. Grudgingly he commented, 'America has become necessary . . . only in the most negative sense: I don't like exile and I have my doubts about exiles.' Eventually hostile articles in the collaborationist press made him decide to get out as soon as possible and by October he and his wife were at the Committee's centre waiting for a visa. Not until February 1941 did he manage to get passage to Martinique and then on to New York.

Saint-Exupéry was also undecided. The fall of France found him in Algeria. Eventually he wound his way to Vichy, where he even managed to interview Pétain. After a trip to Paris in the company of Drieu, he returned to the Unoccupied Zone where he found an invitation from his American publisher.

In December 1940 he sailed from Lisbon, sharing a cabin with Jean Renoir. Demobbed in autumn 1940, Jean Gabin hoped to resume his film career. But when a German film company operating in Nice offered to take him, he refused. Instead he followed René Clair, Max Ophuls, Jean-Pierre Aumont and Michèle Morgan to Hollywood. As the risks for Jews in the Unoccupied Zone increased following the Vichy government's adoption of ever stiffer anti-Semitic laws, Maurois, Lipchitz, Chagall and Masson, whose wife was Jewish, decided to leave. Some of them nearly did not make it. In Marseille, awaiting passage to New York, Chagall was picked up in a surprise round-up of Jews in April 1941 and was saved only by the urgent intervention of Varian Fry.

The flight of so many admired artists naturally enraged collaborators, who derided them as good-for-nothing fortune-seekers. 'This pretentious idiot, this literary demagogue. In America that is all there are. And this is what they call fleeing the country.' Such was Léautaud's malediction on learning of Jules Romains's arrival in New York. Obviously exiles were anything but a good advertisement for the Happy France that German and Vichy authorities wanted to create. By the end of the summer the German-controlled Paris press began attacking 'those lousy French émigrés living in Anglo-Saxony'. From Vichy Pierre Laval, at the time deputy premier, announced, 'It is not by leaving France that she will be saved.' But it was not until 1942 that flight was made difficult and exiles punished by being officially deprived of their citizenship and property.

Although the number of distinguished exiles was substantial, many of the big names in French culture chose to remain. A few notables even decided to return to France from abroad. One of them was the novelist Paul Morand, an attaché at the French embassy in London. He took, as it were, French leave from his post in a mad rush to get to Vichy – and, he hoped, high office in the new government. Not long after the armistice the Germans began releasing a few prisoners and, as a propaganda gesture, gave preference to cultural figures. Drieu, already working closely with German authorities, submitted a list of writers to be freed. Out came figures like Brasillach and Anouilh. A few, such as Malraux, had in the meantime escaped and settled on the Riviera. And some, like Sartre, Desnos and Messiaen, got out through subterfuge.

By the terms of the armistice France was divided into two parts, or what the poet Fernand Gregh referred to as 'une zone occupée et une zone préoccupée'. And so the second question facing refugee artists was whether to return to what Poulenc in a letter to Milhaud called 'that zone of mystery'. In terms that many another artist might have echoed, he announced his own decision in what was his final letter to Milhaud until after the war. 'I hesitated somewhat to return to the capital. . . . But after all I suppose there are intellectual values to defend. Now one can only live on hopes and future projects. I envy you more and more.' Apprehensive but resigned, Poulenc concluded his letter, 'It is now necessary to find some way to live.'

Typical of other artists who saw little to fear and much to welcome in the Occupation, Jean Cocteau could scarcely wait to get back to Paris. 'I find these days terribly exciting', he wrote to one friend. 'Miracles are happening every day, and I am intensely interested in this unreal Paris', he wrote to another. To a third he commented, 'I shall return after trying to restore my balance, and I assure you that our hearts will not be as heavy as they have been in these last weeks. . . . It was a losing game. I knew it and did not want to say it.'

The Occupiers themselves made it fairly easy to return to Paris. Instead of romping around like Attila's legions as they had in Poland and as the French had expected, German soldiers amazed everyone by being friendly, well behaved and courteous – less like conquerors than tourists, spending their time sightseeing, photo-snapping and shopping. The Occupied responded in kind. No longer were Germans *boches* but now the inoffensive *fritz* or *fridolins* or, in reference to the colour of their uniforms, 'men in green-grey' and even 'green beans', while female personnel were nicknamed 'gretchens' and 'grey mice'. 'Green bean' was not the only agricultural allusion; *doryphore* – potato beetle – was another, as the Germans were aware. Early in the Occupation there was a plague of potato beetles; when the editor of *Aujourd'hui* – mischievously or not – let pass an article recommending the extermination of *doryphores*, he was sacked.

That was probably as close as any publication came to raising a conscious laugh during those unhappy years. The Wehrmacht did not arrive in Paris bubbling over with wit and whimsy. So it is scarcely surprising that within a few weeks of their arrival German censors found French humour so far beyond them they deleted anything suspiciously resembling it. To be sure, they offered to let the satirical *canard enchaîné* reappear 'without interference', but the proprietor was canny enough to realize the offer was fraudulent. Happily, however, a variety of mock *canards* appeared to keep alive the flame of irreverent humour. The nearest to the original was the *Caneton déchaîné*, printed in England and 'distributed' from the air by the RAF. Among domestic underground offspring were a *Canard clandestin*, a *Coq enchaîné* and even a *Canard embaumé*. In Algeria there was a *Canard sauvage* and in Beirut a *Canard libre*.

Although it became quickly apparent that life would go on without much risk to the average person, artists and intellectuals were not average and they had no idea how free they would be to write, act, paint, compose, sing and so on. Would theirs be the lot of the *doryphores*? Before they had had a chance to think much about it, they found that culture had been enthroned as a central element of Occupation policy and that an elaborate infrastructure had been set up to carry it through. This was not out of any humanitarian concern for the French. Hitler did not want problems on his western flank and, while France was to be exploited materially and made to behave politically, the population was to be anaesthetized by means of a rich cultural life. No newspapers, books, plays, art exhibitions or films that were anti-German or by Jews, Freemasons and (later) communists were allowed. Otherwise – a big otherwise, to be sure – French artists were to enjoy a preferred status, be cultivated, even fêted, but largely left to themselves.

Nonetheless, some artists – writers in particular – believed that the atmosphere under the Germans would be uneasy, if not unbearable, and stayed in the Unoccupied Zone. Gide, Malraux, Roger Martin du Gard and Paul Éluard were some of the best known. Others did so because they felt at risk for political or racial reasons – Louis Aragon and Elsa Triolet as communists, Julien Benda and Tristan Tzara as Jews. Several who had held out in Paris eventually found life there intolerable and fled – Giacometti to Switzerland, Beckett to Provence, Duchamp to New York. The academic and cultural institutions that had moved after the declaration of war remained where they were. The musicians of the National Radio settled in Marseille. But by and large the attraction of Paris was too great to resist and most cultural figures returned, however warily, to the capital.

Paris in the late summer of 1940 was likened by Serge Lifar to 'a huge, deserted theatre where the stagehands were busy shifting the scenery and preparing for the next act'. No one was more anxious for the show to go on than the Germans themselves. A lively cultural life, they thought, would help to create the impression that everything was back to normal. And life-as-though-nothing-had-changed was a key element of their pacification programme, the psychological foundation for a contented – or at least quiescent – population. For their part most French reckoned that the Germans had won the war and there was no alternative but to make the best of it. After all, as the pianist Lucienne Delforge said, 'If someone were to ask me to define collaboration, I would say, "It is Mozart in Paris." ' In this way collaboration, in the guise of cultural cooperation, started right away. Even before the audience had returned – after falling from its normal two million to 700,000 in late June, the population was only back to 1.3 million – the curtain had risen.

Cabarets and music halls revived during the first week of July. Theatres followed a short time later. 'La noble maison de Molière', the Comédie-Française, was soon on its feet again under the artistic management of Jean-Louis Barrault. Cinemas had reopened almost immediately, though the three largest – the Marignan, Rex and Paris – were reserved for the Wehrmacht.

British and American films were immediately banned and replaced with dubbed German ones – the dubbing often done to such unintended comic effect that audiences were regaled. With the Invader's encouragement the great musical institutions were soon in operation, the Opéra-Comique on 22 August and the Paris Opera two days later.

Most museums reopened in the course of the autumn. The Louvre, with most of its paintings stored in various châteaux in the Loire valley, had little more than sculptures to exhibit. The Salon d'Automne was held as usual and displayed works by both established and new young painters. Further down avenue du Président Wilson at the Palais de Tokyo, the Salon des Indépendants also went ahead with its annual show. The private art galleries, except for those whose owners had fled, were back in business almost immediately. Instead of the anticipated struggle for financial survival, they were soon enjoying an unparalleled bonanza as rich black-marketeers, Germans with pockets full of cheap francs and speculators sent prices soaring. During the twelve months following the armistice galleries held twenty-four exhibitions.

On a less exalted cultural level nightclubs and cabarets thrived and by 1942 there were more than a hundred of them in business. Other places where Occupied and Occupier met in a friendly atmosphere were the whorehouses, which reopened in July, with the same girls. The most luxurious were le Sphinx, le Chabanais (Edward VII's favourite) and le One-Two-Two at 122 rue de Provence. Here were to be seen the glitterati of the Wehrmacht, the glitterati of the arts – Sacha Guitry, Georges Simenon, Maurice Chevalier, Fernandel and Tino Rossi, to mention a few – as well as the glitterati of the underworld – torturers from the Bonny-Lafont gang, who would torture and kill members of the Resistance and then hang out with the girls to unwind. In her memoirs, Fabienne Jamet, the châtelaine of le One-Two-Two looked back on that time with nostalgia. 'You could have thought it was before the war', she remembered. 'Those nights! I am almost ashamed to say it, but I never had so much fun in my life. But it is the truth, those nights during the Occupation were fantastic.' For many others in the cultural and social life of Paris in those years did she speak. In fact she might have taken those words right out of the mouth of Florence Gould or Marie-Louise Bousquet, two society hostesses who promoted collaboration on a less overtly carnal level.

'The population easily accepted the Occupation. Paris had never been so brilliant culturally.' So said Véronique Rebatet, wife of Lucien Rebatet. Unintentionally she was identifying the great fault line of social collaboration. For her 'the population' was the great and good, the aristocracy, the rich and well-placed who did indeed easily accept the Occupation. The 'Paris' of which she was speaking was the social Tout-Paris and the cultural grandees. These included the *noblesse de l'épée* – le comte Étienne de Beaumont, la duchesse

Antoinette d'Harcourt, la marquise de Polignac, la vicomtesse Marie-Laure de Noailles, le baron Seillière – as well as such rich socialites as the Dubonnets, the Mumms and their like. Take the example of Étienne de Beaumont. His residence, wrote Serge Lifar, 'was wide open for Franco-German intellectual contacts which were much encouraged by Marie-Laure de Noailles, Marie-Louise Bousquet, Antoinette duchesse d'Harcourt at the head of the writers, and Georges Auric as the leading musician. Their special darlings were Friedrich Sieburg and Herbert von Karajan.' Although little in Lifar's memoirs is reliable, here he spoke sooth. Robert de Rothschild had fled to New York, but his butler stayed and served his new master with equal loyalty. His new master was Luftwaffe General Friedrich-Carl Hanesse, who had scored brilliantly in the great Wehrmacht property sweepstakes by winning the palatial Rothschild residence in the avenue Marigny. In a revealing slip of the tongue the butler remarked to Jean Cocteau who had come to attend one of the general's lavish receptions, 'I am not unhappy here with Monsieur le baron – excuse me, General Hanesse. He receives all the same people as Monsieur le baron.'

Life in high society therefore went on much as before. Thanks to their connections with the Invader, these people did not go hungry. The Tour d'Argent, Maxim's and Lapérouse went on serving them splendid meals as though there were no war or occupation. For those whose preferred dish was raw collaboration, there were such nightspots as the Montmartre, which Lifar labelled 'a veritable Franco-German club', and the Cercle Européen on the Champs-Élysées, known as 'the supper club of the *collabos*'. Some of the South American ambassadors remained and threw glittering parties. Dior, Fath, Balenciaga and Nina Ricci resurfaced to clothe the guests and Coco Chanel to scent them. Yet simply because they wanted to maintain a semblance of social life, Lifar complained without conscious irony, they 'were quickly dubbed "pro-German" '. Imagine! When New Year's Eve 1940 came round, most of them trooped off to a reception at the German embassy to celebrate. The actress and socialite Corinne Luchaire, who had spent the previous end-of-year entertaining British and French air force pilots, had a marvellous time. The airmen were now German – to her an irrelevant difference – and could not have been pleasanter. 'As busy as bees', they served drinks and chatted up the guests. 'The buffet was groaning. Champagne flowed', she raved. 'Here was le Tout-Paris in the sphere of literature, the arts, politics, the theatre.'

Not quite. Across the Seine on the Left Bank existed an entirely different Tout-Paris, the left-wing artists and intellectuals. At the centre were the denizens of the Café de Flore. The Flore must have been a curious place. *Collabos* despised it as a haven for Jews and homosexuals. The Resistance considered it a den of Gestapo spies. But, according to de Beauvoir, the regulars were 'resolutely hostile to fascism and collaboration and unafraid to conceal it'. So unafraid, in fact, that the art critic Gaston Diehl felt unnerved whenever he went there or to the Deux Magots and heard patrons broadcasting anti-German opinions loud enough for everyone to hear. Apparently the Germans were well aware of the mood and stayed away. De Beauvoir recalled seeing a young Wehrmacht officer enter the Flore and, sensing the hostile atmosphere, quickly leave. The mood of defiance seems to have pervaded the Left Bank. 'In Montparnasse and in Saint-Germain-des-Prés, I never saw anyone wear a yellow star', de Beauvoir wrote. Her Jewish friends never changed their habits, she said, and ignored regulations forbidding them to enter restaurants, cinemas, libraries and so on.

People in dire circumstances cling to one another and the Flore developed into a virtual club where like-minded artists and intellectuals met in a congenial atmosphere. De Beauvoir likened Paris to 'a vast stalag' and found that the only way to endure the prison regulations was to meet friends, drink and chat. There was a certain excitement to it. 'Because the pleasure was so furtive, it seemed illicit.' A sense of camaraderie developed which some of them later recalled almost fondly. These were 'days of friendship and confidence', François Mauriac said later.

At times they were days of fun and even hilarity. The best-known coterie of the 'Flore set' – Picasso, Sartre, de Beauvoir, Éluard, Robert and Youki Desnos, Camus and Michel and Louise Leiris – periodically held what they called 'fiestas'. On a notable occasion in 1944 they joined friends in a play-reading – immortalized in Brassaï's photograph – of *Le Désir attrapé par la queue* (Desire Caught by the Tail), a divertissement written by Picasso during his days in Royan. With characters holding such names as Onion, Thin Anguish and Tart, the play spoke to the problems of the time – hunger and cold, chilblains and sore feet. Camus directed, more or less, and orally described the imaginary stage-sets based on Picasso's sketches. Michel Leiris, Sartre, de Beauvoir and Queneau were some of those reading parts and the large audience included the likes of Barrault, Braque, the psychoanalyst-philosopher Jacques Lacan, the poet Henri Michaux, the actress Maria Caserès and the polymath Georges Bataille. While the play was a neo-Surrealist period piece of no great consequence, the players and audience formed as stunning a group of cultural figures as could be jammed into a single room in a Paris apartment. 'A year earlier,' de Beauvoir remarked, 'we would never have imagined meeting to spend such a noisy and light-hearted time together. . . . Overcome by a sense of the joy of living, I regained my old conviction that life is and should be a pleasure.'

It was such small, private amusements along with mass, public entertainments that helped people to carry on. 'Glittering Paris' was the Invader's paramount propaganda stratagem. It would create the impression that in France – in the cultural sphere especially – nothing had essentially changed, that life was as exciting as ever and that the material hardships could be compensated for by aesthetic pleasures. And all this, the Germans liked to insinuate, was thanks to their tolerance and, indeed, encouragement – in contrast to the philistine and prudish authorities in Vichy.

Of course, the putative normalcy and glitter were fake. What could have been less normal and glittering than a Paris and all it stood for under the boot of an occupation army? As Picasso once commented to his friend Brassaï, 'Paris would almost be a charming town if signs pasted all over the walls with [German] commands, lists of hostages and names of those executed did not bring one back to reality.' And the reality was that Occupied France, as de Beauvoir said, had become a gigantic prison. As time passed the inmates increasingly resembled the panther in Rilke's eponymous poem: 'He was so exhausted looking through the bars that he could take nothing in; it was as though there were a thousand bars and behind the bars no world.'

The antidote was mass mental narcosis – induced by the hard and soft drugs of culture – which kept the people entertained, diverted, numbed, pacified. People read as never before. Even publishers were amazed; one remarked that he could have reissued the phone directory and it would have been snapped up. Titles of some popular books – *Raising Rabbits, Family Beekeeping, The Potato* – make clear what was on people's minds. As early as September 1941 a survey undertaken for Occupation authorities reported that 'some people, we were assured, even read at the table, to forget their appetites'.

The public flocked in unprecedented numbers to art shows, museums, concerts, films, plays and operas. The Salon d'Automne and the Salon des Indépendants continued their stately courses, presenting works of Braque, Matisse and other Modernists. Private galleries did a thriving business, exhibiting and selling whatever they wished, although in some cases with discretion. Music was especially popular and more than any of the other arts brought French and Germans together. The exterior of the Paris Opera was now symbolically bedecked with swastika banners. Inside, Alfred Fabre-Luce, the millionaire author, found an equally symbolic setting. 'In that old monument, the Garnier, the dinner jackets of the collaborators and those of the remaining Americans mingled with the grey-green uniforms [of the German military].' This was exactly the scene the Germans wanted – the Invader and the Invaded happily mingling and imbibing culture, preferably German.

So what about Véronique Rebatet's claim that 'Paris had never been so brilliant culturally'? It is a myth. Some historians cite high attendance at events as evidence. But with no cars to drive, with the entire Atlantic coastline off limits for holidays, with the demarcation line difficult or impossible to cross, with no food for dinner parties and social life cramped by a curfew, there were few alternatives. Films, the theatre, concerts and exhibitions may have been a pleasure in themselves but they were equally a way of forgetting the grim realities of life. Another spurious argument referred to the sheer number of works – more than four hundred plays, two hundred new feature films, countless documentaries and so on. But quality was something else. Music was hampered by the absence of those instrumentalists who were excluded because they were Jews or in a stalag. On the stage were only a handful of outstanding new plays; a high proportion were revivals. Some painters did not exhibit. Few new books of merit appeared. De Beauvoir described the literature of those years as 'dormant', 'stagnant', in a 'vegetative state'.

Claims that in cultural matters the Germans were tolerant in comparison to the prissy, reactionary Vichyssois is an exaggeration amounting to another myth. To be sure, there were art exhibitions that would have been inconceivable in the Third Reich. But these very exhibitions – exclusively of French paintings – had been rigorously purged. The whole of twentieth-century German Expressionist painting was excluded – excluded from shows, excluded from sales. Any number of plays never got to the stage and any number of films were never made, any number of books were either rejected or refused paper to be printed on or had to be revised. Those works that did reach the public after German censorship and pre-emptive self-censorship by artists themselves often had an artificial quality about them. You cannot write poems about trees, Brecht pointed out, when the woods are filled with police. Faced by German censors, some writers refused to publish, some limited what they published, some published with embarrassment. Publishers also played it safe by turning down any manuscript that risked trouble. So artificiality was also a product of silence – the silence of books and films and plays never born.

Cultural freedom was stifled in another way – by the French themselves. Vicious quarrelling over ideas was a sacred French tradition, the necessary condition of a society that took products of the mind with the utmost seriousness. But during most of the interwar period right-wing writers and critics had felt themselves sidelined in a cultural world dominated by the intellectuals of the left. Now, with the downfall of the Third Republic, their hour had come and they would have their revenge. It would be, to adapt a phrase of Stanley Hoffmann, the revenge of the outsiders. To get even for the past, they wanted not mere influence but power – power to set the intellectual tone, to determine what books might be published, what films shown, what plays performed and even who might act in them. This power was to be exercised through writings, agitation, character assassination, moral blackmail and at a later stage the physical thuggery of the Milice, the French fascist police. In May 1944 Jean Marais gave a stunning performance in his own production of Racine's *Andromache*. A few days later in an evening broadcast Philippe Henriot, Vichy's version of Goebbels, declared that this 'massacring of Racine was no less a sacrilege than the RAF's bombing of the cathedrals of Rouen and Orléans'. The offence? Marais and other male actors wore tights that were considered provocatively revealing. The next morning the local head of the Milice demanded that the police should stop any further performances. The Paris police as usual sided not with the victims but with the thugs.

In the *bouillabaisse* of the minds of these fanatics, there was a great variety of ingredients. One was simple vindictiveness, the settling of personal scores. Another was counter-revolution, to do in culture what was being done in political life. Then there was collaboration, though not with Vichy, which they despised as confused and weak, but with the strong and determined Invader. There were varying amounts of pacifism, romanticism, elitism and Anglophobia, and more than a soupçon of a virility cult. Of course, there was a huge chunk of raw anti-communism and lots of vintage anti-Semitism. Not to mention homophobia. All this was immersed in a broth of hatred.

Hatred, pure and unalloyed, had in fact already become a pervasive characteristic of public life in the late Thirties. So bad was it that the novelist Georges Simenon, a man of the right and by no means a public-spirited figure, decided to organize a movement to neutralize it. Badges were made with the slogan 'Sans Haine' (Without Hate) and posters were printed with the message 'I have my ideas, you have yours; let's express them without hatred'. The president of France, Albert Lebrun, was a member of the sponsoring committee. The project had no noticeable impact, but it testified to the foul state of mind in France at the outset of the Occupation.

Just as in Germany after Hitler's rise to power, long-pent-up forces of reaction erupted following the defeat. The old proto-fascist, anti-Semitic, anti-liberal, anti-Modernist sentiment typified by Charles Maurras's highly influential political organization Action Française merged with a straight-laced puritanism coming out of Vichy to rise in a flood of recrimination. Tony Judt put it concisely: 'What had been thought before 1940 could now be said, what had previously been said could now be done.' What was said was that artists and intellectuals rather than politicians and generals were responsible for the moral state that had led to the disaster of 1940. And what was now to be done was to destroy their ideas, if not the perpetrators along with them. In setting the intellectual tone of the new France, these critics transformed culture from a matter of art into one of 'morals'.

Painting was one of the first targets. To help matters along, German authorities lost no time in organizing an exhibition of photographs and documents intended to demonstrate the rottenness of Expressionism, Surrealism, Dadaism and other 'degenerate' schools. Like glove-puppets, right-wing critics happily joined in. Everything produced during the past fifty years, they said, had been not just bad art but bad morals. Fauvism, for instance, innocently known to art historians for its unimpeded expression of chromatic energy, was now described by one critic as 'Judaeo-Masonic sadism, hysteria, raving looniness and incoherence'. The main target was Picasso, whose works were routinely reviled as epitomizing the worst perversions of the Third Republic. In a critique of the Salon d'Automne of 1940, the art critic of the prestigious review *L'Illustration* had some ominous advice to offer. 'As artists start work again, they should know what is expected of them.' And what was expected of them? 'A renewal of moral values.'

'Moral values' was the issue in accusations against Gide and a number of other writers who were condemned as practitioners of what is historically known as 'unnatural vice'. Inevitably the old charge against Socrates reared its head. The ultimate anathema was now the 'P' word, which had a long and honoured tradition in France as a term of abuse for homosexuality. 'Only pederasts and snobs could enjoy *Pelléas et Mélisande*', claimed an opera conductor in the 1930s. Even earlier Paul Claudel had proclaimed that Dadaism and Surrealism were 'for pederasts only'. Vlaminck, in a filthy mood that lasted throughout the Occupation, accused Modernist painters of sexual visions involving 'onanism and intellectual pederasty'.

The issue was brought into the open only a few weeks after the armistice when the distinguished daily *Le Temps* – now published in the Unoccupied Zone – ran an anonymous article on 'The Youth of France' which damned Gide as a public menace because of his enormous and baneful influence over young people. Several weeks later *Le Figaro littéraire* chimed in with a series of articles accusing 'decadent elements' of having 'corrupted society' and, more than anyone else, for having 'caused the debacle'. The attack left some of *Figaro*'s editorial staff so queasy that the paper opened its columns to a debate on whether the literature of the 1930s had in fact been morally corrupting and should now reform itself. Claudel expressed himself strongly in favour of this view. Mauriac defended the accused writers. Gide's response was not to respond, saying it was up to young people to comment. But in his diary he noted that the accusation was based on two of his earliest works, *The Treatise of the Narcissus* of 1891 and *The Immoralist* of 1902, and remarked that for all their having been corrupted and enfeebled, the generation that read those books 'had fought rather valiantly in 1914'.

Even more than Gide, Cocteau was the writer the right-wing critics loved to hate. He and his lover, Jean Marais, were victims throughout the Occupation years of an abusive vendetta led in particular by Alain Laubreaux, the venomous theatre critic of the fascist weekly *Je suis partout* and other papers. Cocteau had already been under fire in 1938 for his play *Les Parents terribles*, which was misrepresented as a portrayal of incest. 'Believe it or not,' Cocteau now wrote to a friend, 'those worthies have decided that Gide and I are to blame for everything. . . . They go so far as to say that *Les Parents terribles* is responsible for the defeat.' When his next play, *La Machine à écrire* (*The Typewriter*), appeared in 1941, it was roundly lambasted for its critical picture of the French people. Leading the pack, Rebatet published a ferocious attack suffused with homophobia in *Je suis partout*. The work, he said, typified 'the usual sort of pervert's theatre', which epitomized 'twenty years of abasement and the indulgence of all the depravities of body and mind'. He concluded, 'This clown could have been charming. At fifty, the age of full maturity for real men, he is no more than a degenerate simpleton.'

Rebatet's crude remark touched on an issue that troubled even some writers of the anti-collaborationist left. Jean Guéhenno put it this way in his diary: 'Sociological problem: Why so many pederasts among collaborators?' Cryptically he referred to those he had in mind as 'C . . ., M . . ., F . . . and D . . '. He raised the question with Mauriac, who responded even more cryptically, 'You do not understand because you are not Catholic.' Considering this unenlightening, Guéhenno cogitated and eventually believed he had found the explanation. 'Solution. . . . They are like the residents of a brothel in a small town who get their pleasure when a regiment passes through town.'

Risible comments by a number of gay writers themselves seemed to lend almost literal support to Guéhenno's theory of crass, carnal attraction. It was not exactly subtle of the popular writer Marcel Jouhandeau to claim that, in the interests of Franco-German understanding, 'I wished to make of my body a fraternal bridge between Germany and us.' Since the writer was at the time enamoured of a (male) German poet, the remark was all too picturesque. And while there was a certain metaphorical truth to Brasillach's statement – 'Whatever their outlook, during these years the French have all more or less been to bed with Germany' – his choice of words was lewdly suggestive. Montherlant also regarded the relationship in male-female terms. Because the French were weak and decadent, they had to submit to virile German troops 'streaming with sweat'. Picking up on such remarks at the end of the war, Sartre came to the sensational conclusion, in an article entitled 'What Is a Collaborator?', that there had been a 'mixture of masochism and homosexuality' in the collaborationism of cultural figures.

In fact, the number of prominent gays in the arts during the Occupation was by no accounting large. Of writers some six or seven – Gide, Cocteau, Jouhandeau, Roger Peyrefitte, Montherlant, Jean Genet and the larvated homosexual Brasillach – come to mind. Only Jouhandeau and Brasillach were out-and-out *collabos*. Gide and Genet were opponents of Vichy and the Germans. If any group was psychologically suspect it was the heterosexual collaborationists – whether officials of the Vichy government or the most outspoken of intellectuals, such as Drieu, Rebatet, Céline, Fabre-Luce and their like – who exalted virility and sweat no less than Montherlant and who wallowed in masochistic abasement before the ruthless German Invader. Sartre himself pointed out that a frequent metaphor of such *collabos* as Châteaubriant, Brasillach and Drieu was France as a woman submitting to male Germany. The fact is, all France was a psychological wreck as a result of the defeat and one of the main neuroses was a feeling of submissiveness, self-hatred and masochism. One of the greatest bestsellers of the time was a book that mercilessly excoriated the French individually and collectively – Lucien Rebatet's *Les Décombres*. A full psycho-sexology of the Occupation did not appear until 2008 when the television journalist Patrick Buisson published his *1940–1945: Années erotique*, an exhaustive – and exhausting – exposé of life in those years as one big love-in.

The debate was important primarily in reflecting the intellectual tone of Occupation France. It marked the beginning of a campaign of journalistic intimidation and remorseless browbeating. It is a historical characteristic of ultra-conservatives in every country to look for scapegoats in times of crisis. In this case they were Jews, Freemasons, homosexuals, foreigners and ultimately everyone who was not French and right-wing. Leaders of this agit-prop operation such as Rebatet, Laubreaux and Brasillac were clever and effective writers. They were regularly read by many thousands. Like harpies in a Greek tragedy, they kept up such a screeching chorus of vilification that untold numbers of intellectuals were reduced to silence. Victims had no other way to defend themselves than to flee – as Gide and Breton, among others, eventually did. The result was the pre-emptive cringe and the self-censorship that were central traits of cultural life during the Occupation. In this way collaborationist intellectuals became a virtual political force that worked side by side with – and that was usually more fanatical than – the Invader and Vichy.

If the cultural mood of the Occupation was set in the autumn of 1940, it was upset almost as abruptly in the summer of 1944. In a way the end of the Occupation was similar to its beginning, with another military defeat followed by another mad flight. Life in France in 1944 was like a film being run in reverse back to 1940. People held their breath for a battle they knew was soon to occur. But, again, there was not much more for them to do than to hold their breath and wait. Even on D-Day life went on as usual except for the postponement of a championship football match. Cafés, nightclubs, cinemas and all the regular meeting places were as jammed as ever. While the British,

Canadians and Americans were fighting and planning to break the German defence line in Normandy, Édith Piaf was singing to full houses and Sacha Guitry was making plans for his next season. Although electricity was sporadic and limited to a few hours a day, theatres continued to thrive with plays – often performed in candlelight – by Anouilh, Shaw and Strindberg. On 8 June the members of the Académie Française held their weekly meeting to discuss the Prix Née. They decided to award it to Léautaud, who turned it down.

Even the hardcore *collabos* kept their nerve. A week or so after the Normandy landings, Drieu, Rebatet and their friends met at Lapérouse for their regular lunch-discussion and talked of the future. Although Drieu had long been convinced that Germany would be beaten, many of his friends retreated ever further into a fantasy world, somehow believing or pretending to believe that the Occupation would go on for ever. Florence Gould continued to hold her weekly salons, though one by one her German boyfriends were taking their leave. Despite everything *la vie parisienne* followed its usual exciting course. 'The military appear to be killing one another everywhere and destroying Italy while here we crush one another at Gallery X, where the painter Y presides over his vernissage in drag – powdered, made-up, in a Lanvin dress, silk stockings, high heels', ran one description. This was grotesque only in its exaggeration.

At the Vieux Colombier rehearsals went on undisturbed for the premieres of Camus's *Le Malentendu* (*The Misunderstanding*) and Sartre's *Huis clos* (*No Exit*). Of the latter, the actor-playwright André Roussin commented, 'I shall never forget the oppressive summer heat. In the tiny and overcrowded room everyone was sweating and mopping his brow, which gave a certain topicality to the play since it took place in hell.' He went on to comment on the incongruity with the real world. 'Sainte-Mère-Église was under siege and masses of soldiers were being killed at the foot of the sea cliffs in Normandy; but the event of the month was Jean-Paul Sartre's play.' Everything went well for Sartre and the play had good notices, even in the German-language papers. A few days later the author agreed to participate in a conference on the future of the theatre, along with Camus, Cocteau and Barrault. At a time when Caen and Oradour-sur-Glane were no more than smoking ruins and convoys of deportees were on their way east, the future of the theatre was being chewed over in a salon by the Seine.

In a final sweep of Jews, communists and suspected members of the Resistance, the Milice helped the Gestapo to pick up and deport Robert Desnos, the poet Max Jacob and a number of other artists. Surrealist incongruity again intervened. While Desnos was being shunted from one detention camp to another, a film was being shown in Paris cinemas with the credit 'scenario and dialogue by Robert Desnos'. It was a weird time and Galtier-Boissière caught the mood when he commented, 'We now have some conception of what life was like during the Terror. While the guillotines were busy chopping off heads every day, daily life, business and pleasures never stopped, cafés and theatres were full. Today people live between two dangers, the Gestapo and [Allied] bombings – but one goes on living, surviving; one lives without making plans but one lives.' In a bizarre replay of the panic of May–June 1940, the Allied military invasion of Normandy at the end of July occasioned another exodus. In fact, there were two exoduses. Some noted opponents of the Germans and Vichy hurried into the countryside to evade the revenge of the Milice and the Wehrmacht, now more brutal than ever. At the same time the *collabos*, on the run from the liberators and the Resistance, headed for Germany.

Already back in July 1941 Galtier-Boissière had remarked that when France fell, many had become collaborators because they believed Britain was finished. 'Today they cling to collaboration,' he said, 'because if the *fridolins* lose, they know they will be shot or hanged.' This was precisely what many now faced.

CHAPTER 3

OH, WHAT A LOVELY WAR!

At dinner in July 1942 at the most famous of Parisian restaurants, the Tour d'Argent, a German officer recalled that Henri IV had dined there several centuries earlier on pâté of heron. The officer was feeling a bit like a king himself. 'In times like these,' he commented in his diary, 'to eat, to eat well and copiously gives you a sense of power.' The officer had arrived in Paris in April of the previous year and written in his diary at the end of his first day,

> In the evening with a military friend to the Rôtisserie de la Reine Pédauque . . . then to the Tabarin. There we watched a revue of naked women before an audience of officers and officials of the Occupation army who were downing oceans of bubbly. . . . Then to the Monte-Cristo, a little establishment where you sit on low cushions arranged around a narrow track for the singers and dancers. . . . I had a conversation with a melancholic young woman, a bit overcome by champagne, about Pushkin, Akasakov and Andreiev, one of whose daughters she knew.

Captain Ernst Jünger, exemplary hero of the First World War and widely admired writer, had fought in the French campaign in 1940 and was then assigned to a variety of duties for the Wehrmacht commandant in Paris. Renowned for his cold, steely demeanour, he looked at the world with gimlet-eyed detachment. Hitler, for example, he regarded not so much as monstrous as ridiculous and 'a man with no sense of refined cuisine'. The detailed diary he kept of the Occupation years chronicles the pleasures of dining not just at the Tour d'Argent but also at Maxim's, Drouant, Lapérouse, Prunier and the Ritz, as well as of taking tea at the Café de la Paix, sitting in the sun at the Brasserie Lorraine in the place des Ternes, shopping in the Faubourg

St-Honoré for gifts for women friends and purchasing rare books and auto-
graphs for himself. His circle of French friends was limited to such prominent
collabos as Abel Bonnard, Paul Morand, Jacques Benoist-Méchin and Sacha
Guitry, and the diary records some snippets of their table talk – Fernand de
Brinon's anti-Semitic gibes in front of his Jewish wife, Céline's taunting of the
Germans for failing to exterminate every Jew in Europe, Arletty's hooting
when she heard the word 'cuckold' and Florence Gould's priceless aperçu that
the essence of political wisdom is 'Don't be afraid'. Although he once went to
see Picasso and called on Braque and Jean Fautrier, the writer-captain steered
clear of the artistic and intellectual set, ostensibly never read any of their writings, avoided such places as the Café de Flore – in fact, rarely ventured onto
the Left Bank – and assuredly never met a Gaullist.

Occasionally he had a bad moment. He mentions his shock at seeing
Parisian Jews wearing a yellow star and at witnessing one of the round-ups.
Shock? Where had he been since Hitler came to power? Otherwise he took no
notice of arrests, executions or deportations. Everyone in Paris knew about
the torture that went on at the Gestapo offices in avenue Foch and rue de
Saussaies, but this too went without note. Equally telling, he stayed aloof from
the Paris end of the anti-Hitler conspiracy of July 1944. Yet Jünger has been
praised by some literary critics as being typical of 'the good German'. Probably
his skill as a writer blinded people to his character. Some even argued that his
Auf den Marmorkklipen (*On the Marble Cliffs*), published in 1939, was a coded
anti-Nazi work. In fact, Goebbels' only objection was his use of a quotation
from a Psalm. And in any case after the war he himself firmly quashed the
claim. Jünger was typical of the fun-loving Germans in Paris, untypical only
in the relative sophistication of his artistic and gastronomic tastes.

'A larger version of Switzerland' is how Germans looked on France during
the Occupation. And Paris, the finest trophy of the war, was theirs. The
Conquerors began as they meant to go on. Whatever their rank or station, they
had the time of their lives. The most eminent confiscated imposing residences
in the capital and country estates nearby. For the commander-in-chief an
ancient abbey near Rambouillet was remodelled as a summer retreat. Göring
reserved part of the Luxembourg Palace for himself. General Hanesse, not
content with the Rothschild residence for himself, installed his command
headquarters in the Château de Rambouillet, the country estate of the presi-
dents of France. Less senior officials requisitioned family homes or confiscated
those that had been abandoned by their rich British or Jewish owners. In the
outskirts whole neighbourhoods were sometimes taken over, owners thrown
out or confined to part of their house. To fit out their new residences, the
higher-ups helped themselves to furniture, kitchen equipment, linen, cutlery,
the contents of wine cellars, glassware, refrigerators, radios, carpets and

whatever else caught their fancy. They lived and entertained in grand style – served by soldier-servants in white gloves, dining on tables fitted out with the owner's linen and china, drinking the owner's wine from the owner's Baccarat crystal and otherwise living in a style considered appropriate for a conqueror. Smaller fry made do in luxury hotels, the best of which had been commandeered. Suites were reserved at the Ritz for visiting officials. To ensure there would be familiar food, Maxim's and a number of other restaurants were taken over by Göring's favourite restaurateur, Otto Horcher. The noted German chef Alfred Walterspiel managed some thirty or forty bistros. After dinner, reserved seats at the opera and theatre were always available to German officials at no charge. At weekends the racing at Auteuil and Longchamps was enormously popular with the Invader. Stands were reserved for German personnel and at Longchamps the box of the French president now belonged to the German commandant.

This was not occupation. It was vacation in grand style. It was also shopping sprees à gogo. Thanks to the artificial exchange rate, everything was cheap for the Invader, who emptied shops of items that had not been seen in Germany for years. *And* it was ultimately all free since the Wehrmacht was financed by the French people in the form of occupation costs. 'I was very often in Paris', the sculptor Arno Breker recalled. 'My headquarters was at the Ritz; I had a suite there, and I paid nothing for it. I invited friends there. During the war you could eat as well as in peacetime, or even better, only you had to know the right addresses.' His own private address, by the way, was an apartment on the Île St-Louis that had been confiscated from the Jewish cosmetic entrepreneur Helena Rubenstein. Albert Speer recalled that he and Breker enjoyed dining at the Coq Hardi, a restaurant on the Seine outside Paris much favoured by German generals. 'We were served by Maître François like old friends,' Speer recalled. 'We sat in the sunshine, a loose group of Germans and Frenchmen, on the terraces of a garden laid out on the side of a hill. Here there was nothing to recall war, enmity, the Resistance.'

It was not just the high-flyers who disported themselves. Twenty-one-year-old Ursula von Collenberg worked as an assistant to the historians who were pilfering French diplomatic archives. 'I never lived so well anywhere,' she recalled years after the war.

We went to the opera or the theatre; we saw Jean-Louis Barrault and Sacha Guitry and the Grand Guignol; we visited exhibitions in the Orangerie and the Musée de l'Homme. Weekends were free and we went sightseeing everywhere. We had a young Frenchman come to give us language lessons. There was lovely material to be bought for clothes, and I found a little White

Russian dressmaker. We could buy what we wanted, much more than the French. It was the most wonderful and unforgettable time of my youth.

Even the overtly disrespectable had a wonderful time. Eighteen-year-old Fritz Molden, who worked for an agency that dealt with the underworld to procure goods on the black market, recalled his Paris days fondly. With young German friends he spent his free time exploring Paris. 'We talked about books and art, went to plays, visited museums and art galleries and sat for hours in the cafés of the Champs-Élysées. . . . I doubt if I ever enjoyed anything so much in my youth as those three or four months in Paris.'

And of course there was a flood of VIPs, so much so that an important Gestapo official jested that the acronym for the most important German wartime operation was EOTP – Everyone Once To Paris. Bars, restaurants, nightclubs, brothels and so on were favourite sites. For the more high-minded there was art and architecture. One such was a professor from Berlin University, the famous philosopher of National Socialism Alfred Bäumler. It was his first visit to Paris and he could not have enjoyed himself more. With the head of the German Institute as his guide, he spent a week seeing every notable site, taking coffee at every famous café, visiting every museum, browsing in bookshops and at the flea market, attending the theatre, the Folies Bergère and cabarets, and even looking in on the fashion houses. De rigueur for the Invader-tourists was a circuit of the cathedrals, and off went Bäumler to Reims, Laon, Senlis, Strasbourg, Amiens and Rouen, whose architectural features he expatiated on to his German host at great length. Still raring to go, Bäumler was persuaded to attend a performance at the Grand Guignol. Hardened Nazi though he was, the sanguineous spoofs at the famous theatre proved too much for him; he turned pale and was sick. At last sated, he returned to Berlin.

These are just a few of the countless examples of the holiday mood that have been recorded in book after book and manifested in photo after photo. Even in the relatively soft occupation of France, the shameless exploitation of a helpless population resembled the worst side of old-fashioned colonialism. The natives were tolerated so long as they behaved; apart from prominent collaborators, they ranked as hardly more than bystanders in this happy playground. Sometimes they were literally bystanders. Jean Guéhenno described what he and his family found when they went on an outing in the Bois de Boulogne on the first Sunday of May in 1941. 'On the lake in the Bois, veritable flotillas of Germans were massed. We queued up at the rental office for a boat. But the Occupation authority claimed priority for their leisure and pleasure, so only two or three French couples eventually had their patience rewarded. . . . One little girl near me asked her father, "could she get into one of those boats, too?" He replied, "Yes, when there are no more Germans." '

The little girl and her father were unaware that kindly Herr Hitler wanted them and their countrymen to have a good time too. Until he had finished with the Soviet Union, Hitler needed a peaceful and contented France that would cause him no trouble. Beyond that, German Occupation policy, so far as it could be called a policy, essentially consisted of a series of exigent demands. The German economy required French material resources, agricultural products and industrial goods. German industry needed French manpower for its factories and the military needed it for its construction projects on the Atlantic coast. The Gestapo turned to the French police for help in ridding the country of Jews, Freemasons, German refugees and resisters. The Foreign Office sought Vichy's cooperation in French colonies in the war with Britain.

How to bleed the country without causing a popular uprising? It would be necessary, officials in Berlin realized, to carry out a massive pacification programme, an operation that the historian Henri Michel aptly characterized as a 'vaste entreprise d'intoxication'. Culture was to be the key element in creating a *contre-monde* where the French would be distracted from political affairs and the hardships of occupation by indulging in a rich cultural life. So German authorities not merely permitted but strongly encouraged a revival of the arts. Within a matter of weeks of the capitulation, theatres, the two opera houses, concert halls, cinemas, cabarets and music halls, art galleries, museums and publishing houses were all again in full swing. 'Everything back to normal' was the slogan, and to an amazing extent it was true.

The Occupiers did not leave it at that. The invasion of the Wehrmacht was to be followed by an invasion of German opera companies, orchestras and soloists; Luftwaffe raids by an offensive by theatre groups; Gestapo operations by recitals by German soloists. Throughout the country were to be established German cultural institutions offering lectures, receptions, libraries and language lessons. German pianists, choral groups, opera companies and orchestras would regularly be shuttled in. German books would be translated and made available in libraries and bookshops. Theatres would show German dramas, cinemas German films.

Considering that the two countries were still at war, with fighting going on all around them, this was an extraordinary proposition. Hitler was right. Never before in history had a victor framed a cultural policy for a people it had just vanquished, much less one that aimed to make them happy. It seemed too good to be true. And of course it was. The French were to be entertained by German culture but in being entertained they were to come to recognize that Germany was as supreme culturally as it was militarily. France's belief in its civilizing mission in the world would be uprooted and 'the intellectual monopoly held by France throughout the world', as the Germans phrased it, brought to an end.

A memorandum outlining these ideas was approved by Hitler several weeks after the armistice. Its author was Otto Abetz, whom Hitler a short time later appointed ambassador, in that way taking political affairs out of the hands of the Wehrmacht and making them the responsibility of Joachim von Ribbentrop and the Foreign Office. It was an unusual arrangement, to say the least. France could not have been extinguished like Poland and Czechoslovakia. But it could have been autocratically administered by a harsh governor, as were Norway and the Netherlands, or it could have been ruled by the Wehrmacht, as was Belgium. Instead, like Denmark, it was allowed a certain amount of latitude to run its own affairs. In this way the Occupation would be made palatable with a minimum use of force. It was left to Abetz to figure out how to do it.

Although only thirty-seven and without diplomatic experience, Abetz thus became the grand impresario of Franco-German relations. It seems unlikely he was ever a sincere Nazi; but a sincere opportunist he certainly was. Along with the military commander and the Gestapo chief, he was the most important German in Paris. While the generals passively guarded France as Albericht defended the gold of the Rhine, Abetz pursued his mission with the fervour of Siegfried lusting for deeds of heroism. He knew France fairly well, spoke decent French and was married to an ambitious Frenchwoman. Francophile in his way, he had for years cultivated French intellectuals, artists and heads of political associations. Now he looked forward to a new National Socialist Europe in which France would occupy an important place. He intended to teach the French to accept a cooperative but subordinate role, while trying to convince the Germans that France would be a loyal subject state. From the first he carried out his mission with such energy and panache that Céline nicknamed him 'King Otto I' and referred to France as 'the Kingdom of Otto'.

In his youth Abetz had displayed an aesthetic bent, at least to the extent of being good at languages and liking poetry. Above all, he was adept at drawing and in 1926 was appointed drawing instructor at a gymnasium in Karlsruhe. Around the same time he became increasingly active in youth movements and in this way developed contacts with similar French groups. In 1931 he helped to organize a large meeting of French and German youth at the Black Forest town of Sohlberg, out of which grew the so-called Sohlberg Circle, a group dedicated to reconciliation between the two countries. At these and other meetings Abetz emerged as someone who knew the French, enjoyed a wide range of contacts and could organize and mobilize.

When Hitler came to power in January 1933, Abetz immediately realized that he had found a way of giving direction to his talents. Eagerly taken up by Nazi officials, he was back in Paris within weeks to organize a meeting to cast the National Socialist revolution in a favourable light. On the French side the sessions were attended by a broad array of intellectual and political figures such as Fabre-Luce, Drieu, Bertrand de Jouvenel and Jean Luchaire – pacifists now taking their first steps towards what became collaboration. The meeting, which largely disarmed French concerns and evoked remarkable openness towards German developments, was a great success for Abetz personally. And it marked a critical moment in the Franco-German equation. Reconciliation now meant conciliation not with a country but with a totalitarian ideology. Some French participants seemed not to notice; others were aware but felt that friendship between the two nations was too important to fall victim to ideological differences. The success of the meeting was reinforced by a similar one in Berlin, attended by Drieu and de Jouvenel, among others, after which Abetz arranged for Drieu to meet the party ideologue, Arthur Rosenberg.

By 1934 Abetz was not only directing French affairs for the Hitler Youth but was picked by Ribbentrop to be the Nazi party's advisor on France. When the latter was appointed foreign minister in 1938, he automatically became the government's chief expert on France and was given a diplomatic passport. Abetz's charm offensive now went into high gear. Journalists and other opinion leaders were his main target. One of Abetz's seduction techniques was a favourite of dictatorships – the guided tour. Carefully prepared, all expenses paid, first-class travel and hotels, these junkets took participants to the Nuremberg party rallies and in 1936 to the Berlin Olympics, to conferences and to cities and factories and other sites showing the glories of the new Germany. Those taken in by this wheeze included Luchaire, de Jouvenel, Louis Bertrand, Thierry Maulnier and Jules Romains – all of them influential writers. Another stratagem was to give authors large royalties for the translation rights of their books. The journalist Fernand de Brinon hit the jackpot: he not only got royalties and great publicity for his *France – Allemagne* but was also the first French journalist to be allowed to interview Hitler. For some, Germany continued to mean not totalitarianism, concentration camps and anti-Semitism but Goethe, Beethoven and Nietzsche. For others, Nazism appeared to hold answers or at least hope.

Jules Romains was a good example of the sort of innocent who was drawn into Abetz's web. At the time he was, with Pirandello and Shaw, one of the three playwrights most performed in the world. As of 1936 he was also president of PEN International. Deeply scarred by the Great War, he feared that another European conflagration would mean the end of Western civilization. Despite his anti-fascism and left-leaning political views, he supported Franco-German reconciliation at any cost and was lured into the France–Germany Committee, which had been founded in Paris in 1935 to promote contacts between artists and intellectuals in the two countries as the counterpart to a similar German–French Society. The very title of his principal novel, *Hommes de bonne volonté* (Men of Goodwill), says much about the man himself and the naïveté that left him prey to Abetz.

Abetz's missionary work coincided with a period of great intellectual ferment in France. The ambassador was fascinated by Parisian intellectual circles and by no means restricted his contacts to proto-fascists and Germanophiles. As an adherent of the Old Catholic sect – which in itself implied a certain amount of nonconformity – he showed particular interest in groups of religious inspiration centred on publications such as *Ordre nouveau, Esprit* and *Plans,* even though they were opposed to Hitlerism, fascism, Bolshevism and American capitalist fascism. In these idealistic circles he came to know such up-and-coming intellectuals as Robert Aron, Henri Daniel-Rops, Denis de Rougement, Claude Chevalley and Alexandre Marc. Step by step Abetz led his prey from pacifism to Franco-German reconciliation and on to swallowing Nazi propaganda whole.

Consequently the collaborationist state of mind did not suddenly take shape in the summer of 1940. 'Nous ne sommes pas des convertis', was the cry of Brasillach and other pan-Germanists. They were not converted after the defeat, they were already living in the faith. The original impulse – never again such a blood-letting – was honourable enough, but in the succeeding years it became ever more encumbered with anti-Semitic, anti-democratic, anti-British, anti-communist, anti-liberal accretions. To be sure, the annexation of Czechoslovakia, coming after the absorption of Austria and Kristallnacht, was such a shock that it finally propelled some, such as Romains, to bail out. Even so, there remained an impressive number of journalists, intellectuals and leaders of various social groups who continued to regard friendship with Germany as vital, and the discipline and other traits of Nazism as a model for France.

By the eve of the war Abetz had built up an elaborate structure of contacts to exploit in ways favourable to the Third Reich. That is exactly what he tried to do at a critical moment in 1939 by making a brazen attempt to destabilize the French government and keep France out of a war in Eastern Europe. Venturing to Paris in June 1939, he sought out politicians, journalists and other opinion leaders of his acquaintance to convince them that their country was being dragged into a war by Britain for British interests, that Danzig was not worth a fight and belonged to Germany anyway, and that a war would wreak devastation on France. An outraged French government expelled him. His prestige in Berlin and with Hitler personally was now higher than ever.

While it is difficult to quantify the extent of Abetz's influence in prewar France, the expulsion order, which neither Ribbentrop's fury nor repeated German diplomatic pressure succeeded in having withdrawn, speaks for itself. Thwarted in France, Abetz returned to Berlin, where he worked on French journalists until the war began. In January 1940, as plans for the invasion of France went forward,

Hitler consulted him, primarily to ask whether there was any chance the French might yet pull out of the war. Abetz said no. In the course of the following weeks he began assembling the team that would work with him during the coming occupation. Most were men in their late twenties and early thirties who already knew France, spoke French well and admired French culture. They were also marked by the humiliating defeat of 1918 and, though in some cases not Nazi party members, were inspired by a determination to destroy the Versailles Treaty and construct a united Nazi Europe in which German culture reigned supreme.

Less than twenty-four hours after the Wehrmacht marched into Paris, Abetz arrived at the Hôtel de Beauharnais behind the Quai d'Orsay, since 1814 the Prussian and later the German embassy. His duties were at first unclear. The military held complete physical control; Abetz held merely a title. However, the old Prussian generals had little desire to get involved in Franco-German political relations. Abetz had every desire and knew the ground well. Where they disagreed was over which of them would control the media and wider public affairs. After some toing and froing, Abetz conceded the military's authority over censorship while the Wehrmacht agreed to his primacy in political affairs, propaganda and cultural activities. But in the face of all the competing authorities – Wehrmacht, Gestapo and representatives of Göring and Rosenberg – his authority was circumscribed. Henri Michel summed it up in a phrase: 'Abetz had more prestige than power'.

Before getting started, Abetz had other, more urgent business to attend to. If, after the war, he had written an honest c.v., it would have listed as his initial activity 'looting'. Like other eminent Occupation officials, he looked on Paris in the way a Saracen pirate had looked on a helpless Mediterranean hill town. In his case he immediately sent out teams to seize property belonging to Jews and anyone else who had fled. The best of the loot he earmarked for the pirate-in-chief back in Berlin, with whom he was always seeking to ingratiate himself. For himself and the embassy he stole valuable furnishings and paintings from the Rothschild residence in the Faubourg St-Honoré. These thefts were but the beginning of what became the biggest art heist in history as German agents plundered homes, bank vaults, galleries and any other site where works of value were to be found.

While managing the Franco-German diplomatic relationship from the Paris end, Abetz also oversaw the entire realm of public affairs. Before 1940 his objective had been to destabilize the country. Now it was to stabilize it as a satellite. Goebbels himself, although he never gave Abetz credit personally, was convinced that Germanophile propaganda had played an important role in exciting the defeatism that led to the fall of France. If cleverly managed now, 'Paris will be ours', he said. That was precisely Abetz's aim. And to assist in his efforts, he brought with him several of his colleagues from the German-French Society.

As his deputy and chief administrator Abetz chose Rudolf Schleier, a wounded veteran and former French war prisoner. In the opinion of Hans Speidel, chief of staff of the German Commandant in Paris, he was the strongman in the embassy. A convinced Nazi – having joined the party prior to 1933 – Schleier must have been somewhat sinister, judging by a colleague's comment after the war that he was not a person with whom others on the embassy staff felt at ease although he would not have denounced a friend. The colleague was Ernst Achenbach, whom Abetz selected as his political counsellor. The only member of the team with prior diplomatic experience, Achenbach had been a junior official on the embassy staff just before the war. With a good understanding of French politics and a broad range of contacts – though with the liability of an American wife – he managed embassy affairs with a competence that allowed Abetz to concentrate on high diplomacy.

To create the impression that they were separate from the embassy, two other agencies were established *extra muros*. One was a high-powered cultural-propaganda operation called the German Institute. This was under the direction of Karl Epting, who had been in charge of student exchanges before the war. The other agency was an Information Section, responsible for press and propaganda. To buy off journalists, publishers and anyone else who was useful, it could draw on secret funds of a billion francs, which were charged to Occupation costs. The director was a wheeler-dealer and social smoothie named Rudolf Rahn, though Rahn was not the only name he went by. A Foreign Office troubleshooter, he spent much of his time running around Europe, North Africa and the Middle East shooting trouble in a series of rocambolesque adventures. Together these men formed the core of what in a short time expanded into an embassy complement of around six hundred officials and staff.

Abetz also had two senior advisors. Friedrich Sieburg was, in the eyes of the German reading public, Mr France. The long-time *Frankfurter Zeitung* correspondent in Paris, he had published in 1929 *Gott in Frankreich?* – issued in France the following year with the title *Dieu est-il français?* – extolling the *douceur de vie* of a country of which he was deeply fond but which he found rotten inside. The book is said to have been the most popular ever written by a German about France. The other advisor was Friedrich Grimm, whose surname did not belie his character. Thanks in part to his moustache, he bore a remarkable facial resemblance to Hitler. This may have lent his speeches – his *pièce de résistance* was about the Führer's concept of a future Europe – added force. A professor of law, he had defended German industrialists during the French occupation of the Ruhr and was to be the prosecuting attorney in a planned trial of Herschel Grynszpan, the young man who in November 1938 had murdered Ernst vom Rath, an official at the German embassy in Paris – the event that prompted the Nazis to stage the notorious Kristallnacht. Grimm saw the murder as part of a plot to derail an effort by those in the French government who wanted to avoid a war with Germany. He was also a prolific writer of Nazi polemics. Their anti-French tone can be gauged from his *Volk ohne Raum* (People without Space), a tome of 1,229 pages published in 1926 which argued that the French were not of the white race. Grimm also acted as the embassy's legal advisor, counselling Occupation officials to be ruthless, 'because that's just what the French population expects'. Ever the lawyer, he recommended holding a few spectacular show trials of those elements in France – civil administrators, Freemasons, Jews and 'corrupt politicians' – who were Germany's 'natural enemies'.

On his return to Paris in 1940, Abetz encountered a society so disoriented by a defeat so sudden and catastrophic that he believed he could guide its ideological evolution. Getting his hands on the press was the vital first step. Although this inevitably provoked a tug of war with the Wehrmacht, he succeeded in asserting his authority over the print media and in no time established and bankrolled a variety of newspapers intended to appeal to the main sectors of society – *La France au travail, Illustration, La Gerbe, La Vie nationale* and *Aujourd'hui*. That was just a start. The embassy's Information Section, responsible for all forms of publishing as well as radio and propaganda, was so aggressive that by September 1942 it was managing six dailies, eleven weeklies, four bi-monthlies and seven monthlies while also issuing four daily press bulletins.

Nearly everyone likes a show, and Abetz saw in this an opportunity. Hardly had he installed himself in Paris than he and Bernard Faÿ, the country's leading anti-Freemason, organized an exhibition in the Petit Palais to 'expose the nefarious conspiracy of Freemasonry'. Hated for centuries as secret plotters and enemies of the Catholic church, now the Freemasons were pilloried as the economic and political buttress of the Third Republic and as warmongers who had manoeuvred France into conflict. Not only were they accused of being philo-Semites, they were looked down on by some as worse than Jews. Pétain was one of these. 'A Jew cannot help his origins,' he told Faÿ, 'but a Freemason has chosen to become one.' The show's theme was that this occult and conspiratorial power had contributed to the decadence that had led to the defeat. Evidently German authorities were not troubled by the paradox of an exhibition deploring the very reason for their presence in Paris. If nearly everyone likes a show, no less does nearly everyone like conspiracy. Coming only a few months after the debacle, the exhibition was a terrific success, attracting nearly a million visitors who carried away zillions of propaganda brochures explaining why France had fallen. The exhibition followed by two months the outlawing of Freemasonry and the dismissal of fourteen thousand public officials, and was no doubt staged to justify the arrest, and to look forward to the deportation and even execution, of some members.

No one could have been more surprised by this success than Abetz. To keep up the momentum, he next arranged *The New Life*, a show illustrating how merry life was going to be in a Nazi Europe. That in turn was followed by an exhibition with the title *European France*. It was inaugurated with great fanfare by the Vichy government representative in Paris, Fernand de Brinon, and the military commander of Paris, Otto von Stülpnagel, as well as Pierre Laval and a representative of the archbishop of Paris. Held over a four-month period, it drew 635,000 visitors. How many of them grasped that the point of the show was that their country no longer had a future as an independent national entity but only as part of a larger Nazi Europe? Just as that exhibition was closing, a third one opened, *The Jew and France*. This turned out to be a huge flop. Abetz had expected a million visitors. Only 250,000 attended, some of them German military personnel. By now it was the autumn of 1941 and in the wake of the German invasion of the Soviet Union, propaganda had no more urgent theme than that the French faced an inescapable choice – support Hitler or see the Bolshevist hordes sweep across Europe. An exhibition, *Bolshevism against Europe*, opened in Paris in March 1942 and eventually travelled throughout France, closing in Toulouse only two days after D-Day, having been seen by around 750,000 people.

Of course, the Invader's propaganda programme was far broader and more sophisticated than merely staging crass exhibitions. Abetz and Epting calculated that of all the cultural activities that would calm anti-German feeling and demonstrate German cultural dominance, music would be the most effective. 'It is beyond war, beyond nations' – Fabre-Luce's comment was precisely the naïve response the Germans hoped for. Their strategy was as tactful as it was duplicitous. Disguising their propagandistic intent, Occupation officials stayed in the background and allowed French groups to sponsor concert performances and even decide on the programmes. When a noted *collabo* suggested introducing a performance with remarks about cooperation between France and Germany, the Germans objected. The notion was not only heavy-handed, it missed the point. And the point was not that France and Germany should be friendly partners but that the French should recognize German culture as superior.

Within a few months of the armistice France was hit by a second assault, this time by German musicians. Herbert von Karajan led off with a performance of Bach's B-minor Mass by the Aachen Orchestra and Chorus. He came back in June 1941 and wowed audiences with the Berlin State Opera in Mozart's

Abduction from the Seraglio and Wagner's *Tristan und Isolde* as well as a concert at the Palais de Chaillot. In the months and years that followed, to mention only a few of the events, there was a Beethoven Festival, a Lehár Festival, a Mozart Week, two Wagner celebrations and a Richard Strauss birthday celebration. The Mozart event commemorated the 150th anniversary of the composer's death and was celebrated in a week-long ceremony with a variety of lectures and concerts. The highlight was a performance by Hans von Benda and the Berlin Chamber Orchestra held in the courtyard of the Palais Royal.

Another commemorative event took place in May 1943 to mark the sixtieth anniversary of Wagner's death, the 130th of his birth and the fiftieth of the first Paris performance of *Die Walküre*. In a remarkable joint production, musicians and singers from Berlin, Vienna and Paris gave three memorable performances of the work. There were also concerts by the Berlin Philharmonic around the country, tours by chamber music groups and a choral concert at Notre Dame cathedral in Paris by the Regensburg Domspatzen, the boys' choir financed from Hitler's personal funds. Wilhelm Kempf, a great favourite, played the piano from one end of France to the other, and the fanatical Nazi Ely Ney performed at the Beethoven Festival. In addition to the tremendously popular Karajan, most of the leading German conductors appeared – Eugen Jochum, Hans Knappertsbusch, Clemens Krauss, Franz von Hösslin and Wolfgang Abendroth. At the request of the Wehrmacht commandant, Willem Mengelberg came from Amsterdam to conduct the full cycle of Beethoven symphonies in both 1941 and 1942. The list could go on and on. In a telling statistic, Philippe Burrin points out that in the period from mid-1942 to mid-1943 there were fully seventy-one concerts by German musicians – thirty-one in Paris and forty elsewhere. Never in peacetime, much less in wartime, had there been such a massive cultural assault.

Having destroyed Modernist paintings and sculptures at home, the Germans had nothing to send forth as propaganda in the visual arts – with one exception. Taking shape in the mid-Thirties was a heroic 'Third Reich sculpture' with no equivalent elsewhere. And thus it was that in May 1942 Occupation authorities arranged what turned out to be the cultural summit of the Occupation years and the ultimate *collabo* jamboree. This was an exhibition in the Orangerie of gigantic sculptures by Arno Breker, a disciple of Maillol and, more relevantly, Hitler's favourite artist. It opened with a brilliantly imaginative, magnificently symbolic act – Alfred Cortot and Wilhelm Kempf playing the same Mozart works simultaneously at two pianos. One could have sworn, said the wife of the head of the German Institute, that the sound came from a single instrument. 'I could scarcely believe that joint playing in such perfect harmony was even possible.' The political meaning could not have escaped the meanest dolt.

Lending the event an official character, three Vichy officials, Abel Bonnard, Benoist-Méchin and Laval, gave inaugural speeches in the presence of Abetz, the Wehrmacht commandant of Paris, the local head of the Gestapo and other assorted German officials. Present also were all the leading collaborationists in the cultural field. From the visual arts were Derain, Despiau, Van Dongen, Segonzac and Vlaminck. To pay homage the eighty-one-year-old Maillol himself came all the way from his home in the Pyrenees. Never willing to miss a party, Guitry, Arletty and Cocteau were there too, as were Brasillach, Drieu and the publisher Robert Denoël. In an accolade that he never quite lived down, Cocteau published an effusive 'Salute to Breker': 'I salute you from the lofty realm of poets, a realm where nations exist only to the extent that they contribute to the artistic treasure of the nation' – and on and on in that Pseuds Corner vein. Breker and Cocteau had been lovers during Breker's Paris years in the 1920s and the testimonial may have been as much a celebration of their old relationship as of the works themselves, which were seen by some as embarrassingly homoerotic.

The vernissage was only the beginning of the week-long festivities. Laval hosted a lunch, de Brinon a reception, Abel Bonnard a party at the Ritz, Derain a champagne breakfast at Fauchon. The German embassy and the German Institute threw parties while Brasillach organized a conference on Breker's work and a few days later a reception. The sculptor was also received at the École des Beaux-Arts and the Rodin Museum as well as privately by Van Dongen and Vlaminck. Guitry introduced him to the theatre crowd. In addition to the stunning musical evening at the Orangerie when Cortot and Kempf played, Germaine Lubin sang songs alternately in French and German. Kempf also performed the Goldberg Variations at an afternoon concert at the German Institute. The press gave the event full and effusive coverage. Eventually even Cocteau was sickened, commenting in his diary: 'The Breker event has taken on proportions similar to those of his statues. It went to his head to an unbelievable extent. He was received like a sovereign. Official dinner after official dinner. Article upon article. Advertisement after advertisement. Speech upon speech. In comparison to a spectacle like this, it would be better to be ignored, insulted, thrashed. If I were Breker I would see this not as a triumph but as a disaster.'

De Beauvoir erred in claiming that the exhibition was boycotted by 'almost the entire intelligentsia'. But she was right to the extent that the Left Bank crowd never gave it a look. Picasso and Braque were also notable for their absence. Derain at least had the decency to be so embarrassed that, when newsreel crews filmed the opening, the camera caught him trying to hide behind the genitals of one of Breker's enormous horses. Gigantism was in fact the most notable feature of Breker's works. Maillol himself felt that their size disguised their emptiness. Michel Ciry, painter, engraver and designer, complained, 'I record with sadness the spinelessness of my compatriots before the boring and colossal academicism of Arno Breker.' He might have been even sadder had he known that the bronze for the statues had come from melted-down statues confiscated from around France and that much of the workforce at Breker's atelier outside Berlin comprised French POWs who were said to have been badly treated and who found the sculptor insufferable. For all the hoopla, the show, although it had lasted two and a half months, drew a derisory 60,000 visitors, plus 45,000 German military who were no doubt encouraged to visit.

But most of these various programmes were an undoubted success, so much so that repeat performances often had to be arranged. In the provinces they frequently offered a cultural lifeline, providing the sole cultural activity held in the area. For the cynical Epting and Abetz, however, these events were primarily an enticement to attend the receptions afterwards when German officials had an opportunity to win friends and influence people – or at least the elite that mattered. How far they succeeded is impossible to know. Parisians, at least, appear to have been as cynical as the Germans. On his visits to Paris Speer found that the French guests were either bored or cowed by such events. 'Cocteau showed none of his charm and wit; fragile Despiau sat glumly in a corner of a sofa; Vlaminck stood around scarcely opening his mouth; Derain talked with French colleagues; Maillol seemed embarrassed; and Cortot, too, seemed visibly constrained.' Such was the architect's account of one embassy function.

One of the cunning practices of totalitarian governments is to take advantage of the naïveté, gullibility and vanity of artists and, step by devious step, to manipulate and corrupt them. Nazi authorities did this in Germany herself and then did it again in France, where they were on the lookout for prominent figures susceptible to flattery and favour. One of the main techniques was the old stand-by – visits, meetings and talks in praise of Franco-German friendship. These were a speciality of Dr Goebbels. Management was in the hands of the old German-French Society, run out of Berlin by the particularly disagreeable Friedrich Bran. As before the war, the organization's principal remit was to arrange tours of Germany for individuals or groups. Now it organized guided tours for writers, film people, musicians and painters. Every non-German artist in wartime Europe knew that to appear in the Third Reich was to be tainted. In the case of France, a state of war still existed, Germany was still the enemy, a million-and-a-half men were in prisoner-of-war camps, thousands were being hauled off into forced labour and still more thousands were being deported to death camps. To accept the hospitality of that country was moral treason. 'When writers and painters went to Germany to assure the conquerors of our intellectual support, I felt personally betrayed', was de Beauvoir's reaction. Sometimes the invitation was combined with a vague offer to release a few war prisoners. But in the end, as Jean Galtier-Boissière remarked, 'The fritzes did not keep their word.' And that was pretty much the story of collaboration across the board. Some French sincerely wanted it, most Germans sincerely did not.

The first to go, in October 1941, was a group of writers, ostensibly to attend a Goebbels-organized Congress of European Writers in Weimar but in fact to take a three-week junket around Germany to see the wonders of National Socialism. Declaring they wished to reaffirm their links to Germany, Drieu, Ramon Fernandez, André Fraigneau, Brasillach, Jacques Chardonne and Abel Bonnard signed on. Morand and Marcel Arland backed out. Jouhandeau hesitated but went, commenting in his diary: 'Night thoughts. For whom or for what am I here? Because from the time I knew how to read, understand and feel, I have loved Germany, her philosophers, her musicians and I think that nothing could serve humanity better than our understanding with her. In 1940 I observed very closely what happened and it is undeniable, unless one is less than honest, that the Germans could have treated us worse after their victory.' Then fell the remark – 'I would like to make my body a fraternal bridge between us and the Germans' – that caused those in the know to laugh up their sleeves. On his return Jouhandeau could not forbear praising his nation's subjugators, writing in the *Nouvelle Revue Française*, 'I was finally able to live for a few days close to people who were yesterday our enemy but whose tact towards us amazes me.'

During the day the multinational group went sightseeing and in the evening attended dinners with inevitable toasts and speeches praising love among nations. In Vienna a banquet in the splendour of the Hofburg was hosted by Baldur von Schirach, governor of Vienna and de facto poet laureate of the Third Reich. In Berlin the writers were received by Goebbels, who recited his favourite theme – that Europe faced a simple choice, Germany or Russian Bolshevism. Jouhandeau was bowled over by Schirach's charm and deeply impressed by Goebbels's 'intelligence, determination and clear-sightedness'. More than a bit of the shine was taken off the trip when at one point the train stopped along a stretch of railway line under repair. Leaning out of the windows, the group saw that the workers were French war prisoners. The sight of the wretched men contrasted so sharply with their own pampered state that they were struck dumb when the prisoners asked what they were doing in Germany. So ashamed were they that when the tour continued on towards Strasbourg, the French members of the group adamantly refused to set foot in the now-Germanified city and were shunted off to the Black Forest, presumably to listen to the cuckoos.

When a second trip to Weimar was arranged for the autumn of 1942, the Germans found few willing to go. Pierre Benoit pleaded a sick cousin, Morand was working on a speech, Montherlant was indisposed, Giono would need to be chauffeured from his home in rural Provence. Even Jouhandeau declined. In the end Drieu, Fraigneau and Chardonne went and were joined by André Thérive and Georges Blond, who labelled himself and his fellow travellers 'guests of Goethe'. In the meantime similar junkets had been arranged for figures from the worlds of music, painting, theatre and cinema. Plans for tours by architects and academics never came to fruition.

It is impossible to know whether these *voyages de propagande* had any value as *propagande* or were no more than *voyages*. Those few artists who went were in most cases already practising *collabos*. Those many who read about them – the cold and hungry population of France – were unlikely to take vicarious pleasure in the high life enjoyed by a select few.

The cultural traffic was all one-way. French films, music, plays and art shows had been proscribed in Germany at the beginning of the war and remained so, though in November 1943 Goebbels permitted some French music to be broadcast. Throughout the war, despite Vichy's persistent efforts, no French theatrical group, orchestra or opera company was ever invited to Germany. No French cultural institute was allowed to operate, no French speakers were asked to give talks, no French students were allowed to enrol at a university, no exhibition of French art was held. In the hope of getting these restrictions eased, Vichy even agreed to censor and ban French schoolbooks that displeased Occupation authorities. To no end. In the cultural as in the political field, collaboration was a swindle. The whole point of German policy was to combat French cultural influence. Vichy never caught on to the fact that the Germans were engaged in cultural warfare and that French artists were in their own way war prisoners.

From the first day of the armistice, collaborationist circles began working inde-pendently in the same direction as the Invader. Before the war they had been devoutly pro-German, in some cases pro-Nazi. Now they saw an opportunity to show their countrymen that the Germans were decent people who wanted nothing more than a happy relationship – 'marriage' was a frequently used figure of speech – between the two nations. Some of them were noted artists, intellec-tuals and social leaders with contacts well beyond Abetz's reach. By giving collab-oration a friendly face, they were enormously useful in Hitler's grand design.

One of the dottiest of the species was the writer Alphonse de Brédenbec de Châteaubriant. Of conservative Catholic Breton gentry, winner of the Prix Goncourt in 1911 for his first novel and author of a runaway best-seller between the wars, he was one more of the French artists and intellec-tuals whom the First World War left convinced that France and Germany had to reconcile. In his case, however, the form of reconciliation rested on a romantic medieval notion of an organic society in a unified Europe in which a mystical Catholicism would be amalgamated with a mystical Nazism. On meeting Hitler at Berchtesgaden in 1938, Châteaubriant was convinced he had met the new messiah and later said he had fantasized the Führer with one arm outstretched in the Hitler salute and the other holding the hand of God.

Following the fall of France, he launched a weekend cultural review, *La Gerbe*. It got off to an impressive start with a first issue containing not only the text of an interview with Marshal Pétain but also articles by Giono, Morand, Cocteau and Guitry. Colette and Montherlant were among later contributors. Its circulation eventually reached 100,000. At the same time he also organized the least disreputable of collaborationist organizations, the Groupe Collaboration, whose sponsors included members of the Académie Française, the rector of the Catholic Institute of Paris, the head of the Opéra-Comique and the curator of the Rodin Museum. Its aim was to encourage understanding between the two countries on an essentially cultural basis through its journal, *Collaboration*, and by arranging visits of artists and intellectuals, cultural events, book readings and lectures by such figures as Sieburg, Grimm and Bran. The programmes were so successful that in mid-1942 a gleeful Abetz reported to Berlin that, with encouragement, collaborators would soon overwhelm Gaullists in the battle for public opinion.

The organization's appeal was to some extent due to Châteaubriant personally. With his squirearchical demeanour and ample facial shrubbery – part country gentleman, part bearded prophet is how he came across – he conveyed such a solid respectability that his organization enjoyed a certain social cachet among the quasi-cultured middle class and clergy. In arranging meetings, he could mobilize the local notables – the prefect, church representatives and officials of the main social bodies. So, though its membership was insignificant – 26,000 in the Occupied Zone and less than half that number in the Unoccupied Zone – the organization's appeal extended beyond its own ranks.

In March 1941, when the Groupe arranged for Grimm to give a speech in Bordeaux on 'France and Germany: Yesterday and Today', the hall was filled to capacity and the speaker was given a warm introduction by the mayor, Adrien Marquet. The meeting evoked such interest that when Grimm returned a month later, twice as many people turned up as could be accommodated. The embassy claimed that 200,000 people attended the Groupe's events in the first three years. To some extent such figures create a false impression, however, since by all accounts attendees were largely the same several hundred people who went to meeting after meeting. And that the places were packed indicates not necessarily that the speaker was wildly popular but that the halls were small.

Grimm gave over a hundred talks, from Lille to Toulouse and from Bordeaux to Nice. He went on talking right to the end – in Nîmes in June 1944 after the D-Day landings and in Nice several weeks later. Strange to say, instead of being run out of town, he was evidently well received. After the war he himself confessed to being astonished at 'how loyal these audiences remained in their firm conviction about the right course'. But how much of an impact did he have? Little or none, apparently, when he spoke to a general audience. The prefect of the Côte d'Or department recorded the bad taste left by his speech at the inauguration of the German Institute in Dijon. 'Yet again, it is curious to note the extent to which German propaganda misunderstands the psychology of the French.' That was also the reaction on a similar occasion in Besançon. When Grimm spoke to members of the Groupe Collaboration, however, his message was well received. It never varied throughout those years and was as deceptive as it was simple – France and Germany must avoid war with one another and work together for a new Europe. Not for a second can any of those dear bourgeois have dreamt that what was in store for France, in whatever form it continued to exist, was to be a mere satrapy in that 'new Europe'.

For most members, as for for Châteaubriant, collaboration had the quality of a religion that demanded self-abnegatory, blind devotion. They never wavered in their dream of a new 'organically united', Aryanized Europe free of communism. At the end the dream turned to nightmare. Come the Liberation, some local leaders of the group were summarily shot. Châteaubriant himself fled, became 'Dr Alfred Wolf' and vanished into Austria. There he ended his years, appropriately, in a monastery in the Tyrol.

Also valuable to German authorities were the collaborationist Parisian hostesses, most notable among whom were the three Maries – Marie-Louise Bousquet, Marie-Blanche de Polignac and Marie-Laure de Noailles. Their salons and soirées offered a discreet way for the *gratin* of the Occupation to meet the *gratin* of the cultural collaboration. This is the way it worked. At one of her soirées the márquise de Polignac, for example, might introduce the collaborationist editor Ramon Fernandez to Gerhard Heller, the officer responsible for censoring books, who would in turn be introduced to Marie-Louise Bousquet, who would invite the German officer to a private recital in her residence on the place du Palais-Bourbon, where the collaborationist cellist Pierre Fournier would play to a collaborationist audience. There Heller would meet, among others, the collaborationist Marcel Jouhandeau who would introduce him to his close *collabo* friend Florence Gould, who would incorporate him into her collaborationist 'literary' salon. This is almost exactly the way Heller infiltrated Parisian high society.

'How come it is', Harold Nicolson once asked himself about a prewar London society hostess, 'that this plump and virulent little bitch should

hold such social power?' In the case of Gould there was no doubt about
the answer. Money – American and tons of it. Behind her back Jünger and
Heller used to joke about her wealth and its power to buy anything or anyone.
While Sylvia Beach and some three thousand British and American civilians languished in an internment camp, Gould remained at liberty. Although
others found it impossible to get a pass to cross into the Unoccupied
Zone, she went back and forth at will. While the rest of the population went
hungry, she kept the best table in Paris. As Heller noted, she may have been a
cultural nullity but she had 'one appeal that in those days was not to be
underestimated – nothing was lacking at her table. Some of the guests . . . had
difficulty managing these opulent meals with their refined wine, champagne and – rarest of all – coffee, because their stomachs had become so
unaccustomed to such things.'

Florence Gould was born of French parents in San Francisco, which she
abandoned for France following the 1906 earthquake. After a marriage and
divorce, she became a singer and caught the attention of Frank Jay Gould, the
seriously rich son of a corrupt American railway mogul, and married him in
1923. Frank lived on the Riviera, and that is where the armistice had found his
wife as well. Florence quickly returned to Paris, however, and in no time was
cultivating Wehrmacht officers and Gestapo officials. She received every
Thursday afternoon but was also At Home to the right people at almost any
time. Jünger was often there, with Heller. Also Helmut Knochen: it is hard to
think of a more abominable character to have as a guest. A fanatical Nazi, head
of the Gestapo in Paris, Knochen was the protégé of the famous Gestapo chief
Reinhold Heydrich, who had rewarded him with the Paris post for his brilliant
espionage work. Knochen it was who directed the rounding-up of French Jews
and who ordered the blowing-up of seven Paris synagogues in October 1941.
And it was he who ordered executions of hostages by firing squad in reprisal
actions. When an outraged Otto von Stülpnagel, the military commander,
appealed to Berlin to have him recalled, such was Knochen's prestige inside
the Nazi party that it was the general who had to walk. The Gestapo official
was not Florence's only friend in the German intelligence network. Jünger and
Heller were with her late one evening, sipping 1911 champagne, when there
arrived a friend whom she introduced as 'Colonel Patrick'. The colonel turned
out to be a good friend, the head of German counterintelligence in Lyon.

Florence liked to think of her salon as a literary one. In reality it was nothing
more than a meeting place for hardcore collaborators, fascists, Nazis, anti-
Semites, Anglophobes and vociferous anti-Americans who were enticed by
her food and wine. Her favourite pet was Marcel Jouhandeau, the ardent anti-
Semite who in 1938 had published *Le Péril juif*, a peril epitomized for him by
Léon Blum and his Popular Front government. Needless to say, the Left Bank

crowd had nothing to do with her; indeed, as Camus's biographer observed, Sartre and Camus rejected invitations from society hostesses, 'above all from Florence Gould'. Although figures such as Giraudoux, Montherlant, Marcel Arland, Cocteau, Morand and Pierre Benoit looked in once or twice, the most important names in French culture snubbed her. Léautaud went but grumbled to his diary that he found his hostess and her other guests frivolous and the conversation trivial. He returned home 'disturbed, weary and hoping that the night and sleep would erase the memory'.

There was one writer whom Florence admired but could not entice to call – Céline. On occasion she went to him, uninvited, and stayed to dinner, which she brought with her. 'She was absolutely insistent on buying my manuscripts', the writer said later. 'I refused, not wanting to owe anything to an American multimillionairess. In her rush to leave one evening – she was drunk and it was dark – she slipped on the steps at the bottom of the staircase and broke her leg.' Her unwilling host refused to visit her in hospital. Céline was not without a certain respect, though, characterizing her as 'amazing and not stupid, a snob'.

But why did cold-blooded Gestapo officials like Knochen and 'Colonel Patrick' call on someone so vapid? To hear the latest gossip in artistic circles? To guzzle her boundless supply of vintage champagne? Or was it simply her company? Florence enjoyed the pleasures of the bed, a bed that Jünger and other German officers came to know well. As Céline later testified, 'She was enormously compromised with the Luftwaffe – where she had at least three young lovers and was very much at home in the German military headquarters.' Come the Liberation, she was hauled in for interrogation. Asked about it later by Galtier-Boissière, she responded flippantly, 'I forget the charge but I still remember the date.' All was well, however, that ended well – thanks to having lots of money and a passport of the country she betrayed.

CHAPTER 4

'I GET A KICK OUT OF YOU'

The name of Cole Porter's famous song of 1934 would be a good title for a book about German occupation policy. As Pierre Lazareff, self-exiled editor of *Paris-Soir*, explained on arriving in New York in 1940, 'So long as the Germans occupy France, our collaboration with them will be like the relationship of a pair of boots to a pair of buttocks.' Phrased less poetically, the Invader set down the rules and the Invaded obeyed them or got a hefty kick. In the cultural sphere, the kicks were withal judiciously administered. Cicero's famous maxim, *inter arma silent musae* – in the face of weapons, the arts are silent – was not to be Occupation policy. At all costs German authorities wanted to avoid the kind of popular discontent that might lead to open civil disorder. A vigorous cultural life was therefore not so much a means of beautifying the Occupation as the principal way – effectively the only way – to ameliorate the material hardships of occupation. The bedrock of the Wehrmacht's policy was therefore to allow just that amount of cultural freedom that would make life bearable but not undermine the absolute imperative of civil order. The *musae*, far from being silent, were to be encouraged to speak. But – a huge but – they would say only what the Occupier allowed. In reality cultural freedom was therefore a tactic in a stratagem of repression.

To carry out this pacification programme the Wehrmacht set up what it unashamedly, if appropriately, called a Propaganda Department. Its job was to manipulate public opinion in a way that would make the German presence palatable. On the one hand it encouraged cultural activities, but on the other draconically controlled every aspect of them. Whatever might be considered as anti-German or reflecting the influence of Freemasons, Jews or communists was automatically barred. Wehrmacht officials vetted radio programmes, newspapers and journals, books, film scripts and documentaries. The Department worked through branches, called *Staffeln*, located in Paris, Bordeaux, Angers and other cities in the Occupied Zone. Every month these pre-censored an average of some 87 private art galleries, 35 museums, 60 plays, 750 arts programmmes and 50 music programmes. To guard against evasion, they followed up with spot checks. They employed 32,000 informants (colloquially known as *mouches* – flies) and opened around 1,500 letters a day. They had snoops in lycée and university classrooms. In short, all forms of expression were at the mercy of Wehrmacht bureaucrats whom Abetz and his embassy colleagues frankly described as 'uneducated officers, dyed-in-the-wool party functionaries and fourth-rate journalists'.

There were some 1,200 such cretins. Their boss was Major Heinz Schmidke, a misassigned, stiff-necked infantry officer who spoke no French and had no interest in culture. He was so universally unpopular in the Wehrmacht that he almost arouses sympathy. 'A square head', commented one colleague. 'He had no knowledge whatsoever of France, and no one took him or his rages too seriously.' Goebbels, to whom he was also answerable, considered him 'a total washout'. It is not surprising that his Department was regularly outsmarted by Abetz and his staff and steadily lost influence, until in 1942 most of its responsibilities, except for media censorship and paper distribution, were transferred to the embassy. In typical military fashion, Schmidke was then promoted.

For obvious reasons radio and press were of most immediate concern to the Invader. Accompanying the first troops into Paris on 14 June were German officials and journalists who headed straight for the offices of the National Radio, newspapers and news agencies. On the newsstands could soon be found a vast array of dailies, weeklies and monthly journals, some old and some new. Journalists needed little imagination to know what could get past the censors and were only too happy to censor themselves. Still, they needed to be fed. So several times a week the Propaganda Department held meetings to hand out the line to be taken on current events. Editors never bothered to attend and fewer and fewer journalists showed up. Hermann Eich, the head of the section, described those who came as 'very visibly bored'. He went on to recall that piles of handouts were passed around. 'In Berlin, half a dozen offices were manufacturing words for us, all blaming the Jews, et cetera, in idiotic journalese.' Needless to say, readers took for granted that newspapers – and their correspondents – were German-financed, censored and controlled. 'He has been in the pay of every government in the past and is now on the take from the Germans,' Galtier-Boissière said of Jean Luchaire, editor of *Les Nouveaux Temps*. 'Tomorrow he would touch the Mongols if the Mongols were camping in Paris.'

So though no one believed them, everyone read them, and altogether they enjoyed a circulation of around two million. Yet dishonest and twisted reporting was the least noxious feature of the Occupation press. Worse was the prevalence of hardcore ideological pornography. This was the speciality of a dozen or so weeklies, best known of which were *Je suis partout* (I am everywhere) – popularly known as *Je chie partout* (I shit everywhere) – *Au Pilori* (To the scaffold), *Aujourd'hui* and *Gringoire*, an age-old organ of the Catholic right. There was little to distinguish among them. They were ultra-*collabo*, of course, but the collaboration they wanted was with the tough Germans rather than the namby-pamby Vichyssois. Their vocabulary was vile. Their message was odious. Their targets were democracy, parliamentarianism, Jews, Freemasons, the British and anyone connected with the Popular Front and indeed any of the governments of the Third Republic. Culture was no less an object of their terrorist operations. Anyone and anything – play, book, film and so on – was fair game. Worst of all, they made a profession of lethal denunciation. In her book about the career of Robert Brasillach, Alice Kaplan shows how low some human beings can sink. Referring to the plight of Jews, Gaullists and members of the Resistance, she writes: '*Je Suis Partout* published a column each week entitled "*Partout et ailleurs*" (Everywhere and elsewhere) revealing the identities and locations of those trying to save themselves. . . . Often their exact addresses were given.' *Au Pilori* was just as bad. It not only informed its readers of the address of the agency to which to send denunciatory letters but, if that was not convenient, it invited readers to send them to the newspaper's own office and it would forward them on their behalf.

At the opposite end of the respectability spectrum was the cultural review *Comoedia*. Founded in 1906 as a weekly journal of arts and letters, it enjoyed a distinguished period in the Twenties, went into decline and finally died in 1937. To create something similar without giving the impression that it was a new, German-invented publication, Abetz 'revived' it in 1941 and appointed René Delange as editor. Delange, a well-regarded prewar journalist, recruited a team of intellectually reputable correspondents for the whole range of the arts and welcomed independent contributions. Articles about contemporary political events, to say nothing of the hysterics of *Je suis partout* and its brethren, never sullied its pages. Many years later a scholar analysed 3,396 of its articles and found that only 5 per cent betrayed overt political bias. 'Overt' was the key word.

The first issue set the tone. On the front page appeared articles by Montherlant, Jean-Louis Barrault and Honegger as well as a report on the return to France of Saint-Exupéry. The second page carried a long, enthusiastic article by Sartre on *Moby Dick* and an interview with Paul Valéry. During the years that followed many of the great names in French cultural life gave lustre to the review's image. More than any other publication, *Comoedia* presented the respectable face of collaboration. That was its danger. In reply to a question about the review's objective, Delange was frank enough to acknowledge that 'the principal aim is to work for complete Franco-German collaboration'. He played his hand honestly, but the game itself was rigged. Pierre Assouline alembicated Delange into a phrase – 'A figurehead of the intelligentsia under the jackboot.'

Yet *Comoedia* might be reckoned one of Abetz's greatest cultural successes. By its very nature, the journal created the impression of a France as culturally flourishing as in the best of times and as intellectually free as ever. So it coincided perfectly with the German design of roping in – and corrupting – distinguished French intellectuals and artists. That had been the technique of the Sohlberg Circle. And now again 'innocent' French intellectuals were tricked into compromising themselves. Sartre wrote about Melville but would not have dared to write nor would the censors have passed a piece about Thomas Mann. The arts correspondent Gaston Diehl wrote freely about Matisse but would never have risked mentioning the name of Emil Nolde or any other German Expressionist. In fact, the journal's contributors corrupted themselves twice – once by writing for the publication and later by their casuistical double talk justifying what they did. Sartre at least saw through the façade and after reviewing *Moby Dick* declined to write for the paper again.

With a controlled press and little or no postal or other contact with the outside world, including the Unoccupied Zone, the Occupied Zone was effectively sealed off. But there was an invisible hole – the airwaves. The Germans did their best to popularize their Radio-Paris, but it was hopelessly tarnished. In his travels around France Friedrich Grimm found that people thought of Radio-Paris as German, Radio-Vichy as collaborationist and the BBC as '*our* radio station'. Throughout the country, tuning into the news from London – the volume kept low because of the harsh sanctions for listening – was a daily devotion. 'It was listened to religiously at 8 in the evening with every family member sitting closely around the receiver as though around an altar.' This is the scene as described by Henri Michel, but it can be found in account after account of the Occupation years. So effective were BBC broadcasts that German authorities candidly admitted that their propaganda was completely outclassed by what was beamed in from London.

It was easy to control the press, art exhibitions, music events and films. Books were a different matter. To begin with, libraries, bookshops and publishers' warehouses were filled with hundreds of titles that a totalitarian invader of any stripe was bound to consider objectionable. With their rich experience in combating free thought, German officials had brought with them a list, the 'Bernhard List', of 143 titles – such as works on Hitler, the Third Reich and Nazi racial policies – which they ordered booksellers immediately to turn over for destruction. This cull was just the beginning.

Throughout the Occupation the Germans did their best to avoid giving the impression of being the brutal Invader; even the Gestapo usually had the delicacy to make its arrests during the curfew between midnight and dawn. So wherever possible they inveigled the French to do their dirty work for them. When it came to banning books they had no difficulty in recruiting volunteers to help. To compile a comprehensive list of books for liquidation, they found a willing executioner in Henri Filipacchi, a leading employee of Hachette, which put on an annual bibliography of every book published in French. Filipacchi drafted a preliminary list, which he circulated to Paris publishers for their own suggestions. On the basis of this document, the Propaganda Department, the German embassy and the Gestapo compiled a catalogue, the so-called 'Otto List' – not named after Abetz, as is commonly believed. The heading of the list – 'Works Withdrawn from Sale by Publishers' – loaded responsibility onto the French themselves. Only in its small print did it add 'or forbidden by German authorities'. Further underlining the French lead, a preface declared that it was publishers themselves who had 'decided to withdraw from sale . . . books which, by their lying and tendentious spirit, have poisoned French public opinion'. To remove any remaining doubt, the preface concluded, 'German authorities have noted with satisfaction the initiative of French publishers'. In a final touch, it was not the Propaganda Department but the Publishers' Guild that distributed the list – in 48,000 copies.

Bad as that was, it was not the worst of it. Scarcely had the armistice been signed and well before the Otto List had been drawn up, French publishers were grovelling before the Invader by anticipating his demands and volunteering to bind themselves to a censorship agreement – an agreement to censor themselves before even being asked to do so. The evil genius behind this idea was the noted publisher Bernard Grasset. Before having so much as laid eyes on a German official, he was advising his colleagues to accept German censorship and to do so willingly. With this thought in mind he hurried to Vichy and secured Laval's consent to offer the Germans a censorship accord. To anyone with a belief in free thought – or thought at all – the resulting document is sickening to read. Candid enough at least to call itself a censorship agreement, the document set down 'the limits within which a publisher can exercise his activity'. It promised that 'French thought' would be permitted to 'pursue its mission', but immediately added, 'while respecting the rights of the victor'. After giving with one hand and taking with the other, it said publishers should voluntarily censor themselves by 'eliminating undesirable works' from their inventories and by publishing nothing which 'in any way whatsoever [might] damage German prestige or interests'.

'This was the system used in prisons where a selected inmate supervises the other prisoners.' Such is the icy comment by Pierre Assouline in his biography of one of the self-censoring publishers, Gaston Gallimard. The contract was a clear example of art imitating politics à la Vichy, where concessions were offered even before demanded and in this case even before political collaboration had been formally sealed with the famous Pétain–Hitler handshake in October 1940. What is shocking is how quickly, easily and unanimously 140 publishers signed an agreement that turned them into major executors of the German cultural strategy for France. 'Evidently no problem of conscience kept Denoël or almost all the other Parisian publishers from reopening their doors, no matter under what conditions,' Assouline remarks. And so, in return for their willing collaboration, they retained their firms, their staff and their lists, and placed themselves in a position to make solid profits by publishing books acceptable to the Invader. Nothing was lost save honour. Theirs was one of the most disgraceful acts in the cultural sphere during the whole of the Occupation.

As for works already published, the Otto List condemned to destruction over a thousand titles. Most of them – in the main unknown works by unknown authors – were published after 1930 and were in one way or another incompatible with Nazism. In the course of history, indexes of proscribed books have always made themselves laughable in one way or another. In the case of the Otto List one of the outstanding follies was the entry on page 2 that read: 'Hitler, Adolf. Mein Kampf (Mon Combat)'. An entry on a subsequent page listed extracts from the same work. Yet perhaps the ban was not so ridiculous. If they read it, the French would know that Hitler despised them and admired the British – whom they were now being instructed to hate. The inclusion of a pro-Nazi book by the English journalist G. Ward Price was one of many further absurdities. In the irony department, the three most unabashedly collaborationist publishers saw their inventories significantly depleted by the ban – Grasset lost 35 titles, Denoël 29 and Fernand Sorlot 40. Several writers who had become arch-*collabos* immediately after the defeat found their earlier anti-German works on the index.

The list was essentially limited to anti-Nazi titles by French authors or French translations of foreign authors. In the latter category were primarily political refugees and German Jews. These were singled out for having, as the document phrased it, 'betrayed the hospitality that France has accorded them . . . and unscrupulously promoted war, from which they hoped to profit for their egotistical ends'. So, irrespective of content, out went popular novels by notable anti-Nazis such as Heinrich and Thomas Mann, Franz Werfel, Erich Maria Remarque and Feuchtwanger, as well as titles by such Jewish writers as Sigmund and Anna Freud, Stefan Zweig and Vicki Baum. Not mentioned, however, were Jewish writers of nationalities other than German – for example, Irène Némirovsky, even though she was well known as a Jewish writer of 'Jewish' fiction. Scientific works by Jews were allowed, though not Einstein's political commentary *How I See the World.* Not until 1941 did the authorities let it be known that, while not formally prohibited, the publication of works by French Jews would be considered inopportune. A high proportion of titles on the new list were of a political nature, mostly books and tracts that had been published in the Thirties about German policies under Hitler. Churchill made the list, as did John Foster Dulles, Anthony Eden, H.G. Wells, Lloyd George, de Gaulle and former premiers Reynaud, Daladier and Blum. Because of the alliance at the time with the Soviet Union, the confiscation of communist literature was limited; even so, certain arbitrarily selected works by Marx, Lenin and Trotsky (*Défense du terrorisme*) were included.

Like various lists of proscribed books, paintings and music in the Third Reich itself, the Otto List was amended and expanded. In July 1941, following the invasion of the Soviet Union, books of a 'communist nature' were banned wholesale. Forbidden at the same time were translations of English-language books except for classics, as well as works by Jewish authors and biographies of Jews, even if by non-Jews. A year later a second Otto List was circulated, essentially codifying earlier criteria. In May 1943 a final one was issued, but it was no longer marked 'withdrawn from sale' or 'banned' but the considerably less exigent 'undesirable'. Heinrich and Thomas Mann along with Freud were now promoted to having 'all [their] works included'. The famous Swiss Protestant theologian Karl Barth, previously unlisted, was placed in the same category, presumably not for his theology but for his outspoken personal opposition to Nazism. To clear up any confusion about who was Jewish and therefore 'undesirable', a list of names was attached as an appendix.

Even in terms of combating ideas by outlawing books, the lists accomplished little or nothing and are mostly of interest for what was not on them. Here was a case of throwing away the bath water and leaving the baby. The entire Western intellectual and cultural legacy was left essentially untouched. French classics and French fiction were ignored entirely. The Surrealists were not proscribed, nor were most writers in exile, normally an especially despised category. Gide was there, but solely for his book hostile to the Soviet Union and only remained there during the brief time that Germany and Russia were allied. Similarly, only a few political books by Louis Aragon and Roger Martin du Gard were barred. Otherwise not a great – or even near-great – name in French letters was mentioned, not even Proust, despite his partly Jewish mother. To be sure, La Fontaine's *Fables* was included, but only in the form of a light-hearted satire, *Jean de La Fontaine et Hitler.* By and large the lists were little more than a petulant, petty attempt to settle scores with opponents of the Third Reich, especially those Germans who had fled. The most serious consequence for the general reading public was to be deprived of the works of such popular German writers as the Manns, Baum and Zweig. Later on, as censorship tightened on translations of American and British books, readers also had to do without such bestsellers of the early Occupation period as Louis Bromfield's *The Rains Came*, Margaret Mitchell's *Gone with the Wind* and Melville's *Moby Dick* – works that had been highly praised by critics across the political spectrum.

So publishers actively collaborated. Restrictions on what might go into print steadily increased. But officials of the Propaganda Department were by no means appeased. Like surly schoolmasters berating dumb schoolboys, they summoned representatives of publishers several times a week to criticize, advise, direct. They reprimanded them for errant ways, past and present. During the Thirties publishers had brought out books by German émigrés and by other writers unfriendly to the Third Reich, they said. Now they must clean up their book lists, promote collaborationist works and publish German books in translation. If they behaved, they might be rewarded with some precious paper for other titles. They behaved. Putting profits above principle, publishers turned themselves into what the noted writer Julien Gracq scorned as 'a propaganda department'. In that spirit and despite the paper shortage, the publishing trade flourished – in fact more profitably than in the Thirties.

In addition to browbeating by the Germans, some publishers had to contend with a barrage of vituperation from the right-wing writers and intellectuals who had felt unloved by the important publishing houses. In the new political climate they could at last settle old scores. Gaston Gallimard was a prime target. 'Gallimard? Where have we seen that name? At the bottom of books by André Gide, Malraux, Aragon and Freud; Surrealist books, suspicious books afflicted by necrosis.' This was the *Liebesgruss* of the book critic of *Au Pilori*. In a classic expression of the resentments of the far right, he promised revenge on 'a gang of malefactors [that] has operated in French literature from 1909 to 1939 under the orders of the gang leader, Gallimard'. He concluded, 'Gallimard, murderer of the mind! Gallimard, bringer of rot! Gallimard, chief malefactor! French youth vomit you!'

And how did the malefactor respond to these eructations? More or less pretending to be unaware of them, Gallimard simply carried on carrying on. 'But to eliminate the obstacles created by the Occupation,' his biographer observes, 'he had to resort to double talk and to moving in circles where collaborators and their masters were to be met – for it was there that power (censorship, paper supply, and safe-conducts) was to be found.' So he made his way to the German embassy and the German Institute. He dined with Propaganda Department officials. All the while, however, he allowed the firm's offices to be used for secret meetings of the underground communist publication *Les Lettres françaises*. Such were the ambiguities of literary life during the Occupation.

Not every publisher hedged his bets. Bernard Grasset committed himself wholeheartedly to collaboration – even envisaging himself, according to Assouline, as 'commissar of publishing'. No slouch, by November 1940 he had already got a book into print praising 'the creative power of the Führer'. In the years that followed he often dined at the Brasserie Lipp with Heller and other officers of the Propaganda Department. And so often did he invite high-ranking Germans to his house in the Paris suburb of Garches that it was nick-named Garchesgaden. His publishing list included most of the political *collabos* of note and even excerpts of Hitler's writings published under the title *Principes d'action* (*Principles of Action*). Unlike Gaston Gallimard, however, he would sometimes turn the tables and threaten the Occupation authorities. With a touch of reverse blackmail, he warned them on one occasion that if they failed to provide paper to those 'who are loyal to you', some authors would 'defect' and publish in the Unoccupied Zone. A bluff, but these were sometimes successful.

And what about the object of it all, the books themselves? Booksellers hung on to as many proscribed books as possible and to some extent compensated for their losses by selling them under the counter at exorbitant prices. In a city famous for its countless bookshops, bookstalls and private vendors, it is anything but surprising that the German ordinance was so widely disregarded that authorities had repeatedly to threaten 'very serious sanctions'. Despite the evasions, however, a horrendous total of 2,242 tons of books were collected up and dispatched to death row – a huge garage in the avenue de la Grande Armée – en route to being pulped. Inspecting the books was the responsibility of Heller as head of the literature section of the Propaganda Department. 'In the dim light that came through the dusty windows,' he later wrote, 'it was with a heavy heart that I saw all the stacks of dirty and damaged books that were for me sacred objects.'

However sacred the books and however heavy his heart may have been, Heller was the German official who held French literature by the throat. And this was not just because he vetted its destruction but also because he was the principal official to decide whether new works should even be born. Any author who hoped to see his work in print in the Occupied Zone had to submit it to him in manuscript for approval. A civilian with the military rank of lieutenant, Heller was typical of many Germans engaged in cultural affairs – educated, even cultivated, with some knowledge of France and French culture. Although his academic background lay in Italian language and literature, he had eagerly taken up a travel grant to spend the academic year 1934–35 studying philosophy in Toulouse. On returning to Germany, he was picked up by Berlin Radio and employed in its overseas service as an Italian specialist – writing Nazi propaganda to be beamed to Italy. Upon the fall of France, he jumped at an offer from the Propaganda Ministry to work as literary censor in Paris, arriving there on his thirty-first birthday in November 1940.

In 1981 Heller published an account of those years, *Un Allemand à Paris*, with a subsequent German version, *In einem besetzten Land*. Survivors write the histories and the illustrious censor waited thirty-six years, until all the other allemands à Paris were dead and could not contradict him, to tell his story – and to stick the knife into all his former colleagues. His book, a masterpiece of the *suppressio veri* and *suggestio falsi*, has hoodwinked many readers. On the one hand he omitted compromising personal facts, such as having joined the Nazi party very early – in February 1934 – when it was still a voluntary act of ideological commitment. On the other he catalogued his alleged enlightened actions on behalf of French writers without citing a single verifiable fact. Admitting he was infected with a slight touch of anti-Semitism caught from contact with Nazis, he claims to have been healed of it while in Paris. Yet when Youki Desnos appealed to him in 1944 to save the life of Max Jacob, he told her, 'Max Jacob is a Jew, Madam, those people, they are like vermin.' And, as Philippe Burrin found in examining German documents, Heller it was who took the lead in banning books by Jewish writers. Come the Liberation, he made no effort to exculpate himself, because he felt he had done nothing to require repentance. Even forty years later he could not see the incongruity of being a Francophile and a censor of French literature, an Occupier in a country that had been crushed and someone who enjoyed every minute of his time there.

As he presents himself in his book, Heller was less an Occupation official than a man about town – albeit in the bizarre way of the time when even *collabos* rarely invited him to their homes and did not want to be seen with him in public at all or at least not until he had changed into civilian clothes. He was amazed and touched when Drieu once insisted on their going to a restaurant together even though he was in uniform. The memoir tells of dining at the Ritz – where he complained that the food got more and more basic as the war went on – cultivating *collabo* writers and frequenting the salons of the two *collabo* queens, Marie-Louise Bousquet and Florence Gould, both of whom he held in awe.

Although the bulk of the 216 pages is devoted to his social conquests, Heller nevertheless gives a few, almost inadvertent glimpses of the operations of his office. On arriving in Paris, the Wehrmacht had stopped all book publishing. Heller's first job was to deal with the submissions that had accumulated in the intervening four months. He said he was aghast on being shown to his office and first beholding the mountain of waiting manuscripts. 'They were piled up everywhere, on bookshelves, tables and chairs, even on the floor. I was simply told: "read them all" . . . For weeks I did nothing but read manuscripts.' And read he did. The only authors sure of getting his approval, however, were those who supported the Occupation. Of the first batch of manuscripts he licensed, all were works by notorious arch-*collabos* – among them Marcel Arland, Jacques Benoist-Méchin, Abel Bonnard, Henry Bordeaux, Drieu, Fabre-Luce, Chardonne and Brasillach. Other writers and publishers sometimes had to abase themselves and plead for approval. Only three of seventeen manuscripts submitted by Mercure de France in 1942 received his approval. Humiliation was often the price to be paid for getting a work in print, as even as distinguished a writer as François Mauriac found. On finishing his novel *La Pharisienne* (*A Woman of the Pharisees*) in 1941, he was advised by Grasset to check with the German Institute before the text went into print. Epting authorized publication but with a print run of only five thousand copies. In the view of the author this was almost tantamount to rejection. Although accounts differ, Heller apparently intervened and, in return for some textual concessions, the initial print run was raised to 25,000. After the war Mauriac found it difficult to live down his dedication in one copy of the work: 'To Lieutenant Heller who took an interest in the fate of *La Pharisienne*, with my gratitude.'

Some writers were treated far worse. Heller himself cited the case of Georges Duhamel, the distinguished intellectual and permanent secretary of the Académie Française, whose book about the mass flight in 1940 was forbidden by German authorities. When Duhamel asked for reconsideration, Heller told him curtly, 'You are our enemy and that is enough reason for our decision.' Sometimes a problem could arise over a single word. Roland Dorgelès wanted to reprint his *Les Croix de bois* (*Wooden Crosses*) about life in the trenches during the Great War, the book that had made him famous on its appearance in 1919 and nearly won him the Prix Goncourt over Proust. But when he adamantly declined to delete the word *boche* from the text, Heller refused a licence. Dorgelès and Heller were again at loggerheads over a reprint of his 1937 book on dictatorships, *Vive la liberté*. Not surprisingly Heller would authorize only the part about the Soviet Union, and not surprisingly the author refused to make any cuts. There was also the case of Charles Péguy, the famous essayist and freethinker, whose popular *La France* was sanitized by Gallimard so that Heller would authorize a reprint. Of this Pierre Assouline acidly remarked, 'One is moved to meditate on the unjust posterity of Péguy, killed in battle by the Germans in 1914 and then mutilated by them twenty-seven years later – with the help of the French.'

Heller as well as Abetz liked to brag, both during and after the war, that the number of books published in France had not only actually increased during the Occupation but also exceeded the figures for Britain and America – in

1943, 9,348 titles appeared, compared to 8,320 in the US and 6,705 in the UK. The claim was disingenuous, to say the least. Print runs of most French books were tiny and much of the French output comprised collaborationist works, German propaganda and translations of German books. Anything having to do with the real world in which the French people lived was out of bounds. The consequence of German policies was an impoverishment – perhaps more accurately, a near-starvation – of the literary scene.

While the aim of the Wehrmacht's Propaganda Department was the negative one of preventing any undesirable information or ideas from reaching the French, the objective of Abetz's team was the positive – or more positively negative – one of radically changing the French concept of both themselves and the Germans. It was never Occupation policy to Germanify the French in the way that French language, culture and customs were suppressed in Alsace after the armistice. But they were to be made to feel so defeated, so humiliated, so inferior, so dependent, that they would see no alternative but to acknowledge Germans as their superiors and willingly collaborate. 'In terms of political power, France is at our mercy. We must now try to dominate her in spirit.' These were words from an official report by Abetz's close subordinate Friedrich Bran, who was now appointed head of the German-French Society. With equally brutal frankness he defined France's new position as that of 'a docile participant in the new European Order'. In his wartime novel *Le Silence de la mer* (*The Silence of the Sea*), Jean Bruller (Vercors) puts words in the mouth of a Wehrmacht officer that could just as well have been spoken by Bran or any other Occupation official: 'We have the possibility of destroying France and destroyed she shall be. Not just her power but also her soul. Her soul, above all. Her soul is the greatest danger. That's our aim at the moment. Our smiles and our solicitude are mere camouflage.'

The high command for this offensive against French culture was the German Institute under Karl Epting. After receiving his degree in German studies at Tübingen University in 1928, Epting had been active in an international student exchange organization in Geneva. Thanks to this connection plus a semester spent at Dijon University in 1926, he was appointed director of the German student exchange programme in Paris in 1933, which he ran until the outbreak of war. A conservative nationalist, Epting had welcomed Hitler's coming to power as a way of making Germans, as he expressed it, more ideologically cohesive and conscious of their German-ness. In his hands the exchange programme was not intended to help Germans understand France or even to introduce German culture to France. It was to make every German student, professor, speaker or artist who visited the country more consciously German. This cultural chauvinism was reflected and even magnified in his official reports and published articles. Towards the end of the Thirties, French police came to suspect Epting of being an agent for German intelligence, though a postwar search of German archives produced no supporting evidence.

On returning to Paris to take up his duties in June 1940, Epting, like Abetz, began with a brief career in grand larceny. In his case it was pilfering the archives of the Foreign Ministry, the Socialist party and the political leaders of the Third Republic. His great coup was finding the original of the Versailles Treaty and even the table on which it had been signed, and sending them off to Berlin to be presented to Hitler. He then tracked down the painting collections of the Louvre and, when the French authorities were slow in supplying inventories, threatened to break open the containers and inspect the contents himself. He also participated in the looting of private art collections until Wehrmacht officials objected.

For its headquarters the Institute confiscated the eighteenth-century Hôtel de Sagan, the former Polish embassy, with handsome rooms for offices, receptions, meetings and a library. The staff was organized into divisions for literature, schools and universities, and language training, as well as music, theatre, painting and film. For largely devious purposes, two additional divisions were added in 1942. One was devoted to art history, probably with a view to inventorying French art works for later seizure and export to Germany. The other dealt with agriculture, with the unstated intention of improving French agricultural production for German benefit. Branch institutes were subsequently opened in major cities of the Occupied Zone and after 1942 in what had been the Unoccupied Zone as well. These branches proved to be so popular – normally they were welcomed to the area by the prefect, the mayor and the bishop – that by 1944 fifteen of them with fifty-six sub-branches had been established.

The institutes were staffed by persons with an expert knowledge of French cultural and intellectual life. In Paris, Epting's deputy, Karl-Heinz Bremer, was a scholar of French language and literature. He was a personal acquaintance of Montherlant – who described him as 'brusque, plain-spoken, jovial' – and had translated his works into German. From 1936 to 1938 he had been a lecturer at the École Normale Supérieure in Paris and after that at the Kiel Institute for Politics and International Law. A hardcore Nazi, Bremer was arrogant, tall, blond and blatantly Aryan. His good looks were said to have caused 'tremors in the homosexual milieu of Paris' – specifically on the part of Brasillach, who nearly worshipped him.

Even though he and his team knew French culture, especially literature, extremely well, this expertise did not make them friends of the French people – and in fact they were not. This distinction is often missed by historians. Beneath a carapace of Francophilia, both Epting and Bremer were good Nazis and strongly anti-Semitic. Epting it was who pressured the Propaganda Department to proscribe all Jewish authors outright in the 1943 edition of the Otto List and who proposed that children of Jewish background should be segregated and in their own schools.

Epting took up his duties a few weeks after the armistice and knew his job would not be easy. Of all the countries in the Western world with a cultural superiority complex, France was leader. Her deep, centuries-long sense of *mission civilisatrice* was central to the French sense of national identity. This is what he and the German Institute intended to destroy. 'French intellectuals must give up the idea of being world leaders', Epting told an audience of them to their faces in one of his earliest speeches. 'They must not pretend to speak in the name of principles valid for every country and they should not try to spread these principles beyond France.' At the same time Bremer was busy berating other audiences for having fallen prey to decades of distorted writings about Germany by hostile historians and Jews. That was why the French disdained Germany, particularly National Socialist Germany, as 'a country that is barbaric and above all dangerous'. Only when the French surrendered their pretensions to intellectual superiority would the two nations be able to get along. That was the message repeated over and over again.

With Abetz's support, Epting made the German Institute *the* centre of cultural and social activities in Paris. Going there became a critical gauge of a person's attitude towards the Occupation. People like Camus, Guéhenno, Galtier-Boissière, Picasso and the entire 'Flore set' would not have been seen dead there. Others went and were seen – alive and to their acute embarrassment. Like encountering someone you know in a brothel – such was the reaction of one of those who was caught *in flagrante*. But many in the cultural world could resist everything except temptation and gladly accepted its invitations. One such was the ubiquitous Serge Lifar, who welcomed the revival of social life after the inconvenient interruption of the war. 'At its receptions there crowded a mass of "intellectuals" and artists', he recalled, 'among whom were Count Metternich, the German responsible for all the art treasures in occupied France, Jean Giraudoux and Count Etienne de Beaumont.' As he went on to say, 'the Institute's visitors-book contained a fine long list of names belonging to the most outstanding personalities in Parisian artistic, literary, scientific and Society circles.'

Indeed it did. Fifty-six writers, 35 journalists, 18 publishers, 47 musicians, actors and painters, 18 politicians, 6 clergymen, 36 professors, 14 other educators, 6 physicians and 31 other figures from public life – such was Epting's postwar accounting of those who participated in the Institute's activities. His wife, Alice, published her own little book of memoirs with family-type photographs of some of the habitués of the Institute – among them Arno Breker,

Charles Despiau, Abel Bonnard, Ernest Fourneau of the Institut Pasteur, Paul Belmondo, Alfred Cortot, Wilhelm Kempf, Serge Lifar, Robert Brasillach and Mgr Mayol de Lupé, the priest who concluded mass with a rousing 'Heil Hitler'. Still other guests – Céline, Jean-Louis Barrault and his wife, Madeleine Renaud, José Sert, Montherlant, Cocteau and Châteaubriant – she remembered fondly in her text.

In addition to its rich array of imported German musicians, the Institute also sponsored a lecture programme in Paris and the provinces. According to surviving records, some 109 talks were held during the first three years. Roughly a quarter of these were on the 'achievements' of the Third Reich, another quarter on German culture, twelve on German-French cultural relations, ten about the Second World War and the remainder about the new Germany and the Europe to come. Propaganda Department officials considered the Institute's various cultural programmes as so much pandering to a defeated nation. Relations between the two, tense from the start, had become so frayed that Schmidke blocked the planned visit by the Berlin State Opera in 1941. Abetz had to appeal to Hitler personally to have the veto overruled.

In the early years, lectures attracted relatively large audiences – between three and four hundred people – and in reports to Berlin officials of the embassy and Institute raved about the success of the programmes. Among themselves, however, they had no illusions. At least a third of the audiences, they reckoned, comprised the same old crowd. Even so, people came, listened and went away – *basta*! Schleier complained that a few Vichy officials would attend a meeting but never be seen again. Speakers felt equally frustrated. A German professor who gave talks in Paris, Orléans and Dijon in May 1942 found that everyone had been very polite, 'but *politesse* is the armour the French wear as protection against everything German'. He went on, 'The French have always felt that their culture is superior to that of Germany, as everywhere else, and that they have nothing to learn or take from us. German culture does not interest them.'

And then there was language instruction. A second language is a sign of the cultural and even the ideological leaning of a nation, or at least of its educated class. In France between the wars the favoured language was English. Making German the primary second language was therefore a major objective of the Institute's greater mission of reorienting France culturally as a critical step towards realigning it politically. The Institute put tremendous effort into it. Lessons were free and offered with transportation vouchers. Following an intense advertising campaign in Paris newspapers in the summer of 1940, five thousand people quickly signed up and a large number had to be turned away. Epting was so pleased he extended the programme throughout the Occupied Zone and after 1942 into the formerly Unoccupied Zone as well. In the early years the programmes were so oversubscribed that Epting anticipated having twenty thousand students in classes at any one time. 'The French condemn collaboration but study German; clearly they believe it [the Occupation] is going to last', Fabre-Luce commented in 1941 at the height of German military successes. True enough; so it is not surprising that attendance should have steadily declined from 1943 on, as the days of the Occupation were now clearly numbered and studying German carried the stigma of collaboration. From a high of 15,000 in the autumn of 1942, the number of students slipped to 11,000 six months later and to 9,000 in 1944. Still, 9,000 is a not an insignificant number in light of the military situation. And what explains the fact that in Toulouse in April 1944 within the space of a week 330 signed up and in Paris in June 1944 1,000 enrolled for the summer course?

Why did people take lessons at all? The best answer is the answer to another question – who attended? They were a rough cross section of the urban middle class – businessmen, secretaries and general office workers who had commercial contacts with the Germans. In Paris and other cities, there were a fair number of students from secondary schools and universities who wanted German for academic reasons. It fails to surprise that very few labourers or farmers and no church figures enrolled. Attendees must have included *collabos* and persons who wanted to know German for cultural reasons. How else to understand why, among the 1,055 who signed up in Dijon in late 1941, 162 were without a profession, eight were retirees, nine doctors, four pharmacists, three judges, two lawyers, three architects and three painters?

Since the great mass of the French people was obviously not going to be able to speak or read German any time soon, Epting set out to encourage them – or a cultured elite – to imbibe German literature. Given the demand for books throughout France, he saw a great opportunity. But he faced two problems. The Invader had undone himself by banning precisely the German authors whom the French most liked. And in any case French taste in foreign books ran overwhelmingly in the direction of Anglo-American works. To reorient the reading public, Epting made the translation of German authors a top priority. Selecting the works was politically delicate. So he formed a committee of representatives of the Propaganda Department, the Foreign Office language service, collaborationist publishers (Grasset, Payot and Plon), literary critics, professional translators and even *collabos* like Châteaubriant, Drieu and Benoist-Méchin.

Eventually around five hundred titles were chosen, mostly classics, with relatively few Nazi works included. The selections, compiled in the so-called 'Matthias List', were criticized by the Propaganda Department for being in some cases too politically neutral and in others too highbrow. Once again French publishers disgraced themselves. They went right along with the project, bringing out not only German classics – in Gallimard's case Goethe and Theodor Fontane and some of Wagner's correspondence – but also Nazi propaganda. Some 330 titles got into print at a rate of about a hundred year, a figure roughly comparable to the interwar period when a total of slightly more than 2,300 German titles had been published. To encourage as wide a circulation as possible, Epting ensured that the translations had priority in the allocation of print paper and cultivated his contacts with literary critics and journalists to get helpful reviews.

Financially the project was a swindle. Like a hostess telling her dinner guests at the end of the meal that they had to pay for what they had just eaten and drunk, the Germans informed French publishers that, in addition to their publication costs, it would be for them to cover the expense of translation and royalty fees. The only concession was to offer a modest subsidy for books – on such topics as racial issues – that were expected to find few readers.

Another way of making German literature available was to open a large bookshop. The project was carried out with such brutality, however, that its reputation was sullied from the start. As punishment for the minor student uprising on Armistice Day 1940, the military had seized a building on the place de la Sorbonne housing the students' favourite café, the D'Harcourt. Here Epting installed his bookshop. Although the Rive-Gauche, as it was named, purported to be a French business, the embassy owned a majority of shares. As cover, management was placed in the hands of Henry Jamet, a proto-collaborationist of the Thirties; Brasillach, Châteaubriant, Rebatet and Maurice Bardèche were members of its board of directors. Despite its smelly background and occasional acts of sabotage, the shop quickly became the largest and flashiest bookshop in Paris. Indeed, it was said to be the largest bookshop in Europe. But Galtier-Boissière, who lived across the street, said he only ever saw German officers going there.

People who think for themselves are a nuisance to any government. So it is unsurprising that the Invader was leery of the universities, seeing them as potential centres of opposition. There was little need for concern. Fearing that their institutions might be closed or staffed with ill-qualified *collabos*, heads of academic and cultural bodies offered concessions – firing noted anti-Nazis and Jews – even before being asked. Roger Seydoux, head of the Political Science Institute, sought out Epting soon after the armistice and continued to cultivate good relations with the German Institute by attending its lunches and lectures. Epting and Bremer of course knew the academic scene quite well from the Thirties and were the Gestapo's prime informants, fingering some 125 professors who were Jewish or hostile to Nazism. Four particularly well known as anti-fascists were arrested. Epting also succeeded, against stubborn academic resistance, in choosing replacements and in injecting German lecturers into the Sorbonne and various provincial universities.

In such ways the German Institute was making some impact on the French cultural scene. By 1942 around fifteen thousand students were in language training, the book translation project was going at full gallop, attendance at receptions and lectures was excellent, German musicians were enjoying a series of stunning successes. Abetz and Epting finally won total control over cultural affairs when the Propaganda Department agreed to surrender its literature, music, theatre and visual arts sections. And the Institute's publication, *Deutschland-Frankreich*, with articles by collaborationists, finally got off the ground.

Then suddenly the whole operation imploded. In the course of the summer of 1942 Epting and the entire top level of the Institute staff were withdrawn, many to be sent off to the Russian front, where Bremer, among others, was killed. Documents found in German archives make clear that the purge – which has been widely misinterpreted by historians – was a straightforward bureaucratic manoeuvre by the 200-per cent Nazis in the Foreign Office to take over the Paris operation. The long years that Epting and his colleagues had lived in France and their expertise in French culture were presented as evidence of their political unreliability and uncritical Francophilia. Back in Berlin Epting was subjected to a scorching interrogation about his alleged ideological failures.

The upshot was that Epting, the 100 per cent Nazi, was replaced by an example of the 200 per cent variety from the now-Germanified University of Strassburg, Gerhard Krüger. Alas, the new director's habit of molesting ladies finally caught up with him. Not long after his arrival he groped a foreign diplomat's wife at a dinner. 'The job of a diplomat is to seduce, not to rape', was Abetz's lapidary remark in a telegram to Berlin. The witticism aroused such guffaws in the Foreign Office that Ribbentrop sent Krüger back to Strassburg and replaced him with none other than Epting.

But it was now the spring of 1943 and the Wehrmacht was on the defensive everywhere. The Institute and its branches were as active as ever, no longer as symbols of German cultural triumphalism but as beleaguered outposts of a forlorn German hope of victory. People stopped participating in its programmes, some in protest against the growing brutality of the Wehrmacht, some in fear of later being considered *collabos*. Despite all its efforts, the Occupier had failed to win the hearts and minds of the mass of the Occupied. As Grimm went about France on his speaking tours, he discovered – as he frankly reported to Berlin – that at best 20 per cent of the French supported collaboration, that most people believed the British would eventually win, that they listened to and believed the BBC, that crowds sometimes sang the Marseillaise or shouted 'Vive le RAF' when

French cities were bombed, and other such discouraging facts. Officials of the military's Propaganda Department sent in similar reports.

Berlin reacted by instructing Abetz to draw up a list of suspected dissidents to be arrested. Among the thousands identified were figures in every area of cultural and intellectual life. Convinced that arrests and deportations would incite open resistance, Abetz and German intelligence officials in Paris took no action. Civil order was in any case fraying. It was now 1944. Writers such as Louis Aragon and Elsa Triolet went into hiding. Maurice Goudeket, Colette's Jewish husband, concealed himself in a maid's room in the Palais Royal. Max Jacob and Robert Desnos were deported. In Provence the noted Jewish historian Marc Bloch was arrested, tortured and shot as a member of the Resistance. In Paris Philippe Henriot, the Vichy propagandist, and Georges Montandon, a noted anti-Semitic ethnologist, were gunned down. Outside Paris Georges Mandel, a prewar interior minister, was killed in reprisal. Léautaud's prediction years earlier – 'The day is perhaps not far off when we will enter in a period of reciprocal assassinations' – now came true.

Epting remained in Paris to the last and then despondently accompanied the Wehrmacht out of France. His final responsibility was to persuade cultural and intellectual figures who had been collaborators to flee with him. Some of the most noted – Drieu, Brasillach, Suarez, Lubin, Lifar – refused. Others straggled off. Céline was one of the first out – railing against the *boches*, members of the Resistance and almost everyone else – and as usual found in the experience material for a book. Another writer, Jean Hérold-Paquis, waited until he had put the finishing touches to his magnum opus *L'Angleterre comme Carthage* (England like Carthage) in which he predicted the downfall of the 'Judaeo-plutocratic Anglo-Saxon nation'. Hérold-Paquis, an honorary member of the Waffen SS, had been a broadcaster for Radio-Paris and had always concluded his commentary with 'Like Carthage, England will be destroyed'. The hopelessly compromised – Luchaire, Abel Bonnard, Rebatet, Châteaubriant, the actor Robert Le Vigan, the director of *L'Illustration*, Jacques de Lesdain, the pianist Lucienne Delforge and miscellaneous journalists – decamped with the Germans. The arts critic Alain Laubreaux and Vichy's commissioner for Jewish questions, Louis Darquier de Pellpoix, followed Laval into Spain.

Bitterly disappointed that so many had remained, Epting traced this to their naïvely mistaken notion that cultural life would, as he put it, be as free under the British and Americans as it had been under the Germans. He consoled himself, however, by anticipating a brighter morrow. That the Institute would soon be returning to France to resume its mission he had no doubt, and so he advised Berlin to keep the entire staff intact. Perhaps it was necessary at that point to be slightly insane to stay slightly sane.

The miserable, terrified exiles settled in the Hohenzollern family castle at Sigmaringen on the edge of the Black Forest. What went on there – the Monty Python atmosphere deftly caught by Céline, himself an inmate, in his *D'un Château l'autre* (*Castle to Castle*) – resembled nothing so much as a children's game of make-believe. The site enjoyed extraterritorial status and flew the Tricolour from one of the ramparts. The 'government' even maintained 'diplomatic relations' with Mussolini's equally comedy-of-the-absurd Republic of Salò. Suitably enough for a fantasy regime, the key ministry was a Commission for Propaganda and Information with a staff of no fewer than 220. It operated a radio station (Ici la France) and put out a four-page newspaper (*La France*). Presumably the paper was read only by the inmates; since Goebbels forbad radio sets at the castle, it is not clear who listened to the broadcasts.

The irrepressibly energetic Epting cranked up the *machine intellectuelle française* and organized a *congrès intellectuel* which took place in all apparent seriousness in early November with talks by – who else? – resident intellectuals such as Rebatet and Châteaubriant. In the audience were Mme Abetz, the Eptings, the three Friedrichs – Grimm, Sieburg, Bran – and even a representative of the Japanese embassy at Vichy. In concluding this three-day seminar, the participants agreed to establish a Committee for the Defence of the French Spirit. The madness went so far that Epting seemed seriously to believe that the new centre of French intellectual influence would be in Germany and would spread from there to France and the rest of the world. As its final act, the participants adopted a resolution deploring the 'persecution' then under way in France of collaborationist cultural and intellectual figures. Reports of executions reached Hitler himself. Angered that it was impossible to take appropriate reprisals, he suggested exchanging cultural collaborators in Paris for Gaullist prisoners in Germany. By spring fantasy had turned into nightmare and with the approach of the Allied armies Céline, Bonnard, Hérold-Paquis, Le Vigan, Châteaubriant and Luchaire had slipped away into the night.

It was an appropriately squalid end to the concept of Franco-German understanding as propagated by Abetz in the interwar period and as promoted by the German Institute after the fall of France. The Institute's objective had been to demonstrate how jolly the world was going to be when ruled by the cultured, hospitable Germans. But in the end, how much collaborationism had French guests actually imbibed with their champagne and petits fours at the Institute's receptions? All three seem to have been quickly forgotten by most of the guests. Years later an embittered Alice Epting cited Sacha Guitry as one of the ingrates. A frequent and ebullient guest at the Institute, after the war he flatly denied he had ever had anything to do with it or indeed any Germans. And Guitry, she observed, was far from the only person 'whose name is world-famous' who needed to be forgiven for a poor memory.

Yet nothing could better testify to the Institute's importance as the centre of cultural collaboration than the fact that, after the Liberation, purge committees regarded attendance at its activities as *prima facie* evidence of collaboration. This emerged at the treason trial of Robert Brasillach. Accused of having compromised himself by his frequent appearances at the Hôtel de Sagan, the writer gave a devastating response.

At the German Institute I met quite a lot of people, some of them writers, most of whom would perhaps be quite embarrassed if I did not have the good grace to keep their names to myself. Nonetheless, I can say that the only time in my life when I met M. Gallimard, today the eminent publisher, was at the German Institute. I can say that everyone who mattered went there. M. Duhamel [laughter in the court], I saw him at the Institute. . . . I lunched with Jean Giraudoux at the German Institute and I do not think Jean Giraudoux was a traitor, celebrated as he is today by Resistance papers practically as a martyr.

'Everyone who mattered went there.' Brasillach's sensational claim was bolstered by Abetz. In 1956 the former ambassador told an investigating commission that it would be 'difficult to name any notable French artist who had not stood on the side of collaborationism'. Leaving aside that this was a ludicrous exaggeration, it also missed the cardinal point – and one the Germans did not want to face up to – that most of those who went to the Institute went for the champagne and petits fours and were not so much *collabos* as opportunists. Unlike Guitry and the others Alice Epting had in mind, the real collaborators were not shy in owning up to their commitment even when doing so was life-threatening. Brasillach's response when sentenced to death was, 'It is an honour.'

CHAPTER 5

BONJOUR TRISTESSE

Radiant sunshine, a luminous azure sky, white sailboats bobbing in a sparkling Mediterranean Sea. The scene in French Railway travel posters and magazine ads for pastis beckoned to countless thousands as they fled the Wehrmacht. One of the fugitives was Roland Dorgelès. He arrived in Marseille in mid-July and found the city so welcoming that his pen, he said, 'felt as though it was caressing the very name when it wrote it'. The noted author was merely one of what he described as 'a motley crowd of rich people, poor people, people without a trade, people without a country, soldiers, boy scouts, prostitutes, nurses'. When they got there, they – Paris – did not take over Marseille; instead, as he nicely phrased it, 'Paris melted into Marseille like a piece of ice in a glass of pastis.'

Scarcely a city or town in southern and central France was untouched by the wave of refugees. Everywhere the scene was the same, even down to the cloudless sky during that exceptionally fine summer and autumn. But Marseille was unique. *La cité phocéenne* was both the country's oldest city – founded by Phocaean Greeks in 600 BC – and its second largest in population. As such it was a congenial site for displaced artists and intellectuals, offering on the one hand opportunities for professional work and on the other relative concealment for those who needed it. France's biggest port, it was also now the single great harbour not in German hands, and hence an escape route for those who wanted or needed to get out. In all, how many refugees arrived? There are no reliable figures but some estimates speak of 500,000. And they all had their own adventure story to tell.

Henri de Montherlant was one of them. A war correspondent at the time, the author had retreated with the French army until he reached Marseille in early June. 'Sans peur et sans espoir' – without fear and without hope – was how he viewed France and perhaps himself as well. After rolling up his military uniform, he dossed down in a small hotel and spent several months writing *Solstice de juin*, a series of boring, stream-of-consciousness meditations inspired by the defeat. Montherlant was a writer who admired naked force in various guises – war, bullfighting, boxing and other violent sports – and derided the French army for being insufficiently bloodthirsty. 'I do not like people when they enjoy themselves, when they make love, when they work, when they show off. But I like them when they make war.' His book, with several positive references to Hitler, launched him on the road to collaboration and in no time he found himself one of the German Institute's favourites.

Of an entirely different sort was Fernand Léger. Far from desiring the company of the macho Enemy, he wanted nothing more fervently than to get out of his clutches. Until he found boat passage he spent his time at the Old Port. The sight of dockworkers diving and falling into the water during their breaks fascinated him. 'I was immediately spellbound by the motions of these tanned bodies, first in the sun and then in the water. Fluid, marvellous movements. These divers inspired everything that followed in my paintings – acrobats, cyclists, musicians. My style became more supple, less rigid.'

A more typical refugee was Countess Consuelo de Saint-Exupéry, wife of the author-pilot, who ended up in Marseille via misadventures in Pau and Carcassonne. She arrived with no possessions, no address and almost no money. She did not know whether to cry or scream, beg or be silent, stay or go – 'but go where?' In any case, 'I was alive and free', and that was what was important. Soon she found her way to the Cintra, already Marseille's version of the Café de Flore. 'There were all the painters and writers of Paris. Without money, without means to paint or write, they still preferred exile in the Free Zone to their old surroundings in Paris. Their freedom was grounded on a flat refusal to share the air of Paris with the Germans. It was a NO to the acceptance of shame.' But for her, as for thousands of others, the price of that freedom was hunger, homelessness and loneliness.

Many there were who would happily have settled for hunger, homelessness and loneliness. These were the Germans, Poles, Czechs and others who for political or racial reasons had been on the run for years. Now they had to flee for their lives, either because Vichy did not want them or because the Gestapo did. For them it was not sunshine, blue sea and pretty boats that brought them to Marseille but a desperate hope of escape. Yet those who arrived in hope soon found danger lurking around every corner as officious cops patrolled the streets, railway stations, hotels and cafés, interning anyone without proper documents. 'Our very existence is hanging from slender threads which may break at any moment,' was how Victor Serge described the mood. He was an old hand at exile. This was his third since Stalin had sent him to Siberia. He was also a specialist in flight. This was his seventh in twenty years. The pain and numbed despair felt by these poor wretches was powerfully expressed at the time in a chilling relief, *Maimed and Stateless*, by Hans Arp, himself psychologically maimed and legally stateless. Moulded from cast-off newspapers – in itself symbolic – the work depicted the wounded and bandaged hulk of a person floating in space against a sinister black background.

Because of the war and the problems of getting the necessary documents, it became more and more difficult for the maimed and stateless to get out. In May 1940, 406 ships with 135,000 passengers had sailed. In June the figures fell to 279 and 6,000, and declined from there. Refugees had little choice but to wait for something to turn up. 'They pass hour after hour on the terrace of cafés in front of a glass of mineral water, keeping an eye on their meagre baggage, while waiting for some news of a berth on a ship', was how the head of the Marseille Historical Institute described the scene to a friend. For those who had money, it was sometimes possible to bribe an official for a visa and exit permit – a transaction Victor Serge likened to 'selling lifebelts on a shipwrecked continent'. For those who could not get passage on a boat, there were trains into Spain. And for those who had no papers or visas, there was a rough land route over the Pyrenees where, with luck, it was possible to cross the frontier on foot and bribe Spanish border guards with cigarettes. Some made it out on their own; some were helped out by American refugee agencies; some were arrested and deported in the opposite direction. One of the famous unlucky ones was Walter Benjamin, who struggled up a mountain to the border and, on being refused entry, killed himself.

One of the famous lucky ones was Claude Lévi-Strauss. After retreating from the Maginot Line to the Midi, he was demobbed in Montpellier. He had in his pocket, thanks to the Rockefeller Foundation, an invitation to the New School for Social Research in New York. Having heard that a boat was about to leave, he trudged to Marseille and made his way from dock to dock, shipping office to shipping office. 'Yes, a boat existed; yes, it was going to leave; no, he could not get on it. Why? The man could not explain.' Imagining he could hear the gates of a concentration camp closing behind him, he persevered. Finally on 15 March 1941 he got passage to Martinique – one of 350 passengers on a boat with two cabins and a total of seven berths – sailing with André Breton, Victor Serge, the painter Wilfredo Lam and the German novelist Anna Seghers. In his *Tristes Tropiques* Lévi-Strauss described the month-long passage on a boat from hell to an island from hell that was run like a concentration camp managed by especially vile sadists.

Breton was typical of those who were not Jews, foreign exiles or in flight from the Gestapo who wanted out because they wanted to feel free. Consuelo de Saint-Exupéry remembered a dinner table conversation among refugee artists at the time:

> Why leave, I say, wearily. If we all leave, where will France be? . . .
>   Obviously you do not have anything to fear here, Maurice said. . . . For us it is different.

To uproot yourself – in the case of German artists, a second or third time – and to leap into the unknown was anything but easy, even when it was possible. 'As for us,' Sophie Arp wrote to a friend, 'we are very tormented. We have all the papers for America and must decide in a few days. There is some hope that in New York we may little by little rebuild our lives. . . . Here for years to come any activity will be impossible, that is to say sales, exhibitions, and so on.'

Marseille was not just an escape route. 'Everything that was tragic in the rest of France seemed almost forgotten or at least of no concern to those living under a blue sky and in obvious freedom. Life revived with a fury.' While not quite as carefree as André Roussin made out in his memoirs, life in Marseille as elsewhere in the Unoccupied Zone was far freer, politically and culturally, than in Paris. Despite its gangsters and prostitutes, its dirt and rats the size of cats, it was a cosmopolitan and tolerant city with a polyglot population of Arabs, Spaniards, Italians and immigrants from the Asian and African colonies. Politically it was well to the left, with a socialist mayor, supported by the communists. In 1936 it gave nearly half its vote to the Popular Front.

It is therefore a measure of the ideological convulsion that followed the armistice that even a city like Marseille should overnight become wildly Pétainist. When the Marshal visited the city in December 1940 the reception he was given was rapturous. Buildings and streets were festooned with flags and every church bell tolled on his arrival. The main dock at the port was renamed Quai du Maréchal Pétain and both a steamer then under construction and an important lycée were also named in his honour. Showing that the intellectual community was as much behind him as everyone else, the Marseille Academy of Science, Letters and Fine Arts hailed him 'saviour of France' and unanimously appointed him their 'Protector', a title not bestowed on anyone since the eighteenth century.

How did this affect cultural life? It didn't. Or only slightly. 'Culture' may not be the first word that leaps to mind in thinking of Marseille, but the city had more to offer than just the best *bouillabaisse* in the world. Before the war it had enjoyed an active musical life, the centre of which was the opera, which staged nearly a hundred performances a year. A symphony orchestra had been formed in 1938 and was highly popular. Visiting artists had included Casals, Menuhin,

Monteux and Cortot. There was also a chamber music group with a small but ardent audience of devotees. The city was very proud of its museums and most of all of its library, the second library of France. Marcel Pagnol's film studio was also situated there. 'After a long sleep, Marseille seemed to wake up in an atmosphere transformed by the presence of refugees', Jean-Michel Guiraud wrote in *La Vie intellectuelle et artistique à Marseille*. 'The city took on the allure of a cultural capital.' Its position was reinforced when the cultural service of the National Radio was moved there. This included five complete orchestras and a choral group of two hundred choristers. They were installed in the opera house, which became in effect a broadcasting studio.

Marseille swarmed with refugee actors, playwrights and theatrical producers who, along with their local counterparts, could hardly wait to get an active theatre life going. As an encouragement, a Vichyite organization, the Centre Culturel Méditerranéen, was established in November 1940. Although intended to be a catalyst for the arts throughout the Unoccupied Zone, it primarily promoted the theatre in Marseille. The Comédie Phocéenne was established as an equivalent of the Comédie-Française to promote good old safe works from the classical repertoire. But there were also experimental groups – such as Rideau Gris (Grey Curtain), a joint effort of Louis Ducreux and André Roussin. Some of their plays, such as Roussin's *Am-Stram-Gram*, were so successful they were performed throughout France.

Of great importance in Marseille's cultural life were the activities of a number of devoted patrons of the arts. The most important was Countess Lily Pastré, who used her considerable fortune and ample estate, the Château de Montredon, to help refugee artists. Shortly after the defeat, she established an organization, Pour que l'Esprit Vive (So the Mind May Live), to help those most in danger by offering housing and funds. She it was who had advanced the money to get Rideau Gris started. As many as forty people at a time – writers, painters and especially musicians – were lodged on the estate and provided with meals. André Masson stayed in a hunting lodge there before emigrating. When the publisher Jean Ballard looked him up, he found the artist 'enjoying a rare state of bliss in his retreat, where the singing of the wind in the pine trees incited him to work'. Masson himself described the winter as having passed 'in a feeling of brotherhood all round'. The Czech painter Rudolf Kundera lived for three years in a *dépendance* on the estate. The noted Jewish pianist Clara Haskil was another guest and, when ill with a brain tumour, received medical care paid for by Pastré. Eventually, through the countess's connections, Haskil was able to emigrate to Switzerland.

Pastré's passion was music, and at Montredon there were daily recitals, frequent conferences and every afternoon a concert. Casals, Haskil and Monique Haas were among the soloists. To add a bit of excitement she offered a prize of 5,000 francs for the best performance of piano works by Brahms. On one occasion, to try to raise spirits as the Occupation ground on, she arranged for a gala public performance by moonlight of *A Midsummer Night's Dream*. With a cast of fifty-two in appropriate costumes, stage-sets and incidental music played by the Orchestre National under a Jewish conductor, it was a memorable event.

Late in 1940 another art patron, Cécile de Valmalète, started Heures Musicales, an association to organize conferences and concerts for young people and to encourage popular interest in serious music. The septuagenarian de Valmalète, a serious painter who had exhibited in the Salon d'Automne, was also a devoted music lover with a partiality for chamber music. She organized small public concerts and established an École des Arts Réunis, a private school where courses were run on art history, drama and the piano. A third patron was Marguerite Fournier, who arranged meetings of musicians, poets, writers and the like. It was with her that Charles Munch, conductor of the Orchestre National, found refuge on leaving the Occupied Zone.

Culture in its various forms was a vital element in the psychological recovery of Unoccupied France. In a society where church and state were telling people that they had been debauched and must now repent, cultural activities carried a positive message. They said that, despite everything, beauty and pleasure were still to be found in life. And they reassured artists that there was still a role for them and that they should continue to think for themselves and be creative. André Breton put it this way: 'What appears to me as the task of intellectuals is not to let this purely military defeat, for which intellectuals are not responsible, carry with it the debacle of the spirit.'

The large number of artists and intellectuals from Paris and northern France who had settled in the Unoccupied Zone gave a tremendous impulse to cultural life throughout the Midi, stimulating new artistic activities, theatrical groups, publications, musical societies and the like. Even in resorts such as Cannes and Monte Carlo, theatrical life flourished and a number of art dealers were still showing and buying. Of course, not all of it was high culture. 'Nice experienced a period of extraordinary boom', Maurice Chevalier recalled. 'Overwhelmed with refugees, all sorts of high-powered and mysterious business affairs went on every hour. Trafficking in gold, in gems. Trafficking in everything imaginable. Bars, restaurants, cabarets were jammed with people who had no concern for money.'

After the defeat some noted painters – Matisse, Bonnard, Rouault and Picabia – remained in the Unoccupied Zone and went on working undisturbed. In fact, Picabia prospered in a way that he later had to answer for. As far as Vichy authorities were concerned, you could paint and exhibit whatever you wanted, providing it was not downright insurrectionist. The real issue was not *what* was painted but *who* painted it. Artists who were foreign nationals, Jews and communists were not at first hunted down, but they were subject to internment if found by the police. The tense atmosphere was almost unbearable even for those not on the endangered-species list. 'I put myself in front of a mirror so as to analyse my torment', Masson said. The result was *Homme à la corde* (*Self-Portrait on a Hangman's Noose*), showing a terrified man awaiting execution.

Practising one's art became a way of surviving. But it was not easy. Just scrounging the necessary materials was the most immediate problem. Matisse and the collector Aimé Maeght did their best to help Bonnard and a number of others with supplies. Some artists found it so difficult to get their hands on canvas they had to make do with newspapers, wood and cardboard. Citing the examples of Hans Arp, Hans Bellmer and Max Ernst, Michèle Cone points out in her *Artists under Vichy*, 'For the Surrealists, these shortages acted as stimulants to the discovery of new techniques.' One of these was gouache, which became a favourite medium in those years, used by Sonia Delaunay, Chagall and Masson. Even the emotional hardship in itself had its artistic benefits. Strangers became friends and that in turn brought about a revival of old Surrealist collaborative projects. Working with three others on an album of lithographs, Arp commented, 'The tragic hours during which these lithographs were conceived compelled modesty, the sacrifice of all vanity, the effacement of any overtly individual expression.'

The most curious example of artistic collaboration was an experiment in communal living at Oppède, a crumbling medieval village not far from Avignon. The project was initiated by several architects who, unemployed after the war, discovered the site when they went to the area to do farm work. Living in hunger and poverty, a number of painters, writers and architects saw an opportunity for a novel artistic adventure by using their talents to rebuild the site. The prime mover was Bernard Zehrfuss, an architect and recent winner of the Prix de Rome. He explained their intention. 'Out of this abandoned village we wish to create an immense atelier, a great community of the arts and a professional community of builders. . . . We wish to animate lifeless areas by attracting artists, workmen, artisans, and making sure they have adequate material living conditions.' Almost by necessity the group used only local talent and local materials. As Zehrfuss explained, 'At Apt, thanks to its ochre, there are glassblowers, stained-glass makers, mosaic specialists to work with; at Gordes, painters, poster artists and decorators; at Vaucluse, miniaturists and engravers, and at l'Isle sur la Sorgue, there is a river with remarkable properties for work in iron and steel.' Gradually the experiment attracted the interest of painters, architects and writers throughout the area. Consuelo de

Saint-Exupéry had run into Zehrfuss in Marseille and went along with him, later writing a small book, *Oppède*, in homage to those who settled there and recounting their adventures.

In such ways artists made the best of things and in some cases even managed to squeeze a little joy out of living in exile. Long after the war, Hans Arp recalled the final two years of his wife's life in Grasse, a hill town above the Riviera. 'She was in love with the land. It was her paradise on earth. She always pressed me to explore the area. Her eyes never let go of the silvery green of the olive trees. . . . Each day brought with it a new richness of light and of happiness, and Sophie revelled in it.' Otto Wols, an impoverished German refugee artist without much to be happy about, recorded his delight at living on the Mediterranean coast following his release from internment. 'At Cassis the stones, the fish, the rocks, the salt of the sea and the sky . . . showed me eternity in the small waves of the port repeating themselves without repeating themselves.'

Less eminent painters scattered around the Unoccupied Zone had a desperate time just scratching out an existence. 'Life is especially hard for us because we have no relatives with nice farms', Arp wrote to Paul Sacher. 'We are beginning to suffer from hunger. I am not saying this in jest.' A few good souls helped them by buying one or two of their paintings. Paul Sacher and Peggy Guggenheim sometimes donated money. A particularly heart-rending case was that of the German Jewish painter Otto Freundlich. For a time a few other refugees paid for his hotel room in exchange for paintings. His situation was not unique. As Cone comments, 'It is likely that in the French provinces there is still today, not yet accounted for, refugee art that was once bartered for favors.' Eventually Arp and a number of other painters were taken in by the Swiss. Chagall, Lipchitz, Ernst and Masson managed to reach the United States. Sonia Delaunay, though Jewish, remained safely in Grasse. Freundlich was picked up by the Gestapo in 1943, deported and died soon afterwards.

An important stimulus to cultural and intellectual life in the Unoccupied Zone came from newspapers and reviews. Many of these were Paris exiles. More or less typical was *Le Jour-Écho de Paris* whose staff of one hundred left Paris at 4 a.m. on 11 June, stopped briefly in Poitiers, moved on to Bordeaux and then to Clermont-Ferrand – where they intersected with other Paris exiles such as *Figaro*, *Le Temps*, *Paris-Soir*, *Le Journal des débats*, *L'Oeuvre*, *Candide* and *L'Illustration* – until finally landing in Marseille in October, without having failed to publish a single issue during the entire migration. *Le Jour-Écho* decided to stay in Marseille where in the meantime two socialist ex-deputies founded *Le Mot d'Ordre*. Like *Le Jour-Écho*, this new daily was suitably equivocal for the time – loyal to Pétain to the end but with a cultural section that was open to anti-Vichy views. It ran articles by Stanislas Fumet, an intellectual close to the Catholic church and a member of an organized group of Resistance writers. René Tavernier contributed poetry, as did Aragon, whose *La Rose et la réséda*, which he had just written and which surprisingly – 'by what miracle?' asked Guiraud – passed the censors and was published under his own name in May 1943. Aragon had earlier published other poems under the cover name of François la Colère. In such ways an apparently Marshalist paper could become a vehicle for opposition ideas.

Le Jour-Écho de Paris and *Le Mot d'Ordre* were Vichyite but otherwise respectable. Collaborationist and grossly unrespectable were two important weeklies that had also moved to Marseille, Horace de Carbuccia's *Gringoire* and Jacques Doriot's *L'Émancipation nationale* – both pro-German, crassly anti-Semitic and of course anti-Gaullist and Anglophobe. *Gringoire*, which Carbuccia founded in 1928, had been so vociferously opposed to the Popular Front that its defamatory campaign was credited with having helped to drive Interior Minister Roger Salengro to suicide in 1936. During the Occupation the paper criticized what it considered Vichy's inadequate support for collaboration and its leniency towards communists, Freemasons and Jews. Yet the publisher and his paper were also among those characteristic anomalies of the Unoccupied Zone. Carbuccia convinced himself he was not anti-Semitic and gave two Jews responsible positions on his staff and published a laudatory obituary of Henri Bergson. To help Irène Némirovssky professionally and financially, he published no fewer than seven of her short stories prior to her deportation in February 1942.

But the media centre of the Unoccupied Zone was Lyon and it was there that *Le Temps*, *Le Figaro*, *Paris-Soir* and most other of the established Paris dailies settled. Though publishers and journalists found life in the provinces excruciatingly boring, even those of the far right preferred to submit to the light hand of Vichy's censors rather than return to the capital and work under German control. Some were outspokenly collaborationist, some were mere vehicles of Vichyite propaganda, but a few maintained an independent and even a cautiously critical voice.

Lyon was home not only to such popular journals as *Confidences*, a 'true romances'-type magazine, and comics such as *Pim Pam Poum*, *Félix le chat*, *Mandrake* and Walt Disney's *Journal de Mickey*, but also a number of critical journals. *Esprit*, a revived version of the prewar journal of the same name, was under the editorship of the leftist Catholic intellectual Emmanuel Mounier. Its political ideology was ambiguous, initially sympathetic to Vichy but increasingly critical of certain of its policies, in particular its anti-Semitism. It was ferociously attacked by the right-wing press and warned to stop its 'double game' and in August 1941 it was banned. More interesting was René Tavernier's poetry review, *Confluences*. Initially its political line was so fluid that it floated between the extreme right and the communists. Tavernier finally plumped decisively for the left to the point of even giving Aragon and his wife, Elsa Triolet, an apartment in his own house overlooking Lyon. Aragon continued to live and publish openly until one of his poems, 'Les Nymphées', provoked the censors to suspend publication of the review.

The importance of these various publications lay in their keeping intellectual life going and then acting as a threshold to the Resistance. Of no publication was this truer than *Les Cahiers du sud*. Edited by Jean Ballard and considered the most outstanding literary and philosophical journal outside Paris, the review had for a quarter of a century published criticism by the likes of Gide, Valéry, Montherlant and Benjamin. Ballard had been a pacifist until a visit to Germany and Czechoslovakia in 1938 convinced him that 'it is impossible to get anywhere with gangsters'. Moved by the misery of the flotsam and jetsam of humanity in a shipwrecked continent, he gave what help was in his power. After the fall of Barcelona, he began publishing 'lettres catalanes' and saved at least one political figure, Ventura Gassol, from extradition and certain execution. In 1939 he managed to get Walter Benjamin released from an internment camp. A short time later he befriended two other Jewish Resistance figures, Marcel Abraham and Simone Weil, and published articles by them under pseudonyms. The offices of *Les Cahiers du sud* became a site of intellectual exile in more ways than one, supporting any number of disoriented refugee writers and artists, Jews among them, and reorganizing and enlarging its staff to include them.

Ballard constantly pushed the boundaries of what he could get into print. Rather than deal with a local censorship office, he sent his material directly to Vichy, where one of the officials, René Massat, had been a contributor to the *Cahiers* and turned, if not a blind, at least an astigmatic eye to some of the articles. Only rarely were deletions required. Most remarkably, in May 1942 Ballard got away with publishing a poem, 'Exil', by Saint-Jean Perse. The title itself was provocative and the author, a former ambassador and Foreign Ministry official who had fled to the United States, was one of Vichy's earliest outcasts – deprived of his citizenship and expelled from the Legion of Honour. Yet authorities did not lift a finger and the issue quickly sold out. Not only did Ballard also get articles by André Breton and André Masson and poems by Federico García Lorca past the censors but even succeeded in publishing Kafka's *Aphorisms* along with an article about its author – and did so even after the Germans had invaded the Unoccupied Zone. Once he did go far too far, sending Massat an article allegedly by Kleist. In fact, it was a translated extract from Kafka's *Trial*, in which a character complained about the occupation of his town by 'nomads from the North'. In forbidding publication, Massat warned Ballard that had 'such an inopportune and flagrant' text been published, it would have had grave consequences for the *Cahiers*.

In the face of countless worries, Ballard managed to keep the review going. Circulation slipped from a meagre 4,500 in 1941 to an even more exiguous 3,000 in mid-1942. There were constant financial problems. A request for a continuation of a subsidy from the city of Marseille was turned down on the grounds that the articles did not convey the ideals that should animate youth – a response that Ballard described as 'a revenge of mediocrity, which is a sign of the times'. Interviewed in 1972, Ballard said simply, 'I ask myself how we held on.'

Les Cahiers du sud was the most important but only one of many such reviews. Isolated from Paris and liberated from its cultural domination, intellectuals throughout the Unoccupied Zone started their own little reviews. Circulation was paltry when compared to *Gringoire*'s 470,000. But they offered an ideological refuge for an intellectual public and in so doing helped to sustain cultural life. They followed no common line. Though none was collaborationist, some were strongly Pétainist; but most were at least critical of Vichy and became increasingly so. They were published in cities, towns and even villages. There were several in Algiers, the most notable of which was Max-Pol Fouchet's *Fontaine*. For poets the centre was in Provence, at Villeneuve-lès-Avignon. There, at the outbreak of the war, Pierre Seghers had started a poetry journal for men in uniform, *Poètes casqués* (Poets in Helmets). After the defeat he brought out an annual – *Poésie 40, Poésie 41* and so on, and published works by war prisoners as well.

On a trip around the Unoccupied Zone in the summer of 1941 de Beauvoir and Sartre were so delighted to find cinemas in Marseille showing American films that they stayed for several days just to see them all. 'We decided to go to three a day. As though they were old friends, we met Edward Robinson, James Cagney, Bette Davis; we saw whatever was being shown, just for the pleasure of seeing scenes of America.' As they discovered, cultural life functioned in two separate geographical spheres. With the armistice, a nearly impenetrable demarcation line of a thousand kilometres cut France in two. For a time virtually no letters, phone calls or physical contact were possible across the line.

'This demarcation line is diabolical,' Jean Ballard commented in March 1942. 'The moral consequences of two years of occupation explain, I believe, the gulf we feel between us. . . . It is therefore not strange that this state of mind, the result of our moral suffering, is reflected in the poetry being written at the present time.' Yet the division also had a positive effect by encouraging a richer cultural life in the area than before, when everything was centred on Paris.

There was something like a reversion to the Middle Ages, when intellectual activities were dispersed throughout France. In the centre, Clermont-Ferrand enjoyed an unprecedented intellectual and cultural life following the installation there of Strasbourg University. Small Provençal towns like Lourmarin and Villeneuve-lès-Avignon became magnets for poets. Even the Riviera compensated for the disappearance of tourists and foreign residents with an expansion of the film industry in Marseille and Nice.

By and large cultural life in the Unoccupied Zone, as de Beauvoir and Sartre found, went along essentially as before the war. In certain cities Swiss and a few other foreign newspapers were on sale. International mail was largely unhindered. There was no Otto List. Books were not banned, confiscated and pulped. British and American books continued to be freely sold. *Gone with the Wind* was a bestseller for adults and Mickey Mouse remained all the rage for kids. Jewish and communist writers – Julien Benda and Louis Aragon are examples – lived and worked freely, if discreetly. Until late 1943 Jewish instrumentalists continued to perform. Works by Jewish composers were not explicitly prohibited, and Offenbach's opera *La Belle Hélène* was performed – and performed in July 1942 in the casino at Vichy, no less. A jazz club was authorized and installed itself next to Pétain's offices and residence in the Hôtel du Parc. In cinemas Hitchcock's *Foreign Correspondent* and Sam Goldwyn's *Boom Town* and such colour films as *Gone with the Wind* and *The Private Life of Queen Elizabeth* enjoyed enormous popularity. Formal censorship there was, of course. But, newspapers aside, it was light, aleatory, occasionally ridiculous and as much for moral as political reasons. The relatively few cases of banned books were, paradoxically enough, those by far-right authors, the most notorious being that of Rebatet's *Les Décombres* which was condemned for denigrating the French people and army.

For the most part artists ignored Vichy, as Vichy ignored artists. The regime was too short-lived, too bedevilled by political and economic problems, and too much a prey to transient ministers to develop a cultural policy. During the four years of its tenuous existence there were fully five ministers of education, into whose remit cultural affairs fell. Two stood out. Jérôme Carcopino, the distinguished archaeologist-classicist, was remembered for trying to reform the educational system. Abel Bonnard, literary figure and member of the Académie Française, was notorious for his radical pro-Nazi views and administrative incompetence.

Nonetheless, Vichy had certain cultural aims. Most immediate was keeping the nation's cultural institutions and artistic heritage in French hands. Here was the one sphere where Vichy did not collaborate but resisted, doing its best to prevent musical institutions, museums, educational establishments and film companies from being taken over by the Germans or run by their puppets. Vichy authorities also saw in the arts an instrument to promote the principles of the 'National Revolution'. To give focus to such activities, Pétain appointed the renowned pianist Alfred Cortot to be commissioner for fine arts – in effect culture minister.

Since his immediate goal was to get a grip on musical life, Cortot allowed cultural affairs otherwise to rest in the hands of the director of the Beaux-Arts, the mild-mannered mandarin Louis Hautecoeur, professor of classical architecture and member of the Académie Française. Certainly no fascist, though a loyal marshalist, Hautecoeur believed that it was through the arts that the nation's morale could be raised and the distinctiveness of French culture in the new Europe preserved. He also took it as his mission to foster French art as the embodiment of French nationalism while at the same time protecting the cultural patrimony not only from the Germans but also at times from Laval, who would have given away the nation's artistic treasures to please them. Hautecoeur even managed to get a modest increase in funding for cultural activities and channelled much of the money to painters and sculptors through commissions and purchases of contemporary works for the national collections. His choices were often prim, cautious and conservative – like himself – but he probably did the best he could under the circumstances. He was never in good odour with Laval or the other ultra-*collabos* in Vichy, much less the Germans, who suspected his office of being the centre of a 'secret resistance' – as indeed it was in the sense of fending off German encroachments. In March 1944 Hautecoeur was replaced – according to some accounts, at Göring's insistence – by a Laval creature, Georges Hilaire. His job qualifications? He came out of the Interior Ministry and was associated with some of the most repressive actions of the Vichy government. It is not surprising, then, that, as Stéphanie Corcy has commented, 'His principal intervention lay in denouncing artistic freedom.' To be fair, he could claim one other achievement – the establishment of an Office of Good Taste.

Everyone had a general notion of what was permissible and, if they didn't, the wink and nod usually sufficed. When it appeared that the Prix Goncourt, for example, would be awarded to a prisoner of war who had written a story about the terrible suffering of a person dying of cancer, officials let it be known that such a depressing subject would be unsuitable in the difficult times. The award was duly given to the author of a back-to-the-soil book praising a healthy rural existence. Critical views did have an outlet, however, in a variety of new literary-intellectual publications. Circulation was tiny, which no doubt meant that the authorities could tolerate them and allow them to provide a harmless escape valve for malcontents. Poetry became a favoured literary form because it was too slippery to pin down to a single, objective meaning and therefore difficult for censors to deal with. Louis

Aragon in particular developed the double entendre to a fine art as a mode of veiled political criticism.

In practice it was hardcore *collabo* art critics more than Vichy censors who acted as cultural watchdogs, and who brought down the wrath of scurrilous fascist rhetoric on the miscreants. That explains why caution and self-censorship prevailed. If you know a thought is dangerous, you do not write it down and even begin to stop thinking it. In late 1940 André Breton had tried to find a Marseille gallery to show Surrealist works. Despite his best efforts, gallery owners refused to display them – not because Surrealist art was forbidden but because it was considered out of step with the mood of the times.

A more dramatic example is provided by the experience of Peggy Guggenheim. Bored, rich and sexually voracious, she had been in Europe for some years collecting both art works and male friends. Her collection – of paintings – was in Paris at the outbreak of the war. Fearing German bombs or German soldiers, she followed the advice of Fernand Léger and asked the Louvre to store it. The stodgy museum told her that her collection was not worth saving. Among works not considered worth saving were ones by Kandinsky, Klee, Picabia, Braque, Gris, Léger, Delaunay, Severini, Balla, Mondrian, Miró, Ernst, de Chirico, Tanguy, Dalí, Magritte, Brancusi, Lipchitz, Giacometti, Moore and Arp. Fortunately, just as the Wehrmacht was about to enter Paris, Guggenheim shipped them off to a friend near Vichy who stored them in her barn. But wanting to see and exhibit them, she approached André Farcy, the head of the Grenoble Museum and a great admirer of modern art. The unfortunate Farcy had his own problems. He himself had nearly been sacked by Vichy authorities – in fact, he eventually landed up in prison – and in anticipation of a visit by Pétain to Grenoble had hidden all the museum's modern works. 'He gave me perfect freedom in the museum to do anything with my pictures except to hang them', Guggenheim remarked. A year later she dispatched them with pots and pans and bed linen as household effects to New York.

The charge against Vichy was less that it oppressed or harassed artists than that it was dull and its interventions quixotic – at one time reactionary and prudish, at another progressive and tolerant. On the whole the cultural world looked on the authorities as preposterous, not so much to be feared as laughed at – literally. 'At Vichy tragedy turned into comedy which occasionally made us laugh', de Beauvoir recalled. 'We learned to our sheer delight that *Tartuffe* had been banned in the Free Zone.' In a way it is odd that she was surprised. With its story of phoney morality and hypocritical double-dealing, Molière's comedy provided an apt metaphor for the Vichy government. And in prohibiting it, the authorities were following the notorious precedent set by Louis XIV after its premiere in 1664.

Although Vichy officials had little positive impact on cultural life, which revived largely on its own, Pétain himself had an indirect influence. In the months following the defeat almost everyone in the Unoccupied Zone had rallied to the Marshal. The war was over. He was at least French and not a German governor. And in their chastened and insecure mood, people needed a reassuring figure. With his dignified, grandfatherly appearance, Pétain was that. What they also got was a man whose ego was almost as big as Louis XIV's. To promote his personal image, the government mobilized the arts. For the place of honour in public buildings and schools, a student of Rodin, Léon Drivier, sculpted an official bust. Constantin Le Breton painted an official portrait. Two writers of popular chansons, André Montagnard and Charles Courtioux, composed an anthem, 'Maréchal, nous voilà!' (Marshal, Here We Are!), which school children sang first thing every day.

Pétain himself was turned into an art form in ways that would have made Hitler and Stalin blush. An Art Maréchal office encouraged the development of industries that spewed forth a fantastic wonderworld of kitsch – Sèvres vases of all sizes, some decorated with his image or his lapidary sayings; small busts in plaster and Sèvres porcelain; images in Baccarat crystal; medallions of various types as well as ashtrays, pens, cups, dishes, paperweights, posters, calendars and so on. Postage stamps as well, of course. An Atelier Maréchal manufactured tapestries picturing him or scenes featuring *imagerie Maréchal*. Some objects were emblazoned not with an image of the Marshal but with the iconography of his regime – the double-bladed battle-axe that had been a symbol of Germanic and Frankish tribes. In one way or another, everything had a propagandistic aim. Even ashtrays were decorated with homilies quoting such inspirational words of the Marshal as 'A new France is born'. Dinner plates were a favourite gift – an irony, as Michèle Cone points out, since there was less and less food to put on them.

Being a general, Pétain was anything but an aesthete. However, he cultivated a façade of literacy that in 1931 won him membership of the Académie Française in the old seat of Marshal Foch. During the Vichy years he ordered a few command dance and music performances. That was all. He was no friend of the cultural establishment. His three favourite artists were outsiders, not to say mavericks – François Cogné, a sculptor; Robert Lallemant, a ceramicist who directed the Art Maréchal office; and Gérard Ambroselli, who produced an album illustrating the life and heroism of the Marshal. For reasons of vanity rather than aesthetics, Pétain was extremely finicky about his portrait and on no point was he more insistent than that it had to catch the precise colour of his china-blue eyes.

Pétain did, however, encourage a movement that had a very brief impact on the culture of the Unoccupied Zone. Of all the ideals of the 'National

Revolution' that he and his government dreamed of imposing on France –
work, family, soil, homeland, regionalism – the last was especially dear to his
heart. Within a few weeks of coming to power he announced his intention of
re-creating the regional provinces of yore and a few months after that spoke of
reviving regional cultures of even greater yore. To some extent this reflected the
traditional fascist view that the simple rural existence is virtuous and urban life
one of debauch. It now took the form of reviving the sentiment, customs, folk-
lore, dress and language of a medieval past. Forward-to-the-past or backward-
to-the-future? In either case the effect was to turn cultural revival into cultural
regression.

The regional ideal found a receptive audience among cranks and separatist
fanatics in various parts of the country, most notably in Brittany. In the
Unoccupied Zone it was in the Midi that it drew the greatest response. Rooted
in a quirky movement going back to the late nineteenth century, regional
feeling was largely inspired by the work of Frédéric Mistral, who had worked
to resuscitate the customs and language of the medieval Provençaux. Pétain
chose the occasion of the 110th aniversary of the poet's birth in September
1940 to send a warm message to the assembled celebrants in Maillane, his
birthplace. The text, read by Henri Massis in the presence of Mistral's widow
and a huge crowd, exalted regionalism as a key element in the 'national revival'.
Mistral was, said the Marshal, 'the outstanding promoter of the new France we
want to establish'. The speech was printed and displayed in every school and
lycée in Marseille and other parts of Provence. Regional associations organized
an annual pilgrimage to commemorate Mistral's death day on 25 March. A
mere six months following the defeat, one Marseille folkloristic organization
had already launched thirty-one celebrations in his honour.

In Provence there were those who believed that Vichy's school reforms would
open the way to a *respelido de la langue d'Oc*, or renaissance of the Oc language.
In fact, all that was eventually authorized was one hour's teaching a week
outside class time and only eleven schools in all even permitted it. *Les Cahiers
du sud* published special issues on 'The Genius of the Oc' and 'Mediterranean
Man' in which intellectuals of the area or refugees living there were asked their
views. The replies amounted to a veiled argument, escaping Vichy censors, that
Oc civilization was long dead but that its spiritual values, directly opposed to
Nazism, deserved to be cultivated.

For the most part Vichy's youth policy was also typically fascist. It discour-
aged reading and cultural activities in favour of sports and strenuous outdoor
work. Authorities made the lives of thousands of young people miserable,
adding to their hunger and other deprivations by requiring them to undergo
eight months of harsh, compulsory labour when they reached the age of twenty.
There was, however, one enlightened initiative in the cultural domain, the

establishment of an organization called Jeune France (Young France). Although some of its officials had lofty notions of 'remaking men' and 'reshaping minds', it was not narrowly propagandistic. Its intention was rather to reconcile artists and intellectuals to the National Revolution by demonstrating Vichy's great liberalism in promoting cultural activities and in doling out encouragement and financial support. In certain large towns it established centres to promote popular culture and encourage young people to paint and so on. The Maison de Provence in Marseille, for example, offered courses in acting, popular dance, singing and painting. Jeune France published two journals, organized theatre performances throughout the Unoccupied Zone and North Africa, and arranged art shows and 'poetry days', including one in Algeria. One of the most successful was a poetry festival at Lourmarin in September 1941 that brought together writers of a variety of political views from the Unoccupied Zone and North Africa. It went so well that a similar meeting was held in April of the following year in Villeneuve-lès-Avignon.

Following the Allied landings in North Africa in early 1942, the Wehrmacht invaded the Unoccupied Zone, except for a corner of southeastern France left to the Italians. The easy-going Italians generally behaved themselves but elsewhere people now felt the full lash of Occupation. The Invader requisitioned public and private buildings, cinemas, theatres and residences. They took over school buildings and displaced children from their classrooms. In Marseille the archbishop himself came within an ace of being evicted. Countess Pastré had Wehrmacht troops billeted in Montredon, bringing to an end this haven for refugees. Everywhere the Gestapo was now actively hunting German exiles, Jews and resisters.

The invasion drastically changed the cultural scene and set off a new wave of emigration. Many of those who had been unable to stomach living in Paris under the Germans now saw no reason not to return. For a time the atmosphere was still relatively relaxed, however, and many stayed. Benda remained happily in Carcassonne. Ballard continued to put out *Les Cahiers du sud*. But cultural life was being strangled. An 8 o'clock evening curfew drastically curtailed theatrical and musical life. Cinemas, where American films had been banned shortly before the Wehrmacht arrived, lost their audiences. By 1944 the Germans and the Milice were becoming steadily more menacing. Cultural figures, who up to now had lived an almost normal life, retreated into clandestinity or joined the Resistance. The Occupier became steadily more repressive. Léon Bancal, a long-time writer for the *Petit Marseillais*, was arrested in March 1943 for apostrophizing Mickey Mouse in an article, 'Adieu à Mickey', which protested the sudden ban on American films: 'You are no longer in style, according to the Vichy censor.' Around the same time the director of the Marseille opera was summoned to Gestapo headquarters and instructed to forgo any further performances of *Madame Butterfly, Boris Godunov* and *William Tell.*

The relative popular indifference towards the Germans turned increasingly to hostility as the Gestapo and the Wehrmacht became more ruthless. In the largest police operation ever mounted in France, the Gestapo, Wehrmacht and nine thousand French police sealed off the Old Port of Marseille at 6 in the morning on 24 January 1943, rounded up everyone living there and then dynamited the area. Over the centuries the Old Port had developed into a notorious labyrinthine warren of passageways and tunnels where were to be found bars, brothels, the opium dens of Chinese Annamites from Indo-China – indeed, almost any type of illegal establishment. Under the circumstances, it offered fugitives a perfect place for hiding. Jean Cocteau, who knew the area first-hand, described the scene as he learned of the round-up: 'The amazed Germans saw emerging whole farms with cows and dairies. When they threw in tear gas bombs out appeared Chinese with tons of opium, intoxicated blacks, forgers of dollars, queers, lepers and a camp of English aviators.' Although figures of how many were caught in the net vary, some six thousand were arrested, many of them the exiled foreigners, resisters and Jews the Gestapo was looking for.

To camouflage their brutality, the Germans once again turned to the arts and launched another cultural charm offensive. They brought in German films and music. Knappertsbusch conducted the Berlin Philharmonic in a concert of Schubert, Liszt and Wagner. Lucienne Delforge opened a conference on 'Wagner and France' at which she played musical selections. The Luftwaffe band blared away in parks. The German Institute held conferences on cultural topics. Cultural programmes while the Nazi Reich was collapsing? Precisely because it was collapsing, the Germans were determined to forestall any weakening of the civil order by making clear they were in charge and intended to remain so.

CHAPTER 6

SONGS WITHOUT WORDS

'Blut und Schande' – blood and shame – Thomas Mann insisted, stained everything published in Nazi Germany. Getting into print, whatever the content, amounted to complicity – complicity in creating 'window dressing for absolute monstrousness'. There were those in Occupied France who were equally categorical. Jean Bruller, better known by his pseudonym Vercors, posed the choice starkly: 'When the Nazis occupied France after the defeat of 1940, French writers had two alternatives: collaboration or silence.' For certain others the issue went further still: 'Today in France legal literature means treasonous literature.' That was the motto of the underground publication *Lettres françaises* and the creed of communist intellectuals.

The opponents of Vichy and the Germans were not the only ones who believed this. André Gide's one-time secretary Lucien Combelle, himself a recent convert to collaboration, put it this way: 'When you wrote something, it was submitted to censorship. . . . In the eyes of the Germans, we were already an intelligentsia on their side.' In other words, subjecting your work to censorship was not merely subjecting your thought to censorship and it was not just subjecting your thought to censorship by your enemy. It amounted to complicity with him. Were books, then, to be like those piano pieces of Mendelssohn that cried out to be sung but that had no words?

What was someone to do, however, whose only possibility of earning a living was to be published? Most journalists saw little choice. And within days of the Wehrmacht's arrival, those who had not fled immediately jumped ship, reviving the old barb that some people could change their politics as quickly as they could change their shirt. For an author of books, however, there was a way out. As a result of the division of the country, some old publishing houses in the Unoccupied Zone expanded and a number of new ones – notably Robert

Laffont in Marseille – were established. So those unwilling to submit to German censorship could publish there, as did Louis Aragon, or in Algiers, as did Gide, or in Switzerland, as did Malraux.

Another possibility from 1942 on was the underground press. The most important of these tiny publishers was the famous Éditions de Minuit, established in 1941 by Jean Bruller. Before the war Bruller was a little-known graphic artist and satirist – *21 Recettes pratiques de mort violente précédées d'un petit manuel du parfait suicide* (21 Practical Ways of Violent Death Preceded by a Short Manual on the Perfect Suicide) was his earliest satirical album. So stunned was he by the defeat that he was left with only one thought. He must preserve, in his words, 'if not my freedom, at least my integrity'. And that meant in professional terms refusing to publish under the Occupation regime. So he took up carpentry. 'I was a bad carpenter and did not earn much money', he said later. 'All the same, I think writers could have earned their living from other work, teaching for instance.' But as he looked around, he could see only an artificial normality perpetrated by a seemingly friendly Invader and passively – or actively – accepted not just by the general public but also by prominent writers, artists and intellectuals. The French had expected the brutal *boche* but found instead the friendly German. This very friendliness Bruller regarded as an insidious trap. Even though many of them may also have been innocent victims of Hitler's grand design, the German Occupiers remained an enemy, a murdering enemy, a plundering enemy, an untouchable enemy, an enemy to be shunned, looked through and not even spoken to.

This train of thought Bruller worked out in what became a famous minor masterpiece, *Le Silence de la mer* (*The Silence of the Sea*), in which silence in the presence of the Invader was commended as the only acceptable behaviour and in itself a form of resistance. Since it was obvious that no publisher would have anything to do with it, he knew the only way of getting the text into print would be to publish it clandestinely. So, with the help of a journalist friend, Pierre de Lescure, money from a banker named Robillart, an underground printer and paper from the black market, Bruller and his friends banded together and managed by February 1942 to produce some 350 copies of his ninety-six-page work. The editor Jean Paulhan slipped it into underground circulation. And not just underground circulation. Thumbing a provocative nose, Bruller sent copies to Abetz and Drieu la Rochelle as well. Even more defiantly, he attached to each book a publisher's statement on what was at issue and how high the stakes were. 'In France there are still some writers . . . who refuse to obey orders. They feel that they must express themselves . . . because if they do not express themselves, the mind will die.' The work was published under the name Vercors. Bruller told no one, not his friends nor even his mother and wife, that he was the author. Guessing the identity of the writer became a popular game. It was thought to have been too well written to be by Malraux. Was it by Gide, then? Aragon jested that it was the best-kept secret of the Occupation. Only after the war did Bruller identify himself.

By that time Éditions de Minuit had brought out twenty-five works. Manuscripts had arrived in a flood from the likes of Paulhan, Sartre, Gide, Aragon, Jean Guéhenno, Jacques Maritain, Jean Cassou, Éluard, Camus, Mauriac and even John Steinbeck, whose story about the Resistance in Norway, *The Moon Is Down*, was published in translation. The biggest problem was finding paper. Since the only printing press available was one that printed death announcements, the books had to appear in that size and shape. They were printed at night, page by page on a hand press, and then stitched by hand. The works circulated as *samizdat*, mostly in Paris and several large cities in the south. Copies even made their way to London and New York – where *Life* magazine published an English-language version – and then back to Europe through the Low Countries. The Germans were troubled, but the only response they could think of was the childish one of trying to discredit the series by getting into circulation a ridiculous work called *Les Prophéties de Nostradamus*.

Bruller and other underground authors were exceptions. The vast majority of authors felt they had not been published at all unless they were published by a Paris house, even though this meant submitting to German censorship. Camus could have published *Le Mythe de Sisyphe* in its entirely, with a chapter on Kafka, in the Unoccupied Zone and considered doing so. But wanting the work to be widely known and being in ill-health, he deleted Kafka and published both *Le Mythe* and his novel *L'Étranger* (*The Stranger*) with Gallimard under German licence. Other anti-collaborationists tried to square the circle. Aragon published some writings without censorship in the Unoccupied Zone, some with Gallimard with German approval and still others clandestinely in *Lettres françaises*, the journal that damned those who published with a Paris house as treacherous. His wife, Elsa Triolet, gave her novels *Mille Regrets* (*A Thousand Regrets*) and *Le Cheval blanc* (*The White Charger*) to Denoël, publisher of such delicious titles as *Comment reconnaître le juif?* (How to Recognize the Jew?). After having travelled around France with Sartre to try to organize a resistance movement, de Beauvoir published *L'Invitée* (*She Came to Stay*) with Gallimard while Sartre himself submitted his plays *Les Mouches* and *Huis clos* to the Propaganda Department for approval. Perhaps none of this qualifies as collaboration, but it certainly did not amount to resistance or the coded message of opposition that the authors and their admirers claimed after the Liberation.

Very few writers of note – only six or seven come to mind – refused categorically to submit to German censorship. The most prominent abstentionist was the most prestigious living French writer. In 1939 André Gide was the Grand

Old Man of French letters, enjoying all the perks of GOMhood – praised, panned, revered, reviled, honoured, dishonoured. Now in his seventies, he was an institution and a symbol, respected and pilloried over four decades for his views on politics, society, morals and sex. Feelings went so deep that one of his most devoted critics, the devout Catholic Paul Claudel, on once witnessing crêpes being flambéed at dinner, cried out joyously, 'And that is how Gide will be flambéed in Hell.' Some of his friends feared that something similar might happen when the Germans came to dinner in June 1940, so they sent him a telegram urgently warning him to hide in the Pyrenees. As a well-known left-liberal, a famous homosexual and a public critic of Hitler and the Third Reich, he was presumed to face immediate detention.

Gide had publicly denounced Hitler within weeks of his coming to power. Any understanding with the German dictator, he argued, was neither possible nor desirable. When noted German Jews were fired from their positions, he had rallied support in French intellectual circles for offering one of them, Einstein, a chair at the Collège de France. And several times in the early Thirties he had travelled to Berlin to plead for the release of prominent political prisoners.

Gide was not sufficiently frightened by the Wehrmacht to flee. 'I haven't the heart to go and leave [my friends] behind. The danger is no greater for me than for them.' A short time later he spurned several offers by the Emergency Rescue Committee and others to help him go abroad. Instead he lived some-times with his daughter in Cabris and sometimes in Vence or Menton with his English translator, Dorothy Bussy, all the time trying not to think about the war but 'not able to think of anything but *that*'. He read voraciously. He had a passion for Goethe at the time and would sit with a German dictionary on one knee and Eckermann's *Gespräche mit Goethe* (*Conversations with Goethe*) on the other. Tedious going, he admitted, but it induced 'a semi-forgetfulness of the present anguish'.

It is characteristic that what Gide found repellent in Nazism was as much moral as political. No one who had made a virtual religion out of the primacy of the individual could have stood in anything but categorical opposition to it. 'And that is especially the point, it seems to me, on which Hitlerism is opposed to Christianity, that incomparable school of individualization, in which each is more precious than all,' he argued. 'Negate individual value so that each one, fused into the mass and adding to the number, is indefinitely replaceable – so if Friedrich or Wolfgang gets killed, Hermann or Ludwig will do just as well – and there is no occasion to be greatly grieved at the loss of this one or that.' It was his belief in the supreme value of the individual that had in earlier years led him to condemn French colonialism in Africa and, having first embraced communism, to denounce the Soviet Union after what he had observed there during a visit.

But Gide never doubted Hitler's popular appeal or his genius. On hearing his speech at the 1938 Nuremberg party rally, he foresaw what was coming. 'It is easier to lead men to combat and to stir up their passions than to temper them and urge them to the patient labours of peace.' It was impossible to deny that Hitler was playing the game masterfully, not letting himself be bound by any scruple. 'Hitler is sole master of the circus ring.' The dictator recognized the weaknesses of France – internal divisions, social discontent, political disorder – and played on them brilliantly. France herself had given him the opening. The punitive Versailles Treaty was the original sin. It would have been better had France not won the Great War, Gide was once moved to say. Unlike most other guilt-ridden intellectuals, however, he opposed reconciliation or cooperation with Germany once it became a totalitarian state.

Like the majority of Europeans, Gide breathed a sigh of relief when the Munich Agreement was signed in 1938. But he soon decided it was wrong and when war was declared the following year, he supported French entry. 'In this dreadful struggle now beginning everything for which we live is at stake, and the sacrifice of those dearest to us may not be sufficient to save those values. One would like to put them in safe-keeping, like the stained-glass windows of the churches.' He sank into despair. 'There is no acropolis that the flood of barbarism cannot reach, no ark that it cannot eventually sink. One clings to the wreckage.'

The fastidious Gide had always maintained there was no point in howling with the wolves. The time to speak up was when you had something to say that was not being aired. So he declined to give pep talks to the public in favour of the war in 1939. 'No, decidedly, I shall not speak on the radio. I shall not contribute to pumping oxygen into the public. The newspapers already contain enough patriotic yappings. The more French I feel, the more loath I am to let my mind be warped. If it regimented itself, it would lose all value. . . . Why should I express in an undertone what others excel in shouting?' A mere six months later, in the wake of Hitler's attack on the west, the news from the front so filled his heart 'with tears and horror' that he was unable to record his feelings.

At the time of the debacle, the septuagenarian Gide was weary. The suddenness and totality of the collapse left him staggered. Like everyone else he speculated on the reasons; but, unlike almost everyone else, he rejected the notion that France fell because it was morally rotten. The German victory was a military success and that success was inevitable. 'Hitler had educated his generals in a series of easy victories; they came already tried in combat. Their forces were superior in their arms, in their numbers, in their discipline, in their impetus, confidence in their leaders, unanimous faith in their Führer. What had we against that? – disorder, incompetence, negligence, internal divisions, decay.' Beyond that, he refused to apportion blame. 'There is doubtless no shame in being conquered when the enemy forces are so far superior.' But over and over he maintained that it was Hitler personally who was the great victor, who had acted 'with a sort of genius'. Everything had taken its course 'exactly as he had foreseen it, wanted it'. With all too much truth, he added, 'Soon the very people he is crushing will be obliged, while cursing him, to admire him.'

Still, for all his cool analysis, Gide so lost his bearings that he had trouble thinking straight. At one point he himself referred to 'my torment', 'this vacillating state of mine', 'the oscillation of my thought'. So on the one hand he said, 'To come to terms with one's enemy of yesterday is not cowardice; it is wisdom and accepting the inevitable.' But on the other he expressed hope that the French fleet, if not France herself, would fight on. When this did not happen, he accused the navy of being 'useless and dishonoured'. To him it was 'perfectly understandable' that the British should sink the French naval squadron at Mers-el-Kébir in July 1940 to prevent its falling into German hands. Later, when the remainder of the fleet at Toulon was scuttled by the French themselves, he commented, 'Alongside the English, that fleet might have rendered very great service; now it serves merely as an example of the evils of obedience.' When Vichy turned against Britain and entered on a path of collaboration, Gide was again struck by Hitler's 'consummate cleverness'. Britain and France were like two puppets in his hands and, after having conquered the one, he now amused himself by playing it off against the other.

Similar alternations marked his attitude to Pétain. The Marshal's speech announcing the armistice and ascribing the defeat to the fact that 'the spirit of enjoyment had won out over the spirit of sacrifice' Gide found 'simply admirable'. Yet he himself had been preaching something like the opposite for nearly fifty years. Pétain's next speech left Gide aghast. 'Can it be? Did Pétain himself deliver it? Freely? One suspects some infamous deceit. How can one speak of France as "intact" after handing over to the enemy more than half the country? . . . How can one fail to approve Churchill? Not to subscribe to General de Gaulle's declaration? Is it not enough for France to be conquered? Must she also be dishonoured?' Then two years later he came to think that Pétain was 'playing a difficult game as best he can'.

Yet he never wavered in his moral opposition to Vichy and the Germans. Without hesitation he agreed to become a member of the Patrons' Committee of the Emergency Rescue Committee. But organized resistance he considered futile under the circumstances. When de Beauvoir and Sartre went to see him in the summer of 1941 to enlist his support for a resistance organization, he gave them no encouragement. Where he erred was in assuming that some degree of free expression was still possible. Shortly after the armistice Drieu la Rochelle asked him – along with such other non-collaborationists as Paul Valéry and Paul Éluard – to contribute to the *Nouvelle Revue Française*, the distinguished publication Gide had helped to found in 1909. Not realizing that Drieu intended to turn it into the intellectuals' collaborationist journal, he proffered two articles. This provoked a pained outcry. 'You do not know', one critic wrote to him, 'what support you are giving enemy propaganda by this; your collaboration will be presented by them as proof of their liberalism.' Recognizing his blunder, Gide broke off all contact and wired Drieu, 'Grateful for your cordial letter and regret I must ask you to remove my name from the cover of your review.' In 1939 he had published the first volume of his diary; not until after the Liberation did he again publish a book in France.

If Gide thought he could live quietly in the south of France with his friends and his beloved Goethe, he could not have been more mistaken. The attacks on him in *Le Temps* and *Le Figaro littéraire* as well as in a book about his malign influence by the reactionary Catholic Henry Bordeaux left him neither amused nor frightened. To his diary he confided, 'That old accusation, "corrumpere juventutem", is more likely than praise to assure fame . . . and how ill-founded it usually is.' Some people had a 'strange idea' about the effect of his works. Here he was being more than a little disingenuous. In 1940 Gide was, as he had been for decades, the most controversial and influential – or at least thought-provoking – literary figure in France.

His break with conventional mores had begun at the end of the nineteenth century when a visit to Algeria had the effect of liberating him from the moral restraints and inhibitions of both his strict Protestant upbringing and the social and moral orthodoxy prevailing among the French middle class. In *Les Nourritures terrestres* (*Fruits of the Earth*) of 1897 and *L'Immoraliste* of 1902 he had exhorted young people to think for themselves and follow their instincts, wherever these might lead. In a way his early books did what Ibsen was doing in drama, what Kandinsky was doing in painting, what Schoenberg was doing in music, what Freud was doing in psychology around the same time – breaking chains, habits, conventions, orthodoxies. He challenged youth to go its own way, to succeed and fail, rise and fall down, but to live free – free of religion, of conventional social morality, of family. 'It is being free that is hard', says a character in *L'Immoraliste*. By the time of the First World War his work was widely read and even more widely discussed, exerting an influence upon the aesthetic and moral values of the interwar generation that steadily deepened. He might be esteemed as a prophet or denounced as a subversive, but he was never ignored.

By no means did his stoking of controversy end there. In 1924 he published *Corydon*, which was not so much a defence of homosexuality as a forthright insistence that it was a perfectly natural instinct that did no harm to the individual or society. Around the same time his political views were becoming equally unconventional and unwelcome. A long trip to the Congo in the summer of 1925 led to two books condemning French colonialism in Africa and campaigning for decent treatment of the natives. A passion for social justice led him to communism, though not the Communist party, and made him a hero of the Marxist left. But after touring the Soviet Union for four months in 1936 he commented in his *Retour de l'URSS* (*Return from the USSR*), 'I doubt that in any other country today (even in Hitler's Germany) the mind is less free, more bowed, more terrorized, more vassalized.' And so over the years he had antagonized, among others, Catholics, communists, Nazis, Italian fascists, Spanish Falangists, colonialists, homophobes and xenophobes.

By the same token he occupied a position for literary and political critics similar to that of a village lamppost for the neighbourhood dogs. From all directions they came and let loose. In the early Twenties the accusations were in full flow. The universal charge was that he exerted a 'baneful influence' on youth. Along with Proust and Freud, he had poisoned French literature with homosexual ideas. So malign was his influence, so sick were his views, that most major crimes committed by young people were attributed to him. Now, with the defeat in 1940, the long intellectual tyranny of Gide and his mouthpiece, *La Nouvelle Revue Française*, would be brought to an end.

It was probably only to be expected that most of Gide's old enemies should become noted collaborators. Yet Vichy did not – or did not dare – move against him even after he published a ferocious attack on a pro-German book by the fascist writer Jacques Chardonne in *Le Figaro* in April 1941. He also got away with – and must have had fun – writing a series of 'interviews imaginaires' in the same newspaper. The 'interviews' were ostensibly on purely literary topics but the 'interviewer' was a bit of a Pétainist and the answers were written in a teasing style that made fun of both the Marshal and his National Revolution. Varian Fry was so struck by the anti-collaborationist message embedded in the subtle ironies and double entendres of these pieces that he was moved to write an essay on the subject.

In the end it was not Vichy that sought to break him but the fascist-oriented Veterans' Legion. In May 1941 Gide was to give a lecture in Nice about the poet Henri Michaux. Objecting not so much to the lecture as to the lecturer, the Legion forced the event to be cancelled. 'I like being a "victim" of the Legion', Gide remarked. But being muzzled he did not like. North Africa, the place of refuge of his youth, beckoned. In May 1942 he betook himself to the less oppressive atmosphere of Tunis. There he continued to work on several critical writings, completed his translation of *Hamlet*, contributed to the Algiers publication *Fontaine* and kept a close watch on what was going on in France. After less than a year, however, he was warned to go into hiding from the Gestapo. Although he found it difficult to think he was in danger, he grew a beard and went underground so as 'not to run the risk of a forced voyage and sojourn in Germany or Italy'. He continued to work, founding *L'Arche*, an Algerian version of the *NRF* and writing the story of Theseus, the founder of Athens. In a remarkable gesture, de Gaulle invited Gide to dinner in Algiers in June 1943, after which the two had a long private talk. All in all Gide was impressed, foresaw an important role for the general in a future France and concluded, 'I shall not find it hard to hang my hopes on him.' In October 1944 Gide decided to return to Paris but, with executions and deportations in mind, feared that 'many of those I should have taken the most pleasure in seeing again will not be [alive]'.

For all his gravitas, Gide was, if not a corrupter, certainly a troublemaker, an agitator, a disturber. He opened Pandora's boxes and cans of worms; he stirred up hornet's nests and threw torches into tinder. It was for this – being 'an emancipator of the mind' – that he was twice honoured. In 1952 the Vatican ordered his *Opera omnia* to be added to its *Indicem librorum prohibitorum*. And in 1957 the Swedish Academy awarded him the Nobel Prize for Literature. 'I call a book a failure when it leaves a reader intact', he had proclaimed. 'To disturb is my function.' These words could easily have been written by the much lesser-known novelist, historian, quondam painter, bibliophile, bookseller, publisher and investigative reporter – a.k.a. muckraking journalist – Jean Galtier-Boissière.

At the time of the armistice Galtier-Boissière was the publisher-editor of *Le Crapouillot*, a weekly review of politics, culture and just about everything else. He had founded the journal in 1915 while a corporal in the trenches, naming it after a mortar that in profile resembled a *crapaud* (toad). The intent was to make the home front aware that life on the battlefield was unimaginable hell – 'une perpétuelle catastrophe' – not the glorified heroics painted in the daily press. In addition to descriptive articles about the fighting – some deleted by army censors – the paper included poetry, fiction and satirical sketches. From the start it was an independent voice: iconoclastic, satirical, provocative, serious, ironic, humorous.

After being discharged from the army, Galtier-Boissière kept his review going, despite urgent warnings from professionals in the field that the weird name alone ensured failure and that sales would be so poor he would lose his shirt. He recruited a set of lively, young contributors, to whom he paid nothing, and launched the paper with money made from the sale of twenty-five of his wartime sketches, windfalls from betting on horses and lucky speculation in Russian oil stocks. Given his own artistic interests – he was uncertain at the end of the war whether to be a painter or a writer – *Le Crapouillot* was as much a cultural as a political publication. A personal, private venture, it was in chronic financial difficulty. French papers in the interwar period depended on newsstand sales, advertising from large corporations, covert financing from the French and foreign governments and even blackmail. Being the sort of paper it was, *Le Crapouillot* had to depend solely on sales and these were dicey. Circulation never exceeded eight thousand copies and only the exceptional sales of special issues provided a financial cushion.

Galtier-Boissière has sometimes been labelled an anarchist. In reality he was a compulsive freethinker, instinctively irreverent, incapable of taking people or institutions as seriously as they took themselves. He looked for trouble, he was suspicious of everything. *Le Crapouillot* consequently purveyed no ideological creed and its contributors came from various political backgrounds. The paper's politics were the politics of truth-telling – a bit like *Private Eye* and *I.F. Stone's Weekly*. It sniffed out and exposed corruption, deception, illegal activities and anti-democratic behaviour wherever they could be uncovered. The interwar Third Republic – indeed, interwar Europe as a whole – was a field ripe for harvest. Galtier-Boissière looked on it all as Gibbon had looked on Rome, with never-ending amazement and bemused detachment in witnessing humanity's endless follies.

In addition to the regular weekly issues, Galtier-Boissière published several special issues every year featuring articles by experts, prepared from solid research and marinated in deliberate provocation. A fair number of these special issues were about the First World War; one sold 120,000 copies. In 1922, to take an example, there were issues on cinema (which initiated movie reviews in France), fashion and art exhibitions. In 1937 various issues treated such diverse topics as the Vatican, modern ideas of sexuality and phoney news stories. Other issues investigated the wine industry, gastronomy, the French press and the famous 'two hundred' who 'owned' France as well as 'The Mysteries of the Secret Police', 'From Lenin to Stalin' (portraying Stalin as a monstrous dictator who ratted on the Revolution) and 'Genuine and False Nobility' (showing that nine out of ten aristocratic titles were bogus). Two issues in particular caused a sensation. 'The Germans', published in January 1931, immediately sold 49,000 copies. 'The English', which came out the following November, was confiscated at the request of the British government – ostensibly because it included an exposé of the intelligence services – but not before fifty thousand copies had been sold, some at ten times the cover price. Although it created less of a stir, Galtier-Boissière brought out a remarkable seventy-five-page issue in July 1933 about Hitler under the title 'Does This Mean War?'. For its time the text was an astonishingly prescient analysis of Hitler's character, policies and intentions.

It might be thought that Galtier-Boissière's sceptical view of people and institutions and his desire to rake muck resulted from his unspeakable years in the trenches. After fighting on some of the worst fronts, he had suffered shell shock in 1916 and was hospitalized for about a year. He left the army a fervid pacifist but without hating the world or his superior officers and with a lasting sympathy for his fellow *poilus* – veterans of the trenches. Galtier-Boissière's independent character was, à la Freud, clearly formed during childhood. His family was respectably nonconformist. On the mother's side they were academics, poets and painters of the Barbizon school; on the Galtier de la Boissière side – the particle was dropped after the Revolution – they were Protestants and liberals in both temperament and politics. His father, a physician, was the author of *Le Larousse médical*. From an early age Jean was an intellectual loner, writing of himself as a child, 'I lived in a world apart.' Although good at studies – he attended the same Protestant École Alsacienne as Gide – he was considered by his parents to have 'un caractère très difficile' and he himself admitted to being instinctively rebellious in the face of authority. In a revealing anecdote, he related that his parents sometimes punished him by denying him dessert at dinner. His response to this 'injustice' was for years afterwards to refuse to take dessert at all. Reductive perhaps, but it would be obtuse not to recognize that from refusing dessert under a parental regime to refusing to publish under an Occupation regime was not a huge psychological step.

Although a man of the left, Galtier-Boissière was far from a socially recessive left-wing grouch. In fact the term joie de vivre might have been coined for him. He was a man about town, a bon vivant, an oenophile who kept a good cellar whose contents he enjoyed – sometimes at all-night drinking parties. He seems to have known almost everyone and revelled not only in the company of the cultural Tout-Paris but the denizens of the demi-monde of the *maisons de tolérance* and the rough *boîtes de nuit*. He was someone who could find humour in a handful of dust. There was high indignation but little or no hatred in his character or in his writing. A sketch of his head, in the style of a street artist, by his close friend the artist Jean Oberlé is entirely in character, showing him with a wry smile on his face, clearly about to break into a sceptical laugh.

Galtier-Boissière was a polemicist, with all the strengths and weaknesses of that profession. When it came to the critical question of how to deal with the dictators, his views lacked clear direction. Like many another militant pacifist at the time, Galtier-Boissière was caught in an agonizing dilemma – how to oppose war under any circumstances and yet resist aggressive totalitarian powers. He first confronted the conundrum at the time of the Spanish civil war when he and those like him supported the Loyalists but opposed any military support to fight Franco. He faced it again at the time of Munich when he wanted to stand up to Hitler but refused to support an alliance with Stalin to resist him. In August 1939 he apparently would have liked to see France stay out of any conflict over Poland but all he had to say in his memoirs about the declaration of war was that he was 'sickened by human stupidity'.

Having witnessed the marauding German army in the First World War, Galtier-Boissière decided to evacuate his family to central France in June 1940 but he returned to Paris not long after the armistice. Back only a few days, he was visited by a French businessman named Leperche:

L: Well, *mon cher*, when is *Le Crapouillot* going to reappear?
JG-B: After the war.
L: But the war is over. Now Europe will take shape. You have a role to play; Franco-German reconciliation opens the door to magnificent opportunities. At last we pacifists have realized our dreams.
JG-B: But the war isn't over.

Then and during all the dark days that followed, Galtier-Boissière never lost his conviction that the war was not over and that in the end the British would prevail. He never explained this *refus absurde*, the absurd refusal to accept the 'fact' that Hitler had won the war, to make no secret of his belief and to bear almost universal derision as a result. At lunch with Drieu in October 1940, the latter's reaction was typical: 'He shrugged his shoulders and, with a superior smile, treated me like an idiot.' For a time all that gave him hope was broadcasts from London. 'That's what raises morale.'

Never did he relent in his refusal to restart *Le Crapouillot* or to publish anything requiring German approval. Yet he was itching to write. He would have loved to do an exposé of the French press – a press that did somersaults not only during the phoney war but even more spectacularly after the Germans arrived. There were all sorts of temptations. The very morning after his return to Paris he was approached by Abetz through an intermediary with an invitation to edit a new 'polemical newspaper'. After he spurned the offer, Drieu pressed him at least to go along to dine with the ambassador, whom he described as 'a man full of charm'. Another friend offered to introduce him to officials in the Propaganda Department who could ease his way to publishing again. He brushed the offers aside. But when his anti-collaborationist friend Henri Jeanson invited him to contribute to *Aujourd'hui*, a new 'independent' daily, he agreed. The Germans scrapped Galtier-Boissière's first article and within no time scrapped Jeanson as well.

The autumn of 1940 found Galtier-Boissière bankrupt. *Le Crapouillot* was closed. He had no income from writing. A book business he had run on the side lost three-quarters of its customers when the colonies were cut off. 'I realized I was ruined,' he wrote in his memoirs. 'As a result I decided to sell my library, keeping only my collection – unique – of dictionaries of slang and several beautifully illustrated works of the Romantics, in particular Grandville.' Giving up a library, built up over many years, of rare books, first editions, original drawings and historic documents could not have been easy.

Once the Otto List came out, it became risky even to sell books. Characteristically Galtier-Boissière treated this as a challenge. He would submit to censorship neither what he wrote nor what he sold. Thumbing his nose at the Invader, he made a point of including in his weekly sale catalogues such provocative titles as *Crime de boche*, *L'Autriche martyre*, *Les Atrocités alle-mandes en Pologne* and de Gaulle's *La France et son armée*. Before long he had a caller whose furtive demeanour left no doubt he was either a plainclothes *flic* or a Gestapo agent. 'A friend gave me your catalogue. I assume if you circulate this list of banned works that you sell them under the counter to good clients. I would like to have some of these titles,' he said. 'Unfortunately I had to disappoint this connoisseur of forbidden books,' Galtier-Boissière commented. Afterwards he felt ashamed not to have confronted the man. In fact, he could have been arrested. Two years later he could not resist another provocation by printing on the front of his weekly catalogue the names of former *Crapouillot* writers who had fled or were in prison. But the worst moment occurred when two French police turned up in the *Crapouillot* office in the summer of 1943 and asked Galtier-Boissière's secretary her name. 'Madame Vacher,' she answered. 'And what was your maiden name?' they asked. At this she broke down and replied, 'I lied. My name is Lucienne Bloch. I am Jewish.' To her amazement the two men laughed and told her that when she thought up a good Christian name, she should phone it in to the local police. Luckily they were covert Gaullists.

And so Galtier-Boissière survived. But even apart from having to give up writing and publishing, these were horrible years. On the most immediate physical level – aside from ever-present hunger – was the terror of the heart-stopping ring of the doorbell late at night. 'There is always fear of the Gestapo,' he wrote. It is surprising in fact that his 1933 commentary on Hitler did not earn him an appointment with Himmler's representatives. In addition to personal danger, he suffered the constant torment of observing German soldiers strutting around Paris and treating it as their own city, seeing swastika flags flying from public buildings, hearing about the execution of hostages and worrying about friends when he had not seen them for several days. He spent as much time as possible at the old family home in Barbizon.

Though Galtier-Boissière would not write for the public, he could write for himself. So he kept a diary, later published as *Mon Journal pendant l'Occupation*. It opened on a note of perfidy. 'Today, 7 July 1940, the official French radio proclaimed that Hitler was right, that France had declared war on Germany to defend British hegemony and to ensure the revenge of the Jews.' From there on the diary is a veritable catalogue of examples of dishonour, betrayal, rampant opportunism, greed and all the other sins that raged like an epidemic throughout French society. It is also a treasury of anecdotes, comic episodes, bons mots, jokes against the Invader and the Vichyites, and vignettes about everyday life.

Galtier-Boissière was completely unable to reconcile himself to the Invader's presence. It would not have crossed his mind to dine with a German, much less to put in an appearance at the German Institute. He disliked the Occupiers, individually and collectively, and in his diary and memoirs of this period even avoided the word 'German', always using instead *fritz* or *fridolin*. Never did he have a good word to say for any of them, considering them imbeciles, oafs, thugs, disciplined barbarians or, in the case of Gestapo agents who ransacked his office, plundering brutes. Had it been published by then, he would have found Camus's *La Peste* (*The Plague*) perfectly apt, with its metaphor of the Invasion as an infestation of rats.

His attitude towards collaboration can be imagined. From the outset of the Occupation he let it be known that he was a Gaullist *jusqu'au-bout* – a supporter of de Gaulle and an opponent of Vichy and the Germans to the very end. Writers such as Rebatet, Brasillach, Suarez and their like – blatantly pro-Nazi and anti-Semitic, who applauded the persecution, deportation and execution of communists, Jews and members of the Resistance – were to him beyond the pale.

Collaboration he regarded as not just reprehensible but also ineffective. It was, he said, a matter of 'Give me your watch and I'll tell you the time'. The French, he was convinced, would get nothing by falling at the feet of the conqueror. Having a *Gauleiter* would have been better because he might have made concessions to gain personal popularity. Instead it was Vichy that made all the concessions. Vichy was to him a contemptible vassal regime and, though noting the quarrels among its bigwigs, he wasted little ink on it. Running into an acquaintance who wrote newspaper articles attacking the 'Judaeo-Masonic regime' of the Third Republic – a regime that had appointed the man to a lucrative job before the war – he was asked, 'Well, my friend, are we following the Marshal?' To which Galtier-Boissière replied, 'Not me. Your Marshal is a traitor who will be hanged.'

Yet with some *collabos* he could be remarkably patient. He was bemused by the three Leperche brothers, wealthy landowners and international traders

who are as sincere as they are unmercenary, representing the collaborator in his purest form. For twenty years all intelligent Frenchmen advocated Franco-German rapprochement, they say, and, well, now the hour of recon-ciliation has come. If they believe in Hitler's mission on earth, it is because they often travelled in Germany between 1920 and 1939 and, after seeing

the misery and desperation of the German people, they witnessed its resurrection thanks to the 'Führer'. If Hitler could transfigure Germany, they
conclude, he can put France back on its feet by organizing Europe ration-
ally. They have faith.

Seated next to one of the brothers at dinner, Galtier-Boissière was treated to
an outburst of 'flamboyant Hitlerism' about the wonders of the Third Reich,
which he had observed in his prewar travels around Germany – 'its urban
policies, its social reforms and its swimming pools'.

> But for heaven's sake, I reply, there are more important things in life than
> swimming pools. There is also freedom of thought and expression. I try in
> vain to open his eyes to the horror of a police state, of concentration camps,
> of racial persecution. 'That is all propaganda,' he responds. And when I
> maintain that the fritzes would be beaten, he doubles up with laughter and
> exclaims, 'Oh, these literati, these artists; no use talking to them – they live
> in their own world.'

Although philo-Semitic – or probably because of this – Galtier-Boissière
was aghast at Jews who somehow managed to get themselves Aryanized and
then became Nazi *collabos*. One of them told him, 'I really do prefer the
Germans to the English. We simply must come to a better understanding
with Hitler and conclude peace.' Another was a newspaper editor who, on
hearing about Mussolini's anti-Semitic measures in 1938, had broken down
in tears.

> Since discovering he is Aryan, he has taken advantage of the elimination of
> Jews to earn a lot of money. 'We should find what good we can in the Nazis,'
> he told me very matter-of-factly. 'It is what our Marshal is doing. Let us
> follow him. It is amazing the work of this great soldier, the number of laws
> he decrees, his magnificent modification of the legal code.' Yes, I reply, in
> particular the racial laws, don't you agree?

That the Occupation brought out the worst in people did not in the
slightest surprise the sceptical Galtier-Boissière. He simply amused himself by
compiling what he called a 'Dictionnaire des girouettes' (Dictionary of
Weather Vanes), quoting comments by people whose views and behaviour
changed with every shift in the political wind. He was disgusted by the self-
hatred of the defeatists, as when an old friend declared that the best way to
deal with the chaos and decadence of France would be for Germany to annex
the country. The open expressions of anti-Semitism left him speechless. While

dining with Jewish friends at the Brasserie Lipp shortly after the armistice, he was accosted from an adjacent table by a right-wing journalist whom he knew vaguely. The acquaintance shouted that he now had a newspaper column where he could at last freely 'take it out on the kikes'. And Galtier-Boissière was sickened by the meretricious style of life that had emerged within a few months of the defeat. It pained him to go into restaurants crowded with fritzes guzzling champagne and eating steak – forbidden, therefore concealed under fried eggs – and French fat-cat profiteers swilling Château Margaux. 'The rich are triumphant in the New Order. With money you can get anything while poor housewives have to stand for hours in the snow for a bit of swede.'

He knew of an old gentlewoman who had fallen on hard times and advertised for work. Several days later she was invited to German headquarters where they offered her 60 francs a day to denounce people who made anti-German remarks. A friend told him of a prisoner of war who had escaped and made his way back to Paris. No sooner had he returned to his old apartment than his landlord demanded back rent; the man was of course unable to pay so the landlord reported him to the German authorities. As time passed Galtier-Boissière's diary recorded news of more and more arrests, executions and deportations.

What humour he could find, he noted, though it was usually gallows humour. A man who had been released from prison after six months related that he had been told on arriving, 'On Friday mornings we execute and on Friday evenings we have theatricals to show that we didn't give a damn about what had happened to them.' An old friend made a point, whenever he dined at a restaurant favoured by the Wehrmacht, of loudly asking for every dish to be served with *sauce anglaise*. A worker impressed into labour service in Germany told his family that if he wrote to them in black ink, everything was fine, but if it was in red, life was miserable. His first letter arrived, written in black ink, saying, 'The food is excellent, the people are great, work is fine. The only problem is that there is no red ink.'

Then came the Liberation and, with the shifting wind, the weather vane again changed direction. He ran into one of the Leperche brothers several weeks after Paris was liberated.

JG-B: Well, my friend?

L: I am an idiot. That's all. I am an idiot. Those damned Germans really fooled me. Their Atlantic Wall was of cardboard! So, from today on, no more discussions, no more bets; I'll keep my mouth shut forever.

JG-B: And your brother?

L: Amédée? Oh, him! He is a Gaullist now – even a communist fellow traveller.

Given his political stance during the Occupation, Galtier-Boissière had good reason to want to see the guilty punished after the Liberation. But he did not always find it easy to know what counted as guilt, and in any case he was opposed to the wave of blind revenge, which he regarded as imitating the Germans. It was the destruction of moral values as a result of the Occupation that he deplored most. He did not object to purge by trial but was offended by the lenient treatment of major offenders and the summary punishment of minor miscreants. His diary relates the plaint of the mother of one victim of head-shaving. 'My little Josiane; it's horrible! They cut off her hair, sir. Poor little Josiane! If she slept with the Germans, it's because she was seventeen. You understand, sir? She would have been just as willing to sleep with Americans!' It also records the case of a contractor who, having made 40 million francs' profit doing military construction work for the Germans, was punished by being fined half the amount and allowed to keep the rest. About such things, he quoted with approval Fabre-Luce's comment that 'France, in time of revolution, is a country where hysteria is tempered with corruption'. The final entry in his diary of the Occupation years tells of a conversation he overheard in a café between two smartly dressed wheeler-dealers who had clearly made a killing during the war. Speaking of an article in that day's newspapers about investigations into fortunes acquired during the Occupation, one said, 'For four years we were left alone!' To which the other replied, 'Yea, and now the trouble begins.'

One of Galtier-Boissière's closest friends was Henri Jeanson, journalist, newspaper editor (for six weeks), film scriptwriter, actor, provocateur, syndicalist, pacifist, anarchist, jailbird, etc. Galtier-Boissière laughed in the face of authority; Jeanson flung pie in it. It was typical of him that, following dinner at Galtier-Boissière's not long after the defeat, he went to the window and shouted into the place de la Sorbonne, 'Vive Churchill, vive Churchill.' His ebullience, reckless at times, was expressed in the title of his posthumous memoir, *70 ans d'adolescence*. The book – a collage of pointillist recollections – might as well have been entitled, 'How I Laughed My Way Through Life' or 'How I Saw the Humorous Side of Everything'. Not that everything in his life *was* humorous. For what he wrote he was arrested twice by the prewar French government and twice by the Gestapo. 'But what always saved me in the most disagreeable situations was that I never took myself seriously or got indignant.'

Unlike Galtier-Boissière, whose character was formed in his youth, Jeanson's was prenatal. 'I was born with a lack of respect. No one taught me to be insubordinate. Instinctively I began very early to rebel.' His youth – he was born in 1900 – coincided with the early days of aviation. His favourite pilot was Georges Legagneux, whom he idolized for his 'celebrated escapades, his street slang, his bad character and his impeccable vulgarity'. Much later he worked for a newspaper editor whom he loved 'for his defects, his amorality and his outrageousness'. Reverence for the disreputable may have been a reaction to his father, a professor of political economy in Paris, who was a man of excellent character and impeccable respectability. His mother by contrast was pleasantly wacky. When he was quite young she used to take him for daily walks along a street that intersected with routes to two different cemeteries. When there was a funeral cortege, they would follow the mourners, attend the interment ceremony, duly express sympathy to the deceased's relatives and then resume their stroll. Because of his instinctive mistrust of authority, even as a child he had a particular dislike of the police. Passing a policeman's home on the way to school in the morning, he would always shout, 'Down with the cops.' To which the policeman, at first furious, after a time came to respond, 'Well, it must be a quarter to eight.' But it was not all a matter of prenatal instinct. When you had two grandfathers who were labourers, worked twelve hours a day all their lives and died poor, Jeanson felt you were bound to be against the established order.

Humour plus disrespect for authority guided him through life. He was ten when his father died of tuberculosis and he was honest enough to admit – to his shame – that he welcomed the resulting sense of independence. Although a scholarship student at the prestigious Lycée Henri IV, he was now free to quit school to follow his ambition of being a comic actor. He took whatever roles he could find in vaudeville, revues and theatre, and would act, dance and sing. He was often desperately poor and said that he learned little about the theatre but a lot about life. When unemployed, he sometimes spent the whole day chatting with the 'jolies créatures' at what he referred to as 'ces maisons que la police tolère et la morale réprouve'. As the Great War ground on and manpower became ever scarcer, he was offered a job with the main trade union newspaper and wrote articles not just on theatre but on military developments as well. 'Yes, I did! I signed myself General N. My articles, amateurish as they were, were no more stupid than those of the famous Colonel Rousset or General Cherfils. And my articles were no less frequently commented on by the foreign press.' He was now all of seventeen.

After the war he abandoned acting for journalism and worked for a variety of left-wing papers. For none of his mentors did he have a higher regard than Maurice Maréchal, founder-proprietor of Le Canard enchaîné who 'for thirty years gave his colleagues a lesson in courage, truth and independence – not that he developed many disciples'. Jeanson was now enjoying success and notoriety as a satirical journalist, especially for his articles in Le Canard enchaîné and Le Crapouillot. He was rising in the world and one evening was invited to dine at Maxim's. He did not own the requisite dinner jacket and lacked the means to hire one, but he had an idea. Henri Bernstein's latest play was having its premiere that day so he rushed to the theatre during intermission. Seeing someone he knew vaguely who was his size, he approached him:

That's a handsome dinner jacket.
Yes, isn't it?
Would you lend it to me?
You want to borrow my dinner jacket?
Yes, just for one evening.
Borrow my dinner jacket? What evening would you want it?
Now, this evening, right away.
But you would have to go home with me after the play.
But why?
If you want to borrow my dinner jacket, I would have to put on something else.
I'll lend you my suit; that way you will have collateral. It is really not so much a loan as an exchange.

And so they exchanged clothes. Looking as elegant, he said, as Lord Byron, he crossed the threshold of Maxim's for the first time. But there was a hitch. The next morning he realized he knew neither the surname nor the address of his benefactor. And owning only one suit, Jeanson had no choice but to wear the dinner jacket everywhere. After several days the lender finally tracked *him* down and the episode ended with thanks and smiles.

During these years journalism did not monopolize his writing. His first play was staged in 1929. He sat with the audience at its premiere and the first comment he heard was, 'Let's get out of here; it's too idiotic.' The critic of *Comoedia* declared it 'the silliest, most inane, the dullest of comedies' and prayed it would be the author's last. Far from the last, it was only the stuttering start. Jeanson now entered his most successful period, writing film scripts for a variety of European producers. *Pépé le Moko* and *Carnet de bal* in 1937, *L'Entrée des artistes* and *Hôtel du Nord* in 1938 made him famous.

Throughout the interwar period Jeanson also did straightforward political reporting, venturing to Italy in 1923, where he interviewed Mussolini, and to Spain at the outbreak of the civil war. In 1938 he published an article in *Solidarité internationale antifasciste* defending Herschel Grynszpan, the young Jew who had recently murdered Ernst vom Rath. Jeanson argued that Grynszpan had been distraught as a result of the Nazis' treatment of his parents. The French government considered the article 'justification of murder'. Jeanson was tried and given an eighteen-month suspended sentence. Then in August 1939 he returned in the same publication with a harsh attack on the premier entitled 'Non, mon Daladier, I Won't Fight in your War'. He had not fought in the First World War and had no intention of participating in the Second. His logic was flawless. 'The best way to return from war is not to go.' A month later he was one of a number of writers and intellectuals to sign a manifesto, 'Peace Now!', drafted by the pacifist anarchist Louis Lecoin. Nonetheless, when war was declared, he obeyed the call-up – 'general immobilization', as he referred to it – and went into the army. Although it is unlikely his article or the manifesto had the slightest public impact, the authorities were in such a panic over pacifist feeling and German efforts to destabilize the country that they arrested Lecoin immediately and Jeanson some weeks later. Following a trial he later compared to the surreal trial scene in Camus's *L'Étranger*, Jeanson was sentenced to five years in prison.

Even now his sense of humour did not desert him. On the way to his cell, he passed a general who, for whatever reason, was also under arrest. 'The dream of my life! Could archbishops and government ministers be far behind? I gave the general a smile of delight.' A prostitute in the next cell did her best to cheer him up. 'Don't worry, dearie, the five years will pass fast.' Loyal friends intervened so persistently that six months later, with the Wehrmacht on the outskirts of Paris, he was released.

So what were his views when the war began? Muddled. Back in the early Thirties, when Jean Renoir, a close friend, was flirting with the Communist party, Jeanson rejected that course for himself. 'I was already against everything. I remained that way.' Here he did himself an injustice. He had positive views – for which he was willing to go to prison – but would not bind himself to a political party or a political doctrine. He detested ideologues, singling out Rousseau and Ignatius of Loyola as proto-fascists. Like his friend Galtier-Boissière, he did that rarest of things – he thought for himself. So he could not be a this or a that. He supported the left but was not a socialist or communist. He opposed everything about Nazi Germany but was not willing to sacrifice his life to fight the Germans. Hitler, he thought, was the result of French stupidity – 'the natural son of Poincaré and Clemenceau, born at Versailles on 28 June 1919, as everyone knows'. But his pacifism trumped his hatred of Hitler and he wanted France to stay out of any war. Feeling hopeless and helpless, like most of his countrymen in 1939 he fatalistically awaited his nation's fate.

Jeanson welcomed the armistice and at first – 'for several days' – had hopes for Pétain. But these were quickly dashed. Vichy, he decided, was nothing more than a reactionary clericalist regime in the hands of 'the big business crowd' and 'the Pius XII gang'. Ever the naïve pacifist, however, he also seems to have believed for a brief time that a degree of coexistence with the Invader might be possible. Certainly he failed to take their measure. Nothing summed up his attitude better than a comment by Hermann Eich, head of the press section of the Wehrmacht's Propaganda Department: 'With Henri Jeanson, whom I knew, I always had the impression he was a constant cabaret turn; he took nothing seriously, as though we were running an assembly of lunatics who by some misfortune had settled themselves in Paris.'

One of the lunatics was Otto Abetz, who, as self-appointed czar of the press, decided Parisians should have at least one paper that was lively and satirical. When Galtier-Boissière showed no interest, he turned to Jeanson and promised there would be no interference in who wrote and what they wrote. Jeanson took the bait, and so was established *Aujourd'hui*, with writers who included the likes of Galtier-Boissière, Robert Desnos and Jean Anouilh. Despite problems from the start with the censors, Jeanson published a few articles on the fringes of the politically permissible and offered an outlet for Jews to write under a pseudonym. Naturally he was destined to fail. Six weeks on, he was ordered to follow an explicit editorial line in favour of collaboration. He refused and was sacked. At this point he should have fled to the Unoccupied Zone – he later reproached himself bitterly for not doing so. Paris was a vicious place, scores were being settled and for months the collaborationist press had been calling for the Germans to imprison 'the apologist for the Jew Grynszpan'. Jeanson spent two days burning incriminating papers but stayed. 'Why didn't you flee, you imbecile?' he later asked himself. 'You knew very well that Laubreaux, that specialist in anonymous letters and denunciation, swore to get your scalp. And when two Gestapo agents arrived, guns in hand, you were not at all surprised. You were waiting for them, you fool.'

'You again!' was the jailer's greeting when Jeanson arrived at the prison. This time he was not a simple prisoner. Now his name was on the hostage list, meaning that he was part of a pool of people to be executed whenever the Wehrmacht might want to retaliate for the shooting of a German soldier or other act of resistance. Under the circumstances even Jeanson's sang-froid rose several degrees, and he admitted 'this worried me a bit'. Since he had little contact with other prisoners and was refused pencil and paper, he spent his days trying to think up 'last words'. But when everything that occurred to him seemed either too serious, too melodramatic, too superficial or too lighthearted, he gave up. The sole respite from boundless boredom was an interrogation every ten days by the same Gestapo official, who banged his fist on the same table with the same violence and asked the same question:

OK, that article!
What article?
The article in *Solidarité internationale antifasciste*.
I don't know what you mean.
Where is it?

Curiously neither the Gestapo nor Jeanson's haters had been able to locate a copy of the offending article. To remove an obvious source, Jeanson had had the fore-sight to send his wife to the Bibliothèque Nationale where she got hold of the bound volume of the paper and, when the invigilator was distracted, tore out the article, chewed it up and swallowed it – 'proof that my prose is digestible', Jeanson boasted. Tempting as it must have been, he refrained from telling the Gestapo that the last-known whereabouts of his article was his wife's stomach.

What saved Jeanson, now as in 1940, was primarily the intervention of friends, in particular Gaston Bergery, a noted leftist politician who had moved steadily to the right into fascism and collaboration. Bergery appealed to Ernst Achenbach, whom he knew, and after four months of imprisonment Jeanson was released, though forbidden to work on films. But that was still not the end of it. In July 1942 Laubreaux, one of the supreme rats of the dark years, published an article reminding the Germans that the 'hoodlum' who had defended 'the Jew Grynszpan' was still at large. The effect was not long delayed. 'On 28 July I woke up in a cell in prison', Jeanson commented. And indeed for two weeks he was back in solitary confinement, continuing, as he said, the meditation he had begun the year before. After a fortnight he was consigned to a vast dormitory with 'Jews, resisters, wheeler-dealers, saboteurs, drug dealers, down-and-outs and the simple poor'. The stories they told him of betrayal and denunciation and other forms of unvarnished wickedness taught him whatever he still had to learn about how awful human beings could be.

Once again Gaston Bergery went to his rescue and after several months he was released but forbidden to write for publication or film. Needless to say, he went right on writing covertly for both and at the same time contributed to various clandestine publications. Then, after narrowly escaping yet another arrest, he went underground until the Liberation.

Henri Jeanson thought of Occupied France as a madhouse run by the lunatics. To Jean Guéhenno it was a prison run by murderous criminals. 'I cannot express the tremendous anguish that overwhelmed me when I went and locked myself in that prison', he said of crossing the border into the Occupied Zone after having fled from the Wehrmacht. The sense of being an innocent man in a prison without bars but also without escape plagued him throughout the Occupation years and guided his every thought and action. 'The job now is to paint the walls of the cell. I don't know what I shall paint mine but I am sure it will reflect all my old dreams, all the images of my ideals. The prison term will be long. I shall work slowly.'

Guéhenno had returned to Paris to resume his position at the Lycée Louis-le-Grand where he taught modern French history and literature – or, as he presented it, the history of ideas. He had grown up in a town in Brittany where his father was a cobbler. The family was so poor he had to drop out of school at fourteen to work in a boot factory. He studied on his own with such diligence that he gained a scholarship to the elite École Normale Supérieure. A decorated infantry officer in the Great War, he was invalided out before the end and left the army a pacifist. During the interwar period he was a passionate Europeanist and for some years edited a noted cultural review, *Europe*, and later founded a weekly, *Vendredi*.

From the moment Pétain sued for an armistice, Guéhenno felt the full emotional force of the defeat and feared the Occupation would last his lifetime. As an outlet for the flood of despair that swept over him, he kept a diary. It is one long, loud scream of anguish. The free-flowing emotions he recorded suggest at times more the utterings of a person on a psychoanalyst's couch than a professor's diary. The vocabulary alone is revealing. 'Misery', 'suffering', 'servility', 'sadness', 'anger', 'shame', 'cowardice', 'despair' and especially 'servitude' appear over and over. The impact is heightened by the stark simplicity of his style. The mood is one of heartbreak as he observes the tragedy around him. Not a single smile, much less a laugh, is to be found in these pages. 'This diary is sombre, too sombre,' he himself commented in a preface to the published text, *Journal des années noires* (Diary of the Dark Years). 'The original manuscript is more sombre still. I have refrained from publishing many pages of it.' In constant fear that the police would discover his notes, he concealed them as soon as they were written. And in the eventuality he might be arrested for his underground activities, he omitted whatever he knew of the identities and activities of friends and students who were in the Resistance or in hiding. Despite these omissions, he said, 'The average Frenchman will recognize himself here – that is all that a witness can hope for – and will remember his shame, that terrible shame that devoured us and almost made us lose a taste for life as well as the sense of contamination that the traitors inflicted on us.'

'It's over', are the diary's opening words, written after Pétain's appeal for an armistice on 17 June. But if the war was over for France, it had just begun for Guéhenno. During the next four years he was engaged in a titanic inner struggle to lead a free and honourable life as a Frenchman, professor, writer and liberal humanist in a world he found all but unbearable. In the weeks following the ceasefire he was overwhelmed by a sense of despairing loneliness as he saw people around him accommodate themselves to the Occupation and to Vichy. 'I am filled with sadness, anger and shame. I cannot bring myself to speak to anyone whom I suspect of looking at events differently from me. At the first word that reveals their wavering, their acceptance, I hate them. I experience a sort of physical horror and I withdraw.' For himself, there was only one course. 'I intend to sink into silence. I must conceal everything I think. Already we are accepting servitude. . . . Perhaps few people really need freedom.'

Servitude was the supreme evil to Guéhenno. By this he meant not simply moral capitulation to Nazi and Vichyite ideals but also an attitude of deference, obedience and visceral subordination to authority. 'To preserve your freedom in a world of slaves', was the blunt way he defined the central challenge facing every Frenchman. In his moral code, liberty was always associated with fraternity, however, and he added, 'It is not just one's own freedom, it is also the freedom of others. In a world of slaves, any true man feels himself a slave. He cannot bear to live.' Again and again he contrasted 'servitude' with 'honour', by which he meant integrity and self-respect – qualities as vital to a nation as to an individual. And these he feared could be destroyed by the defeat and Occupation.

This was the point of an article he wrote for *Marianne* – 'my last as a free man' – just after the defeat and before German censorship had taken hold. Pleading with his countrymen not to fall prey to shame, he wrote, 'Be proud. You are not conquered.' He contested the view coming out of Vichy that France had been defeated as a result of the moral laxity and defects of the old republic and so needed to repent. The worst thing that could happen, he insisted, would be to let disgust for the failures of the old political system lead to an attitude of servility and a belief that the French deserved their misery. The most dangerous invasion was not territorial but an invasion of the mind. 'My country, my France, is a France that no one can invade.'

True though that may have been intellectually and morally, there was another France – the one he had to live in every day. Almost immediately that France became intolerable, as several diary entries in late 1940 show. 'I close myself in my house and go out as little as possible' (16 September). 'All my projects seem ridiculous under the circumstances' (19 September). 'I cannot think of writing right now – don't have the heart for it' (27 September). 'I have not been able to write in this diary for days – silence and misery over the entire city' (4 October). 'Liberty is dead; France is also dead' (24 October). 'I do not believe much in myself any longer. I do not feel attached to the world, to life' (16 November). 'Sometimes I believe I have reached the bottom of despair' (23 December).

In a desperate desire to see beyond the dark days ahead, he told himself that even if you are not physically free, you can nonetheless think freely. However bad things became, he reassured himself, 'I can remain loyal to my beliefs.' He would take an inner journey and get to know himself better. He would lose himself in his work. 'I cannot write great novels or great histories. I don't have those gifts.' But he could write an autobiographical essay and he could also write about Rousseau – 'the exemplary life of a man who did not give up'. And to divert him there was always his favourite subject, the history of ideas in France in the eighteenth and nineteenth centuries. In the meantime he turned for solace, like many before and since, to Montaigne. Though he had lived during the bloody and irrational time of the religious wars, 'when outrageousness was triumphant', Montaigne's essays were nonetheless a model of reason and moderation. 'I try to imagine what he would be like today.'

The Invaders – 'our guests' – were an abomination. He referred to them as marionettes, robots and rats. He hated the very sight and sound of them. Later on he wrote:

> To the German I pass on the street: I do not know exactly what I feel when I am near you. I don't hate you; I no longer hate you. I know that you will never be my master. I pretend not to see you. I act as though you don't exist. . . . When you get on the Métro, we press together to make room. You are untouchable. I lower my head a bit so that you cannot see where I am looking, to deprive you of the pleasure of an exchange of glances. You are there, in the middle of us, like an object, in a circle of silence and ice.

In December 1941, when the Wehrmacht's invasion of Russia was halted, he came across a book on Napoleon's retreat from Moscow in 1812 and was ashamed of the malicious joy he felt at the parallels. 'The book came out last March but the Occupiers have banned it – too many French readers will delight in reading it and will find the account of the horrors a source of comfort and hope. Such are the sentiments that servitude inspires in us.' Later on, when Hamburg, Berlin and other cities were blasted by air raids, he was uncharacteristically indifferent to the suffering of the victims. More ruins and more misery were the only way France would be saved, he told himself. The Germans and Italians were responsible for their misfortunes and should learn that nationalism does not pay. 'For two years I have seen hate grow like a tree. Now it will bear fruit. And what fruit!' Yet he never fell prey to a blind Germanophobia. During some of his darkest hours he, like Gide, read and enormously admired Goethe. And as the Wehrmacht's defeat became clear, he thought of the years to come when a postwar Germany would be integrated into a new European system.

The Germans were contemptible. Pétain – 'an old man who no longer has even the voice of a man but of an old woman' – and the Vichyites were beneath contempt. While he never spelled it out, he thought France should have fought on from her colonies. 'Collaboration is nothing more than a nice word for servitude.' He was appalled that Frenchmen did the Germans' dirty work for them and it enraged him when Pétain condemned the assassination of a German soldier but was silent about the frequent executions of French civilians. It was not merely Vichy's policies but also its lies that he found intolerable.

Although for several years world news horrified him, he faithfully listened to German, Vichy and British radio broadcasts. He never missed a speech by

Hitler or Churchill, and on occasion got up in the middle of the night to hear Roosevelt. He reduced the war to a simple, personal duel – 'Hitler versus Churchill'. It was Churchill more than any other figure who offered inspiration and even a glimmer of hope. He was awed by his rhetoric – the 'impressive grandeur' of a radio address at the height of the Battle of Britain in September 1940 and the Miltonian reference to 'the unconquerable will'. And when in February 1942 Churchill announced the disastrous defeats in Asia and the fall of Singapore, he did so in language of 'incomparable nobility'. 'Everyone in the entire world who is attached by love and hope to the great humanistic tradition of Europe feels himself close to this old man.'

As the Occupation went on with its round of arrests, deportations and reprisal executions, Guéhenno was sometimes too desperate even to record his feelings. 'I refuse to put down in this diary all the awful things that happen these days', he wrote following the bombing of Paris synagogues and a series of new executions. And on 10 December 1941, after the military catastrophes suffered by the Americans and British in the Pacific, he wrote, 'I am too overcome by my emotions to write much here.' One did not live, one merely survived. 'Rarely does a thought open its wings.' In addition to moral agony, he suffered the sheer physical misery of the winter, when cold sometimes made it impossible to concentrate sufficiently to write or even think. But he always linked the two – famine *and* servitude, cold *and* servitude.

When the military news about the British and Russians got steadily worse in the course of 1941 and early 1942, Guéhenno became almost wild with despair. 'For the first time I tell myself that our defeat is permanent and wonder what life will be like in this prison. A life sentence for people my age anyway. . . . Most urgent is to maintain one's honour. . . . At all costs strive to regain honour and freedom.' His desperation reached such a point that he even once thought of prayer. Not prayer as understood by a religious person, which he considered foolish. When Catholics told him it was necessary to be irrational to understand the irrational, he wondered, 'Is it then necessary to be insane to understand the insane?' But he searched for some sense of communion with destiny and appealed to the heavens that he might somehow survive with his honour and integrity whole. 'No sect, no philosophy, no priest can speak for me. . . . I recall nights when I appealed to the beauty of the world to preserve what I loved, to allow it a few more years. . . . Beauty of the world, I said, preserve what is beautiful! Delights of the world, save what is delightful! . . . But I have not found my prayer and am afraid of passing my life in a search for it.' And so he accepted that there was no solace.

Several times he returned to the Unoccupied Zone, to Montolieu, his adoptive village in Languedoc. He was shocked by what he found. On the first occasion – just two months after the defeat – instead of dancing in the streets, as there had always been on summer evenings in the old days, there were now religious processions and confessions of sin. 'So quickly submissive, so obedient', was his terse reaction. The atmosphere was such that he decided to stay indoors to avoid meeting people and having to converse with them. On going back two years later, he was left with the impression that France had become two countries. Vichy had successfully insulated the Unoccupied Zone from the rest of France and the world beyond. When he told villagers about Gestapo activities in Paris and showed them newspaper articles, they were not only annoyed but even treated him with suspicion. One of the village barbers refused to cut his hair – 'he would really have liked to cut off my head' – and the other seemed inclined to denounce him to the police as a republican or a communist. 'War veterans, Franciscans, Jesuits, sneaks, informers – what a show!' When he returned the following year, after the Germans had at last occupied it, he found life physically difficult; poaching small field animals was almost the only source of food. The selfishness of many of the village folk distressed him and he ruminated on what makes a healthy society.

It was against this background that Guéhenno led his professional life. And of all cultural figures, it is he who is most widely known for categorically refusing to write under German licence. He argued that if you are in prison, there are things you should not do. Chiefly, you must refuse any form of cooperation with the jailers. He wanted to write; he needed to write, emotionally if not professionally. But he considered it wrong, if not immoral, to pretend that nothing had changed. This was just what the Occupier wanted. 'If you are in a prison, you should live like a prisoner, at least maintain the dignity of a prisoner. But you must never play the jailer's game, never do what he would like you to do – living and enjoying oneself as before, when you were free.' If you could not say what you wanted, it was better to be silent – unless, he added as a vital qualification, 'absolutely obliged by the need to earn a living'.

He was vexed therefore to see an announcement in November 1940 that Gide, Giono, Jouhandeau, Valéry and Montherlant – established writers who were not obliged to write to survive – intended to publish articles in the *Nouvelle Revue Française*, now in the hands of the prominent *collabo* Drieu La Rochelle. 'The man of letters is not the highest type of human being. Incapable of living long out of sight, he would sell his soul to see his name in print. Several months of silence, of invisibility drive him to the very limit. He can hold out no longer. . . . "French literature," he says, "must go on." He thinks that he is literature and French thought and that they would die without him.'

Barely two months later he received a pencilled note from Drieu asking for an article on Voltaire. This triggered a mordant comment.

We have no way of telling these people what we think of their activities. They could at least leave us in peace. The worst of it is that they try to pass off our silence and our decision not to publish as something reprehensible. 'Fortunately,' one of them writes in the NRF, 'neither Voltaire nor Diderot would think like that.' These people who hold out their hands in chains take themselves to be Voltaires. Nothing to be done except grit your teeth. Impossible to reply without entering the prisons of the Occupier.

Nearly a year later he reverted to the subject, with like asperity. He noted that writers – like artists generally – enjoyed greater prestige in France than anywhere else. But under the Occupation they had become vain and selfish. 'Under the surveillance of Goebbels they go right on with their work. "Is it their fault", they ask, "that their merchandise must nowadays have a Hitlerian stamp of approval if it is to be publishable?"' Guéhenno had no objection in principle to publishing in the Unoccupied Zone, where books were not censored. He himself once thought of doing so but was warned he risked arrest by the Germans. It was much to Malraux's honour that he had published *La Lutte avec l'ange* (The Struggle with the Angel) in Switzerland, 'as a free man should do'. And once the Éditions de Minuit got going, Guéhenno published sections of his own diary there. But his essays and his work on Rousseau had to await the Liberation. Behind the scenes Guéhenno was increasingly active with the Resistance and in May 1941 was one of the founders of the anti-*collabo* National Writers Committee.

In a world he found abhorrent, Guéhenno had one great consolation – his students at Louis-le-Grand. It was their situation in 1940 – young men his age when he entered the First World War – that forced him to face the dilemma of the pacifist. 'Above all I thought of young people. It was cruel to see them go to war. But is it less cruel to force them to live in a dishonoured country? I shall never believe that people are made for war. But I also know they are not made for servitude either.' And servitude, he felt in June 1940, was a greater threat to young people than fighting. After the defeat he considered it Pétain's unforgivable crime to force youth to disobey the civil order if they were to maintain their honour and integrity. When the students demonstrated on the first anniversary of Armistice Day in 1940, he was so appalled by the police actions against them that he could not bear to record in his diary what he had seen.

Teaching, he said, 'was my last resort, my refuge. I really devote myself to it, I lose myself in it.' The only time he felt good was when he stood in front of his fifty students. 'I enter [the classroom] and immediately I am sure that all the miseries of this country are temporary. ... We lose ourselves in the thought of Racine and the torments of Pascal and for several moments it really seems as though the current idiocies are completely abolished.' He read them long passages from Montaigne's essays and Walt Whitman's *Leaves of Grass*. Both were men he admired because they were individualists who thought for themselves. At another time he turned to Voltaire and discussed his *Lettres anglaises* and his poem on liberty of 1734. 'At four o'clock I suddenly realized that the class had fallen into a profound silence. In their attention the students had turned pale. None of them even thought of taking notes. . . . They listened, did nothing but listen. . . . When I left at five my heart was filled with joy, though I was close to tears.'

Teaching was by no means without risk. One day Guéhenno learned that the Germans had that morning arrested a professor at another lycée. He was a teacher of German literature who had given his students a passage of Schiller on liberty to translate. One of his students had denounced him for the 100-franc bounty paid by the Occupation authorities for such denunciations. 'What will happen to me reading fragments of Voltaire?' he wondered. 'What will I do in the months to come? But I cannot stop – Voltaire, Rousseau, Diderot, Danton, Robespierre, Chénier, Hugo, Michelet.' However, by January 1943 he was perplexed to find that the mood of the class was becoming morose and unresponsive. When he spoke of freedom and honour, they were annoyed. Weeks later, for the first time in his teaching career, he felt a sense of discord between himself and the class. He was devastated. 'I feel alone and old.' Eventually he discovered that one of the students had been taking notes on whatever was said in class that might be considered subversive, terrifying his classmates. Once the snitch and his several accomplices had been exposed, the class again came alive. Guéhenno was lucky: three professors at his lycée were arrested. Even so, he did not escape punishment. Instead of firing him outright, Vichy officials demoted him to the position he had held at the outset of his career and required him to teach for seventeen hours a week instead of the usual six.

Far worse was the situation facing students as they became liable for forced labour in Germany. Guéhenno was deeply embittered that it was the French authorities who were implementing the German order. As a result the only choice facing the students was to comply or to go into hiding – without papers, without identification, without food rations. 'I do not find pleasure or honour in the French mind any longer, only an immense sadness.' Early in June 1943 all the students of the 1940–42 class were informed they would be required to leave for Germany on 1 July. Some decided to flee to Spain, others to hide in the mountains in Savoy or central France. A few volunteered to work in coal mines rather than go to Germany. But most were resigned to going, fearful of causing trouble for their parents if they fled. So respected and trusted was Guéhenno that those of his students who went underground kept in touch with him and went to see him on clandestine visits to Paris. And when he came to publish his diary after the war, it was his students he thought of. 'This diary of our misery I dedicate to those of my students who – imprisoned, tortured, deported, shot or killed in combat – testify, through their suffering or their death, that we were not mistaken, that that vague thing we talked about together, in anguish but also with fervour – liberty – exists.'

Students and young men in the Resistance were the last sort of people Alfred Fabre-Luce would have had contact with, much less have dedicated a diary to. But then Fabre-Luce was just the sort of person Guéhenno said he would have fled from had they met. Not that there was much chance of that. Since Guéhenno was a lycée instructor active in the Resistance and Fabre-Luce was a wealthy intellectual and a devout pro-German collaborator, their paths would never have crossed geographically or intellectually or morally. For all their differences, however, both shared the dream of a peaceful Europe without nationalistic rivalries in which France and Germany would be friendly part-ners. But for Guéhenno, it was to be a Europe based on Enlightenment ideals, for Fabre-Luce a Europe based on fascist principles led by the Third Reich.

Although he was too young to have served in the Great War, the mad slaughter had made Fabre-Luce a fervent pan-Europeanist, a supporter of the League of Nations and a promoter of Franco-German cooperation. After studying law, history and political science in Paris, he served very briefly at the French embassy in London. Being wealthy – a son of the founder of Crédit Lyonnais – he was free to pursue his interests independently and abandoned diplomacy for a career as an author and journalist. By 1922 he was already in print with *La Crise des alliances: relations franco-britanniques* followed two years later by his widely read *La Victoire*, a condemnation of President Poincaré's harsh German policy. He went on to write biographies of, among others, D.H. Lawrence, Talleyrand and Constant. A trip to the Soviet Union turned him into an ardent anti-Bolshevist, a view elaborated in his *Russia* in 1927. He later visited China, about which he wrote a novel. A spokesman for the extreme right, he was the founder-editor of the weekly *Pamphlet*, an editor of *L'Europe nouvelle* and a member of the editorial board of *Je suis partout*.

Fabre-Luce was not a *converti*, who suddenly became a collaborator after the Wehrmacht had arrived in Paris. Nor was he one of those plutocrats who was so terrified of the Popular Front government that he turned to the far right on the eve of the war. At least as far back as 1930 he was fascist in ideology and, a friend of Oswald Mosley, was quietly active in European fascist circles. Against the twin dangers of Bolshevism and social disorder he saw two great bulwarks – fascist Italy and Nazi Germany. Why then be disturbed by political repression, anti-Semitism, the absorption of Austria, the annexation of the Sudetenland and the seizure of Czechoslovakia? And when it came to France, between a Popular Front government that gave the workers a paid vacation and occupation by the Germans who would keep them in their place, the choice was easy.

At the outbreak of the war Fabre-Luce decided to keep a record of the events of the time, and it is this for which he is now best known. The document is not an account of daily life in those years but a chronicle of high politics, a commentary on how he viewed the course of major events. Implying that his account was not so much a personal interpretation as a testament of how *le bon Dieu* himself would have seen things, he gave it the magisterial title *Journal de la France*. Suitably enough, the writing has the oracular quality of a mandarin's all-knowing and condescending wisdom. A number of perceptive aperçus notwithstanding, it reveals a world-weary cynic who knew neither the value nor even the price of anything. Though verbose and repetitive – a mark of a man enchanted with his own words and thoughts – the *Journal* is impersonal, saying little or nothing about his own life until near the end. His views are evident only obliquely through what and whom he berated or defended. Out of the text emerges bit by bit a hate list that reveals Fabre-Luce's intellectual orientation. It included the principal politicians of the Third Republic – above all Blum and the Popular Front – the BBC, America, de Gaulle, the Café de Flore set, French intellectuals, communists, 'bourgeois Anglophiles', university students, the RAF for its 'terror bombing' of France, and the Resistance and 'Resistance authors', to name a few.

His paramount villains were the British, Churchill specifically. Every reference to the prime minister was written in bile; the Britain of the *Journal* was the caricatured perfidious Albion of French historical lore. 'They pushed us into war and then did not follow' is typical. After the French surrender he hoped Britain would suffer the same fate and rejoiced in every British defeat and regretted every German setback. What could have been more in Britain's treacherous character than the sinking of the French ships at Mers-el-Kébir, which he claimed had killed more French sailors in one day than did the Germans during the entire length of the war. British wickedness continued with a blockade of French Atlantic ports. To Fabre-Luce it was perfectly natural that 'to continue its war against Britain, Germany should control the coastline and lines of communication', but intolerable and in violation of international law that the British should seize French cargo on the high seas and bomb German ships in French ports.

Most dastardly of all was the British plot to annex French colonies. Whatever the man's faults, lack of imagination was not one of them. When Rudolf Hess flew to Scotland, Fabre-Luce foresaw negotiations between Germany and Britain in which the dismemberment of the French empire in

Africa would figure. In fact, as he saw it, this had already begun with the seizure of French Equatorial Africa and continued with the invasion of Syria in June 1941, an operation described as being part of a British effort 'to extend its tentacles into Iran and the Caucasus'. The fact that the invasion was one that de Gaulle had long proposed and was carried out by a largely Free French force and that the action had been provoked by Vichy's granting the Luftwaffe landing rights in the country went unmentioned.

It is scarcely surprising that, after Churchill, the person Fabre-Luce most hated was de Gaulle. He was the enemy of Pétain, the enemy of Vichy, the enemy of collaboration, the enemy of the Germans and the enemy of France. He wanted war instead of peace, divided the French nation, sought to stir up insurrection and was as much a collaborator with the Anglo-Saxons as was Pétain with the Germans.

By contrast, Fabre-Luce's references to the Germans – never called 'fritzes', 'fridolins', 'Nazis' or other irreverent terms – are at the least neutral, usually sympathetic and often favourable. He even put a good face on the 1940 invasion itself. When the Wehrmacht attacked, it did so 'without hatred', he maintained. 'It conquered without unnecessary massacres, respected monuments, spared and sometimes repatriated with paternal care those who fled in the exodus. For a time it was the force for order in a hysterical nation.' After their victory German officials in their wanderings around France were 'almost timid, as the Romans might have been on conquering Greece'. And when they went off to fight in the east, the French people regretted their departure. 'They had not behaved badly. It is a shame they are going off to get killed,' was how he described the sentiment – perhaps a transference of his own feelings onto others. Fabre-Luce even took a benign view of the German invasion of the Unoccupied Zone in November 1942, maintaining that it had occurred without serious incident and that 'German troops avoided disturbing the way of life of the population'.

Fabre-Luce's contempt for the Third Republic – the subtext of his *Journal* – was so intense that he welcomed the Occupation. To begin with, the French had no right to complain. They had brought their plight on themselves; it was they who had declared war, not Hitler. The defeat was salutary in any number of ways. In its wake France was cleansed of undesirable elements – to wit, 'the compromised', 'the Freemasons', 'the doctrinaire', 'the Jews', 'socialists and communists'. With the passage of time there came hunger and cold, as food and coal supplies diminished. But Fabre-Luce always saw a silver lining, however black the cloud. Having to stand in queues for food and tobacco offered a way for different classes – though not forsooth Fabre-Luce – to get acquainted. 'People accepted the waiting and the boredom as a way of calming their nerves.' And by confiscating motorcars, the Invader had taken Paris back to the unspoiled world prior to 1900. Fabre-Luce waxed lyrical. The silence of the city was overwhelming; the monuments more magnificent than ever; the gardens seemed to submerge the buildings; the air was fresh and nicely scented; you could cross the street without fearing for your life. Sometimes you could almost believe you were in Versailles or the Vatican, Angkor Wat or Baalbek. The old atmosphere of the city had been restored.

But a far more important benefit of the Occupation was bringing together the French and Germans 'in a sort of reciprocal compassion'. Historically, occupations were the way one nation civilized another – the Greeks, the Romans; the Romans, the Gauls. The German presence was therefore not so much a burden to be borne as an opportunity for a better future. 'French Europeanists' were convinced that Hitler was well on his way to creating a united Europe and it was vital for France to be a part of it. 'This will not sanctify our defeat but on the contrary overcome it. Rivalries between countries, that were such a feature of nineteenth-century Europe, have become passé. The future Europe will be a great economic zone where people, weary of incessant quarrels, will live in security. . . . The Germans do not want slaves but clients.' However, slaves are what the French would be if they were not smart enough, as he put it, 'to accept the invitation to participate in Europe's construction'.

By opening the way for Pétain to come to power, the Germans had done France a historic service. The aged Marshal is the hero of the *Journal*. Actually, 'hero' is an understatement. Veneration of the head of state was far from uncommon at the time. But Fabre-Luce's fawning praise for the Marshal resembled nothing so much as the gush spouted at a boozy testimonial dinner. His Pétain had not sought power for personal glory, he had accepted it in a self-sacrificing effort to diminish the suffering of the nation. The esteem in which he was held for his military past and the way he radiated justice and humanity, even at the age of eighty-four, were proof of his lack of personal ambition. 'The true measure of his grandeur is his power to symbolize in his person the fate of the nation.'

Fabre-Luce described the relationship between the people and Pétain in several ways. One was as between 'a believer and his god'. 'In this mystical exchange, the essence of French patriotism will take shape.' Another was like that between a father and his children. Rather than commenting on his daily activities, the Marshal was 'similar to a father who cannot tell his children what he is doing for them'. In his functions as head of state, he was wise and he was competent. He appointed his ministers based on their 'moral foundation' and 'their abstention from political corruption'. Unfortunately the old guard had followed him to Vichy. So, for example, when Pétain wished to protest the British government's support for de Gaulle as an 'intolerable gesture', the old Foreign Ministry officials changed the wording to 'unfriendly gesture'.

How to salvage France's role in world affairs preoccupied much of Fabre-Luce's thinking. In her geopolitical position, he felt she had her trump card. 'He who is master of the Mediterranean will be the one to win the war.' And it was France with her North African empire who held that mastery in her hands. By collaborating with Germany, she could ensure German control of the continent; by keeping open the Mediterranean, she would allow Britain to control the seas. 'Materially and spiritually we would find ourselves at the fulcrum. Rather than being victors, we could be arbiters. In that final hope resides our ancient dreams of grandeur.' What stood in the way of this grand design? The British, of course, by continuing to fight. And then to make matters worse they and the Americans put their troops into North Africa, prompting the Germans to defend their position in France. 'Had the Anglo-Saxons not provoked the total occupation of all France by establishing . . . a "second front" in Africa, he [Pétain] could at an opportune moment have led a united France, in command of her fleet and army, into war.' But on which side? Fabre-Luce did not say, but presumably he meant on the side of the Allies – a betrayal of the Germans that he had roundly condemned in earlier pages.

Fabre-Luce was not greatly interested in what went on inside France. Victims of the Occupation got no sympathy from him. The students who were beaten up by the police on Armistice Day 1940 – leaving Guéhenno so distressed that he refused to write down what he had seen – were so many hooligans and flakes. Because of their antics, the university was closed for several months. After that the students wised up and behaved. Round-ups and reprisal executions found scarcely any mention in the *Journal*. On hearing the news that several thousand foreign Jews had been interned in the Unoccupied Zone, Fabre-Luce remarked, 'These victims do not inspire any particular sympathy; they turned up here as a result of a blind immigration that a wise government would never have allowed.'

The victims he did pity were the dead and wounded resulting from British air raids. By 1944 he was complaining that there was little to distinguish between the one belligerent that took French workers for forced labour and the other that destroyed French factories with bombs. Civilian deaths in 1944 were probably higher than those suffered by the military in 1940, he claimed, and this time the bombs mutilated orphans and killed those who had merely been wounded in the war. In the months before D-Day he bewailed the antic-ipated battle as another case of British and American stupidity: 'The Anglo-Saxon invasion appears to be nearer and nearer, more and more terrible – and more and more pointless. Germany would now willingly agree to evacuate the territories occupied in the West if she was offered peace. . . . Caught between American power and Russian power, she no longer claims hegemony. Is it really necessary to prove this on the ground?'

Collabos were not conspicuous for their sense of humour and Fabre-Luce was no exception. Nothing rises off the pages of his *Journal* to provoke the slightest smile. Coarse irony there is, however, in the case of denizens of the Left Bank, in particular the Café de Flore set. Venturing to Saint-Germain-des-Prés was for Fabre-Luce an anthropological field trip into an exotic land. The natives were all pretty grubby, many looking as though they had spent the day drinking beer. They had dirty hands and fingernails; the males wore sweaters, without a shirt or tie; they had long hair and their jackets were shabby. They gave the impression of expecting any day to be arrested and deported. The Flore itself was the only place where you could simultaneously eat, drink, see friends and work. 'Work? Yes, indeed.' Up on the mezzanine, in a smelly area between the phone and the lavatories, were small marble-top tables and in place of a drink was an inkwell. There patrons wrote, with Simone de Beauvoir in the centre as queen bee. But why work in a café? Because, according to Fabre-Luce, 'French intellectuals love to work in disorder, to interrupt what they are doing to receive an admirer and to try to impress the waiter.'

The *Journal* was published in four chronological parts, the first two celebrating the German triumph. Needless to say, German authorities regarded Fabre-Luce as a propaganda godsend. In preparing the second volume, covering the period August 1940 to April 1942, he worked closely with Peter Klassen, the Wehrmacht Propaganda Department official in charge of anti-Masonic and anti-Semitic propaganda. The Germans were delighted with the result, which they considered ideal for French war prisoners. However, in early 1943, as the tide of the war changed, Fabre-Luce's hopes of a united Europe under Hitler began to fade. The Wehrmacht was on the defensive. De Gaulle was in Algiers with the same old gang of politicians who wanted to re-establish the same old parliamentary government. The communists were on the march. And France herself was a prey to 'the terrorists', as he sometimes referred to the Resistance. The tone of the third volume of the *Journal*, May 1942 to May 1943, was openly apologetic. The armistice of 1940? It had forestalled the German seizure of North Africa – Pétain's defence at his postwar trial. And his own behaviour? 'It will be said that I collaborated. Of course I had good relations with the Germans. It was necessary for business. But unlike the others I do not have any blood on my hands.'

Even this mild degree of 'defeatism' by an influential and socially well-connected *collabo* was bound to displease the Germans. Fabre-Luce was well aware of this but instead of turning to an underground press – 'I do not really like the notion of clandestine publication', he once said – he published the latest volume with the licence number of the previous one. It was printed in two thousand copies in June 1943 and promptly banned by the Germans, though not before Fabre-Luce had distributed a thousand copies with a dedication in the author's hand. Having anticipated trouble, he took a copy to the German censors to assure them that nothing in the text was written with unfriendly intent. Pseudo-naïveté was rewarded with prompt arrest. He spent four months as a prisoner in a comfortable villa in suburban Paris as a guest of the Gestapo.

Later he wrote an account of his experience, which says a great deal about his feelings but very little about his incarceration. His jailmates seem to have earned his respect and in some cases even admiration, though without ever arousing in him respect or admiration for the Resistance itself. About his emotional suffering, he was candid. Even in the comparative luxury of the Gestapo villa, he admitted he was so depressed that the guard who accompanied him on his daily outing commented, 'It is forbidden to cry in the garden.' Yet he seems to have known from an early stage that the Gestapo had decided on his punishment at the time of his arrest – four months' detention and payment of a huge ransom. The German authorities probably had several reasons for wanting to punish him. The book openly admitted that Germany was on the ropes. 'To write such a book is worse than throwing a bomb', his interrogator told him at their first meeting. They were also angered that he had pulled a fast one on them by publishing without a licence. 'You got your book in circulation; that is what you wanted', an angered official commented – meaning that he had got out a book that he knew the Germans would not have approved. Fabre-Luce had to be made an example of, if for no other reason than to forestall other *collabo* writers from defecting.

Imprisonment ended on a sweet-sour note. One day the Germans simply opened the door and let him walk out, suitcase in hand. He had often reflected on how this day would mark an entirely new beginning in his life. 'But then suddenly it seemed to me that it would be a lot more fun to take up my life exactly where it had left off.' So he went into a café and phoned the girlfriend whom he was to have met on the day of his arrest. 'Excuse me for being four months late,' he told her. He then walked on and spied a notice of a piano recital by Wilhelm Kempf. But after a moment he realized it would be impossible to attend. He was bound to run into the head jailer and other German officials involved in his case and 'we would all have thought of one another rather than thinking about Schumann'.

He returned home to write the final volume of his *Journal*, which was issued in a thousand numbered mimeographed copies in the autumn of 1944. It concluded with his version of the final weeks and days, in which he contrasted the orderly behaviour of the Wehrmacht with the rowdiness of the Resistance and the chaos caused by impetuous Parisians. With the Liberation he was once again arrested, this time for collaboration. And once again he wrote an account – almost humorous – of his prison experience. *Double Prison* contrasts the orderliness of Gestapo imprisonment with the anarchy and hypocrisy of the

Liberation purges. Mobs of accused swarmed through the jails. 'The police toyed with the prisoners, at times shuffled them around, swapped them, lost them.' It was the same old disorder and corruption of the Third Republic – *déjà vu* all over again. In the prison yard he ran into old friends – Sacha Guitry, Arletty and Albert, the head waiter at Maxim's – as well as the notorious *collabo* Chave, who used to take the heads of his victims in a suitcase to his even more notorious boss, Pierre Bonny, also an inmate. 'Our wives, our mothers, even our lawyers were refused permission to see us; but the communists, the Anglo-Saxons, the Jews could come to inspect us as they pleased. They were given entry tickets as though to a zoo. . . . The visitors really came to enjoy our humil-iation, which gave them a sense of revenge.' He was particularly bitter, it seems, because having purportedly defended Jews during the Occupation, he thought at least one of them would show up to defend him. But none ever did.

Fabre-Luce certainly had the courage of his quirks. For the rest of his life he continued to rake over the past in an effort to find intellectual and moral justi-fications for the policies he had defended. He remained a fervent Pétainist and insisted, as he had in his *Journal*, that it was the Marshal's policy that had brought Hitler down and saved Europe. The armistice had given Britain valu-able breathing space and had opened the way for Hitler to blunder into the war against the Soviet Union that destroyed the Wehrmacht. De Gaulle and the Free French on the other hand had caused no end of harm by creating perma-nent fissures in French society. Fabre-Luce's vendetta against de Gaulle – linked implicitly to his self-vindication – was so obsessive that in 1963 he wrote a novel, *Haute Cour*, translated into English as *The Trial of Charles de Gaulle*, in which de Gaulle was brought before the Senate, sitting as a high court, to be tried for crimes against the state. The book was a case of wishful thinking *in excelsis*. Undoubtedly to the author's delight, the French government – de Gaulle was at the time president – proscribed the book. It was published in Switzerland, where Fabre-Luce himself had chosen to live.

Fabre-Luce was a solid, stolid *défaitiste*, an unabashed and unrepentant fascist *collabo* whose views rarely changed. One of his close friends was a fascist *collabo* whose views rarely remained the same. Pierre Drieu la Rochelle was a notoriously complicated, conflicted, contradictory figure whose views were in such a constant state of flux that it is difficult to find a consistent thread in his thinking. He has been made fun of for being an anti-Semite who took a Jewish wife, a homophobe with many gay friends, an advocate of an agricultural France who only ever lived in Paris, a proponent of a high birth rate who had no children and a collaborator who hated Germans. His sex life was a neurotic mess, his relations with women were a failure, he despised mankind including himself and was suicidal from a young age. He took sadistic pleasure in the suffering of those he hated – these included 'Jews, liberals, democrats and socialists' (diary entry of 30 May 1940), 'Freemasons, bankers, politicians, journalists, half-breeds, pederasts, drug addicts, artists, Jews, the military and priests' (8 June), not to mention 'Jews and Freemasons, socialists and communists, liberals and capitalists, Christians of all varieties' (13 July). Although a prolific author – of novels, short stories, poetry, *témoignages*, political essays and a play – he could easily be regarded as less interesting to literary history than to clinical psychiatry.

Nihilist though he was, Drieu had a few positive beliefs that he clung to throughout his adult life. Parliamentary democracy was corrupt and inefficient. Only a brutal totalitarian leader could solve the problems of the day. The nation-state was finished and must be replaced by a unified Europe. But even more deeply was he convinced that the world was going to hell. 'French literature is finished, as is literature in general throughout the world, all art, all creativity', was a characteristic gibe. The person who summed Drieu up best was Drieu himself: 'I have always believed in the worst, in the absolute decadence of Europe and the world. My instinct has always been apocalyptic.'

Drieu was never bashful about broadcasting his views. In addition to his political essays, much of his fiction during the Twenties and Thirties was *romans à clef* with a political message. At the outbreak of the war he began keeping a diary, published as *Journal 1939–1945*, that he intended for posterity. It was, he said, not meant to be a work of literature or a political polemic or a defence of his actions but simply a record of how one French intellectual responded to the great events of the time. But, ever self-derogatory, he also dismissed it as no better than graffiti on the wall of a *pissoir*. In fact, the diary has qualities of both, written in a rambling stream-of-consciousness that in its contradictions, nastiness and sheer pixilation sometimes leaves the reader's head spinning.

In light of his fascist political views, it is surprising to find that at the outbreak of the war Drieu was in a highly patriotic mood. Although forty-eight and still suffering from wounds of the First World War, he wanted in some way to participate and criticized Malraux and de Jouvenel for their reluctance to go to the front. He asked Giraudoux to send him to Spain on a propaganda mission. Then he applied to be seconded to the British army as an interpreter. He also dreamed of being in the secret service. But there were no offers and by the end of the year the very thought of rubbing shoulders with grubby soldiers left him cold.

It was only to be expected that French authorities would not want him. Drieu had been active in pro-Nazi Franco-German circles from an early date. Not long after Hitler came to power he had gone to Berlin to visit Hitler Youth groups and to meet the philosopher of Nazism, Alfred Rosenberg. The following year he

1 During his tour of Paris in June 1940, Hitler visited Napoleon's tomb. In this rare photograph he is seen leaving the Invalides with (left) his two principal architects, Hermann Giesler and Albert Speer, and (right) the adjutant Hans Speidel and Wehrmacht chief Wilhelm Keitel.

2 Uprooted from their homes, their lives broken, unwanted by anyone but the Gestapo, tens of thousands of German, Czech and Polish refugees struggled to survive in inhospitable French exile. One of them, Hans Arp, depicted their desperation in his relief, *Maimed and Stateless*.

3 For German soldiers, Paris would not have been Paris without nightclubs performing French *Cancan* by the banned Jewish composer, Jacques Offenbach.

4 Jacques Benoist-Méchin inaugurating the Breker exhibition in the presence of Abel Bonnard, Mimina Breker, the sculptor and Fernand de Brinon. Behind the Brekers stand Serge Lifar and Jean Cocteau.

5 The French film and theatrical world was – falsely – portrayed by the far right as dominated by Jews, led by the playwright Henri Bernstein. Such was the theme of a display in the 'Jew in France' exhibition in 1941.

6 Artists from every sphere were enrolled in an Art Maréchal, portraying Pétain in various guises – revered grandfather, national saviour, self-sacrificing leader. His own preferred image was *Vainquer de Verdun*. For public buildings, offices and homes, 200,000 busts were to be produced.

7 Goebbels invited artists and intellectuals to visit the Third Reich to admire its cultural wonders. About to depart from the Gare de l'Est are several members of an artists' group: Charles Despiau, Othon Friesz, André Dunoyer de Segonzak, Maurice de Vlaminck, Kees Van Dongen and André Derain.

8 Many noted artists fled to New York where Pierre Matisse exhibited their works in an 'Artists in Exile' show: (front) Sebastian Matta, Ossip Zadkine, Yves Tanguy, Pierre Matisse, Max Ernst, Marc Chagall, Fernand Léger; (rear) André Breton, Piet Mondrian, André Masson, Amédée Ozenfant, Jacques Lipchitz, Pavel Tchelitchev, Kurt Seligman, Eugene Berman.

9 In his diary for May 1942 Gide (front) recorded his first impression of Jean-Louis Barrault and his wife: 'Wonderful face, instinct with enthusiasm, passion, genius. In his company Madeleine Renaud, with charming modesty, remains in the background. Neither in him nor her am I aware of any of the actor's usual unbearable shortcomings.'

10 During the Occupation Simone de Beauvoir spent her days writing at the Café de Flore. 'In the face of all the problems of daily life, the Flore took us back to the happy prewar days of peace', she later wrote.

11 Reknown everywhere on the Butte Montmartre for his grace, beauty, street smarts and kleptomania, Bébert was Céline's inseparable campanion.

12 Picasso in front of *Women at Their Toilette*, a cubist cartoon for a tapestry. Distraught at Franco's victory in the Spanish civil war, the artist portrayed his grief symbolically, with the world turning its back on his native country.

13 Serge Lifar and members of the Paris Opera ballet. Why the dancers are smiling is a mystery since they had to survive on a pittance while Lifar made himself the best-paid artistic figure in France.

14 Collaboration in music: in May 1941 the entire Berlin State Opera travelled to Paris to perform *Tristan und Isolde*. Herbert von Karajan conducted, Germaine Lubin sang Isolde.

15 Serge Reggiani, Jean Cocteau and Jean Marais in Cocteau's apartment in the Palais Royal. During the Occupation Reggiani appeared with Marais in Racine's *Britannicus* and later in Cocteau's *Les Parents terribles*.

16 As Tank Commander Moncorgé – his family name by which he was known to his men – Jean
Gabin participated in the liberation of Lorraine and Alsace.

17 The *épuration sauvage* – the spontaneous purge of *collabos* and members of the Milice – began the moment Allied troops arrived and resulted in an estimated 1,600 summary executions.

18 'Normally: (1) a crime is discovered (2) a suspect is interrogated (3) he is charged (4) he is imprisoned. In my case: (1) I was imprisoned (2) then charged (3) then interrogated (4) then considered a suspect (5) but no crime was ever discovered.' (Guitry on his arrest at the Liberation.)

19 Robert Brasillach at the moment his death sentence was pronounced. The trial began at 1 p.m. At 6.35 p.m. the case went to the jury, which reached its verdict twenty minutes later. The judge read the decision at 7 p.m.

20 Picasso's play-reading party: (rear) Jacques Lacan, Cecile Éluard, Pierre Reverdy, Louise Leiris, Zanie de Campan, Picasso, Valentine Hugo, Simone de Beauvoir; (front) Jean-Paul Sartre, Albert Camus, Michel Leiris, Jean Aubier. At the last moment Kazbek joined the group.

came to know Abetz. At his invitation Drieu attended the Nuremberg Nazi party rally in 1935 and was wowed. Although he was now well down the road to fascism – in 1934 he published *Socialisme fasciste* – he condemned Hitler's seizure of Austria, strongly opposed the Munich Agreement, supported French entry into the war and, once hostilities began, hoped and believed France would repulse a German invasion. When Fabre-Luce argued that there was no point in fighting after the fall of Poland, Drieu dismissed him as a dupe of German propaganda. When France and Britain failed to respond by attacking on all fronts, he took that as further evidence of the futility of democracy. 'We should fight for France as long as there is a France and a French spirit', he commented in his diary at the very moment the Wehrmacht was breaching the French lines in June 1940. His chauvinism was such that he did not wish to survive a German victory and, for the eventuality, asked his ex-wife to supply him with poison.

In the wake of the German advance, Drieu hurried to La Roque-Gageac, a village in the Dordogne whose mayor was a friend. From his conversations with retreating French soldiers, he concluded that France had lost the war before the battle had begun. In part, French strategy had not caught up with the fact that air power and the tank had revolutionized warfare. But more important, the French democratic state had been incapable of mobilizing the energy of its citizens. The debacle was tangible proof of the decadence that he had denounced in his earliest books and had foreseen in his novel *Gilles*, published on the eve of the war. The rot was above all moral and those responsible were the Jews, journalists and writers, Freemasons, ecclesiastics, academics and parliamentarians, along with all the bourgeois and peasants who had elected them.

Far from committing suicide after the defeat, Drieu happily contemplated the prospect of the new France and the new Europe that he longed for. Even before the armistice was signed, he worked out his own guidelines for the future. Political parties would be disbanded, trade unions merged into corporatist organizations, foreigners expelled and the press subjected to draconic controls. With typical Drieuian logic, he linked these political objectives with the aesthetic aims of cleaning up Paris architecturally by demolishing structures he disliked, which included the Eiffel Tower, the newly built Trocadéro, the Gares D'Orsay, St Lazare and Montparnasse as well as Les Halles and the Bourse.

He had great hopes for the Pétain government and volunteered to be an intermediary with Abetz. Two visits to Vichy were enough to disillusion him. Pétain, he complained, had been passive as a general in the Great War and was now passive as head of state. His deputy he dismissed as 'this ignoble Laval, this half-breed Jew-gypsy, this bit of crap conceived behind a caravan'. Unlike Fabre-Luce, who believed that Vichy helped bring down Hitler in 1945, Drieu argued that Pétain had played Hitler's game to the end. 'Basically, France has greatly helped Germany. Pétain is a Germanophile without knowing it. The neutralization of North Africa is a great advantage for the Germans.' Needless to say, Drieu also sneered at the 'gargoyle de Gaulle' and, after the general's famous London radio address refusing to accept France's defeat, referred to him as 'the ultimate in national absurdity'. For a time he regarded de Gaulle simply as the stooge of the Anglo-Americans, just as Pétain was of the Germans. Later he did not know where to situate him. At one point he expected the Russians to adopt him. At another he thought the general would do a deal with the Germans. At still another he claimed that the Jews would use him to get back into power.

The German embassy crowd disgusted him. They were 'democrats by birth and nature' who had gone over to Hitler for opportunistic reasons. Achenbach, he was convinced, was part Jewish, Epting was a jumped-up bureaucrat, Heller 'a refined bit of low-life'. Abetz he described as 'weak, irresolute, timid, without much talent' and likened him to a failed French politician who had been rusticated to Rome as ambassador. Bitterly did he reproach Abetz for doubting his commitment to a Nazi Europe and for counselling him not to become a collaborator in 1940. 'He showed me better than anyone else how little Germans themselves really believed in Hitler.' Abetz was really a democrat, Drieu complained, and got carried away playing the role of rich ambassador. In July 1944, as Allied forces were on their way to Paris, Drieu summed up his view of the Occupation: 'The comedy of collaboration has been perfectly human. The Germans, who did not believe enough in Hitler, were responsible for indoctrinating the French, who believed too much.' Occupation officials, he complained, were 'liberal, weak and sneaky, and have constantly duped and betrayed us who believed in Hitler's European revolution'.

But Germans were 'just as idiotic as the French', he argued. 'I have never been a tremendous Germanophile, much less Germanomane. What attracts me is Hitler and Hitlerism.' He never defined what he meant by 'Hitlerism', and his attitude towards the dictator himself went through violent fluctuations – from veneration to denigration, from seeing him as the great hope to bewailing him as the ultimate disappointment. At his best Hitler corresponded to two of Drieu's highest ideals – the great leader who moulded history, and the man who would create a unified Europe. Drieu identified him with two other unifiers, Augustus and Napoleon. Typically he then cut them all down. Augustus was 'mediocre like Hitler'. Napoleon fell prey to hubris but, unlike Hitler, 'at least had some of the culture and manners of the *ancien régime*'. At one moment he commented, '*Mein Kampf* also smells of decadence; the thought of a crude journalist, searching for crude sensationalism.' At another he portrayed Hitler as a great thinker to rival Goethe, Shakespeare, Pascal and Hegel.

Hitler made grave mistakes, it had to be admitted. One of the earliest was to have slaughtered Röhm and his socialist followers, which set the Nazi party on a rightward course. Another was his lack of vision in 1940, failing to invade Italy and Spain and seize Gibraltar, and in that way closing the Mediterranean to the British. 'No imagination, no creativity, impossible to escape the magic confines of the nation, of the shell of the birthplace, of the sclerosis of the old militarist and imperialist diplomacy', is how he phrased it. In summer 1941 he predicted that the German invasion of the Soviet Union would be stopped by the Russian winter. A regular listener to the BBC, he was convinced well before Stalingrad that Germany had lost the war. It was one of Hitler's great misfortunes to be surrounded by men who were incompetent and disloyal. From the Wehrmacht, indeed, he faced downright opposition. Rommel was a traitor who deliberately lost the Battle of El Alamein. Drieu was not surprised by the 'cowardly' July plot against Hitler.

Nothing disappointed him more than the dictator's failure to establish a fascist party in France as part of a unified fascist-socialist Europe that would stand as a bulwark against communist Russia. By the end of 1942 he had realized that Hitler's concept of European unity was simply German hegemony without any social revolution. The best France could hope for, he feared, would be to occupy a place similar to that of Scotland in the United Kingdom – 'the situation of the old servant, well respected – and well exploited'. At worst she would be dumped into 'the trashcan of history'. Yet despite his frustrated hopes, he could never rid himself of a certain admiration for Hitler and, even as Allied forces were sweeping towards Paris, he defiantly commented, 'I regret only one thing – not to have expressed more strongly my love of violence, of adventure, of Hitler and Hitlerism (regardless of their horrible faults and inadequacies).' Hitler had failed, as Napoleon had failed, but it had to be admitted that the forces aligned against him were far greater. 'I like Hitler right to the end, in spite of all his mistakes, all his stupidities, and all his blunders.'

But 'like' is not fear or respect. So eventually the weakness and failures of 'poor Hitler' validated Stalin, whose Red Army had turned the tide of the war. The Soviet dictator promised to be the savage leader that Drieu longed for. Abandoning fascism, which he now dismissed as a mere shield of the bourgeoisie, he declared, 'Nothing separates me from communism, nothing ever did.' As early as November 1942 he looked forward to the coming Russian military triumph. 'It will be great to see the Red Army marching down the Champs-Élysées,' he exulted – a thought spoiled only by the prospect that 'all the rich bourgeois Gaullists will have absconded to the United States and will not get half the punishment they deserve'. Some weeks later, with Soviet forces on the offensive, he fell into a delirium of masochistic anticipation. 'It is with joy that I greet the arrival of Russia and communism. It will be atrocious, atrociously destructive, insupportable for our generation which will perish in a death, slow or quick.' This happy thought culminated in March 1944 – at a time when he was contemplating suicide – with a comment in his diary, 'Oh the splendour of my solitude and my death.' He went on, 'I shall die with a savage joy at the thought that Stalin will be master of the world. Finally a master. It is good that people will know that they have a master who will make them feel the ferocious omnipotence of God.'

Having views that were in constant flux, Drieu assumed that the governments of the contending powers were equally fickle. Throughout the war he loved playing armchair strategist. Over and over he predicted that Japan, the Soviet Union, Germany, Britain and America would come together in every conceivable combination of alliance and then break apart to form some other coalition. He even envisaged an 'international of dictators', with Stalin and Hitler as great pals. And over and over he redesigned the map of Europe and the world. Nobody admired a winner more than Drieu. After having tried in 1939 to be seconded to the British forces, he had switched allegiance at the very moment of the armistice and wished on Britain the same fate as France 'as soon as possible'. A year or so later, when things were at their worst for the British, he declared, 'I can only take infinite pleasure in seeing a moribund world die.' But as the war went on and he foresaw the defeat of the Germans and the Japanese, he came to respect the Anglo-American military forces. Despite its enormous power, however, the United States could never be the world leader he wanted. It was not European. It was a democracy and therefore weak. It was a mixture of races and therefore barbaric and decadent. Nonetheless, he realized that the Anglo-Saxons would be a dominant force in the postwar world. In the last article he ever wrote, 'Letter to a Gaullist Friend', published in Laval's *La Révolution nationale,* he taunted the Gaullists, 'You too will be obliged to collaborate with the victors. I only hope that you will be luckier than we were.' Here at least was an astute comment and a point certainly not lost on de Gaulle. In time Drieu's hope was realized. The need to avoid the stigma of collaboration was one that the general never forgot, then and later, in his relationship with the Anglo-Saxons.

Planet Drieu was an odd place. There you would know nothing of the hardships of Occupation – of cold, hunger, queues for food and tobacco, deportations, denunciations, torture, disappearances, executions, hostages, round-ups of Jews and communists, the impressment of young people for forced labour. Never was there a word of compassion for anyone. A vicious comment was ever on his lips. In Drieu's catalogue of hates, homosexuals were at the top of the list. He saw them everywhere, even suspecting Premier Daladier. At a time when the Wehrmacht was triumphant on all fronts, he feared German soldiers would be infected by the 'disease'. He foresaw the time when 'German pederasts will be walking around the streets of Paris or Moscow wearing make-up.' Homosexuals had infiltrated French intellectual life through the *Nouvelle Revue Française*, which was in the hands of 'all those old Protestant pederasts: Gide, Schlumberger, Paulhan and the Catholic pederast Roger Martin [du Gard]'. The ringleader was Gide, described as 'ce grand impotent'.

And then there were the Jews. 'Pederasty and Jews go well together', he commented after seeing a play by Noël Coward in which, he maintained, half the cast and audience were Jewish. 'I hate the Jews. I have always known that I hated them. Not a single one failed to hurt me.' Did he really mean it? He never explained why he felt that way or who had hurt him. Often his comments about Jews sound like the ramblings of a drunk. It is generally assumed that he despised himself – and the Jews – because he had married a woman of Jewish descent from whom he took money but had not loved. And, in common with most other fascists, he associated Jews with the evils of urban civilization and Modernism in the arts. 'I myself cannot stand Jews because they are par excellence of the modern world that I abhor', a character in *Gilles* says.

Needless to say, Drieu saw them in every corner of society. They controlled the French press. They were in the German embassy in the person of Ernst Achenbach and in Vichy in 'the ugly gnome Laval'. Even those who were not Jews, such as Stalin and de Gaulle, were in the hands of the Jews. To choose between democracy and communism, he said, was to choose between two groups of Jews. In 1939 he predicted that the winner of the war would be either Hitler or the Jews. Weirdest of all, he even had doubts about Hitler: 'And to think that Hitler's anti-Semitism has become dubious!' Some months later he wondered, 'Will the alliance between Hitler and the Jews be reached? Perhaps it already has been.' If Jews wanted to be Zionists, that was fine with Drieu. They would never sever their racial roots and be genuinely French. He even went so far as to claim, 'I would sincerely have liked Jews in their own home. They would make a beautiful people.' He once gave serious thought to writing a book about the Jews. 'You would then see an intelligent anti-Semite; the best friend of the Jews.'

All in all there is something unconvincing about Drieu's anti-Semitism. It does not seem deep or sincere but simply part of his general misanthropy. Nor did it stand in the way of his admiration for Jewish writers such as Bernstein and Benda. And, happily, his treatment of Jews differed from his rhetoric. 'The Jewish friends that I have kept are in prison or in flight', he wrote in February 1944. 'I intend to do what I can to help them. I see no contradiction in that.' And it is a matter of record that throughout the Occupation Drieu used his contacts with German authorities on behalf of Jews – as well as others he periodically disliked such as Paulhan, Malraux and Aragon. But not the pederasts.

Drieu is usually best known as the person who took over as editor of the *Nouvelle Revue Française* after the defeat. Although he had enjoyed a long prewar association with the publication, the relationship had become increasingly fraught for both personal and political reasons. He detested not only Gaston Gallimard, the publisher, and Jean Paulhan, the editor, but also Gide and other regular contributors. Of Gallimard he commented, 'I bitterly regret having done twenty books with a man who is a pluto-anarchist always in fear of the left and who, with all his personnel, is in the hands of the Russians.' Part of this animosity stemmed from Paulhan's refusal to publish extracts from *Gilles*. 'Instead of that it had brought out defeatist poetry and the anti-bourgeois novels of Aragon with notes by Aragon's wife, Elsa Triolet, a Jewish Bolshevist and secret Soviet agent.' By the spring of 1940 Drieu had definitively broken with the publication, complaining that it was 'dominated by Jews, communist sympathizers, ex-Surrealists and all sorts of people who believe in principle that truth is on the left'. So when the Wehrmacht advanced into Normandy – where Gallimard and some of his staff had moved at the outbreak of the war – a delighted Drieu revelled in thinking they were all 'dying of fear'.

That pleasure was nothing compared to the joy he felt on becoming editor of the *Nouvelle Revue Française* following the defeat. 'As for the *NRF*, it will grovel at my feet. That mob of Jews, pederasts, timid Surrealists, pawns and Freemasons will be convulsed in fear.' The appointment had come about when Otto Abetz arrived in Paris with the Wehrmacht and found Drieu almost literally waiting on the doorstep of the German embassy. Abetz wanted a serious literary publication to appeal to intellectuals and wanted it in the hands of someone he could trust enough to promise a minimum of interference. In a cynical deal with the Germans, Gaston Gallimard agreed to turn over the journal to Drieu in return for permission to start up his publishing house again.

Drieu's stewardship was bound to fail. A French literary review was not in good hands when run by someone convinced that French literature had no future. Nor could it attract good writers if they had to work in an atmosphere of censorship and fear of imprisonment. And Drieu could never even make up his mind which writers were good and which bad, which he should publish and which reject. In May 1940 he considered the most outstanding French writers to be Claudel and Valéry. A month later they were Céline, Giono and Georges Bernanos. Although he generally thought well of Valéry, the sole writer whom he consistently admired, personally and professionally, was Malraux. He was one of seven authors whom Drieu thought would last, the others being Bernanos, Montherlant, Breton, Aragon, Giono and Jouhandeau. Drieu also had his hate list, of course, and this included Aragon, Bernstein, Benda and 'the pederasts' led by Gide. Yet he asked Gide – along with Valéry and Fabre-Luce, whom he disliked – to contribute to his first issue.

On realizing the journal was to be collaborationist, Gide, Malraux and their friends refused to have anything more to do with it. To replace them, Drieu recruited some of the most notorious pro-Nazi collaborators – Abel Bonnard, Ramon Fernandez, Bernard Faÿ and Lucien Combelle. Outside *collabo* circles the publication was derisively known as 'NRBoche'. In no time Drieu frankly admitted that very few writers of merit would contribute. 'I rarely see anyone of talent,' he complained in September 1941. 'Apart from a few pages of Montherlant, I have not published anything worthwhile.' In December 1942 he went even further, writing in the magazine, 'Almost the entire French intelligentsia, almost the entire French art world is against us.' In an attempt to rescue the journal, he thought of creating an advisory committee of noted writers and turned to Gide – yes, Gide! – as well as Valéry and Claudel. The proposal got nowhere, of course. In March 1943 Drieu gave up and turned the publication back to Paulhan. In failing as editor, he had also failed to achieve his ambition of establishing himself as the leader of the collaborationist intellectuals.

This double failure was a profound disappointment. Already a year earlier he had contemplated his next career move. Convinced by the autumn of 1942 that Germany would lose the war, he began to feel that the best course was 'a death worthy of the revolutionary and reactionary that I am' – suicide. All his chaotic, neurotic feelings now came gushing out. He regretted he had not fought alongside the SS and been killed in battle. To go into hiding seemed cowardly. There was not much more in life for him anyway. His books were not great or durable. He had always felt closer to the English and Americans than to the Germans. It was fascism and Hitlerism that had caused him to cast in his lot with the Italians and Germans. His sole reason for wanting to survive, he declared in July 1944, was to be able to fight alongside the Russians against the Americans. A few weeks later he commented that he dreamed of being tried in a Soviet-style show trial so he could get up in court and shout, 'I was wrong, Stalin was right. Shoot me.'

Drieu's political essays, his trips to the two Weimar writers conferences, his turning the *NRF* into the 'NRBoche', his contact with Abetz and frequent attendance at functions at the German Institute left him deeply compromised. Obviously he was on various blacklists. He knew this. He could easily have fled: he had a visa for Spain and an entry permit to Switzerland. To stay in France was therefore a conscious choice. In early August 1944 he saw no recourse but suicide and wrote farewell letters to his brother and several friends. To Malraux he wrote, 'I don't want to flee. I don't want to hide. I don't want to be killed by cowards.' To his companion Beloukia he wrote, 'I don't want to repent, I don't want to hide, I don't want to go to Germany and I don't want to be touched by dirty hands.' On 11 August he decided to take the poison his wife had given him in the spring of 1940. But he was discovered by his housekeeper and taken to hospital, where he made a second unsuccessful attempt. Then he went into hiding. Weirdly even by his standards, Drieu later wrote to Malraux offering to serve with him in the French liberation army.

Had the attempted suicide changed nothing? he asked himself. Apparently not. Gradually he resumed his old routine, keeping his diary and working on a new novel. He appeared to regain an appetite for life. 'At this rate I'll start writing again about politics. No, no, not that!' The final entry for 1944 and the first for 1945 were both in English. 'Well, what a year!' he wrote on 31 December. 'I regret nothing; no, I regret one thing: not to have succeeded on the 12th August.' The remainder of the entry betrayed deep depression. 'The temptation comes back, very strong,' he wrote. 'I am sick of that novel, sick of this house, sick of France, above all sick of Europe, sick of the earth.' Finally on 15 March he ended his life.

For all his faults Drieu was professional enough not to let his ideological views contaminate his literary judgement. He respected Aragon, Breton and, however grudgingly, Gide, while despising Brasillach and all the other *collabo* writers – with a single exception. Louis-Ferdinand Céline he considered 'a true author'. Although never friends, they were ideologically on the same page, hating Jews, Freemasons and just about everyone else, ridiculing democracy, admiring Hitler's Germany and exalting violence. But to go from Drieu to Céline is to cross the line between a man who was soft inside and a man who was all edge outside, between competent writer and mad genius. Of the various important artistic figures who embraced fascist ideals, supported the Occupation and hoped for a German victory, Céline was the most notable and the most outrageous.

Outrageousness – in writing, thought and behaviour – was the basis of his well-cultivated notoriety. He had exploded onto the French literary scene in 1932 with *Voyage au bout de la nuit* (*Journey to the End of the Night*). Written in a highly innovative style – vaguely analogous to the experiments of Joyce, Woolf, Dos Passos and others in English – the novel combined street argot, neologisms, obscenity and the like in a frenzied, zany, disgusted satire on life and society during and after the First World War. It evoked such revulsion that it was a tremendous hit. Compared with Rabelais and Zola and considered by some as the greatest French novelist since Proust, Céline sprang in one bound to a central place in the literature of anarchistic revolt.

Céline said of his writing that it had no ideas, only style. This was not entirely true. He was like a crazy chef who invented a new dish and then seasoned it in such a way as to make it disgusting. John Weightman put it like this: 'He was the first foul-mouthed rhapsodist of the twentieth century to proclaim a satanic vision of the godless world, rolling helplessly through space and infested with crawling millions of suffering, diseased, sex-obsessed, maniacal human beings.' In Céline the underdogs had found a voice. And the overdogs loved it. With *Voyage* he became famous and rich.

He had begun as an underdog, born near Paris into a right-wing, anti-Dreyfusard, anti-Semitic petit-bourgeois family named Destouches. It is generally assumed that his family background instilled in him a certain antipathy for Jews and sympathy for the poor and homeless. But what wound in infancy left him feeling so insignificant that he had a compulsive need to shock people in order to attract attention? And the disgust, hostility and anarchism in the writings, where did they come from? Perhaps they were born on the battlefield of the Great War. Céline was a decorated cavalry officer and at an early stage of the fighting was severely wounded, if not quite as badly as he later made out. After the war he knocked about the world before qualifying as a doctor. In 1924 he took a job with the League of Nations in Geneva, serving in the Hygiene Bureau – just the position for a notorious hypochondriac.

After *Voyage*, however, it was all downhill. A play, *L'Église* (The Church), published in 1933 but performed only in 1936, was a flop on both occasions. His second novel, *Mort à credit* (*Death on the Instalment Plan*), though now considered by some to be his best work, horrified his publisher and much of the public. The right lambasted it as decadent, obscene and scatological while the left condemned it as, well, decadent, obscene and scatological. The uproar arose not over the storyline – none of his works had much plot – but over its maledicent view of humankind and its shocking verbal mayhem. 'In 700 pages,' one critic wrote, 'all the misery of mankind screams aloud, oozes out, over-flows, coagulates, sputters.' Céline had worked long and hard; the response shocked him and inflamed his instinctive paranoia.

Rejection goaded him into abandoning fiction for political pamphleteering at a time when France and Europe were in a period of exceptional turmoil. He had travelled on a number of occasions to the United States and disliked it more each time, seeing everywhere the power and influence of Jews. Then, in 1936, he ventured to the Soviet Union to observe the communist system. After two months in Leningrad, he returned and sat down and wrote *Mea culpa*, denouncing the injustices and fraudulence of Soviet rule. If he hated America because of its Jews, after that trip he hated Russia even more for its communists, whom he considered a greater menace than American capitalists. Only Nazi Germany could provide a bulwark against the successors of Genghis Khan.

In *Bagatelles pour un massacre* in 1937 and *L'École des cadavres* in 1938 Céline widened his aim and vented his rage at the whole world, lashing out in every direction. With even more than his usual touch of Savonarola, he brought down his fiery curse on communists and capitalists, Nazis and Jews, Freemasons and Catholics, British and Americans, Léon Blum and the Popular Front, to name a few targets. 'Is there anything left to hate, anything I have not thought of?' he once asked. Actually there was one person, Hitler. And the reason he did not hate him was that he too was anti-Semitic. 'What most people dislike in Hitler – his anti-Semitism – is what I like most', he would say.

In these two tracts Céline laid his anti-Semitic cards on the table. Jews were in control everywhere, in the Soviet Union no less than in London and New York. The Vatican was a ghetto. The pope at the time, Pius XI, was a Jew whose real name was not Achille Ratti but Isaac Ratisch. His successor, Pius XII, was 'equally Jewish'. Nazi government ministries in Berlin were filled with Jews. 'In the whole world there exists only one true International, it is the Jewish racial tyranny, financial, political, absolute. . . . *That* is an International!, it can be said.' Such ravings were obviously so dotty that some critics surmised either that he was writing crass satire or that he intended to bring anti-Semitism into disrepute. Gide, who had been shocked by the vocabulary and crudeness of his earlier works but who believed there were in his writings some pages of genius recalling Rabelais, could not take *Bagatelles* at face value. To him it was a burlesque worthy of Dean Swift.

At the base of all this anti-Semitic delirium was a certain internal logic. To put it simply, Céline hated Jews because of their power, and he feared their power because he had no doubt they wanted to use it to drag the world into the carnage of another catastrophic world war. Having earned attention for his verbal violence, he now gained a name for his preposterous views. His denunciation of Soviet communism had finished him with the left; *Bagatelles* and *L'École* were bound to delight the far right but fell foul of the so-called 'loi Marchandeau', an executive order of 1939 outlawing attacks on religious and ethnic groups. Consequently, on the eve of the war the two tracts had to be withdrawn from sale. Instead of enjoying at least a *succès de scandale*, he found he had produced a *scandale tout court*. By now his career seemed not so much on the skids as having come to a screeching halt.

During the interwar period Céline had been, for all his love of violence, overtly pacifist. When Hitler threatened military action against Poland, he railed, like many others, against 'dying for Danzig'. Yet when the war came, he sided with his homeland and signed up as a physician on a merchant ship, later misrepresenting this as military service. The motivation for volunteering was not patriotism but lust for adventure. And adventure is, willy-nilly, what he got. In early January the ship – no doubt to his delight – collided with a British torpedo launcher off Gibraltar. Afterwards his disabled ship chugged its way to Marseille for repairs and he returned to Paris. Six months later, in the face of the Wehrmacht's advance, he fled the capital and made his way to the mid-Atlantic coast, near La Rochelle. During his wanderings he witnessed the bombing of Orléans and was fascinated by every minute of the chaos and destruction along the way. Squalor and misery were Céline's meat and potatoes, and the tragic exodus was to provide rich material for two later books. A month after the armistice he was again in Paris where he found a job as a doctor in a working-class slum, tending the poor in what time was left over from writing. He rarely went out socially and even more rarely allowed anyone to visit.

With recent adventures still fresh in his mind, Céline immediately got down to work on a new book, entitled *Les Beaux Draps*, which he dedicated – in his childish desire to shock – to *la corde des pendus*, or the hangman's noose. The work interpreted the military debacle as an outward sign of the inward rottenness of the French nation and of course ranted about the menace posed by the Jews and Freemasons, communism and the Catholic church. Again, the mode of writing was shocking. The staccato style, with exclamations and expletives akin to the cries of a hysteric, along with recurrent brutal obscenities, was something new in French letters. Vichy was not amused, liking neither the obscenities nor the derision of the French army. The book was proscribed in the Unoccupied Zone. The German authorities nominally did the same in their zone but apparently – possibly thanks to Epting – did not enforce the ban. Undeterred, Céline went on working fitfully at yet another book using some of the same material. It was published in 1944 with the title *Guignol's Band*. All his writings were in one way or another autobiographical, and this new work offered a kaleidoscope of painful images dredged up from his experiences in two world wars.

Far from being dismayed by the defeat, Céline rejoiced over the end of the Third Republic. The French had only themselves to blame for the mess they were in. But so besotted was he with the notion of apocalypse that the Occupation fell far short of his nihilist expectations, unclear though these were. For all his political blather, Céline was anything but a political person. He had opinions but no thoughts. The nature of Nazism and the Third Reich was, as for most other *collabos*, beyond his ken, even his interest. No party, no political group could claim his loyalty. He was too self-absorbed and self-infatuated, too individualistic and anarchistic – once speaking of 'mon anarchisme fondamental' – to subordinate himself to any philosophy or programme. 'I have always been an anarchist, I have never voted and shall never vote for anything or anyone. I do not believe in people. I have nothing in common with all these castrates.' Despite his lack of commitment he ostentatiously attended highly charged political meetings, wrote inflammatory letters to the *collabo* press and regularly met with fascist fanatics like Châteaubriant, Rebatet and Brasillach. There could be no doubt where his heart lay.

So thrilled was Céline by the German invasion of the Soviet Union that he considered joining the health corps of the Legion of French Volunteers. Later he refused even to visit the French unit. To Châteaubriant he once wrote that he did not fancy killing a Bolshevik for the sake of French bankers and the Catholic church, much less for Pétain and the French bourgeoisie. 'The Germans are horrible,' he claimed to have told French labour service personnel on a visit to Berlin. 'They say they will win the war but I don't know. The others, the Russians, are no better, perhaps worse. It is a matter of choosing between cholera and the plague! Not funny.' Yet in *L'École des cadavres* he had favoured an alliance between France, Germany, Spain and Italy, a confederation of the Aryan states of Europe. 'The hatred between us and the *boches* is artificial, propagated by Freemasons, the press and radio and Jewish money.' But when Abetz and other German officials offered him lavish fees to write about 'the New Europe', he refused, later making much of the fact that he had never taken a sou.

It is hardly surprising that what most engrossed Céline during the Occupation years, apart from his writing, was anti-Semitism. Abetz had a high opinion of Céline's 'scientific anti-Semitism' – that is, seeing it in biological terms – and in March 1941 added his name to a list of writers to be considered for the General Commissariat for Jewish Questions. Céline got no support from Vichy and the suggestion was ignored. A short time later he was invited to the inauguration of the Institute for Study of Jewish Questions and in March 1942 attended a dinner sponsored by the Association of Anti-Jewish Journalists in Paris. Otherwise he held aloof from fellow anti-Semites. He refused to write for collaborationist newspapers, deriding the *Je suis partout* staff as a 'feverish club of ambitious little pederasts'. But he sent them at least a dozen letters for publication, most of them lamenting the inadequacy of Vichy's anti-Semitic measures. The most interesting of these was a response to the question 'Is it necessary to exterminate the Jews?' Céline wrote a very guarded response, saying essentially no more than that his books had been published under the Jews – Premier Blum and Interior Minister Mandel. This elliptical response suggests that when it came down to it, he did not support the 'final solution' and after the war denied he had ever favoured the deportation of Jews.

It is not easy to find a way through the jungle of Céline's thoughts – as distinct from his crackpot babble – about Jews. He insisted that his anti-Semitism was directed not against individuals but against an organized ethnic group. 'It is Jewish racism I am against.' His consistent theme was that Jews were provoking a war against Germany. And his response was: 'I do not want to fight for Hitler, but I do not want to fight against him on behalf of the Jews.' Over and over he portrayed them as a hate-filled group pushing the French into a 'slaughterhouse' where they would be 'massacred' in a repetition of 1914–18.

It was inevitable that Vichy and Céline would despise one another. Vichy was appalled by both the matter and the manner of his writing; Céline liked neither the wishy-washy politics nor the fuddy-duddy morals of Vichy. For Pétain, he had only disdain, once referring to him as 'Philippe the Last'. At least he was not a Jew. That was more than could be said of the loathsome Laval. Needless to say, Céline's all-embracing hatred included Germans in general and the German officials in Paris specifically. Ever the hygienist, he referred to 'les fritz comme parasites'. This by no means deterred him from attending German embassy receptions and the Institute's functions, though. Accompanied sometimes by Bébert, his beloved cat, he was an intellectual catch but also on occasion a terrible embarrassment. As often as not he looked, acted and dressed like a particularly unsavoury bum. Alice Epting recalled a dinner at the German Institute when he shouted across the table, 'Don't you agree, Mme Epting, when I say that if things go on this way, one fine day it will be the Jews who will be dancing on our graves?' There were things one did not shout about, even at a good Nazi's dinner table.

When Céline and Jünger met at the Institute in December 1941, they took an instant dislike to one another. Jünger certainly had his number, commenting of their meeting:

> . . . among others, Céline, large, bony, robust, somewhat oafish but alert during the discussion or rather during his monologues. There is about him that look of a maniac, turned inward, shining as if at the bottom of a hole. 'I always have death by my side. . . .' He said how surprised – astounded – he was that we soldiers were not out shooting, hanging, exterminating the Jews. It is astounding that anyone having a bayonet on him does not make full use of it. 'If the Bolsheviks were in Paris they would let you see how to go about it, they would show you how to cleanse the population, quarter by quarter, house by house. If I had a bayonet on me, I would know what to do.' Hearing him speak continuously like that for two hours, I learned something about the monstrous power of nihilism.

Among German officials, Céline's closest friend was Karl Epting, who had for years been a resolute admirer of his work. Karl and Alice Epting liked him personally as well. Having him often at their home, they found a different person from the outrageous public show-off. 'When we were alone with Céline, he was very easy-going,' commented Frau Epting. 'It was different when we invited other guests. Even when there were large numbers of guests, he would express himself very openly, with the intent of being provocative.' Although he and Abetz disliked one another, Céline deigned to be his guest a number of times at dinner and once for a weekend at the ambassador's confiscated château at Chantilly. The ineradicably selfish never know when they might need a favour.

And that may in part explain Céline's friendship with Hermann Bickler, the head of the Gestapo in Western Europe. Bickler, an Alsatian Nazi, was specifically responsible for infiltrating resistance organizations and protecting important collaborators. He worked directly under Reinhard Heydrich and his successor, Ernst Kaltenbrunner, heads of the Gestapo. Céline and Bickler met fairly frequently. When the notoriously shabby Céline turned up at the door of the Gestapo office in the avenue Foch, guards would phone Bickler and say that a man looking like a terrorist wanted to see him. Despite his heavy responsibilities, Bickler always found time for a walk in the Bois de Boulogne or a chat in his office. 'From the first, Céline was as reluctant to conceal his opinions in our conversations as he was in his writings,' Bickler commented to an American interrogator following the war. 'He told me that after his initial hopes in 1940, the Germans disappointed him more and more. In his opinion German policies towards France were completely mistaken. The German embassy he considered as a nest of dangerous nitwits who were more or less opponents of the Third Reich.' Céline also badmouthed Abetz and his wife, which would hardly have helped the ambassador at a time when he had just been recalled to Berlin in disgrace. Even stronger was his disparagement of Laval – a 'typical yid' who would certainly sell out the Germans if it suited him. And on and on in that vein he would go. 'Although certain of Céline's theories seemed to me extravagant and exaggerated as stated,' Bickler concluded with comic understatement, 'I always met him with pleasure and interest.' The friendship appears also to have become sincere on Céline's part. Although he never otherwise had guests to his home in Montmartre, he occasionally invited Bickler to dinner and once even to attend his wife's dance classes. It is impossible to know whether Bickler got anything out of these meetings apart from intellectual entertainment. The big question is whether Céline ever denounced any of his compatriots. He was later accused of doing so.

What did Céline want from Bickler and other German officials? A lot. Above all, he wanted ample paper allotment so that *L'École des cadavres* could be reissued and *Les Beaux Draps* and *Guignol's Band* could be published. He also wanted permission to travel outside France and to take regular vacations in St Malo on the Breton coast, strictly off limits to non-residents. There he regularly stocked up on food from the black market. Even more unusually he finagled authorization to travel to Amsterdam in the hope of retrieving royalty monies he had deposited in a bank. When the Germans had confiscated the funds in 1940, he was impotent with rage. 'That they should treat Gaullists or Jews like this – all the better', he wrote to Châteaubriant. 'But with their few friends, those who were condemned, pursued, persecuted, defamed for their cause – *not today* but from 1936 to 1939 under Blum, Daladier, Mandel – it is *too much*, a damned nuisance. *What a lesson for their hesitant collaborators!* Despite his furious complaints, German authorities did not relent. But he was one of the lucky few to get fuel to heat his apartment. And when in 1943 he began receiving death threats and miniature coffins in the mail, Bickler gave him very rarely granted permission to carry a pistol to defend himself.

What did the Germans want from Céline? Céline made Nazi authorities uneasy, to put it mildly. Despite his fame as an opponent of Jews and Freemasons, officials in Berlin as well as those in the Propaganda Department in Paris found his pyrotechnic prose, especially its earthy vocabulary, so disgusting that they considered him useless for their propaganda purposes – 'not the person to lead the fight against Jewry and Freemasonry', in the words of the Nazi party expert on French literature, Bernhard Payr. Indeed, they were very critical of Epting for holding him in such high regard. 'The difference between robust and smutty does not seem to be very clear to the gentlemen of the German Institute', a Nazi official complained. Céline's books were not banned by the Germans, but he was not one of those writers whom the Propaganda Department named in its 'List of Writings to Be Promoted'. Céline deeply resented these slights. After attending the exhibition *The Jew and France* in Paris in October 1941, he was angered that the bookstall there had none of his books and that, despite promises, there was no book-signing of *Les Beaux Draps*.

All the same, Céline was an almost unique case of someone who turned collaboration inside out. As practised by him, it meant: you support my writing by making paper available for my books, allow me to travel to forbidden areas whenever I want and give me various other personal favours; in return I will give you . . . a steady torrent of criticism. He refused to join other writers on the trips to Weimar organized by Epting and refused to write pro-collaborationist articles for publication. In fact, apart from Epting and Bickler, who were useful to him, it is impossible to think of any German whom Céline liked. And did he like even them? At the end of his life, Epting doubted it. In 1942 he had written, 'Céline est proche de nous.' In 1963 he wrote, 'Il ne nous aimait pas.'

Self-deception was the outstanding trait of *collabos*, but in the course of 1943 Céline at least could no longer kid himself that Germany would win the war. He felt hopelessly exposed. Friends and acquaintances began distancing themselves. Eventually he felt so threatened that he would not go out without his pistol. Knowing his goose was cooked, he wanted to get out of the kitchen for as long as possible in the hope that the public's appetite for retribution would eventually be sated. So he decided to flee with the retreating Germans and seek exile in Copenhagen, where he had the promise of accommodation and funds from royalties shrewdly salted away in a bank.

On 17 June he left Paris with Bébert and his wife, Lucette, the only two beings he ever loved, and passed several months in the spa town of Baden-Baden. Still without permission to travel to Denmark, in late October he moved on to Sigmaringen. There as usual he found material for another book, to be published after the war under the title *D'un Château l'autre* (*Castle to Castle*). It is in Sigmaringen that we leave him. He was by now a pathetic figure. Witnessing his arrival at the castle, another *collabo* refugee, Lucien Rebatet, recalled:

One morning the rumour spread through Sigmaringen: 'Céline has arrived.' A memorable stage entrance. Still shaken by his trip through a devastated Germany, he wore a bluish canvas cap, like a locomotive engineer's circa 1905, two or three of his lumber jackets overlapping, filthy and ragged, a pair of moth-eaten mittens hanging from his neck, and under the mittens, in a haver-sack on his belly, Bébert the cat, presenting the phlegmatic face of a native Parisian who's seen it all before. You should have seen the faces of the hard-core militants and the rank-and-file militiamen at the sight of this hobo: 'That is the great fascist writer, the brilliant prophet?' I was speechless myself.

CHAPTER 7

ARTFUL DODGERS

What should you do? You are the world's best-known painter. You are rich and well connected. You have invitations to live in the United States, Mexico and Brazil. Any number of other countries would welcome you with open arms. The city where you have made your home for nearly forty years has been occupied by the army of a barbaric power that, as you well know, hates your work and would like to destroy it. You yourself are a committed anti-fascist. Should you go into exile abroad or stay in the Unoccupied Zone, where no one will bother you? Or should you live in Occupied Paris?

Picasso appears to have had little hesitation in deciding to return to Paris from Royan, where he had initially fled. Even to his admirers he was not known for his physical or moral courage. But was it more courageous to stay or to flee? Perhaps the emotional and physical bother of losing friends, home and atelier would have been too much. Or he may have wanted to protect the large cache of paintings in his studio and a bank vault. The explanation he himself gave to his companion Françoise Gilot when they first met in 1943 was simple:

Oh, I am not looking for risks to take, but in a sort of passive way I do not care to yield to either force or terror. I want to stay here because I am here. The only kind of force that could make me leave would be the desire to leave. Staying on is not really a manifestation of courage; it is just a form of inertia. I suppose that it is simply that I prefer to be here. So I shall stay, whatever the cost.

In refusing exile abroad, Picasso chose inner exile at home. By remaining, he may have given comfort and encouragement to others – and some of his admirers have made a great deal of this – but that was not his intention.

Presumably he simply believed he could be free inside his studio even though there was little freedom outside on the streets. For him, no collaboration and no resistance.

And that is more or less what he said on a number of occasions. 'To be left in peace, that is all I ask' – this comment to his confidant Jaime Sabartés. Being left in peace to work was what all painters wanted. They also wished to be exhibited, written about and discussed. What faced them in the summer of 1940, however, was not just the hardships of war and occupation but, for all they knew, interference and censorship, possibly even arrest and deportation. Picasso was a special case, though. On the one hand he enjoyed the security of being the most famous, and no doubt the richest, living painter. On the other he suffered the insecurity of living in a country where foreigners were subject to internment by the French police or arrest by the Gestapo. And despite his forty years in France, he was still a Spanish national.

Picasso had arrived in Paris in 1900 at the age of nineteen. He once observed that, though there had been child prodigies in music, there had never been any in painting. Here he was being somewhat modest because, though certainly not as precocious as, say, Mozart, he was at fourteen considered exceptionally outstanding at the Barcelona Art Academy. And at the ripe old age of twenty, he was already being exhibited by the leading Paris dealer of the day, Ambroise Vollard. As he progressed from his Blue Period to his Rose Period and on to Cubism, he found steadily growing public recognition. There were exhibitions of his work in Munich as early as 1913 and, even more remarkably, in Vienna two years later. During the First World War he ventured into stage design. His décors and costumes for Diaghilev's Ballets Russes production of Erik Satie and Jean Cocteau's ballet *Parade* in 1917 further reinforced his international reputation. By the end of the war he was the most talked-about young painter in France. Success is vital, Picasso insisted ever after. 'It is often maintained that an artist should work for himself or "the love of art" and scorn success. However, he needs success and not just to be able to live but to bring his work to fruition. My success in youth gave me a wall of protection – the Blue Period, the Rose Period were the screens that protected me – with success I could do what I want.' These words say a lot not only about his career as a painter but also about his personal security during the Occupation. Fame was his great shield.

And security was above all what he needed, given his dicey legal status. Only recently has it become known that on 3 April 1939 Picasso submitted a formal request for French citizenship and that eight weeks later it was rejected. The police report declared that 'this so-called modernist painter' was possibly 'an anarchist' – a charge based on a single sheet of paper written in 1901 reporting that he was sharing accommodation with a Spanish anarchist friend – and was sympathetic to communist ideas. In the paranoid mood of the late 1930s foreigners were not exactly popular in France. And in the wake of the German-Soviet accord in August 1939, communists were seen as an internal threat. The police report further commented, 'During the civil war in Spain he sent huge sums of money to [Loyalist] government officials.' It was even rumoured that he intended to leave his entire estate to the Soviet Union. 'This foreigner', it concluded, 'has no grounds for receiving naturalization [and] he should be considered suspect from the nation's point of view.' Picasso himself never spoke of the matter to anyone and the police documents were found only in 2004. But the Germans in all likelihood saw them when they arrived in 1940; they were among records the Wehrmacht took with them when they retreated to Germany in 1944.

Even apart from the nationality problem, Picasso counted as a very dubious character in the eyes of the Germans. Although his dealer and friend Daniel-Henry Kahnweiler described him as 'the most apolitical man I have known', the civil war in Spain had wrenched him out of his indifference and by the end of the Thirties his anti-fascist sympathies were publicly known around the world. He had signed various declarations on behalf of the Spanish Loyalists, had helped to raise funds for Spanish refugees and had done his best to effect the release of Spanish intellectuals in French internment camps. In response to the 'degenerate art' exhibition in Munich, he had co-sponsored an anti-Hitler art show in London in 1938 that had greatly angered the Führer. Needless to say, his paintings were themselves anathema to the Nazis. *Guernica* in particular was regarded as a provocation both as a work of art and as an instrument of propaganda as it travelled through Europe. By the time it reached New York in 1939, it was seen not as a simple cry against war and brutality everywhere, which was apparently its original meaning, but as a specific denunciation of fascist aggression in Europe. All this Picasso knew. And he knew the Germans knew. What he and other artists did not know was that German authorities had no intention of interfering with their work.

At the time of the armistice Picasso was still in Royan and witnessed the arrival of German troops. 'This is a race apart,' he commented to Sabartés. 'They think they are very smart, and perhaps they are. . . . Anyhow, one thing is certain, and that is that we paint better. Fundamentally, if you notice carefully, they are very stupid. So many troops, so many machines, so much power, so much noise to get here!' Picasso's first encounter with the Invader came about thanks to Kazbek, his Afghan hound. A day or two following the Wehrmacht's arrival he was walking with the dog, a lovable but moth-eaten beast, when he was suddenly hailed by a German officer who was hurrying after him. Not knowing what to expect and fearing the worst – but let Sabartés describe the dénouement in the artist's own words:

If you please. . . .

. . . ?

Permit me? Be good enough to tell me your dog's breed.

In a way the encounter might have been a metaphor for the painter's relations with the Germans throughout the Occupation years. He had reason to
be worried, but the worries proved groundless. Picasso's second and more
ominous encounter occurred soon after the armistice, when German authorities inspected the contents of bank vaults throughout the Occupied area and
pilfered whatever took their fancy. In Picasso's case there were three large
rooms in the Banque Nationale pour le Commerce et l'Industrie filled with
paintings, two with his own works and one with Matisse's. According to his
own account, the military inspectors were not very bright. To flummox them,
he rushed from room to room, pulling out paintings and shoving them back
and all the while creating as much confusion as possible until the military
agents decided they had seen enough, assigned a low value to the works and
left without removing anything. From time to time his studio was also visited
by German callers. Some of them he described as 'simple soldiers' who came
'with the pretext of admiring my paintings'. In such cases, 'I used to distribute
reproductions of my *Guernica* and say to them "take it, souvenir! Souvenir!" '
There were also less simple visitors in the form of Gerhard Heller and Ernst
Jünger, who were probably more curious to meet the famous painter than to
admire his works. Jünger described his visit on an afternoon in July 1942 in a
long diary entry. A few brief extracts give the essence:

> I had already once had a glimpse of him, and now again had the impression
> of being in the presence of a magician – an impression that was strength-
> ened by his little peaked green hat. . . .
>
> Among the pictures standing there were two simple portraits of women
> which I liked. . . . Other paintings, such as a series of asymmetrical heads, I
> found monstrous.
>
> About the war he said, 'The two of us sitting here together could reach a
> peace agreement this afternoon. By evening people could put their lights
> back on.'

There are differing accounts of visits by Gestapo agents. Gilot implausibly
maintains that they came 'every week or two' to ask whether he was Jewish. An
often-repeated story has it that they searched his studio and deliberately damaged
a number of paintings. Picasso himself told Kahnweiler that intruders had come
but left his paintings undisturbed. They stole all his bed linen, however, which
he minded more. He told an American visitor after the Liberation that 'the

Gestapo was here three or four times nosing around, but they found nothing'. Whatever the truth, the vital fact is that even inside the Third Reich itself artists were rarely harassed as long as they were not engaged in any sort of subversion. No painters were sent to concentration camps for their paintings, though they might find it impossible to show them. But these facts were not known at the time and, in light of the wholesale destruction of modern art in the Third Reich, it was anything but unreasonable for Picasso to fear for his own safety as well as the survival of his paintings. Gilot's assertion that Picasso was on Hitler's personal hate list is without foundation – no such list has ever been found – but Picasso may have believed it. That he was required, like everyone else, to register for compulsory labour service could only have deepened his insecurity. His Paris residence permit expired in September 1943, with the risk of drawing attention to his foreign citizenship and resulting in his deportation. Fortunately Maurice Toesca, head of the Paris police – a man loyal both to the Germans and the Resistance – had it renewed for three years.

But short of taking pot shots at German soldiers or actively participating in the Resistance, there was not a chance in the world that the Germans would harry a cultural figure of such international stature. In their searches, Gestapo agents would have been looking not at his art works but for evidence of suspicious activities. While Picasso had friends who were to a greater or lesser extent engaged in the Resistance – as the Germans undoubtedly knew – he himself never crossed the line into active opposition – as they must have ascertained. Nonetheless, there could be no doubt where Picasso stood. During the Occupation he donated money and an occasional drawing to underground presses such as Éditions de Minuit and to *La Main à plume*, the journal of a Surrealist resistance group. There was also a story that Picasso had been in trouble for sending money to communists in Spain through Denmark and that Breker had saved him. The teller of this tale was the notoriously unreliable and self-serving Breker himself. 'Help' from the likes of Cocteau and Breker, as has often been asserted, would have been unnecessary for someone of Picasso's fame. In fact, no French painter was ever arrested for his painting. To have interned Picasso would have aroused just the sort of scandal the Germans wanted to avoid. The two sides treated one another with caution.

His daily life during the Occupation? Like everyone else, Picasso's first concern was simple survival – food and heat. 'There was nothing to do but work, struggle to find food, see one's friends quietly and look forward to the day of freedom', is how he summed up those years to his old American friend the photographer Lee Miller when she appeared in September 1944. But anyone as ebullient and gregarious as Picasso was also bound to have an active social life. He often dropped into the Flore and the Deux Magots, dined regularly at the Brasserie Lipp and Le Catalan, occasionally attended the cinema and theatre, visited friends and was visited by them. Somehow he managed to get some coal for heat, bronze for sculpting, canvas and other supplies for painting and sketching, not to mention beef for dinner. Of course, he had the money to pay inflated prices. Canvas to recycle he sometimes found in antique shops that were selling old paintings. Perhaps he also turned to the black market, or 'System D' – i.e., bartered a painting or sketch. In any event he always seemed to have supplies.

To Miller and others he spoke of the irony that his life in those years was so peaceful that he had been able to work with greater concentration than ever before. 'I worked on. They would not let me exhibit, but I worked and all my work is here.' And work he did! Mary-Margaret Goggin, a scholar who studied his output of those years, found that he had painted more oils on canvas in each of the years 1941, 1943 and 1944 than he had in any one of the years from 1932 to 1941, except for 1937. 'And in each of the years 1941, 1942, and 1943, he painted at least twice the number of large size canvases as for any of the years from 1932–1940.' The total number? In his catalogue raisonné, the art critic Christian Zervos credits him with producing 1,473 works from the outbreak of the war to the Liberation. Of these it has been estimated that three to four hundred were oils.

Yet the peace of which he spoke must have been relative. To read Brassaï, you almost get the impression that a day *chez* Picasso was a bit like a *levée chez* Louis XIV. He was daily beleaguered by old friends, collectors, publishers, dealers, people from the art world, people with something to sell, people wanting to buy and not a few strangers. Although Picasso himself was indifferent to this attention, Gilot found it rather sickening. 'The studio seemed the temple of a kind of Picasso religion and all the people who were there appeared to be completely immersed in that religion.' In any case worshippers were not the people he wanted to see. Painters seem to have a greater need of their own kind than do writers and composers. During the First World War they complained of being cut off from one another and during the Second they complained again. There was a deep sense of needing to know what others were doing, see their latest work, talk over their problems, even just meet. The artistic diaspora after 1939 and the subsequent division of the country made this almost impossible. Over and over they deplored, in letter and conversation, the lack of contact and exchange. 'I wonder what Matisse may be doing at this moment?' Picasso said to Gilot one day. Corresponding around the same time, Matisse and Pierre Bonnard were asking the same question of one another.

Painters also long for the gratification of having their new works exhibited and written and talked about. 'No artist can exist without a public', Matisse had said. And bitterly did Picasso resent the limits imposed on him. As he remarked to Sabartés on seeing him for the first time after the armistice, 'I am not permitted to exhibit or publish; all my books are banned, even reproductions of my works.' Gilot even maintained that 'Picasso was the painter who was number one on the German index.' These claims need to be radically deconstructed.

To begin with, censorship was relatively lenient. From the Invader's point of view the visual arts were inherently the least hazardous and the easiest to control. In the Unoccupied Zone the few galleries – in Marseille, Cannes, Monaco and Nice – conducted their business without interference. Vichy's goal was not to regulate established painters but to promote a vaguely intro-verted 'French' art. Even so, officials were not utterly doctrinaire and purchased, for example, several Matisse works for the national collection. In the Occupied Zone curators and gallery owners had a general idea of what was unaccept-able. Propaganda Department officials inspected public exhibitions before their openings and periodically visited private galleries. Their guidelines were simple – nothing by Jewish or Masonic painters. But there were few of these and, of them, Chagall and Modigliani were occasionally shown and sold anyway. No paintings by Klee, Nolde and other German 'degenerates' – but these had rarely been shown in Paris. And obviously nothing that was clearly anti-German, openly Gaullist or pro-Resistance. Most painters, certainly the most eminent, did not fall foul of these guidelines and went on painting as they wished.

So German censors permitted exhibitions that would have been unthink-able in the Third Reich or anywhere else in the Nazi empire. At the opening of the Musée National d'Art Moderne in August 1942 works by such Modernists as Braque, Dufy, Léger, Matisse, Picabia, Signac, Tanguy and Utrillo were on show along with sculptures by Maillol. Earlier in the summer the Galerie de France staged *Les Fauves 1903–1908*. More surprising – given Nazi racism – was an exhibition, *The Influence of African Art on Modern Painters*. Recent works by Braque were shown in 1943 at the Galerie de France and, in a solo exhibit, at the Salon d'Automne. Exhibitions of Cubists and other Modernists were held at the Salon des Tuileries, Galerie Charpentier and Louis Carré. The Jeanne Bucher gallery offered works by Léger, Miró, Ernst and, when the German censors were not watching, Kandinsky. Smaller private galleries sometimes kept such works in a back room and showed them on request.

Harassment of painters and galleries came not from the Germans or Vichy but right-wing art critics. They could not outlaw the art they hated, so they tried to suppress it by intimidation. One of the most rabid of the self-appointed censors was Lucien Rebatet, critic for *Je suis partout*. Another, Camille Mauclair, was author of *La Crise de l'art moderne*, which expounded aesthetic views practically identical to those of Hitler himself. The two were leaders of a campaign not only to rid the French art world of Jews – whether as painters, critics, dealers or even collectors – but also to purge it of all forms of Modernism. Given the subtlety of self-censorship, it is impossible to know just how cowed gallery owners were. There was the example of André Breton in Marseille, unable to find a gallery to show Surrealist works. Yet what could more vividly highlight the anomalies of those days than a sale of Picasso's works at the great auction house Drouot in 1942 that was announced and later written up in *Je suis partout*?

Picasso's nemesis was not the Germans or Vichy but General Franco. As the painter's close friend Christian Zervos wrote to Alfred Barr, director of the Museum of Modern Art in New York, 'At the express wish of Franco's ambassador to France, the Germans informed him that they could not permit him to exhibit.' This was not quite as severe a limitation as it might seem. On the one hand in all the years before the war he never showed at the salons. On the other Drouot and private galleries in Paris, Nice and Cannes occasionally exhibited, bought and sold Picassos. And all the while prices for them went up and up, as people with lots of francs saw art as a way of avoiding taxes and making a safe, inflation-proof investment. The number of Picassos on the art market was small and all were apparently painted before the Occupation. But he sold a not insignificant number of new works to friends, admirers and dealers, both directly and through his friend Louise Leiris, who had taken over from Picasso's old dealer, Kahnweiler.

Nor were Picasso's works entirely excluded from important exhibitions. He contributed to *The Influence of African Art on Modern Painters*, a show whose very subject was daring. He also participated in an exhibit of artists' palettes. Jeune France held conferences about his paintings. Books about them continued to be published, including the provocative *Seize peintures 1939–1943* by the left-wing Surrealist writer Robert Desnos. A year earlier Zervos had brought out the second volume of his catalogue raisonné. Picasso continued to be written about in the daily press, sometimes favourably and sometimes scurrilously. He contributed illustrations to various books, including works by poets who were in the Resistance. In November 1942 he himself published two poems in *Confluences*. The list of his activities could go on.

Although galleries did more business during the Occupation than during the Thirties, for Picasso the exciting prewar days were over. In November 1941 the Galerie Louis Carré mounted a show of drawings by his rival, Matisse, and it must have given him a pang when he read of Braque's one-man exhibition at the 1943 Salon. Dubuffet, Ernst, Fautrier, Kandinsky and Miró also had one-man shows while Picasso was only ever included in group exhibitions. And not even all of them. Like those of other non-French painters, his works were excluded from the opening of the Museum of Modern Art in August

1942 and then equally barred from a show of contemporary Spanish artists at the Galerie Charpentier the same year. In the case of the Charpentier exhibition, Jean Cocteau claimed to have witnessed the removal of a painting that had initially been hung. Franco's revenge again, possibly. Far worse, German authorities destroyed some of his works – along with those of Picabia, Klee, Miró, Ernst, Arp, Dalí, Masson and Léger – in a bonfire of Modernist paintings outside the Jeu de Paume in July 1943.

Picasso had been so widely ridiculed by conservatives over so many years that it is not surprising he was a prime target for the collaborationist press. Just as Gide was accused of having corrupted literature and youth, so Picasso was pilloried for having corrupted French artistic tradition and other painters. Fritz René Vanderpyl, art critic of *Paris-Soir*, and John Hemming Fry, the aged American fascist, were among those who now published books deploring his evil influence. Far more shocking was the behaviour of a fellow painter and old friend. Maurice de Vlaminck was sixty-three in 1939 and had belonged to the Ligue de Solidarité Internationale Antifasciste. He saw two of his books banned by the Germans – *Le Ventre* and *Désobéir*. Yet in June 1942 he contributed an article to *Comoedia* with a caustic *ad hominem* attack on 'this Catalan with the face of a monk and the eyes of an inquisitor who never speaks of art without a private smile showing on his lips'. Picasso's unforgivable sin? Cubism. 'It is difficult to kill what does not exist. But it is true, it is the dead who must be killed. . . . Pablo Picasso is guilty of having forced French painting into the most fatal of impasses, into indescribable confusion. From 1900 to 1930 he led it to negativism, impotence, death.' Cubism 'is as remote from painting as pederasty is from love'. It was anything but news that Vlaminck hated the influence of Cubism and Picasso as its co-founder. But why he chose such a moment to attack him remains a mystery. Although the article did not go over at all well with other artists, only the old Cubist André Lhote sprang to Picasso's defence, responding in the same publication, 'Never, never has independent art been exposed to more idiotic annoyance or deprecated in terms more absurd.' Who could have put it better?

Apart from his close friends, no one knew anything about Picasso's life during the Occupation. There were occasional rumours. Some said he had sold out to the Germans; according to others, he had been consigned to a concentration camp for resistance activities. So with the Liberation, foreign journalists and the artistic laity flocked to his studio. 'PICASSO IS SAFE', ran the blazing headline of the *San Francisco Chronicle*. An art historian has since commented, 'Accounts of life in Paris following the Liberation sometimes give the impression that Picasso ranked with the Louvre as a symbol of French culture.' Gilot recalled that for weeks after the Liberation it was impossible to walk ten feet inside his atelier without falling over the recumbent body of a young American G.I. Picasso the Painter suddenly found himself transformed by the American press into Picasso the Resistance Hero. That he had just joined the Communist party was largely passed over in embarrassed silence. When Alfred Barr trumpeted his supposed heroism in the Museum of Modern Art's bulletin a few months after the Liberation, Zervos brought him up sharp. He appealed to Barr – 'for the love of Picasso' – not to perpetuate a falsehood:

> Everything that has been recounted is bad journalism and for the most part false. The anecdotes are false; the participation of Picasso in the Resistance is false. Picasso simply preserved his dignity during the occupation, as did millions of others. But he never got involved in the Resistance. Bear in mind that his work was itself the greatest form of resistance, not only to an enemy but to millions of pretentious imbeciles.
>
> Do not let yourself be taken in by nonexistent heroics. There were heroes in France, but they either paid with their lives or want their activities to be treated with silence.

Taken aback, Barr sent Picasso a list of questions, one of which asked whether his studio had been a meeting place for the Resistance. The answer was a simple 'no'.

After the war some argued that producing any Modernist work was an act of opposition to Nazism. It was a feeble claim and Picasso himself refuted it when he asked rhetorically, 'Was the number of artists who were insurrectionist so small in comparison to that of writers and poets because of the difficulty of the task?' When all is said and done, the judgement of Paul Éluard can stand: 'He was one of the rare painters to have behaved correctly.'

Yet, strangely, there is often a defensive tone in writings about Picasso during the war years – 'strangely', because no serious charges of dishonourable behaviour have ever been raised. To be sure, his life appears to have been materially easier than the average person's, presumably because of his wealth. When others had fled Paris on foot, he had travelled to Royan in his Hispano-Suiza driven by his chauffeur. He dined out a lot; in fact, he was once caught and fined for eating a steak on a day officially ordained meatless. The paralysing moral agonies suffered by a Guéhenno, for instance, did not seem to afflict him. All the same, he kept his distance from the Germans and the *collabos*. Virtually all his close friends were Gaullists or communists, either in or close to the Resistance. And his record of financial generosity and support for the Spanish Loyalists along with his contributions to underground publishing – Éditions de Minuit and the review *La Main à plume* – speak for themselves.

The impact of the Occupation and the war on Picasso's work is a source of some disagreement. The age-old question of the relationship between an artist's personal life and his creations is especially difficult to answer in Picasso's case because he himself responded in different ways. In his first post-Liberation statement – in an interview with the *San Francisco Chronicle* – he said, 'I have not painted the war because I am not the kind of painter who goes out like a photographer for something to depict. But I have no doubt that the war is in these paintings I have done. Later on perhaps historians will find them and show that my style changed under the war's influence. Myself, I do not know.'

But a month later, in an article entitled 'Why I Became a Communist', he explained that it was the experience of the Occupation that had led him to realize that a political stance had to be expressed both in a public vow of commitment and on canvas and in bronze. Then, a short time later, fell his often-quoted pronouncement: 'What do you think an artist is? An imbecile who only has eyes if he is a painter, ears if he is a musician or a lyre if he is a poet? . . . Quite the contrary, he is at the same time a political being. . . . No, painting does not exist to decorate apartments. It is an instrument of offensive and defensive war against the enemy.'

By general agreement, *Guernica* of 1937 and *Charnel House* of 1945 are his most direct expressions of painting as an instrument of war against the enemy. Even so, there are various interpretations of *Guernica* and the artist himself made conflicting statements. At a minimum it has been considered not so much a symbolic rendering of the bombing of the town but as a general outcry against the horror of war. It was fascists and anti-fascists who turned it into a political manifesto. *Charnel House*, coming when the post-Liberation trials and purges were getting under way, was a more unambiguously political statement. Picasso said the brutal imagery of the horrifying scene was intended as a call for 'justice to be done in honour of those whose sacrifice secured the survival of France'.

Even Kahnweiler, who rarely read politics into the painter's works, commented, 'One could feel the war in Picasso's paintings. . . . Picasso himself told me, "When the Germans arrived in France, I was in Royan, and one day I did a portrait of a woman" – it was Dora Maar – "and when the Germans arrived a few days later, I saw that the head resembled a German helmet." ' Yet, in examining similar material for signs of the war, the art historian Gertje Utley discovered that Picasso 'consistently omitted, and in one case even obliterated, clear references to it'. She cites the *Portrait of Dora Maar* of October 1942 in which Picasso painted over prison bars, thereby effacing what would have been his clearest reference to life during the Occupation. When asked about some of his other works of that period, such as the powerful *Man with a Lamb*, the artist himself intimated that the symbolism was more in the eye of the beholder than that of the creator. In any event, *Guernica* apart, what the general public probably associates with Picasso's 'art as an instrument of war' is paradoxically the postwar emblematic dove used in communist peace propaganda.

Why did a man of such revolutionary creative independence take a step so out of character as to join an organization that routinely crushed any sort of independence? Like *collabos* who hated Germans, Picasso hated communists – and communists returned the compliment by hating his painting. Some believed he was trying to atone for failing to participate in the Resistance. Galtier-Boissière, ever the sceptic, saw it as a matter of raw opportunism, to protect a fortune estimated at 600 million francs. 'As every artist knows, Picasso was in a panic over the possibility of being deprived of his immense fortune. In joining the Communist party, he has taken out insurance.' When Gilot raised the question with the man himself, she received the sibylline answer, 'I came into the party as one goes to the fountain.' She herself likened it to a religious conversion.

In France the arts have always been politically charged, so it not surprising that painting played a central part in the communist campaign to dominate French culture. The party, like a church, was constantly on the prowl for prominent figures who might be candidates for higly publicized conversion. In Picasso's case the prowling began in the early Occupation years when the devout Aragon and Éluard softened him up. The crucial encounter occurred with Laurent Casanova, an important party official then in hiding in Paris after escaping from a German prison camp. Since Casanova was culturally *salonfähig*, unlike others in the party leadership, he was made responsible for cultivating intellectuals and artists. 'As a result of their contacts with Casanova a number of intellectuals entered the Communist Party, Pablo among them', to quote Gilot. The religious nature of his decision was evident in his state-ment in the party's daily, *L'Humanité*, 'Joining the Communist party is the logical conclusion of my whole life and work. . . . I feel much freer, much more fulfilled.' This is the vocabulary of the religious convert. But nothing in the artist's character or work makes it possible to believe the feeling was sincere.

Of course, the party had a field day. *L'Humanité* announced the event on 5 October with a dramatic headline: 'Picasso, the greatest of all living artists, has joined the party of the French Resistance'. The news was manipulated to puff up the party's claim to be the natural home of artists and intellectuals while also puffing up Picasso as a great Resistance hero. The announcement came as a total shock. And since it coincided with the opening of the Salon d'Automne, which was honouring Picasso with a major retrospective, it turned the show into a political event. The exhibition – called the *Salon de la Libération* – had been arranged by the newly installed director of the Modern Art Museum, Jean Cassou, both to celebrate the Liberation and to offer the French public its first opportunity – French museums having been notoriously conservative – to have a look at Picasso's works. It included seventy-four paint-ings and five bronzes and was the first such salon exhibition of the works of a non-French artist. In the best French tradition, it caused uproar. Some viewers were outraged because the state seemed to be sanctioning art they found horrible. Others, especially right-wing students and ex-*collabos*, disguised their political objections as aesthetic ones and protested violently by pulling some paintings off the wall. All the same, the exhibition, and the honour it bestowed, had two consequences. It conferred on Picasso de facto citizenship which in turn soon led to de jure naturalization.

After the war Picasso went to see Matisse, who was then struggling to turn a tiny Dominican chapel at Vence into a work of art – the work of art that became the famous Chapelle du Rosaire. Whether as a tease or a gentle rebuke, Picasso reproached Matisse for taking on the project since he was not a believer. 'You do not morally have the right!' he said with an exclamation mark in his voice. Not pausing for a moment in his work, Matisse calmly replied, 'I do not know whether I have faith or not. Perhaps I am really a Buddhist. The main thing is to work in a state of mind similar to prayer.'

Picasso and Matisse were the great rivals of twentieth-century painting. Picasso form, Matisse colour. So the cliché. Though they were personally as different as two men could be, they were friends. Artistically, too, though they may have been as close as the North and South Poles, as Picasso famously said, they were on the same planet. Each learned from the other. Picasso was always intrigued by Matisse's work and in a way jealous. Once he acquired a Matisse still life precisely because he could not understand it. He said he loved it without knowing why. Witnessing some of their meetings, Gilot commented, 'I felt these conversations were often reaffirmations of their convictions. . . . So even though their voices sounded friendly, and even if the tone was concilia-tory, I sensed an underlying contentiousness. Their confrontational state-ments resonated like the blows of a battering ram. They chatted in a seemingly light-hearted way but I could not escape the painful sense of being witness to a disguised battle rather than a simple conversation.' When Matisse died, Picasso's commented, 'Now I must paint for both of us.'

In any case, prayer is not the first word to suggest itself in thinking of Matisse's state of mind as he worked. Obsession, self-abnegation, courage, grit, self-renewal, among others, are more apt. Tormented by inner demons and beset – partly as a result – by medical and family problems, he struggled all his life to break with the past and strike out on his own. 'When I think of you,' Pierre Bonnard once wrote to him, 'I think of a mind cleansed of all old aesthetic convention.' But to what end? The 'liberation of colour', as it is referred to in art-history books, was a slow process and set in train by no single painter. But, throughout his long career, Matisse had more to do with it than anyone else. Hilary Spurling aptly subtitled the second volume of her biography of Matisse, *The Conquest of Colour*. Matisse took his first steps down this long path when he participated in the Fauve exhibition at the Salon d'Automne in 1905, a show that drew a predictably violent reaction. He soon parted ways with the other Fauvists and went on to invent a new visual language. The results were angrily derided by some and extravagantly admired by others.

Despite his great achievements, Matisse was widely compared unfavourably to Picasso throughout the 1930s. Even his own family let him know they shared the general view that he was an out-of-date decorative painter cut off from the contemporary art world. Slighted by officials both of the city of Paris and the French state, he was the only major French artist not asked to contribute to the 1937 International Exposition. Feeling under attack from all sides, he went on working in solipsistic isolation. He confronted terrible challenges. He was ill. His marriage was breaking up and family relationships with it. He and Job would have had a lot to talk about. Politically he was on the left side of the barricades – signing appropriate open letters et cetera – but he was never really politically engaged. As Europe slid towards war, he appeared cut off from current events in politics as much as in art.

In the face of Hitler's threats to Poland in August 1939, Matisse thought it over and decided to stay at his old studio in Paris – 'like a demoralized dog', he said. But when war was declared, he took fright and left. After some 25 miles he stopped and spent the following month at an inn in the village of Rochefort. There he sketched and read Gide's recently published diaries. With the war in its phoney phase, he decided to move back to his apartment in Nice despite concern about a possible Italian invasion. There, following a painful legal separation from his wife several months earlier, he lived alone except for his two hundred birds and Lydia Delectorskaya, a Russian refugee who came during the day to manage his household.

Matisse had lived in Nice since Christmas Day 1917. For a painter obsessed with colour, the Riviera was ideal. This he had discovered by chance when he went south for a winter's break in December of that year. Like Van Gogh, Gauguin, Renoir, Bonnard, Braque and many another painter, he was enticed to the Midi by its light. The blue of the sea and sky enchanted him. An intended week's vacation stretched into the rest of his life. 'What made me stay was the great coloured reflections of January, the luminosity of the days,' he said.

As the phoney war became phonier and the stress of family problems more stressful, Matisse decided to take a leisurely boat trip to Brazil. On returning to France in April 1940 he went to his place in Paris and remained there until the German breakthrough. Shortly before fleeing, he ran into Picasso, who commented that the conventional thinking of the French generals that had led to the disaster was of a piece with the deadening conventional thinking of the old sticks running the visual arts establishment. 'It is the École des Beaux-Arts all over again.' Matisse managed to find his way to the seemingly safe southwest, beating a path to St Jean de Luz. The town was Ravel's birthplace and, on hearing the town's church bells, he wondered what they might have meant to the composer as a boy. It was there that he learned of the military collapse.

He was devastated by the defeat and in a letter to his daughter, Marguerite, explained how he intended to deal with his feelings. 'Since we can do nothing, let us say no more about it. That will help us to think about it as little as possible, which is essential, so as not to be annihilated.' And speaking for most other artists, he declared that his solution was narcosis – the narcosis of work. 'Each one of us must find his own way to limit the moral shock of this catastrophe. . . . I am trying to distract myself from it as far as possible by clinging to the idea of the future work I could still do, if I don't let myself be destroyed.' And so Matisse enclosed himself in his own universe. Soon enough he realized the external world would not ignore him. To Pierre Bonnard he wrote after finally making his way back to Nice in September, 'I immediately went back to work so as to recover my equilibrium, but here there are such low spirits, such widespread fear that Nice may be occupied at any moment that, through contagion, my work is difficult, unproductive.'

So working even in the relative peace of the Unoccupied Zone was far from easy. 'It is certain that constant worrying is harmful to the unconscious work that generally stays with us when we are not in front of our easel', he commented to Bonnard in November 1940. To which the latter responded drily, 'It is no longer a question of painting but of eating.' Matisse still had his visa for asylum in Brazil but decided to stay in France. He felt, at seventy, too old and frail to cut his ties. More than that, he believed that the French cultural flag must be kept flying and that to leave at such a time would amount to desertion. 'When they told me that Pablo [Picasso] had gone to Mexico, it broke me up inside', he wrote to his daughter. When Varian Fry arrived in Nice and tried to persuade him to leave for his own safety, Matisse refused. He also turned down an invitation from Mills College in California. It was then that he uttered the much-quoted words: 'If all the talented people left France, the country would be much poorer'. To this he added, 'I began an artist's life very poor, and am not afraid to be poor again. I shall lock myself up in Nice with my two hundred birds and paint.' Even the widespread fear at the time that the Italians would occupy the city failed to intimidate him. 'I shall not leave here unless forced to do so. It was even suggested I should go to San Francisco', he told Bonnard. 'I refused. For a thousand reasons – I cannot see fleeing France at this moment – whatever the future may hold for me.'

Despite living in the Unoccupied Zone, he was not entirely immune from the dangers of the Occupation. It was a desperate worry that the Germans might confiscate or destroy his entire private collection, which included works by Cézanne, Courbet and Renoir, stored in a vault in Paris. 'I know what refined and robust removal men the Germans can be,' he commented to his son Pierre. Happily, Picasso was able to let him know that the contents of the vault had not been pilfered. Otherwise his only contact with the Germans was – along with Braque – to receive and reject the German Institute's invitation to tour Germany with a painters' group in January 1942.

'Matisse at War' would make a fitting title for an account of the painter's life during the Occupation. The text would have nothing to do with how he coped with the Invader or living conditions in those years. It would deal instead with the artistic battle within himself. After each breakthrough, he would confront new battle lines to be smashed and new areas to be conquered. But it was a two-front war. Had Matisse been a cat, he would have used up at least seven or eight of his nine lives by the end of 1940. During his life he had suffered one health crisis after another but none nearly so severe as the intestinal cancer that threatened to kill him at the end of 1940. He prepared to die and wrote farewell letters to friends and relatives. The doctors had told him, he said untruthfully, that the operation was necessary but without risk. 'I have accepted matters as they are and shall be happy when it is over,' he wrote to Bonnard. 'I had not believed one could be so much at peace at a moment like this.' To Pierre in New York he sent two letters. One enclosed his will; a second reviewed his life and career, tracing family problems and his own medical condition to his unremitting self-sacrifice to his work.

For a time his doctors doubted he would survive. During the first six months of 1941 he suffered terribly and in his lucid moments wondered whether he wanted to go on. He told his doctors he needed three more years to finish the work he felt he still had inside him. Gradually he recovered. In mid-March he told Pierre that he felt young again – 'like being given a second life'. To Bonnard he wrote that his survival was 'a miracle, they say here'. And to his doctor he triumphantly exclaimed as he quit the hospital, 'Good-bye, I am leaving and I am not going feet first.' By summer he was not only back at work but able to visit his old friends Bonnard and Rouault. This later prompted Rouault's daughter to return the call and present Matisse with the gift of the only work done by her father in the early years of the Occupation. Taking advantage of the occasion, she also let forth a deluge of recriminations about the rotten life of a painter's family. Commenting on the visit to Pierre, Matisse echoed what any great creative artist, whether Giotto or Gris, Michelangelo or Mondrian, might have said in response: 'A man who makes pictures . . . is an unhappy creature, tormented by day and night. He relieves himself of his passion in his pictures but also in spite of himself on the people around him. That is what normal people never understand. They want to enjoy the artist's products – as one might enjoy a cow's milk – but they cannot put up with the inconvenience, the mud and the flies.'

Matisse enjoyed passing the time reminiscing to visitors about his early days, conversations that gave rise to a proposal for a biographical memoir based on a series of interviews. In part the intention was to undertake a casual form of self-analysis that Matisse had long felt he needed. In the course of their meetings, the interviewer noted the painter's obsession with his art and commented, 'He lives only in function of the next picture to be done.' As if to prove the point, once he began working again, Matisse himself complained of complete servitude to his muse, saying ruefully, 'I am chained to my canvas.'

For most painters the lack of food and heat and the difficulties of travel under the Occupation were such a vexation that they became a refrain in their correspondence. Matisse was less troubled; he could eat little and travel less, and his apartment was warmed by the Mediterranean sun. Even so, he too was deeply frustrated. 'I really need to see painting other than my own', Bonnard had written to him. To this Matisse replied, 'I think a visit to you would do me the greatest good. Certainly the sight of your paintings would remove the wall I have in front of me and allow me to handle matters, above all my work, in a simple and direct way.' As time passed Bonnard begged him to send at least reproductions of some of his recent work: 'It has been such a long time since I saw something that I longed to see.'

It was around this time that Louis Aragon, an orthodox Stalinist, inserted himself into the painter's orbit. From the first they got along extremely well. The poet was an inordinate admirer of the painter, who in turn considered Aragon a model of the anti-Nazi Frenchman. Out of this improbable relationship was eventually born *Thèmes et variations*, a volume of the artist's drawings with an introduction by Aragon and a poem by Tristan Tzara. It was a remarkable work in its way, but in the conditions of the time it found few purchasers. Meanwhile Matisse's health steadily declined to the degree that he spent much of 1942 in bed. His life became a daily duel between physical suffering and artistic creativity. 'It was as if', Spurling has written, 'Matisse had gathered all his forces for a last supreme outburst of energy in the autumn and winter of 1942, which his two local doctors predicted would be his last.'

Writing about the first of his many visits to Matisse, the critic and art historian Gaston Diehl caught a glimpse of his life at this period. Arriving from Paris in February 1942 Diehl was immediately struck by the painter's good fortune to live on the Riviera with its colour and sunshine, its profusion of flowers and bright mood, in contrast to the grey, grim and anxious city he had just left. On entering the apartment he was astonished at the sense of joy emanating from the light and bright rooms with their bric-a-brac – magnificent shells from the South Seas, vases from China, huge bowls of fruit, tribal masks from Africa and Oceania on the walls, a glass case with Egyptian funerary masks, gigantic plants and fragrant flowers, cages filled with multicoloured birds and, pinned to the walls like butterflies, a large number of drawings in ink and charcoal. Diehl felt he was in paradise. Of their conversation, he recorded:

> Despite his grave illness about which we spoke at length . . . he looked at me sharply through metal-rimmed glasses and, after excusing himself for being unable to get up from his chair, he asked me in a deep voice about life in Paris and the Resistance. He was particularly interested in the young generation of painters – Pignon, Gischia, Fougeron – who had been so loyal to him. Then he commented in a detached way about the painful trial he had been through – the operation which had left him virtually unable to stand and therefore to paint and able only to draw in the morning on a small, portable table. He concluded with a wink, while stroking his beard, 'I am not dead, that's the main thing and at 71 I still feel young. . . .'
>
> Always the grand seigneur, self-confident, exigent, a bit distant, not very confident of his future health or that of his family, but generous, kindly, he was always talkative about artistic problems. . . . 'I have respect for my materials, respect for the paper, which must be impeccable without any fingerprints or faults, and respect for the paints that are sold to me, pure colour. I do not need to alter my paints because they are transformed by my techniques. A small number is sufficient. After all, is not all music made with only seven notes?'

Following the Allied invasion of North Africa in November 1942, the Italians occupied the Riviera and, when Italy left the war ten months later, the Germans replaced them. To escape the danger of Allied bombardment, Matisse moved into a poky house above Vence, in the hills away from the coast. None of this had much effect on the painter's life since he was now living in a private world that no one could reach. Too frail any longer to stand at an easel and paint, he turned to drawing and the use of such childhood techniques as crayons, linograph and paper cutouts. When Marguerite told him that the art world – to the extent that it knew what he was doing – looked askance if not with derision on his work, he responded defiantly that he regarded all his work up to that point as a preparation for what he felt would be his most creative phase. Whatever the reaction of others, he intended to keep following his new path until he made a fresh breakthrough.

The spring and summer of 1944 were perhaps the most emotionally difficult in a lifetime of emotional worries. The arrest by the Gestapo of both

Marguerite and his estranged wife for Resistance activities left him wild with anxiety. The Wehrmacht had in the meantime requisitioned the basement of his villa and used it as a canteen. His health was now so bad that he was confined to bed, emerging just as the Wehrmacht began to withdraw. While at work one day, his model remarked that through the window she could see soldiers marching away. Matisse refused to turn to look at them, remarking, 'Never let it be said that I stopped work to watch the Germans depart.'

It was in the fallow period during the Occupation that Matisse concluded that his work had reached a dead end and that he must find a new direction. As he later explained to Marguerite, 'Paintings seem to be finished for me now. . . . I am for decoration – there I give everything I can – I put into it all the acquisitions of my life. In pictures I can only go back over the same ground . . . but in design and decoration I have mastery, I am sure of it.' And so originated one of his great ventures, a book of colour experiments eventually published under the title *Jazz*. It turned out to be, in John Russell's words, 'an old man's summation of an activity that he had pursued day after day, without stint or remission, for 60 years'. He had used paper cutouts before but he now made them his preferred technique, slicing into sheets of paper so vividly coloured it is said that his doctor told him to wear dark glasses. He himself remarked that he had a sense of cutting into pure colour. Much of the time he worked in bed – just like Churchill, he liked to point out. Enveloped in white cushions, he created an impression of being, in the happy simile of one of his models, 'like God-the-Father emerging from whipped-cream stucco clouds'. He was launching the final, triumphant stage of his creative life.

In stark contrast to the limits on Picasso, Matisse had works prominently on display in Paris throughout the Occupation – in a solo exhibition in November 1941 at the Galerie Louis Carré, in various group exhibitions at the Galerie Charpentier, at the opening of the Museum of Modern Art, when nine works were exhibited, as well as several nudes at the Galerie René Drouin. He was a central figure in the big exhibition *Les Fauves – 1903–1908* at the Galerie de France in summer 1942. His works were on sale at the Fabiani and other galleries in Paris and at Galerie Seruy in Cannes. He also figured importantly in two books by Gaston Diehl published in 1943, *Les Fauves* and *Peintres d'aujourd'hui*. Diehl published three interviews with him, one in *Peintres d'aujourd'hui* and two in *Comoedia*, of which Diehl was the art critic. An interview with the Cubist André Lhote had appeared in the *Nouvelle Revue Française* in 1941. In 1944 Matisse and Bonnard each contributed twenty-five original lithographs to a sale at a Drouot auction to benefit children who had been evacuated from the Riviera coast in anticipation of an Allied bombardment.

At this point several questions come to mind. Did such shows and publicity not demonstrate the much-vaunted German 'tolerance'? To be sure, the works could never have appeared in the Third Reich. But since in France they were not politically subversive and would be viewed only by the French, even a good Nazi censor could authorize them without risk. Conversely, were artists not playing into the Invader's hands with these exhibits, creating the impression of a normal, happy France inside an ever-expanding German empire? And is this not why they were tolerated? While this was undoubtedly true, it does not invalidate Matisse's rhetorical question whether, if all the artists decamped, anything would remain of France.

Otherwise the Occupation largely passed Matisse by or, perhaps more accurately, he passed the Occupation by. When Diehl had asked what mattered most to him, he did not reply 'the liberation of France' – no doubt he took this for granted. Instead he said simply, 'To work from my model until I have it sufficiently within me to be able to let my hand run while managing to respect the greatness and sacred character of all living things.' His enemy was not the Germans or Vichy or the *collabos* but the demons inside himself. Yet he could not ignore the world around him. He sold or lost his birds one by one for lack of the special food they needed. He worried terribly about his wife, Marguerite and his son Jean, who were in the Resistance, as well as Pierre, who was cut off in America. His health was precarious, to say the least. But none of this seemed directly to affect his art. Or perhaps it did in a reverse way. If signs of the war were suggested by the skulls and so on of Picasso's paintings, defiance of the tragedy of war and occupation was clearly evident in the joy, colour and vivacity of Matisse's work. This fact rather defies Kahnweiler's stricture, 'An ivory tower is a beautiful thing, but a painter in whose work a war like the war of 1940–1945 was not felt, not externally but in almost imperceptible ways – well, he would not be a very great painter.'

Come the Liberation there were no foreign reporters beating down the door of Villa le Rêve. Even if they had managed to find the modest house, they would still have faced the challenge of spotting the painter, who lived in near-complete obscurity. Picasso himself discovered this to his surprise. 'Let's go see Matisse at Vence', he once proposed to Françoise Gilot. 'Wear your mauve silk blouse and your almond green trouser suit; he will love the effect of the colours.' On arrival, the door opened to reveal total blackness. They then passed through one darkened room after another, shutters closed and windows curtained. Exotic birds could be heard singing from cages and white pigeons flying around. Finally, they opened a door to find themselves in a room bathed in light where Matisse was sitting in bed playing with a cat.

Since the two painters had very different experiences of the Occupation, it is unsurprising that come the Liberation they reacted differently to the popular demand to settle accounts. For Matisse there were none to be settled. His wife and daughter survived Gestapo arrest, though in his daughter's case only just. Of the collaborationist painters he was uncritical. 'Basically I do not believe it is up to any of us to torment people with ideas different from our own', he said, naïvely missing the point of collaboration on the one hand and the *épuration* – the positive political purge – on the other. Even years later Matisse was blind to the moral issue, writing to a friend, 'You know that those who went to Germany were driven to it by a kind of fright, and they have already suffered from it.'

Picasso essentially ducked the issue. As head of the anti-collaborationist National Front of Artists, he was nominally responsible for the purge of the visual arts. But after chairing a meeting or two to decide which artists should be put on trial, he excused himself and let André Fougeron take charge. Fougeron, autodidact and communist, was pre-eminently a political artist, both in his commitment to leftist political causes and as a painter of everyday, popular scenes in the style of Socialist Realism. At the outbreak of the Spanish civil war he was on the point of going to Spain to fight but eventually decided he could best work for his principles through painting. He joined the Communist party in 1939 just as it was outlawed following the German-Soviet non-aggression pact in August of that year. With the outbreak of war in 1939 he was conscripted, and in the fighting on the Belgian border in early June of the following year was taken prisoner. He managed to escape and was back home in Paris not long after the armistice. Immediately he began organizing a resistance movement. From then on, his was a typical saga of the Occupation.

On returning to Paris, he had adopted the cover name Marcel and turned his atelier in Montmartre into a clandestine centre for printing Resistance tracts. Security precautions in the early days of the Resistance were pitifully lax and it was not long before a member of the group was arrested. The others fled to the atelier of a sympathetic artist until he in turn was exposed and sent to Buchenwald. Despite these setbacks, the network grew and in early 1942 started issuing *L'Art français*, a mimeographed circular commenting not just on artistic matters but on deportations and other public issues. To Fougeron that was not enough. He wanted to use not just printed words but art itself in the struggle. So he solicited contributions from eight trusted artists for an album – drawings satirizing Pétain, Laval and other collaborationist figures and portraying scenes of German torture and brutality – to be sold on behalf of the Resistance. The project was dogged by misfortune. One of the contributors was arrested and sent to a concentration camp. The courier who was carrying the typescript of Paul Éluard's preface to the printer was arrested and had to it tear up and swallow it before it was discovered. Not until early 1944 was the album, entitled *Vaincre: Témoignage des peintres français* (Triumph: Testimony of French Painters), finally ready for circulation.

Fougeron is therefore interesting both as an example of a painter active in the Resistance and also as an artist who used his own works as a weapon to fight the Occupation. His paintings were stylistically not unlike those being produced in the Third Reich at the time. Poor art about poor people, it has been said. Perhaps this is how he managed to have works included in no fewer than three exhibitions between 1942 and 1944. One such – *Rue de Paris 43*, illustrating the hunger and desperation of the common people – may well have been the most 'political' painting to be publicly exhibited during the Occupation. Sad to say, though, there is much truth in Christian Zervos's remark to Alfred Barr about these Resistance painters – 'unfortunately their heroism was much greater than the quality of their oeuvre'. Some years after the war, when Fougeron berated Picasso as a lousy communist, Picasso riposted by deriding Fougeron as a lousy painter. Both were right.

Like Fougeron, Jean Cassou was a man of the left, though he dropped out of the Communist party after a brief dalliance. In the interwar years he was an art critic and art historian, poet, novelist and museum curator. Like Roger Fry and Herbert Read in London or Albert Gallatin and Alfred Stieglitz in America, he was a passionate early admirer of Modernist painting and tireless in trying to promote it among his countrymen. Already in his early twenties he had begun to write and over the years was astonishingly prolific. At the time of his death the Bibliothèque Nationale credited him with no fewer than 650 entries. Although these were mostly about painting and painters, including introductions to a wide variety of museum exhibitions as well as a ten-volume history of art, he also wrote poems, novels, essays and non-fiction works such as *Origines arabes de Dante et de Pascal*. At the same time, being a militant anti-fascist, he was a fervent supporter of the Loyalists in Spain and an outspoken opponent of the Nazis. In 1936 he succeeded Jean Guéhenno as editor of the distinguished literary publication *Europe*. Politically the journal fell victim to Orwell's dictum that people of the left wanted to be anti-fascist without being anti-totalitarian, so while they hated the Third Reich they were uncritical of the Soviet Union. As such Cassou was a fairly average specimen of the interwar French leftist intellectual.

But the visual arts were always his first love. In 1931 he was appointed inspector for applied arts and the following year inspector of historic monuments. During the Popular Front he occupied a position in the Ministry of Education and Beaux-Arts. On the eve of the war Louis Hautecoeur, then curator of the Museum of Modern Art, appointed him his deputy. Although Hautecoeur was anything but a flaming Modernist, the two got along surprisingly well. After the war broke out Cassou, like everyone else in the museum world in Paris, worked frantically to move art works from the Louvre to various châteaux on the Loire. It was at the Château de Valençay that he heard Pétain, 'an old man reading from a scrap of paper', announce the armistice. 'I remember that I cried.'

On returning to Paris to resume his work at the Museum of Modern Art, Cassou took his first walk around Occupied Paris and was literally nauseated by the sight of German soldiers promenading around the Arc de Triomphe and along the Champs-Élysées. 'But they don't have the right! All that is *mine!*' was his immediate reaction. 'To take what is not yours is possible; that's just a question of force. But to take what is a part of us in flesh and spirit is unpardonable.' He refused to accept defeat, occupation and collaboration. And he decided never to write for publication as long as a censor's licence was required. He was already a resister *in petto*.

Several months later, on 24 September, Hautecoeur appeared at the Museum of Modern Art and announced that that he had just been appointed as head of the Beaux-Arts administration in Vichy and wanted Cassou to succeed him as head of the museum. Hautecoeur went on:

The Minister has signed your appointment. I explained to him very frankly that you had expressed political opinions completely contrary to those of the present government, that you were an official in the Popular Front, that you had supported the Spanish Loyalists and so on but that no one could doubt that your fanatical patriotism and that your qualities as a writer and especially as a writer on art made you my obvious successor. The Minister was fully aware of your background and concluded, saying: 'The Marshal does not want any revenge. . . .'

But then, as Cassou tells it, 'Returning home I turned on the radio to hear: "The communist Jew red Spaniard, part of the Popular Front, Freemason, anarchist Jean Cassou, member of the staff of a Jewish minister in the government of the Jew Blum and a warmonger, has been appointed head of the Museum of Modern Art." The next day I was sacked.' The months that followed were miserable. 'I was out on the pavement with my family during that horrible first winter of the Occupation. I sold some valuable books from my library, some autograph letters and manuscripts.'

In no time Cassou became deeply involved in nascent Resistance circles, writing tracts against Vichy and the Invader. This led him into one of the first Resistance groups which had taken form at the anthropological museum in Paris, the Musée de l'Homme. There he helped to publish *Résistance,* one of the earliest underground newspapers. But as the Gestapo picked up one member of the group after another, Cassou began to feel more and more at risk. One day a friend drew his attention to an article that had just appeared in *Au Pilori*. The headline read, 'What is the Spanish Jew Jean Cassou doing in Paris?' He realized the game was up and slipped away that evening, eventually making his way to Toulouse, where his brother-in-law was a professor at the university. On arriving, he immediately felt a tremendous sense of decompression. 'We were in the Zone, if not Free, at least Not Occupied, the kingdom of Pétain.' But for all that he luxuriated in the relatively carefree life – no curfew, no fear of the Gestapo, no German soldiers – he could not forget that he had friends back in Paris who faced arrest, deportation and execution.

In August 1941 he became 'agent P2' in a major Resistance group, the Bertaux network, but was caught several months later and imprisoned. Deprived of any means to write in jail, he composed in his head the first of *33 Sonnets composés au secret* which, under the cover name Jean Noir, were published in 1944 by the Éditions de Minuit. Demonstrating again the successful double entendre of poetry, the sonnets were broadcast on the Vichy radio. After a short prison term Cassou was released provisionally but was later arrested and put on trial for his underground activities and sentenced to a year in prison.

Recidivist that he was, upon his release he immediately plunged once more into the Resistance. While editing the underground publication *Cahiers de la Libération*, he also became head of an underground network based in Toulouse. During the insurrectionary period that preceded the military Liberation, Cassou was appointed commissioner of the Toulouse region. One night his car crossed paths with a column of retreating Wehrmacht troops. The Germans fired, killing two passengers outright and wounding Cassou so badly he was left for dead. After his recovery and the Liberation he again took up his vocation as a museum curator. He immediately began organizing the Salon d'Automne with its controversial Picasso retrospective. In October 1945 he was formally reappointed head of the Museum of Modern Art, a position he held for the next twenty years.

Cassou's overriding ambition had always been to increase the sparse Modernist holdings of French museums and he longed to have a few Picassos. But when, at the time of the retrospective, he ventured to remark to the artist that there were almost none of his works in French collections – in contrast to the riches of the Museum of Modern Art in New York – Picasso gave him the brush-off. Still, a brush-off is not deliberate torment or cruelty. And torment and cruelty characterized Picasso's treatment at one time or another of almost everyone he knew, not least Daniel-Henry Kahnweiler. The painter's dealer virtually worshipped Picasso, who took petty, even sadistic pleasure in playing him off against other dealers to get whatever he wanted – usually higher prices for his works. It is true that Picasso could easily have found another dealer while Kahnweiler could not have found another Picasso. But it is unlikely that Picasso

could have found anyone as trustworthy or who understood and valued his
works as highly. To be fair to the painter, while the relationship may have been
a case of the cat tormenting the mouse, the mouse did twice inveigle the cat to
give him an exclusive contract.

Kahnweiler was a typical product of an affluent, highly cultivated German –
in this case assimilated Jewish – family. Rejecting a career in business and
without knowing a single painter, much less having any under contract, he
opened a gallery in Paris in 1907 when he was just twenty-three years old.
Stacking the cards even more against himself, he decided to specialize in the
avant-garde. Paris may have been the capital of the Modernist movement then
shaking the art world but this very Modernism was received with philistine
abuse by the public and press when it went on display at the Salon d'Automne
in 1905 and the Salon des Indépendants the year after. The works were those of
the Fauves – Wild Beasts – and, having great self-confidence but little money
to hand, he bought paintings by Van Dongen, Derain and Vlaminck – all then
completely unknown. Not long afterwards he visited Picasso's studio and was
portrayed in a Cubist portrait that now hangs in the Art Institute of Chicago.
Demonstrating his precocious critical insight, the dealer was stunned in
admiration for a strange 'Assyrian' work he had heard about – *Les Demoiselles
d'Avignon* – and came to consider it the painting of the century. In 1912 Picasso
agreed to sell his works exclusively through Kahnweiler, marking the beginning
of a relationship that in one way or another lasted for the rest of their lives. At
the same time it was also the beginning of Kahnweiler's career as the dealer and
promoter of the other noted Cubists – Braque, Léger and Gris.

But fate, as the eminent sage P.G. Wodehouse observed, is always waiting
round the corner to slosh you behind the ear with a sock full of sand. Kahnweiler
was a German national and, come the Great War, an enemy alien. The entire
stock of his gallery was seized and after the war he had to witness it being sold
off as war booty. His biographer, Pierre Assouline, wrote of this experience as a
'descent into hell'. One can believe it. Stabbed in the back by other dealers, especially Paul and Léonce Rosenberg, and abandoned by Vlaminck and Derain and
later by Braque and Léger, he felt stripped naked and despoiled. In the meantime
relations with Picasso became so strained that the painter made Paul Rosenberg
his principal agent.

Only after an uncle in London arranged a substantial line of credit and a
close friend, André Simon, offered both moral and financial help was
Kahnweiler able to pick himself up and start anew. In September 1920 Galerie
Simon – named for the silent partner – opened for business. Kahnweiler again
saw himself not just as a dealer but also as a friend and promoter of *his* artists.
He was firm and unbending about whom he signed up and equally firm and
unbending about the price he offered for their works. Years later he spoke of

his business in terms almost of a religious mission. 'I found an opportunity to help those I considered great painters, to be an intermediary between them and the public, to clear their way, and to spare them financial anxieties. If the profession of art dealer has any moral justification, it can only be that.' These high principles were not easy to uphold through the economic depression of the Thirties. It was the foreign market that kept the gallery going.

Without his unshakeable optimism, Kahnweiler would never have been able to survive. But this trait also grievously deceived him. The man who could infallibly appraise paintings was hopeless in appraising political developments. Until it had actually happened, he refused to believe that Germany and France would go to war in 1914. In the Thirties he refused to believe that the real Germans – the good Germans – would fail to overthrow Hitler. And even after the Wehrmacht seized Denmark and Norway, he could not contemplate a German victory over France. After war was declared in 1939 he wrote to his brother, 'I am too old to live through another war. I no longer have the will to live.' By then he had seen all his sacred values trampled and destroyed. According to Assouline, he was on the verge of a nervous breakdown.

Yet throughout the phoney war he kept his gallery open as a sort of artistic lighthouse. At home in the evenings he and his wife read Dickens and Trollope to one another in an attempt to block out the world around them. Fearing Luftwaffe raids, he shipped some of his stock to a refuge he had found near the village of St Léonard-de-Noblat, not far from Limoges. And it was there that he and his wife fled at the very last minute on 12 June. The shock of the debacle was so enormous that he was unable to get his bearings for a time. According to his biographer, 'he could not at first make an effort to think, much less concentrate his attention for even one hour.' He had several books in mind to write but for a time felt unequal to the task. In his correspondence he could write only about life and death, religion and philosophy.

The political events of the following months destroyed whatever shreds remained of Kahnweiler's hopes and ideals. The art world itself left him aghast. The extravagance of the Breker exhibition, Vlaminck's attack on Picasso and a propaganda tour of Germany by artists enraged him. He felt personally contaminated since three of the painters involved were the first artists he had purchased in 1907. Such was his despair that he had difficulty concentrating on the book he had finally begun about Gris. Instead he busied himself with a book about the origins of modern art and, when he got nowhere, turned back to Gris. This inspired a broad analysis of artistic developments at the turn of the century. Culture, he argued, was indivisible in all its parts and therefore music, painting, architecture and literature had all changed in tandem. Unsure of surviving the war, he treated the Gris monograph as a repository of everything he had to say about modern painting.

In the face of all this tragedy, Kahnweiler was not the only refugee to find a new and even happy way of life in exile. 'I am not nervous at all', he had written to Gertrude Stein soon after the armistice. 'So at least this "holiday", which we did not want, is perhaps doing some good for our health.' He was surrounded by friends, among them Raymond Queneau and his wife, the painter Suzanne Roger, Louise Leiris and her writer husband, Michel. In the months to come he led a simple life – every day walking several miles to St Léonard to chat with the locals and buy food – and quickly felt himself the better for it. 'I am going to tell you something that will amaze you', he said years later to an interviewer. 'Those three years were happy ones for me and my wife. We were together. I worked every day, in peace. I wrote my book on Juan Gris. She was with me, and we were very, very happy.' Still, over everything hung a black cloud. 'Of course, our paradise existed in the shadow of the crematory ovens. . . . We knew that we were in constant danger.'

And indeed in February 1942 Michel Leiris, tipped off by Laurent Casanova, rushed to St Léonard to warn Kahnweiler that he and his wife faced imminent arrest. Leiris found them a place to hide and supplied him with false papers in the name of 'Henri-Georges Kersaint' so that the first letter of his surname would match the monogram on his clothing and other belongings. The couple packed their suitcases. Then at the last minute he balked. 'But in the end I said, "No, I won't leave; we're happy here. We'll take our chances." ' They unpacked and stayed. Eventually the Gestapo did arrive. The Kahnweilers had been betrayed by the daughter of a neighbouring farmer, the mistress of the Gestapo chief in Limoges, who claimed they were hiding arms for the Resistance. The agents looted the house and stole the Kahnweilers' valuables but did not touch the paintings, which meant nothing to them. Now thoroughly frightened, they went into hiding under false names in the home of a family they did not know and who were only vaguely known to the Leirises. There they remained, safely surviving the near-civil war of summer 1944 as the Resistance and Maquis attacked units of the Milice and the retreating Wehrmacht. 'We escaped the massacres,' he later said, 'but there were a great many incidents in the area. One day the Germans surrounded the little hamlet and burned a house, but there was no killing.'

The enforced solitude of the exile years had offered Kahnweiler time for reflection. As he observed the course of events, he was overwhelmed with despair. By now he had come to share Gibbon's view that history is little more than the register of the crimes, follies and misfortunes of mankind. And, like Hobbes, he could only regard life around him as solitary, poor, nasty, brutish and short. The notion of progress in society or the arts he rejected. Much as he admired Picasso, he felt unable to claim that his works marked an advance over the paintings in the Lascaux caves – a view shared by Picasso. Yet, despite everything, there remained one thing of imperishable value, culture in its various forms. This above all had to be treasured and protected. His was a secular, aesthetic faith. When it came to religion, Judaism meant nothing to him. In Assouline's words, 'He never felt Jewish; intellectually he was always more interested in Christianity than in the religion of his ancestors.' To Max Jacob he once said, 'The fact of being Jewish is of no importance to me because I don't believe in the theory of "races".'

That is not how the Invader saw the matter, however. In the previous war Kahnweiler had lost everything because he was German and therefore an enemy alien; in 1940 he had faced confiscation because, though he had become a French citizen in 1936, he was Jewish. In their determination to purge French culture of Jewish influences, the Germans prohibited Jews from being painters, critics, dealers and even collectors. Dealers were the main target. In 1930 there were some two hundred galleries in Paris, a fair number owned by people of Jewish background. Asked about this, Kahnweiler said, 'I attribute it to the fact that, as you know, the Jews had been forced because of the social situation to go into business at the beginning of the nineteenth century. Selling pictures was one of their businesses; but I don't think they have any special gift for it, since the truly great art dealers were not Jewish.' His most notable Jewish colleagues did not inspire his respect. Wildenstein was not interested in painters, only in paintings he said. Paul Rosenberg was nothing more than a high-powered businessman, while his brother Léonce was merely an unsuccessful one.

Although the Depression had taken its toll, there were still 116 galleries officially listed in Paris in 1939 and of these some twenty-six were owned by Jews. Two weeks after the fall of Paris Abetz gave the Gestapo the names of fifteen of them to be sequestered. In addition to Kahnweiler's Galerie Simon, these included Seligman, Wildenstein, Alfonse Kann, Paul Rosenberg and Bernheim-Jeune. Thus was set in motion the process of 'Aryanization', the term applied to expropriation. Jewish gallery owners were replaced by temporary administrators; their collections were then appraised and sold for a derisory figure. Sometimes the procedure was short-circuited when the owner sold or gave the business to a trusted friend or relative. Of the largest galleries, Wildenstein was turned over to Roger Dequoy, a trusted employee; André Weil was placed in the hands of Louis Carré; Paul Rosenberg's gallery was consigned to Octave Duchez. Seligman, Kann and Bernheim-Jeune were confiscated. In every case their personal collections were also plundered. Kahnweiler was lucky. In his own words:

> The gallery was regarded as Jewish property, for my associate Simon was Jewish too. He had gone to England with friends. So at first the gallery was put under sequestration again, but my sister-in-law [Louise Leiris] declared

that she was buying the gallery.* She immediately got an anonymous letter, which must have been from someone we knew, for it was composed of letters cut out of the newspaper. It said that she was my sister-in-law and that consequently the sale could not be valid. My sister-in-law, who is a woman of magnificent courage, went to the bureau of Jewish affairs. She told them, 'It's true, I am Kahnweiler's sister-in-law, but on the other hand I am what you call Aryan, and I have been working in this gallery for twenty-one years, since 1920. Who else would buy it?' Strangely enough, this was language the Germans understood; the sale was ratified, and she was able to take possession of the gallery, which has remained hers ever since.

The Louise Leiris Gallery opened for business in July 1941. The art world was booming and competition was stiff. It was not just the Invaders who were buying but French black-marketeers and Occupation-profiteers with their pockets stuffed with francs. Good paintings, as well as antiquarian books, gems, furs and antiques, were highly sought after as investments. They were not only trophies of financial success but also assets that could be hidden from tax collectors and that would retain their value despite currency fluctuations and inflation. A number of large art collections – such as that acquired by Suzy Solidor, a prosperous nightclub singer – were built up in this way. Thanks to stars like her, vernissages, exhibitions and auctions became popular social events. Dealers prospered. Kahnweiler worried that Picasso might be lured away. Fortunately Leiris was able to sell several of his works at enormous prices. With some daring she also promoted Léger, Masson, Braque and even Klee, a Kahnweiler favourite.

With the Liberation, the bubble burst. There were few buyers and exports were difficult. Americans were unwilling to risk owning a work by that dangerous communist Picasso. But supply also dried up since Kahnweiler's original 'discoveries' were now so rich and famous they were in no hurry to sell. Fortunately the dealer had always had a higher goal than making money. On returning to Paris in October 1944, he found that, in the words of his biographer, 'he had suddenly become a celebrity, a character. His artists were at last triumphant. He was to the world of modern art what Gide was to literature, the Great Contemporary.'

To say that the contrast between two dealers could scarcely be greater would be hyperbole, but no more than hyperbole. D.-H. Kahnweiler was austere, patrician, solemn; Maurice Laffaille was humorous, plebeian, brash. The one was a highly experienced expert, fanatically devoted to his profession; the other took

*Louise Leiris was in fact *la fille naturelle* of Léontine Gordon whom Kahnweiler married in 1904.

life on the fly and became an art dealer by accident. The one dealt only with a
small number of painters whom he felt he had discovered; the other flogged any
art work that came along. If *Juan Gris, his Life and Work* represents Kahnweiler's
response to life in exile, Laffaille's *Chronique d'une galerie de tableaux sous
l'Occupation* tells the story of art life in the surreal freedom of Nice. But however
different in character, the two men were in the same business.

When Laffaille was discharged from the army in July 1940, he was forty
years old, had a total of 200 francs in his pocket and a pregnant wife at his side.
Paris under the Germans was unbearable to him, so he went to Nice where he
at least had an uncle who could give him a room. Although he had trained as
an interior decorator, he had no illusions that there were many people at that
time who would want their interiors decorated. But since Nice was a port city
he reckoned on at least finding a job as a docker. Alas, there were no merchant
ships needing to be unloaded. So he made the rounds of the decorator shops.
Most proprietors thought he was barmy even to ask for a job. One finally took
him on, however, offering as wages a percentage of whatever he sold.

Oddly enough – sadly enough – it was a good moment to be in that line of
business. Unlike Marseille, which was filled with penniless refugees, Nice was
populated by resident Jews and exiled foreigners who had valuables to unload
before going into hiding or exile. Overnight, art-supply stores, frame shops
and decorator businesses became art galleries. And so it came about that, in
Laffaille's words: 'One morning the door opened and a woman entered. . . .
Her whole manner betrayed hesitation and even slight anxiety. "Would you be
willing to place this little picture in your window?" she asked. This simple
question was to change my whole life.' Anticipating the work of a Sunday
afternoon amateur, Laffaille unwrapped the package and to his amazement
found a work by Derain. It sold within a week, whereupon the woman
returned with a Vlaminck. His new career was launched.

The two Fauvist works acted as bait, and paintings now arrived from all
directions. The decorator's shop gradually mutated into a gallery. Laffaille was
frank enough to admit that before then he had only ever regarded a painting
as a work of art, not as an investment. 'I began discovering an entirely new
world of which I had never suspected up to then in its diversity, adventures,
histoires of all sorts – an unpredictable world, often amusing, sometimes bitter
but always enriching and fascinating.' Bitter, indeed. Although he had been
to exhibitions of contemporary art before the war, he knew nothing about Old
Masters. Now he paid the price, so to speak. Because of his ignorance he
passed up a Cranach that was later bought by Hermann Göring for a king's
ransom.

There was also an amusing side. One perambulating junkshop dealer offered
his wares – pseudo-Renoirs, some almost-Douanier Rousseaus and several very

early 'Manets' – all at exorbitant prices, which he reduced in the course of the
day until by evening his prices were minimal and it was sometimes possible to
find a minor painter worth having. One day, while riding in a tram during a
downpour, Laffaille observed the man trudging along the street, head down
and carrying his latest discovery. 'Cézanne?' Laffaille shouted. 'No, Van Gogh,'
the man cried back. Later on the *brocanteur* even discovered the original *Mona
Lisa* and notified the press and the conservators of the Louvre that the one in
Paris was a copy. Of course, he rejected fabulous offers for it; instead, as a
public service he found a hall to display it in and charged admission.

Laffaille's proudest moment came when André Gide passed the shop and,
after spotting a small Braque in the window, went in to congratulate him on
displaying works that were normally seen only in Paris. A few days later there
appeared in a Nice newspaper an article by Gide entitled 'The Museum on the
Sidewalk'. But a public display of avant-garde works could also cause problems. On one occasion a Picasso drawing in the shop window so outraged a
passer-by that she accused both Laffaille and Picasso of being responsible for
the defeat. The Marshal would be hearing from her about it, she left no doubt.

As the war went on, the Niçois could find less and less food, in fact less and
less everything. One by one pigeons disappeared from the squares, to reappear
in a ragout on someone's dinner table. To prevent her pigeon being kidnapped,
one woman attached a string to it while she walked down the street, allowing
the bird to discover what nutriment it could. If you had the money and no
moral objection to the black market, you might occasionally find butter at, say,
the hardware store, fish at the newsstand, apples at a clothing shop. There was
also barter, as Laffaille discovered. His first trade occurred when someone spied
a 1913 Utrillo in the window. After he refused to budge from his price of
320,000 francs, the man went back to his car and returned with a large box.
'310,000 and this ham.' 'Needless to say,' Laffaille commented, 'the Utrillo
somersaulted right into the car, and for the following two weeks we gratefully
thought of the painter whenever we munched our ham.'

Later, not long after the Italian army occupied Nice, an officer named Pizzo
bought a chalk drawing by Derain that he had seen in the window. He
returned some weeks later to buy a second. Some months passed before Pizzo
reappeared and noticed a small Derain oil painting. Although he could make
only a down payment, Laffaille let him take the work on the understanding
that he would return soon to pay the balance. Months passed. Laffaille had
almost given up hope when Pizzo at last reappeared and confessed he did not
have the cash but could pay in cigarettes. Thereupon he disgorged countless
packs that he had managed to hide in his clothing. Then followed any number
of trips from his military camp to Nice until he had discharged in cigarettes
the equivalent of what he owed. 'I don't know whether you can imagine what

seventy thousand francs worth of cigarettes amount to in space, but I saw my office transformed into a cigarette warehouse, and ironically the building was adjacent to a tobacco shop which had no tobacco to sell and was reduced to selling postcards. The further irony was that I have never smoked.' Word quickly made the rounds, and the gallery became a clandestine tobacconist.

Inevitably Laffaille went through the usual Sturm und Drang of authentication. Several dubious El Grecos turned out to be genuine. Several 'genuine' works were found to be forgeries. Once he met a man who had bought a painting in New York with a certificate of authenticity 'valid for four years'. He also learned the fallacy of the saying, current in art circles, that it was better to have a forged painting with a certificate than a genuine one without. This was the lesson he learned from a businessman who had made a killing during the Occupation and invested his fortune in paintings. But suddenly losing confidence in the works, he sold them and put the money in gold ingots that came with certificates from the Banque de France. It turned out that the certified ingots were lead covered with gold leaf and the certificates fake.

Significant in Laffaille's adventures is the fact that it was possible to sell Modernist works without any interference from Vichy or the Germans. He claimed his was the only gallery on a major street in Nice to sell such paintings. There was in fact one other. This was the Galerie Romarain, which openly sold works by Picasso, de Chirico and Rouault. It proved an unnecessarily daring venture because the shop also served as the clandestine headquarters of the most famous Resistance leader, Jean Moulin, himself a collector of Modernist works. Moulin was betrayed and arrested at a meeting near Lyon in June 1943. The gallery closed immediately afterwards.

Laffaille was no more than the humblest minnow in the grand artistic sea. The proud sharks were in Paris and competition among them was ferocious. The situation in which Paris dealers now found themselves was without precedent. An Invader had arrived with boundless greed and boundless funds, along with an equally boundless lack of scruples in how it got the paintings it wanted. The Invader in this case meant primarily Hitler and Göring, and what the Führer and the Reich Marshal wanted were Old Masters. Those they could not steal, they bought and traded through Paris dealers and German agents. One of these agents was the 'Otto Office', a Gestapo operation that combined art trafficking with counterespionage.

Throughout the Occupation some seventy galleries regularly advertised themselves and their shows in the press. The market was so hot that at least half-a-dozen new galleries were established. Drouot auctioned two million artworks in 1941–42 alone. For dealers, the situation – frenzied, insatiable demand and avid, rich supply – was ideal. Four of them, Martin Fabiani, Roger

Dequoy, Louis Carré and Allen Loebl, a Jew under Göring's personal protection, outdid all the others in volume of sales and income. And in lack of ethics. They knew what Hitler, Göring and other Nazi bigwigs liked and knew how to find it. All four sold looted art without any qualms. With the Liberation came the questions. Had their activities amounted to collaboration? Had they amassed illicit profits?

After waiting more than three decades, Fabiani published a book with the promising title of *Quand j'étais marchand de tableaux* (When I Was an Art Dealer). But instead of giving the lowdown on the art market during the Occupation, he produced a brazenly self-flattering memoir that managed in the course of 247 evasive pages to say nothing pertinent. As far as you could tell from this book, the Occupation was no more than a word – and a rarely used word at that. 'German' appears innocuously only two or three times. Unreliable and evasive Fabiani was one of those authors who flirts with facts but never gets a date.

Fabiani had good reason to be evasive. He was a con man. From selling furs, carpets and antique furniture, he had graduated to paintings and in that way came to be associated with the greatest of Paris art dealers, Ambroise Vollard. In July 1939 Vollard was killed in a car smash. In his Paris gallery were around six thousand paintings, with an estimated value of as much as a billion francs. Upon learning of Vollard's death, Fabiani sent his brother, Lucien Vollard – a lawyer in the far-off island colony of La Réunion – a telegram stating that his brother had died and that there was a purchaser willing to pay nine million francs – according to another account, twenty million – for his stock of paintings. Having no conception of the value of the works, the brother was dazzled by the sum, which he immediately accepted. Literally overnight the cunning Corsican had got hold of Vollard's estate.

During the Occupation Fabiani was perhaps the biggest of the dealer-collaborators in terms of sales. Among his German clients was Maria Almas Dietrich, one of Hitler's most important purchasing agents. His main client, however, was the notorious Rosenberg Agency which pillaged private Jewish collections. At some point Fabiani put aside more than six hundred items for shipment to America. A large number were moved to Spain, then to Bermuda and after that to Canada for the duration of the war.

As the war turned against the Germans, Fabiani was careful to cover himself. He donated money to *Lettres françaises* and financed and published Aragon's book on Matisse. He even managed to insert himself into preparations for the *Salon de la Libération*. But in September 1945, following an investigation of the Paris art market by the American military authorities, Fabiani was blacklisted and finally arrested for having been 'deeply implicated in illegal art trafficking in France and specifically in the export of part of the former Vollard collection'. Difficult though it is to believe, he was in the end deemed to be innocent of collaboration and merely fined 146,000,000 francs for tax evasion. The other major dealer-collaborators were also shamefully exonerated and solely taxed on their income at the time of the Liberation. Loebl is said to have emerged from the Occupation the richest of all.

Further scandals came to light in 1995 with the publication of Hector Feliciano's *The Lost Museum*. By drawing public attention to the failure of French museums to return recovered paintings to their original owners, the book provoked acute embarrassment and debate in France and beyond. But it was a *sotto voce* reference to Georges Wildenstein's dealings with Nazi collectors before and during the Occupation that landed Feliciano in a French courtroom. Outraged by the suggestion that the Jewish firm had maintained a profitable business with Nazi dealers, the Wildenstein family sued the writer for damages on the ground that the book was 'manifestly erroneous'. Both a lower court and an appeals court found, however, that there was documentary proof that Wildenstein had indeed done business with Hitler's personal agent, Karl Haberstock, both before and during the war.

Even before the war profiteers had been sentenced, artists themselves were called to account. The premise of the *épuration* was simple, at least in theory. During the armistice France and Germany were still at war and therefore cooperation with the Germans was cooperation with the enemy, hence treasonous behaviour. But what was cooperation? Was it a work of art? The closest Vichy art came to collaborationist art was *l'art Maréchal* kitsch. But there was nothing inherently collaborationist in it as an art form and it was far-fetched to consider it collaborationist simply because its subject was a collaborator. So once content was removed as a basis of guilt, what remained were public, symbolic acts. Hence the paradox that while writers were judged for their work rather than their actions, in the case of painters it was the reverse.

At the time of the Liberation, the National Front of Artists called for the arrest of Derain, Vlaminck, Van Dongen, Othon Friesz and André Dunoyer de Segonzac and the sculptors Henri Bouchard, Aristide Maillol, Paul Belmondo, Charles Despiau and Paul Landowski. They were charged with having collaborated with the enemy in time of war – specifically, for having toured the Third Reich as guests of the Germans in 1941, for being members of the sponsoring committee of the Breker exhibition in 1942 and for participating in the activities of the Groupe Collaboration. Hearings began in early October 1944 with Picasso in charge. The first sentence of most defence statements typically began, 'I have never been involved in politics', ignoring the central point that in Occupied France every public act was a political act. Then came the usual alibis. 'I went on the visit because the Germans promised to release a number of war prisoners.'

And, 'It was not with my knowledge that my name was used to sponsor the Breker show.' And, 'I never actively participated in the Groupe Collaboration.'

It was the tour that caused deepest offence. Most of the leading artists – Braque, Bonnard, Picabia, Matisse, Picasso, Maillol and Rouault – either were not invited or declined to go. Following fanfares and photos at the railway station, off the touring artists had gone in October 1941. During the following weeks they visited most of the major cities of the Third Reich including Hitler's great construction projects in Berlin and Nuremberg. Totalitarian governments do these things well, and everywhere the visitors were treated to banquets and bouquets, hugs and kisses, toasts and flattery. The intention was to demonstrate Hitler's enlightened cultural policies by showing how, in contrast to France, the Nazi state loved and supported its artists. Sure enough, on their return Despiau and Segonzac, among others, had been duly enthusiastic in their praise for the privileged position of artists in Hitler's Reich.

The punishments handed down by the *épuration* courts were hardly severe. Guilty artists were merely forbidden to show or sell for one or two years, which at least appropriately excluded them from the *Salon de la Libération*. The greater punishment was the public disgrace. But soon all was forgiven and forgotten. The purge panels were even more lenient with museum curators and officials of the Beaux-Arts. Although the head of the Rodin Museum, Georges Grappe, was dismissed for his activities as a notorious *collabo*, other museum directors were given sentences that were at best derisory. Although most Beaux-Arts officials were left in their positions, the two heads of the department were hauled before tribunals. Louis Hautecoeur was found innocent of wrongdoing. Because of the stain on his reputation for having served Vichy, however, he decided to take refuge in Geneva. His successor, Georges Hilaire, was sentenced in absentia to five years in prison, though not for his brief tenure as head of the Beaux-Arts but for his earlier activities with the Vichy police when he was a high official of the Interior Ministry. By the time these judgements were announced, public interest in *épuration* had begun to dim. Even a respected leftist and Resistance figure like Jean Cassou believed that the moment for reconstruction had come and appealed publicly for a reconciliation between 'art and the nation'.

While the ten *collabo* artists were in Germany enjoying the hospitality of Herr Hitler, some twenty anti-collaborationist artists who had fled to America were trying to adapt to the noisy, rough and confusing world of New York. *Guernica* had arrived in 1939 and was followed by Mondrian, Dalí, Ernst, Masson, Tanguy, Duchamp, Breton, Léger, Hélion, Matta, Zadkine, Lipchitz, Chagall, Tchelitchev, Ozenfant and Man Ray. In March 1942 Pierre Matisse, the painter's son, held an exhibition, *Artists in Exile*, to celebrate their presence.

Somehow he managed to assemble all of them – as striking as though Van Gogh, Gauguin, Manet, Renoir and their contemporaries had been brought together in one place at the same time – and took their collective photograph. In itself it is a fascinating image, if somewhat disconcerting in its showing not arty eccentrics in smocks in front of easels with paintbrushes in hand but conventional middle-aged men in neat suits and tasteful ties, polished shoes, quietly self-confident and looking for all the world like prosperous members of the New York Stock Exchange. The appearance was deceptive. They were not prosperous; they were not confident. Their lives and careers had just been completely overturned.

Adjusting to a new way of life and salvaging one's career was not easy. American painting had no stimulation to offer; the beauties of American nature intrigued only a few of them. They were on their own and they felt it. Typical was Léger.

My work continues to develop and is in no way dependent on where I am situated geographically. What I am painting here could equally well have been painted in Paris or London. The milieu does not affect me at all. A work of art is the result of an inner inspiration and owes nothing to the picturesqueness of its surroundings. Perhaps the tempo of New York or the climate enables me to work *faster*. That is all.

By no means was the United States new to him. Léger's connection with American art circles began vicariously in 1913 when two of his canvases were in the famous Amory Show and then travelled on to Chicago and Boston. The painter himself had visited New York and Chicago in 1931 and returned four years later for an exhibition of his works at the Museum of Modern Art in New York and the Art Institute in Chicago, shows that helped to establish his international reputation. It was on the latter occasion that he met Le Corbusier, who became a friend and colleague, and, among other American cultural figures, John Dos Passos, who was then becoming popular in France. Cheered by his success and intrigued by the spectacle of American life, he made a third trip in early 1936. Two years later he was back, to execute a commission to decorate Nelson Rockefeller's apartment and to give eight lectures at Yale on 'Colour in Architecture'.

At the time of the invasion, Léger was at his home in Normandy. Fleeing at the very last moment, he followed a circuitous route that eventually took him to Marseille. He was lucky. With a still valid passport and entry visa, he was able to embark via Lisbon for New York in October. There friends helped him to find housing and an atelier. Yale appointed him to a senior position and the following year Mills College did the same. As a sort of welcoming gesture, the

Museum of Modern Art placed his *Composition with Two Parrots* on exhibition. Other museums and galleries – from Oakland to Montreal – were now avidly acquiring and showing his works.

Somehow, perhaps because he was now a resident, he saw the country with new eyes, almost as though for the first time. He took notes. 'Discovery of America', they begin. 'A young country, without a beard, very youthful. . . . Everything is big and high, wide and without borders. There are no native people; hundreds of languages and nationalities find themselves living together. They have founded their union on the reliability of the dollar; as good business people they have imposed themselves on the world.' Fortunately, a few friends materialized. Peggy Guggenheim was one of them. Their friendship was recent. 'The day Hitler walked into Norway, I walked into Léger's studio and bought a wonderful 1919 painting from him for one thousand dollars', she recalled in her memoir. By the time she arrived in New York in July 1941, she found that he knew the city better than she. 'He became a sort of guide and took us to all the foreign restaurants in every quarter of the city. He seemed to know every inch of New York, which he had discovered on foot.'

In reality Léger was finding life in exile emotionally difficult. Separated from friends, without news from France and living in a city utterly unlike Paris physically, socially, culturally and gastronomically, he felt at a loose end. His status was also different now. No longer was he an honoured guest but rather a homeless, rootless exile from a defeated country. In the view of Gaston Diehl, the painter's works during these years reflected a mood of melancholy – anguish even. This could be seen, he believed, in the still lifes with their angular, roughly broken lines and knotty, twisted, gaping, saw-toothed forms. 'On the whole,' Diehl said, 'he borrowed very little directly from the American landscape, except the opulence of nature and piles of rubbish.' Léger turned in on himself. He scrutinized the paintings, drawings and ideas he had brought with him from France and then developed them. The scene he had witnessed on the docks of the Old Port in Marseille, for example, now inspired a series of fugal variants on 'people in space'. *Divers on a Yellow Background, Acrobats in Grey, The Dance, Large Black Divers* and *Polychrome Divers* all portrayed disjointed, tangled bodies in flight.

These were not sterile years, and New York played an important, if serendipitous, role in his stylistic development. During his exile he experimented with separating shapes and subject from colour. One night on the street, it came to him how he could create arbitrary blocks of vivid colour independent of the architecture of the work. He explained:

That is not imagination or invention. I actually saw it. When I was in New York in 1942 I was deeply struck by the floodlights of Broadway which swept the streets. There you were standing and talking with someone, and suddenly he was blue. Then the colour vanished and another came, and he became yellow. . . . I wanted to do the same in my painting. That is very important in wall painting because in that case there are no modulations; but then I applied this to my easel paintings. . . . I could never have thought this up. My fantasy does not extend that far.

Despite his brush with Cubism and Futurism, Léger's work was outside the mainstream of European painting. There was a solid, simple quality about the works as about the man – Guggenheim thought he looked like a butcher, though mechanic was more like it. He painted simple people doing simple things. That was anything but novel, but he did it in a way that was his own. Léger, a man of the left – later a communist – wanted to change the relationship between art and society. That art spoke more to the rich collector than to the man in the street troubled him all his life. It is difficult to think of another painter who tried so hard, through teaching, lectures, articles and even film, to establish a link between art and society.

His down-to-earth simplicity was evident in his fascination with mechanical objects – machines, planes, locomotives, bicycles. Beauty in the conventional sense was not for him. In fact, he once said, 'As for my subjects, I take them anywhere I find them. I like the forms invented by modern industry, and I make use of them – of steel with its thousand colourful reflections. I maintain that a machine gun and the breech of a 75 mm howitzer are more appropriate subjects for a painting than four apples on a table or a landscape of Saint-Cloud.' Although Léger kept Futurism at arm's length, that statement could easily have been made by its great exponent, Filippo Tommaso Marinetti. 'My final goal', Léger said on another occasion, 'is to obtain a maximum amount of power and even of violence on a surface. . . . I am unable to achieve this power except by the ruthless application of the most extreme contrasts, such as flat surfaces in pure colours, moulded components in grey tones and objects treated realistically.' In this spirit he produced some 120 works during his five years in exile.

Léger, badly gassed at the front in 1916, later said that his 'three years in contact with the harshest, most violent reality' had had the effect of revolutionizing his painting. But the experience did not alter his robust, optimistic outlook on life. Such was not the case with André Masson, who had been so gravely wounded both physically and psychologically that he was never the same again, personally or aesthetically or politically. The experience of the battlefield left him with such a profound revulsion for war and violence that he spent the remainder of his life working it out on the easel.

He was both the greatest of the Surrealists and the most ideological. He did not just talk ideals, he lived them. In 1934 he was so anguished by the right-wing threat in France that he exiled himself to Spain. Two years later he found himself in the middle of a civil war. Sympathizing with the Loyalists, he produced a series of savagely anti-Franco and anti-clerical paintings and drawings. But the fighting revived such painful memories of the trenches that he had to retreat to a quiet corner of Normandy to recover. His anguish over the condition of Europe was reflected in the wild and tortured imagery of his works at the time. Most notable of these was *Dream of a Future Desert*, at first sight a Modernist pastiche of a Piranesi prison but with a sense of horror unknown to the eighteenth century. It was now that he initiated four years of labour on his *Anatomy of my Universe*, a philosophical-psychoanalytical self-analysis in text and drawings that pictured desert landscapes, labyrinthine architectural structures, ladders leading nowhere and impregnable walls. Before it was completed, Franco's victory, the war and Occupation inspired his *Self-Portrait on a Hangman's Noose*. Masson was a terrified man and his works were terrifying.

In 1940 he fled to a village in the Auvergne but hesitated to go into foreign exile. Difficulties with the police and Vichy's racial legislation, which threatened his Jewish wife, frightened him and in March 1941 he crossed the Atlantic on a rusty cargo boat to Martinique. There he met André Breton, who had arrived two weeks earlier, and together the two explored the island. Masson was fascinated by everything he saw and made sketches that became a source for many of his American paintings. On finally reaching New York, he decided for linguistic and other reasons to live in seclusion. 'I like New York,' he wrote to a friend when he reached there, 'but it devours me. I hope to live in the country.' For the next four years he resided in Connecticut, leaving it only to visit museums and exhibitions.

Although weighed down by fears for friends and relations in France and by the pain of his country's defeat, Masson now entered a period of extraordinary revitalization. In her encyclopaedic *Surrealism in Exile*, Martica Sawin puts it this way: 'When he started again it was as if a pent-up force had been released, and he entered on a richly productive period and a new stylistic and thematic phase of his art.' She adds, 'His escape, again, from death, as well as the knowledge that he had brought his family to safety, must have impelled him toward an art of affirmation that strongly contrasted with the violent images from the 1930s.'

Masson found inspiration everywhere. A visit to the National Museum of the American Indian in New York aroused an interest in Iroquois mythology and resulted in *Iroquois Landscape*, the first of his 'telluric' works. What he saw in the famous Asian collection of the Boston Museum of Fine Arts became a major source of ideas for the next fifteen years. But it was what he referred to as 'the might of nature' that meant most. 'When Indian summer comes, in October, there is no end to the variety of colours. There are the maples, under a sky of stained-glass blue; they range from yellow to violet, from purple to orange and vermilion, as if the sky had poured cans of paint on the vegetation.' All this, he said on another occasion, 'stimulated me to a greater vivacity of colour'.

Recognition came at last. Masson encountered greater interest in his work in America than he had ever found in France. Within a few months of his arrival, the Baltimore Museum of Art became the first important gallery to mount a major show. After that there were a series of one-man exhibitions that toured the country and took him to the Far West. He gave lectures and attended conferences. 'America has been friendly in the extreme,' he wrote to his friend Jean Ballard, 'and I work like hell. . . . I am amazed to see my paintings in museums, and I have the sense of having become a very respectable gentleman.'

Despite his success, his mind always strayed back to the dark days at home. The titles of some of his works during this period show that no other French painter was so overtly affected – *Hunger, Brutality, Pain, The Partisan, The Résistance, The Victim, Ouradour.* By the end of the war he was homesick and anxious to return. More than any other Surrealist he had benefited from his American experience and was never reluctant to acknowledge his debt. As he wrote many years later, 'It was in the United States that I began to paint in the way I ambitiously call chthonic, belonging to subterranean forces. I did not abandon Surrealism, but I gave it new meaning – telluric.'

What the Iroquois and colours of a New England autumn meant to Masson was what the Hopi and red rock of northern Arizona came to mean to Max Ernst. Ernst had made the discovery by chance when travelling through the area by car with Peggy Guggenheim in the autumn of 1941. The experience had a profound effect on both his life and his work.

Ernst was one of the original Surrealists, his alliance dating back to his meetings with Breton and Éluard in the early Twenties when he abandoned Cologne for Paris. As much at home in literature as in art, he was, in John Russell's words, 'a poet among the poets, a painter among the painters, a prehensile many-sided inventor who gave art . . . a fresh start and a prestige without precedent'. Ernst took a more modest view, regarding himself as someone who merely opened the doors of the unconscious and gave concrete form to the stock of images that came flowing out. In his early years he had studied abnormal psychology, the perfect subject for understanding the mood of the interwar period.

During the last years of peace, he was living in the south of France with the accomplished young painter Leonora Carrington. With the outbreak of war Ernst, as a German national, automatically became an enemy alien and for the next year or so was repeatedly interned and released or captured and escaped until, finally, Paul Éluard arranged for his permanent discharge. Although it was the French police who had interned him, after the armistice it was the Gestapo that he feared, even though he was not Jewish. In early 1941 he went to Marseille and contacted the Emergency Rescue Committee in the hope of finding a way to the United States. There he met Peggy Guggenheim, who was trying to get herself and her collection of paintings to the United States. One of the painters she liked – in more ways than one – was Ernst, and while in Marseille she bought a great number of his works. To celebrate the sale and his fiftieth birthday in April 1941 they had dinner together in the Old Port. 'I felt extremely attracted to Ernst, and soon fell madly in love with him', she wrote in her memoir, *Confessions of an Art Addict*. From then on, she added, 'my only thought was to save him from Europe and get him to New York'. And so it came about that in mid-July they flew across the Atlantic on the Yankee Clipper with her two children and his son. Abandoned and left behind was Guggenheim's previous beau, the Jewish Romanian painter Victor Brauner, who went underground in Provence.

Invited to do time in jail on Ellis Island courtesy of the American immigration authorities, Ernst was released thanks to the intervention of officials at the Museum of Modern Art. Although his work had been shown in New York exhibitions in 1932 and 1936, he had not previously visited the United States. 'I had no idea how famous Max was, and it was great fun going around with someone so well known', Guggenheim said. 'He was also perpetually encountering people whom he had known in concentration camps. To me these people seemed like ghosts, but to Max they were very real, and he always mentioned the dreadful camps where they had been together as though he were talking about Deauville, Kitzbuhl or St Moritz.'

In the search for an appropriate place to open an art gallery, Guggenheim and Ernst flew to California. Unsuccessful, they bought a car and drove back to New York. It was on this return trip that Ernst was overawed by the northern Arizona landscape where he encountered red rock formations bearing an uncanny resemblance to the landscape painting he had been doing shortly before leaving France. It was also at this time that he witnessed Hopi Indian dances and amassed a large collection of masks and kachina dolls.

In December 1941, when the US and Germany declared war on one another, Ernst's legal status became a problem. And so, as Guggenheim phrased it in her usual unvarnished way, 'Soon after Pearl Harbor we were married, as I did not want to live in sin with an enemy alien.' But though they may have stopped living in sin, they did not start living in harmony. She devoted herself to her gallery, Art of This Century, while he painted and flirted. They met in the evenings and as often as not gave a party. The goings-on were sometimes riotous but had the artistically useful purpose of bringing Breton and the other Surrealists together with Jackson Pollock and a large number of other young American painters. Ernst had three shows in 1942, each of which he considered, rather exaggeratedly, a critical flop. In the same year he and Guggenheim organized an exhibition of women painters. The talented Dorothea Tanning was among them. One thing led to another and in the spring of 1943 Ernst left Guggenheim to live with her. They went to Sedona in Arizona and eventually settled there until Ernst returned permanently to Paris in 1953.

Renowned as the man who had painted one of the most famous works of the twentieth century, *Nude Descending a Staircase*, Marcel Duchamp was an eccentric's eccentric who could live almost anywhere under almost any conditions. Almost, but not quite. The Germans and Vichy were too much for him. In the time he could spare from his passion for chess and his artistic projects – he was then working on his miniature *Boxes* – he prepared to flee. Typically, he made his preparations so casually that his exasperated American friends despaired. But he was one of those men of luck, for whom everything somehow works out in the end. To get his art materials out of Paris, he arranged to be authenticated as a cheese merchant required to travel to the Unoccupied Zone on business. In three trips he managed to extricate his materials, which Peggy Guggenheim volunteered to send to New York with her own effects. He then roamed untroubled throughout the Midi and even managed to cross the border to Geneva to collect a debt. After a year-and-a-half's effortless effort, he got passage in mid-May 1942 on a boat from Marseille to Casablanca, where he caught a Portuguese steamer to New York. If you have low expectations, it is difficult to be disappointed, and Duchamp must have been the sole refugee who actually enjoyed the ghastly boat trip into exile.

He already knew and liked New York, so he adjusted easily, so much so that his biographer, Calvin Tomkins, could write, 'Of all the European artists who spent the war years in New York, Duchamp was the only one who seemed at home there.' Staying as a guest with this person and that, he spent his time playing chess, giving French lessons and working on his *Boxes*. He helped André Breton with his art review, *VVV*, and gave him a hand in arranging a grand Surrealist group show – the final one of its kind. In the last gasp of Dadaism, he decorated the exhibition rooms with a mile-long web of string and arranged for a dozen children to run around playing games and annoying the viewers. In the autumn of 1943 he went off to live alone in near-squalor in a one-room walk-up, with neither phone nor private bath and only a packing crate or two to sit on. Having such minimal needs, he was able to survive on the income earned from giving language lessons and selling the occasional *Box*. Apart from that he produced little that anyone else considered art. From time to time he had an exhibition and an entire issue of *View* was dedicated to him. But he and his work were falling out of favour. The paintings of Pollock and other Abstract Expressionists he considered essentially decorative; they considered his productions irrelevant. Gradually, as his biographer has written, his reputation faded to the point of invisibility.

No other exile had as tough, if adventurous, a life during the Occupation as Jean Hélion. In the Thirties he had visited the Soviet Union and become disillusioned with communism. Afterwards he went to New York and, though also disillusioned by the ethos of American capitalism, he stayed. It was there that the outbreak of the war found him. Summoned for military duty, like a good citizen he returned to France. It was a big mistake. A sudden German advance in 1940 trapped his infantry unit and he was taken prisoner. He was sent to work first on a farm in Pomerania and later on a prison boat in the Baltic. In the face of the gratuitous sadism of many of his captors, he found that 'they could not do anything to a thin little smile that meant: "They shall not have me"'. The phrase was both his mantra while in captivity and the title of a book he later published about life as a prisoner. In 1942 he managed to escape and miraculously made his way, via Berlin, Brussels and Paris, back to the United States. With equal daring he then married Peggy Guggenheim's nymphet-daughter, Pegeen – or, as one writer said, he 'rescued [her] from her mother's sex orgies by marrying her'. His painting was similarly adventurous, going from naturalism to abstraction to, following his return to America in 1943, unrelenting realism.

The Surrealist-Dadaist Man Ray had a much easier time of it. He had escaped before the Wehrmacht reached France and made his way to Hollywood. In Tinseltown he had the humbling experience, as he remarked to friends, of encountering more Surrealism in everyday life than all the French Surrealists together could have invented in a lifetime. Be that as it may, the French Surrealists were prospering in the New World. After flagging during the Thirties, Surrealism got its second breath. The horror of the times and the overturning of their lives provoked a reaction that inspired the émigrés to great achievements. 'During their years of exile,' Sawin points out, 'many of these artists produced some of the strongest work of their careers, and at an extraordinary rate of output.'

The presence of the Surrealists in America had a second, longer-term effect. On arriving in New York, they had found American painting in a state of crisis and American painters in a state of despair. Unlike American writers – Poe, Melville and Whitman, for instance – American painters had historically lacked the self-confidence to strike out on their own. They were well aware that they were yet to produce any significant work. They felt lost and directionless. Most great art had been coming out of Paris for a century; Modernism and the École de Paris were so linked they seemed synonymous. Painters everywhere else felt sidelined. And indeed they were. When a number of them protested the refusal of the Museum of Modern Art to acquire and show their works, the assistant director told them, 'You cannot possibly present twentieth-century American painting as we have presented School of Paris painting.'

The sense of inferiority was well described by Lee Krasner. 'In the late thirties there was a feeling that American art could never achieve the status, could never become the aesthetic equal of French art. Absolutely no one thought American painting could rival French painting, then or ever. I don't remember anybody who even *thought* in those terms at the time.' It is said that Arshile Gorky presided over a meeting of young American artists in Willem de Kooning's studio around that time to discuss 'the dilemma of American painting' and opened the meeting with the words, 'We are defeated.' On returning to their studios, according to Krasner, they looked at what they had been working on and threw up their hands in despair. So they did the next best thing. They studied what the exiles had produced by reading the *Cahiers d'art* and similar publications, haunting the Museum of Modern Art in New York and the private galleries, and ransacking what they found for ideas. 'We went with a great sense of hunger', was the way Krasner put it.

Hungry, perhaps, but resentful. It was no doubt inevitable that insecure American painters and critics should react by regarding the French less as exiles than as intruders. Suffering a sizeable inferiority complex – for the good reason that they were inferior – they compensated by dismissing French artists as snobs and elitists. Even the foreign-born de Kooning hated them for their alleged wealth, education and lives of privilege. The resentment was flamboyantly expressed by the young art dealer Julien Levy. 'Matta burst on the New York scene as if he considered this country a sort of dark continent, his Africa, where he could trade dubious wares, charm the natives and entertain scintillating disillusions.' Hard feelings still endure. 'It's amusing', the art critic Deborah Solomon wrote as recently as 1995, 'to think of the Surrealists, with their polished manners and mandarin tastes, roaming New York as the self-appointed aristocrats of culture. For all their vast sophistication, they could not see the revolution taking place right beneath their turned-up noses,

never guessing that they represented the European avant-garde in its final
moment.'

In reality it is anything but amusing to think of the lives of the exiled
French artists. Most had endured harrowing experiences just to get out of
France. While they were usually received with kindness, they were also met
with incomprehension. Those who were socialists or communists – as most
were – were suspected of being dangerous subversives. Max Ernst, having
eluded the Gestapo in France, was not only briefly interned on Ellis Island but
later arrested on suspicion of being a Gestapo spy. When André Masson
arrived in New York a customs agent found among his effects a collection of
erotic drawings. Eroticism happened to be an underlying trait of Masson's
work, but the official pronounced them pornographic and confiscated
those he did not tear up. The émigrés were criticized for being cliquey, but
they clung to one another because they were friends and spoke the same
language in every sense of the phrase. To many Americans, they seemed snobbish because they were sophisticated and worldly. Most exiles did not feel
themselves self-appointed anythings. They were trying to salvage their lives
and their work. In fleeing, they had left family, friends, familiar places – almost
everything – behind. What they did carry with them was the humiliation of
France's terrible defeat. The exiles had to cope with language difficulties,
money difficulties, legal difficulties, harassment by immigration authorities,
not to mention loneliness and the fear they might never return to their homes.
If noses did turn up it was at the American nosh.

The exiles simply wanted to carry on carrying on with what they had been
doing. But what they were also doing – unintentionally – was providing
answers and stimulus to American painters who were at the time questioning
everything. Before the war the Americans had seen the works of European
artists; now they met their creators – having eaten the pâté, they now met the
geese. 'It was the very catalyst they needed', as Solomon observed, 'to take their
own work beyond the cornball style of social realism.'

There were various types of encounters. Art reviews and publications,
including a variety of new critical journals such as the Surrealist *View* and
Breton's even more Surrealist *VVV*, offered intellectual contact. One-man
shows and general exhibitions in galleries like the Pierre Matisse Gallery and
Art of This Century did the same in a different way. But most important were
social encounters. The art historian Robert Lebel explained why:

Everybody met everybody. The influence was collective and this is how
it spread. Each one met someone through another one. The Reises had a party
at least once a month; everyone met at Peggy Guggenheim's parties – Pollock,
Baziotes and Rothko; the Janises invited all of us and there was an open

house at the Askews every Sunday. Later the Americans hid their Surrealist paintings, but when we saw Pollock during the war he was like a little boy in front of Max Ernst.

In his autobiography Ernst describes how he showed young Americans the way to imitate his Surrealist painting technique.

Tie an empty tin can to the end of a piece of string one or two yards long, drill a small hole in its bottom, fill the can with paint. Allow the can to swing to and fro on the end of the string over a canvas lying flat on the ground. Guide the can by movements of the arms, the shoulders and the whole body. In this way amazing lines will trickle onto the canvas. And then the game of free association can begin.

Ernst portrayed the technique of drip painting in his *Young Man Intrigued by the Flight of a Non-Euclidean Fly*, an early version of which Pollock had seen and admired. 'I recognize that the important painting of recent years was done in France', Pollock remarked. 'Modernist paintings simply passed by the great majority of American painters. Also, the fact that many good modernist European painters are here right now is very important, because they brought with them a certain understanding of the problems of modern painting. I am particularly interested in their concept of the unconscious as a source of art.' In this way automatism, the son of Surrealist automatic writing, became the father of what Harold Rosenberg baptized 'Action Painting'.

Some believe Roberto Matta's influence was even more direct. It was he who during the summer of 1941 introduced the Surrealist technique of psychic automatism to Robert Motherwell. Motherwell frankly acknowledged that it was this novel mode of painting that had liberated in him something authentic and inspired. The Surrealists, he said in a letter to William Carlos Williams, 'seemed to understand empirically the solution . . . to those problems of how to free the imagination in concrete terms, which are so baffling to an American.' It was partly through Motherwell that Pollock was drawn into Surrealist automatism as a new approach to painting. Meeting Matta decades later, Peter Busa said, 'It was your presence, Matta, that personalized Surrealism for us. . . . Surrealism was a fuse that lit up the American scene.'

In the view of that quondam primate of art critics, Clement Greenberg, there was yet a more important influence. In his words, 'André Masson's presence on this side of the Atlantic during the war was of inestimable benefit to us. . . . He, more than anyone else, anticipated the new abstract painting, and I don't believe he has received enough credit for it.' All in all, as Ethel Baziotes said of the exiles, 'Their being here was overpowering. Its importance cannot be overestimated. These were fascinating men with highly perfected artistic ways.' Sawin's judicious conclusion is that while there was no single painter and no single technique that held sway, the Europeans together were the catalyst for a process that culminated in new modes of painting and specifically in Abstract Expressionism.

Although no one seemed conscious of it at the time, two revolutionary developments were intersecting. Cut off from its roots, the École de Paris was enjoying its last brilliant flowering and was being succeeded by the first specifically, uniquely American art – the so-called First New York School. In this way, it has been said, Europe's past was projected into America's future. But the French were not the only exiles. From Germany had come such figures as Albers, Feininger, Hofmann, Gropius, Moholy-Nagy and Mies van der Rohe. Thus did New York become by the end of the war what Paris had been before – the centre of an Arts International.

CHAPTER 8

ENIGMA VARIATIONS

On a Saturday afternoon in mid-January 1947 one of the most famous pianists of the century walked onto the stage of the Théâtre des Champs-Élysées and began playing Chopin's *Sonate funèbre*. Suddenly from the second balcony someone shouted, 'Do you dedicate that to your friend Hitler?' Sympathetic cheers and hostile jeers brought the recital to an end. The scandal was by no means the first in the musical history of Paris. Wagner's *Tannhäuser* in 1861 and Stravinsky's *Sacre du Printemps* in 1913 come easily to mind. But in this case the ruckus was over a person, not a work. The person was Alfred Cortot and the uproar was not because of his performance at the keyboard but because of his activities during the Occupation. So mortified was he by the protest that he fled Paris and moved to Switzerland. He never got over the humiliation. A friend has said he would sooner have bitten off his tongue than talk about it.

Born in Switzerland into a genteel working-class family, Cortot began studying piano in 1882 at the age of five. Despite having a weak hand, he made such progress that the family moved to Paris so that he could study at the Conservatory. He was admitted at the age of nine and in the graduation competition ten years later won first prize – plus the gift of a piano. Around this time, like most other French *mélomanes* he fell under the spell of Wagner and was introduced at Bayreuth by one of his teachers. In 1898 he visited Wahnfried and played for Cosima Wagner, who was sufficiently impressed to appoint him initially as a choral coach and for the following two years as an assistant conductor, under Mottl and Richter. With this experience he returned to Paris and in 1902 conducted the first concert performances of *Götterdämmerung* and *Tristan*. His Wagnermania got out of hand, however, and the following year he did something unforgiveable. He conducted excerpts of *Parsifal*, a work which at that time it was illegal to perform outside

Bayreuth. Cosima was furious at what she regarded as his treachery, and he was barred from the Festival for ever. Cortot was so devastated that he stopped conducting for a time and devoted himself to the piano. But like many others, he was to be always marked by the Bayreuth experience. 'On leaving Bayreuth I had the feeling of taking with me something very precious', he said a half-century later. That something was a Germanophilia so intense that it became part of the reason for the fiasco at the Théâtre des Champs-Élysées.

Although known outside France simply as a pianist, Cortot was a tremendously driven man. Among his activities he conducted, taught at the Conservatory and was a director at the École Normale de Musique, of which he was a founder. In 1907, with Pablo Casals and Jacques Thibaud, he formed a famous trio. He also took time off to enter into a cynical marriage with a woman, eight years older, from a wealthy intellectual Jewish family. The marriage – which even his starry-eyed biographer, Bernard Gavoty, admitted was 'based more on reason than on passion' – helped his career by elevating him socially and financially. At the time of the First World War he was put in charge of French cultural propaganda abroad. The interwar period saw him reach his artistic zenith. He came to be regarded as one of the greatest pianists of his time and had a significant, if controversial, influence on piano interpretation in France and abroad. In addition to his teaching and related activities, he gave an average of 110 performances a year, adding up to more than six thousand during his whole career. 'I shall never stop', he said to a friend towards the end of his life. His ardent wish was to drop dead while performing. Linked to this hyperactivity was a hyper-ambitiousness that Casals labelled 'fanatical'. Boundless energy plus boundless ambition added up to the second element that led to the Paris scandal.

With the outbreak of war in 1939 Cortot cancelled all his concert engagements and found a position in the Beaux-Arts administration, dreaming up ways to improve troop morale. As the Wehrmacht approached Paris, he followed the government to Bordeaux and on to Vichy. There, as the archives reveal, he readily fell in with the reactionary political and cultural tone of the new regime and became one of the most ardent Pétainists – or, perhaps more accurately, Lavalists – of all the notable cultural figures. Photographs of him show an extremely controlled man. This discipline was transformed into an organizational talent quickly recognized by authorities, who placed him in the Ministry of Education and Youth. A short time later he was given a seat on the National Council. While this was a powerless conclave of respectable figures designed to give the Vichy government a benign face, real power came to him in early 1941 when he persuaded officials to give him broad control of French musical life. He became the first French artist ever to hold government office.

His political design was simple. Music should play an important role in the new France; the state should control every aspect of musical life from performances to publications; Cortot should be the person in charge. He revelled in his authority. Studies by Myriam Chimènes and the scholar-film composer François Porcile document how conscientiously he took his responsibilities and how intrusive his interventions increasingly became. The decisive step was to require anyone who wanted to practise his profession to be tested and licensed. He passed this off as a way of raising standards of performance and instruction. While there was undoubtedly some truth in this, he had two ulterior motives. As in the Third Reich, licensing was a perfect means of excluding racial and political undesirables from performing and teaching. Audition panels could, if they wished, give such examinees low scores, making it appear they had eliminated themselves. By early 1944 25,000 musicians had been licensed. In the absence of records, how many Jews and other objectionables had been excluded is impossible to know. But certainly Francis Poulenc was in no doubt about the effect. 'The absence of war prisoners and Jews', he wrote to his fellow composer Charles Koechlin, 'has been a serious blow to music.'

The second effect of the licensing stratagem was to give Cortot such power as to make him in effect musical dictator of France. To formalize his status, Abel Bonnard, the fascist education minister, endowed Cortot with a title so flowery it would have raised eyebrows in the ancien régime of the Dual Monarchy – *conseiller technique pour l'étude des questions d'ordre professionnel et corporatif susceptible d'assurer le développement du goût musical en France*. Cortot lost no time in translating this into institutional terms. His model was the Reich Music Chamber that Hitler had established in 1934 to control musical life in the Third Reich. In due course Vichy established just such a body, known as the Cortot Committee. Following the German example, it covered itself with respectability by making almost every prominent figure in French musical life the head of some sham 'commission'. By the time the Cortot Committee got going, however, Vichy was going out of business.

For the student of artists' behaviour in dictatorships, it is interesting to compare Cortot during the Occupation with Wilhelm Furtwängler and Richard Strauss during the Third Reich. While always loudly insisting they were immaculately apolitical, all three were staunchly conservative. Though by no means fascist, they were fed up with the messiness of democracy and welcomed authoritarian government. Dictatorship also offered the potential of advancing their personal interests. Strauss envisaged himself as Führer of music, deciding what should be performed. Furtwängler wanted to be Führer of how it was to be performed. Cortot had dreams of influencing both. All three wanted the state, in the person of themselves, to have the authority to license musicians, to control what was performed, and to have a central agency – in the German case, the Reich Music Chamber of which Strauss was the head – to oversee musical life. In a word, all three wanted power. But there was one important difference. Furtwängler and Strauss never got it and Cortot did. But not enough. His great dream was to follow the example of Ignace Paderewski, the pianist who was interwar president of Poland, and become French head of state.

Despite his heavy administrative commitments, Cortot by no means gave up recitals and recordings. His first post-armistice appearance was in an all-French programme at the Paris Opera in November 1941. The following month he participated in a Mozart festival organized by the Wehrmacht's Propaganda Department. He played and conducted in Vichy and other cities in France, as well as in Switzerland and North Africa. When Sacha Guitry brought out a glitzy book celebrating Pétain's coming to power, Cortot contributed an article on Berlioz. More compromisingly, he played an important role in the Breker jamboree in May 1942, when he performed and was an honoured guest at all the related celebratory events. He even had Breker sculpt his bust. Throughout those years his prestige lent prestige to many *collabo* social events. Cortot greatly enjoyed the company of important Nazis, as a few casual lines from Speer's diaries make clear. 'After these dinners we sometimes went up to the small top-floor apartment of Alfred Cortot. . . . Cortot played Chopin or Debussy.' 'At the Coq Hardi [the favourite restaurant of the Wehrmacht top brass] I had spent pleasant evenings with Cortot, Vlaminck, Despiau and other French artists.'

After exposing himself discreetly, Cortot then did the full monty. In June 1942 he went to Berlin to play the Schumann piano concerto – one of his specialities – with the Berlin Philharmonic under Furtwängler. On returning he was fêted by the Groupe Collaboration, whose new head was the director of the Opéra-Comique, Max d'Ollone. 'The music section of the Groupe Collaboration has the duty,' d'Ollone announced grandly, 'the agreeable duty of honouring eminent artists whose current activities work to the great benefit of Franco-German rapprochement.' Then, turning to Cortot, he added, 'Mon cher Alfred Cortot, you have certainly aided the cause of collaboration in accepting the invitation . . . to be the first French artist to appear before the German public since the armistice.' To this Cortot responded, 'Collaboration . . . in the sphere of music between Germany and France is something I have been engaged in for more than forty years, despite events in other spheres which oppose it.' So pleased was he with the warm reception that he returned five months later to perform in Berlin, Hamburg, Leipzig, Munich, Stuttgart and Frankfurt. Plans for a tour in the autumn of the following year were cancelled, possibly because the massive bombing of German cities made it dangerous.

Shortly after the liberation of Paris, Cortot was arrested. Claude Delvincourt, head of the Conservatory, along with other friends secured his release three days later. In mid-October he appeared before a tribunal to defend himself against charges relating both to his work as a Vichy official and to such compromising activities as his German concerts. In his defence he argued that his perform-ances in Germany had not been for money or self-advancement and that he had also taken time to perform before war prisoners. He further claimed that through Ambassador Abetz he had obtained the release of thirty musicians who were prisoners and had protected both Jews and members of the Resistance. 'I have given fifty years of my life to the service of the cause of France,' he declared, 'and when I was asked to help my comrades I felt I could not refuse.' And then came the inevitable 'I never concerned myself with politics'. With that, a further similarity between Cortot, Strauss and Furtwängler emerged. Even after it was all over, they not only adamantly refused to express any regret but they remained to the end of their days unshakeable in the conviction that they had done nothing to regret.

In the end Cortot was suspended from professional activity for a year, retroactive to 1 April 1945 – in effect a ban of four months. And promptly, four months later, he went on concert tours that took him to various cities in France, Switzerland, Britain and Italy. Not until January 1947 was he finally invited to appear in Paris in a concert with the orchestra of the Conservatory under the direction of André Cluytens. The programme was to have opened with Bach's *Orchestral Suite No. 1* and conclude with Debussy's *La Mer*; between the two works Cortot was to perform Schumann's piano concerto. However, shortly before the concert was to begin the musicians' union instructed its members not to perform with him because of his 'attitude during the years of occupation'. Cortot responded by suggesting that in that case he should appear alone and play his own programme. And so at the first concert on Saturday morning, the orchestra opened with Bach. When Cortot appeared, the musicians left the stage, followed by Cluytens who refused to shake hands as they passed. Defiantly Cortot played to both cheers and jeers. At the afternoon concert the orchestra decided to perform both its works straightaway and then vanish. It was on that occasion, as he began playing the *Sonate funèbre*, that someone shouted about Hitler and set off the rumpus. The following afternoon the orchestra played its two works without disturbance, but when Cortot appeared the audience exploded and the concert ended in pandemonium. Sixty years after the event a young member of the audience was still pained to recall the 'incredible violence', the 'indescribable tumult' and the 'odious shouts'. And as Cortot's car drove away, someone spat at the window by his seat.

Prouder even than most proud men, Cortot was so shocked that he imme-diately withdrew to Switzerland and refused to set foot in France until 1949. In that year he went back to Paris and performed – this time at the Salle Pleyel – in a Chopin commemorative concert that was a triumph. Once again he was a national treasure. And so it was that, within a few years, his past was not only forgiven and forgotten but had become a distasteful subject. Cortot's playing, however, was now feeble. Despite appeals from friends, he continued to perform – frequently in Germany – until 1958, when he appeared for a final time at the Prades Festival. His romantic wish to die on stage during a performance was not granted. He died in 1962 in bed.

Cortot should have ended his days before a firing squad. That is, if more than a dozen writers deserved to be found guilty of treason and sentenced to death or life imprisonment for supporting the Germans in their writings, then Cortot merited a similar sentence for volunteering to perform fifteen times as a guest of the government of the Third Reich, for celebrating the propagandistic Breker exhibition, for being pals with prominent Nazi bigwigs such as Speer, for writing a German-friendly article in a German-sponsored publication and otherwise engaging in publicity on behalf of a country with which France was at war. His celebration of collaboration was not merely voluntary but deliberate, gratuitous and purposive.

After the war Cortot insisted that his friendship with the Invader was not disloyal. As he explained to Bernard Gavoty, his biographer – actually, hagiographer – he did not feel himself properly French. Though his father was a French citizen, his mother came from Switzerland, where he himself had lived for the first six years of his life. It was towards Germany, a land of poets and thinkers and above all composers and musicians, that he looked. Germans reciprocated. He was praised in some circles as the greatest pianist of his time and certainly the leading interpreter of Schumann. When the war began in 1939, according to Gavoty, 'in his heart of hearts he would have preferred a union between France and Germany over an alliance with America'. Symptomatically, at the height of the war, in the autumn of 1942, Cortot wrote an article for the German publication *Cahiers franco-allemands*. In it he praised the musical interchange between France and Germany going back to the Middle Ages with the minnesingers and troubadours, and pointed to this as a model for the future. Harmless? Not really. Under the circumstances the message was propagandistic, the more so since that particular issue of *Cahiers* also carried a message from the Führer to the French people and two letters from the Führer to Pétain, along with an article by Fabre-Luce.

So while Cortot may have been an opportunist, more was he a true believer, a convinced *collabo* who wanted France to be part of a German-led united Europe. But could he have been as *weltfremd* as he pretended? Could he have been unaware that there was no freedom in the Third Reich? Having a Jewish wife, was he not troubled by the persecution and deportation of Jews? He was certainly aware of these since he defended himself at his trial by pressing the dubious claim that he had helped certain Jews in the music field. Another of his exculpatory assertions was that during his trip around Germany he had performed in the stalags of war prisoners. But what did he think about a million-and-a-half men living in the seriously disgusting conditions of a prison camp and forced to do hard labour for the Third Reich? How could he face them? Even the painters who had toured Germany and encountered the prisoners working on the railway line had had the decency to feel mortified.

Despite his various acts of collaboration, Cortot was punished with the merest tap on the wrist. Germaine Lubin was arrested five times, spent months in appalling prisons while awaiting various trials, saw her Paris apartment and her country château confiscated, was sacked for life from the Paris Opera, accused of treason and imprisoned for three years and banished from France. What could she possibly have done to deserve a punishment so savage?

Lubin's singing career began, conventionally, at the Paris Conservatory, where she was, unconventionally, a favourite of Gabriel Fauré, who was then director. With some prescience, he called her 'ma belle statue' and told her, 'I love your voice, it is like no other.' She made her debut in 1912 at the Opéra-Comique as Antonia in *The Tales of Hoffmann*. In 1924 she was invited to sing at the Paris Opera, and for the next twenty years she was the company's most admired dramatic soprano. She had a varied repertory and sang the first French performances of Strauss's *Ariadne auf Naxos, Der Rosenkavalier* and *Elektra*. But it was in Wagner's operas that she felt most at home, emotionally and musically. Her passion for them began at a performance of *Tristan und Isolde* not long after she had left the Conservatory. It was a transcendental experience and her biographer, Nicole Casanova, suggests that she spent the remainder of her life searching for her Tristan. Nature suited her art. Imposing and tall – statuesque was a frequent description – with blond hair and blue eyes, she seemed predestined for the role of Wagnerian heroine. After advancing through the repertoire of Romantic works – Senta, Elisabeth, Elsa and Eva – she reached the *Walküre* Brünnhilde in 1928 and finally, in 1930, Isolde. After that it was Kundry with Lauritz Melchior and in 1933 she was the *Götterdämmerung* Brünnhilde.

Her private life was less successful. In 1913 she married and in 1926 divorced Paul Géraldy, a poet and playwright. She then entered into a deeply neurotic relationship with Jacques Moreau, a co-director at Larousse, that lasted until 1941. By far her most remarkable attachment was to Philippe Pétain, whom she met a short time after the armistice in 1918 during a singing engagement with a French veterans' group. According to Casanova, the Marshal professed his love and asked her to marry him. Although she turned him down, they remained friends ever after. At their last encounter, in 1939, when he was ambassador to Spain and she was in Madrid to sing, he is said to have told her,

'You know that I love you still.' To the end of her days she regarded him as a great knight, the saviour of France, in whom she professed total confidence and whom she revered as 'the greatest man I ever knew'.

It was not Pétain who caused her downfall but Hitler. A quarter of a century after the war, a plaintive Winifred Wagner was still confessing remorse for setting it in train. 'I always tell myself that everything that happened to her after the war was my fault. I am the one who introduced her to Hitler. . . . But how could I have foreseen it?' The tragedy began in 1938 when Lubin was invited to sing Sieglinde in Berlin at the State Opera. After the performance the French ambassador, André François-Poncet, went to her dressing room with Hermann Göring in tow. 'Sie sind wunderbar', the Reich Marshal told her. With that began her involvement with the Nazi leadership. It was not only Göring she impressed that night but also the State Opera's director, Heinz Tietjen, who signed her up on the spot to sing Kundry at Bayreuth that summer. Even before then she had yet another triumph. In May Furtwängler and the Berlin State Opera arrived in Paris to put on a great propaganda show of German culture. The opera was *Tristan*, and Isolde was Lubin.

Wagner can corrupt and Wagner at Bayreuth can corrupt absolutely. So it was for Lubin. Her performance in *Parsifal* was a tremendous hit with Hitler and Winifred Wagner, who swore they had never heard the second act so magnificently sung. Hitler found her personally enchanting as well. At the post-performance reception at Wahnfried he summoned her to dine on his right and was so smitten that he commented, 'Madam, you are a seductress.' The two of them later retired to the salon and a photograph records a beaming Lubin sitting next to the Führer while other guests look on with delight. Afterwards she told a German journalist, 'I had a marvellous time at Wahnfried and found in Winifred Wagner a marvellous German woman. But my most remarkable meeting was with the first man of your Reich. . . . I was amazed to see a man – someone who, through his actions, has left such a strong imprint on the history of the world – yet is so simple and cordial.' She was snared.

After singing Sieglinde and Kundry at the Berlin State Opera in early 1939, she returned to Bayreuth that summer for *Tristan*. On this occasion Hitler went backstage and, taking her hands in his, is said to have exclaimed, 'Never in my life have I seen or heard such an Isolde' – a remarkable statement considering that he had attended more than a hundred performances of the work. In her unreliable memoirs Friedelind Wagner claimed that Tietjen had engaged her 'for "political" reasons' – presumably to please Hitler – and had commented to Winifred, 'She is not up to Bayreuth standards, but she is a very beautiful woman.' If he did say that, he did Lubin a great injustice. 'She was', in the words of Robert Tuggle, the Metropolitan Opera's historian, 'a magnificent singer with a beautiful voice, not quite the powerhouse customary in

Wagner but musical in a way that only Flagstad was.' And indeed it was Kirsten Flagstad who, impressed by their performances together in Zurich, had recommended her to the Met. The Opera company took the hint and signed her up for the 1940–41 season. She was to sing in its first-ever performance of Gluck's *Alceste*, a role for which she was celebrated. Lubin was the most important singer announced for that season and her picture was in all the New York papers.

Meanwhile, as the Wehrmacht approached Paris in 1940, Lubin escaped to the Auvergne. Soon after the armistice she returned to Paris and on 28 October sang in *Fidelio*. Early in January she cancelled plans for her debut at the Met, with the implausible claim that Abetz would not give her a passport. Throughout the Occupation years she continued to sing and was a great hit with Wehrmacht officers. Her performance of the Marschallin in *Rosenkavalier* in February 1941 so bedazzled Colonel Hans Speidel that he insisted on meeting her. They developed a friendship that lasted to the end of their lives. In April 1942, when he was transferred to the eastern front, Speidel invited his closest friends to a farewell party at which Lubin sang Schubert's 'Let Us Make Peace'.

One of the musical – and propaganda – highlights of the Occupation years was a performance of *Tristan* by the Berlin State Opera in May 1941. Mounting it was a gigantic undertaking, which required moving the entire staging and a complement of 250 from Berlin to Paris. Max Lorenz and Lubin sang, as they had two years before in Bayreuth. It opened on the anniversary of Wagner's birth and was repeated the next day at a closed performance for the Wehrmacht, again attended by Winifred Wagner. In his memoirs, Speidel described it as 'a great success' for German culture – the whole point of the venture, of course.

Throughout the Occupation years Winifred Wagner and Lubin continued to correspond. After her son was taken prisoner in 1940, Lubin wrote to Winifred, who turned to Hitler to arrange his release. The courier of their letters was a naval captain, Hans Joachim Lange. He was said to have been smitten by Lubin and for the next four years he was apparently her closest friend. It was through Lange that she was introduced to a number of high-ranking Wehrmacht officers, whom she entertained at her château near Tours. She continued to sing – Isolde in Zurich in June 1941 – to broadcast on Radio-Paris and to make recordings. She was rehearsing *Alceste* as Allied forces approached Paris in the summer of 1944.

On 26 August, the day of the Liberation of Paris, at the very time de Gaulle was marching down the Champs-Élysées amid a jubilant crowd, Lubin had already been under arrest for several hours. According to the terse entry in her diary: 'I return home after ten hours of detention. Arrested this morning by several Free French.' The arrest can't have come as a surprise because she took with her a list of persons she had 'saved' along with some of their letters. After ten hours, her lawyer arranged for her release and escorted her home.

Several days later the *épuration* of the Paris Opera began. It put her in mind of the French Revolution and, as her biographer comments, she was as blithely oblivious of the popular mood as any aristocrat in 1793. '*Dieu*, how patriotic the Opera has become!' she commented with heavy irony to her diary. 'These immaculate artists!' Disgust and outrage were her predominant emotions then and in the months to come. Contempt as well – contempt for the repulsive riffraff who were detaining her. 'The whole affair is as usual in the hands of the obsequious servant class and intriguers. . . . Just a lot of garbage!' What had she done wrong, she wondered. She had not denounced anyone to the Gestapo. She owed the Germans neither her fame nor her fortune. No fewer than twenty Frenchmen had been saved thanks to her. Was it not simply that people were jealous?

Her ordeal was just beginning. Her diary entry for 8 September reads:

Eight days ago I was arrested for the second time. For ten hours I waited on a leather bench with no back, surrounded by dirty men with week-old beards, concierges, laundrywomen, prostitutes. In the corners, garbage was mixed with the hair of women who had had their heads shaved the night before. During the course of the day another four were shaved completely bald except for one on whom, for laughs, they had left a tuft in the middle of her head which hung down like the mandarin's pigtail – so dreadful as to make one shiver. After the fourth woman was shaved, I began trembling in uncontrollable fear of being suddenly delivered into the hands of one of these fanatics and ending up bald.

That afternoon was nothing compared to what followed. Pencilled notes written in prison on small scraps of paper record the events of the next two months. They breathe the atmosphere of the Terror. And, in fact, not since the Revolution had Paris prisons been filled with so many celebrities. On arriving, Lubin had spied someone she knew. 'I greet her and she introduces me to her daughter, the Duchess of C.B. [Countess Cossé-Brissac], like me not knowing why she was arrested. She wonders whether her friendship with the Countess de C. might have aroused suspicion.' No tumbrels, instead there was:

The police van – yes! Like criminals. It is impossible to imagine that police van! I thought I would suffocate in that small metal box. I arrive at 9. I see Fabre-Luce and call to him. We hug and when he goes on his way he says, 'Think of Fidelio!' A woman comes to me, fitted out as though she was going camping. It is the Marquise de P[olignac]. A policeman recognizes me.

'Courage, Madame Lubin; we'll soon be applauding you at the Opera, you'll see.'

Mme de B., Mme J. and I are taken to a cell, apparently the last remaining one, 3 metres long and 2 metres wide, with one straw mattress and one blanket for the three of us. There we lived for three days! And in what hygienic conditions! Two of us slept on the floor while the third tried to sleep on the straw mattress. Horrible!

12 September. Day after day passes and I do not even bother to look at the time. Night, day, everything without shape, without sense, without light, inert, stupid, bleak. . . .

16 Sept. I have not even gone out for six days. I prefer to be a recluse than to have anything to do with this awful bunch, in a courtyard so tiny that it is impossible to take a step – cooped up like sheep.

At some point – she probably did not know the date – she was transferred to Drancy, a prison that had been used by the Germans as a concentration camp.

Ugliness, dirt, selfishness, cruelty, all mingle. I am in my little corner and intend to remain there. It is very cold. . . . As every day, I get up at dawn, exhausted by a bad night. Washing with others in freezing water. The indecency of it. Odious people, nauseating smells, coffee tasting like soup from the night before. I get dressed quickly to escape the putrid sweeping up, the screaming women, the sound of water, the disgusting smells – I run outside over steps covered with filth. . . . Drancy is an immense material and moral garbage heap. I live in a state of perpetual nausea.

And on it went. From time to time it seemed as though she was about to be released. 'Princess Z. came running to me, "Quick, quick, dear, they are summoning you, certainly to let you out." ' Instead she was taken to Frenes. 'Frenes! How to describe the agonizing, the unspeakable impression of this gigantic prison?' When she was made to undress before all the other women and give up everything – watch, papers, face powder – she for the first time broke down and cried. The final leaves of her prison notes record her humiliation and physical suffering. Three weeks later, on 3 November, she was released. Not long afterwards she read that *Boris Godunov* was to be performed at the Opera; in the role that would have been hers, another was to sing. Her greatest anguish of all, according to Casanova, was the deterioration of her voice.

Still worse was to come. Legal action was pending in which she was under suspicion of nothing less than treason. On 3 January 1945 that charge was dismissed, leading her to hope she might soon return to the stage. In early March, however, she learned to her shock that she was still under investigation and at the end of the month received notice that she was dismissed from the Paris Opera with immediate effect and without compensation. A few weeks later she was ordered to appear for trial in a civil court before a jury. Although that case was postponed, she found herself – because of her château in the area – under the jurisdiction of the courts in Tours and Orléans. Early in 1946 she was arrested on suspicion of having denounced her gardener to the Germans. Yet again she was back in prison. 'The most horrifying prison imaginable. A military prison. A cell 2 metres by 2.5 metres, a high ceiling, a skylight at the top, bars, filth, dust, foul odours, a toilet never cleaned. Three women in this cell intended for one individual.' Her notes go on and on in that vein. There she remained from 21 May until 6 June. It was around this time that she read Friedelind Wagner's comment that she had been taken on at Bayreuth to please Hitler, not because of her voice. This may have hurt her more than all the months in prison.

In the face of her disgrace, friends and acquaintances responded as most friends and acquaintances normally do – deserting her, declining to testify on her behalf, refusing to answer her letters. She had never had many friends and was now utterly bereft. Only her ex-husband, the kindly Paul Géraldy, gave her support. In December 1946 her case finally went to trial. There were various charges, among them that she had entertained Lange and other German officers at her château and accepted gifts from them and that she had asked Hitler to release her son from a prison camp. 'Except for having eaten the flesh of children, there was nothing I was not accused of,' she complained without overly much exaggeration in an interview years later with Lanfranco Rasponi. Her social skills did not include friendliness with those she considered her inferiors, and at the trial she made her feelings known with an imperious fervour that irritated judge and jury alike. Some jury members are said to have favoured sentencing her to twenty years of hard labour. The judge's decision was only slightly less severe – the loss of her rights of citizenship for the remainder of her life, the seizure of her assets and banishment from France for twenty years. Eventually the sentence was reduced. But when the Geneva Opera invited her to perform in *Tannhäuser*, the French ambassador mounted such opposition that the offer was withdrawn. It was the end of her opera career. 'She wanted to die', according to Casanova.

Why was she treated with such wanton cruelty? Interviewed years later she said:

I suffered an enormous injustice. They curtailed my career by ten years – my own people! The fact is that I knew some of the Germans who came to Paris during the Occupation. This gave my enemies a chance to satisfy their envy. If I saw Germans in Paris – and they had been more than kind to me

– it was to save my compatriots. It was my way of serving my country. . . .
Nobody knows how many prisoners I had released.

The same old arguments. But not the same old sentence. Surviving the *épuration* was a matter of luck, connections, location of the court and so on as much
as of past actions. Lubin was unfortunate on all counts. The question nonetheless remains why she was punished so draconically compared to almost everyone
else in the cultural field, writers apart. Could her being a woman have been a
consideration? Was it acceptable for a man like Cortot to have important Nazis
as friends but unacceptable for a woman? And Cortot was not the only important male collaborator in the music field to be treated leniently. During the
Occupation Pierre Fournier had given three concerts in Germany. He was
just as much a convinced *collabo* as Cortot and, unlike Lubin, very active in
Parisian collaborationist social circles. It was at private concerts arranged by
Marie-Louise Bousquet that he came to know German officials. And when
Casals left the trio with Cortot and Thibaud, he was replaced by Fournier,
making it a trio of arch-*collabos*.

When Lubin learned that Jacques Rouché, head of the Paris Opera, had also
been dismissed from his position, she wrote him a note of consolation. Both of
them were victims of human baseness, she said. In fact, Rouché was very nearly
not let go because he very nearly did not hold the position in the first place. As
he learned while sitting in a café in the Midi town of Cahors a few days after
the armistice, the head of the Opera Ballet, Serge Lifar, had remained in Paris
and was lobbying the Germans to replace the man who had appointed him ten
years before.

   Now seventy-eight years old, Rouché had been in charge of the Opera – both
as administrator and artistic director – since 1914. To preside over that institution during two wars and a period of interwar political turmoil was challenge
enough. But thanks to his managerial talents and artistic devotion, he had
managed to turn it from a socialite gathering place into a serious operatic institution with high professional standards. Upon the outbreak of war in 1939,
instead of following the example of Covent Garden, he kept the opera going,
despite the loss of personnel and other wartime difficulties. As a gesture of patriotism, he removed most German operas from the repertoire and cancelled a
contract with Furtwängler. Otherwise performances went on right until 10 June,
when the opera house closed with *The Magic Flute*. With the Wehrmacht now in
sight of Paris, Rouché and his company retreated as fast as possible.

   On arriving in France, German officials made clear that it was their intention
to occupy the country not only militarily but culturally as well. This required
breaching the Maginot Line of French musical life and seizing its key stronghold,

the Paris Opera. They regarded the Opera both as a site to display German cultural superiority and as a centre to entertain military personnel. Naturally they wanted it to be in the hands of an emollient figure in whom they had confidence. Rouché was not that person. But he could not be easily dislodged. Despite his long connection with the now-disgraced Third Republic, he was a man of undoubted administrative ability and for twenty-five years had unselfishly devoted himself and a considerable personal fortune to the institution. He could also count on the support of friends like Germaine Lubin, with her connections to Pétain and the Wehrmacht as well as to Hautecoeur and Carcopino, with their bureaucratic authority in Vichy. Eventually Propaganda Department officials gave in. Rouché returned to Paris with an initial two-year appointment in his pocket. The Opera and the Opéra-Comique reopened and remained in French control. Rouché had to make concessions in the years to follow, but he never wavered from his paramount aim of flying the French cultural flag in the face of the Invader. The physical flag that adorned the Paris Opera's ornate edifice, however, displayed a swastika.

On 24 August the Opera celebrated its reopening with a gala performance of Berlioz's *Damnation of Faust* graced by the presence of the German military commander Otto von Stülpnagel. From that moment it became the great showcase of collaboration. Here there was a greater opportunity than at theatres, cinemas or museums for the Occupiers to demonstrate their presence and mingle with the Occupied. Jean Guéhenno noticed how the Germans had – literally and symbolically – insinuated themselves: 'Every evening at the Opera, they tell me, very great numbers of German officers are present. During the intermissions, following the custom in their country, they march in ranks of two or three around the foyer, all in the same direction. The French, in spite of themselves, unconsciously, join the procession and fall in step. The boots impose their rhythm.'

The Paris Opera and the Opéra-Comique were enormously popular. The Germans went there to be entertained, the French went there to forget the Occupation. Attendance was excellent throughout those years; indeed, performances were often sold out. Large blocks of seats had to be reserved for the Wehrmacht – in the case of the Opéra-Comique, three-quarters of the best places, and at the Opera the figure was initially 20 per cent, with all other tickets available to military personnel at half-price. It has been calculated that Germans took more than half the seats throughout the period. As time passed Occupation officials became increasingly exigent, making it more and more difficult for the French public to attend. Rouché did his best to hold the line, but was constantly on the defensive. By November 1943 the Wehrmacht claimed 639 seats at the Opera and 390 at the Opéra-Comique – in both cases, one-third of capacity – and wanted still more. Some performances – such as of *Die Fledermaus*, starring Elisabeth Schwarzkopf – were limited exclusively to members of the Wehrmacht. Moreover, the opera house itself had to be made available to visiting German companies – from Mannheim, Cologne, Hanover and Berlin – as well as for such groups as the Vienna Boys' Choir.

Rouché was also under pressure to add German works to the repertoire. After the Opera had reopened with a piece by a French composer, it was made plain to him that a German work should follow. And so Beethoven's *Fidelio* was performed. From then on Rouché struggled to maintain a balance between French and German works. His tactic, when the Propaganda Department goaded him, was to delay as long as possible – sometimes as much as a year. In all, only four new German works made it to the stage – Pfitzner's *Palestrina*, Strauss's *Ariadne auf Naxos* and Egk's new opera, *Peer Gynt*, as well as his recently completed ballet *Joan de Zarissa*. The total number of German operas increased only slightly, to about 30 per cent of the repertoire, with Wagner's works remaining at around 7 per cent. To be sure, there was also self-censorship, as Rouché dropped plans for any number of operas that he would like to have put on but that risked disapproval. It was a thin line to tread. His colleague Henri Busser, director of the Opéra-Comique, failed. He was fired and replaced by the notorious *collabo* Max d'Ollone. Before long the dreadful d'Ollone also fell out of favour and was replaced by a retired singer, the even more devout collaborationist Lucien Moratore.

And then there was the problem of ridding the opera house of Freemasons, Jews and communists. Rouché himself had to answer the charge of being a Freemason. Although not anti-Semitic himself, he has been criticized for being overly strict in enforcing a German order to rid the Opera of Jews, some thirty in all. In any case he did his best to see that those who lost their jobs received severance pay and at the time of the Liberation were reimbursed for lost income. He also tried to secure the return of war prisoners to their old jobs.

Given the stress of working under foreign occupation, backstage discontent was inevitable. At least one Resistance group of some twenty persons took shape. They were mostly technicians, and their primary concern seems to have been their miserable salaries and administrative practices. In trying to balance the interests of the Wehrmacht, Vichy, the Opera staff and the public, Rouché found himself skating on ever-thinner ice. By early 1944 he was living professionally on borrowed time. But just before time ran out, the Allies arrived and he continued to manage the Opera and saw it reopen on 23 October.

Rouché was one of the first prominent artistic figures to be tried after the war. He was compromised not so much by his managerial work as by his wife's dalliances with the Germans. As Poulenc wrote to Milhaud, who was still in the United States, 'he was very good to the minor personnel, which largely compensates for the *imprudences mondaines* of his wife. [Roger] Désormière,

[Georges] Auric and I stand shoulder-to-shoulder in defending him.' After three interrogations he was acquitted. But the taint of having worked with the Occupation authorities was too strong and he was dismissed in April 1945. 'We all regret the departure of dear old Rouché', Poulenc commented in another letter to Milhaud. 'The *maladresses mondaines* of his wife . . . complicated the record, as you can imagine.'

Rouché would have been out in the summer of 1940 if Serge Lifar had had his way. Scarcely had the Wehrmacht installed itself in Paris than he had installed himself in the director's office and let the Germans know he was available to stay there. Such chutzpah was typical of this self-infatuated man who successfully slithered his way through life. Born in Kiev, Lifar had left the Soviet Union in 1923 to join Diaghilev's Ballets Russes. He was such a success that in 1929 Rouché engaged him as principal dancer and choreographer of the Paris Opera Ballet. Although some considered his choreography derivative and his dancing less than supreme, he was stalked by good luck. That, combined with compulsive self-promotion and undoubted talent, propelled him to be head of Ballet and chief architect of modern French dance.

Scarcely had the Wehrmacht arrived in Paris in 1940 than Lifar started putting round the story that he and Hitler had met when the latter visited the Opera during his brief early-morning tour of the city following the armistice. Perhaps he calculated that this would endear him to the German authorities, who would then appoint him head of the Opera. He may even have said that Hitler wanted this. In any case he was easily caught out and had to admit he had lied.

A liar's liar, a name-dropper's name-dropper, an opportunist's opportunist, Lifar claimed to be on excellent personal terms with just about everybody who was anybody in Europe. Mussolini was so inspired by their meeting that he was moved to confide, 'The highest tree in the world has never reached the sky.' Lifar quotes this aperçu in his autobiography, *Ma Vie*, a book that should have been entitled 'My *Fantasy* Life'. Although widely accepted as a legitimate source, it would easily qualify for a place in *The Guinness Book of Records*, in the category, if there were one, of history's most fanciful memoir.

It was not just the Duce who thought the world of him, according to Lifar. Hitler, he claimed, was so impressed with his work at the Paris Opera that he asked him to stage the victory celebration in Moscow after the capitulation of the Soviet Union. 'I invite you to witness my triumphal entry into Moscow. You will be my guide.' The lies were so ridiculous it is amazing that anyone ever swallowed them. Apparently unaware that Hitler had fallen into disrepute after 1945, Lifar continued to speak glowingly of his hours alone with the Führer. 'Only two men in my life have caressed me like this', he liked to say while stroking the arm of some nearby young man who had caught his fancy. 'Diaghilev and Hitler.'

Once Vichy insisted on keeping Rouché in his position, Lifar shifted his gaze to broader vistas. On meeting Goebbels during his visit to Paris in July 1940, the dancer took it upon himself to invite the propaganda minister to return for the gala reopening of the Paris Opera in August and added that he wanted to discuss the state of dance in Germany. This was the origin of his dream to become 'Führer of the dance', in Burrin's phrase, in a future Nazi Europe. To get what he wanted there was no limit to Lifar's sycophancy. Without a doubt his most disgraceful act occurred in September 1940 when he danced in a ceremony at the German embassy to celebrate the Wehrmacht's triumph over France.

Not long after that he had a bad moment. One morning he awoke to find that the militantly right-wing *Au Pilori* had referred to him as 'the Jew Ralif' – Lifar supposedly being an anagram of his real name. In fact, his baptismal name was Sergei Michailovich Serdkin. But how to prove he was a gentile? Accounts vary. In *Ma Vie* he claimed that he marched into the German headquarters, opened his trousers and produced priapic evidence that he was not Jewish. A document found among his surviving papers indicates a more plausible reaction. In what was apparently a draft of a letter to the German authorities, he denounced the charge as 'calumny'. He had, he pointed out, 'studied at the Imperial Lycée in Kiev, where Jews were not tolerated, [and] during the civil war he had been a volunteer in a group of young people that fought against Jews'. To erase any remaining doubt, he concluded, 'My views with respect to Jews are well known.'

Lifar prospered during the Occupation. Everyone knew he was a scoundrel, a backstabber and a cheat. But in those years he was at the height of his skills as a dancer and choreographer. Ballet evenings were highly popular with Wehrmacht audiences, accounting for more than a third of all performances at the Opera. For him the dark years were a bright time. He insisted on a hefty increase in his stipend, even though his dancers had to scrape by on a pittance. A man about town, he was always in evidence at important functions hosted by the Germans and *collabo* socialites. He was one of the select few to be invited to a reception following a meeting between Göring and Pétain in December 1941. This must have gone to his head. As that promiscuous lover of the arts and artists Misia Sert commented a short time later, 'Serge is still in a state of euphoria. He says to me: "The boss is expecting me in Munich soon." It's Hitler he's referring to.'

Almost certainly Lifar was never a believer in collaboration in the convinced way of Fabre-Luce, Drieu and Cortot. All that mattered to him were his art and his prestige. For their sake he would have made a pact with Mephistopheles without batting an eyelash. Judging by the testimony of *Ma Vie*, it seems clear that Hitler, Stalin, Goebbels, Blum, Pétain, White Russians, Red Russians, de Gaulle, Jews, anti-Semites, George VI and Pius XII were all the same to him and he loved them all. Whether it was the German Nazis, the Russian communists or the American capitalists who united Europe was a matter of indifference. Just so long as he could be in charge of ballet.

After several court hearings, Lifar's behaviour during the Occupation was judged to be so damning that he was banished from the Paris Opera for life. He then took himself to the equally compromised regime of Louis II of Monaco and danced in the Monte Carlo Ballet. But as the fizz behind the *épuration* fizzled out, he was permitted to return to Paris three years later as choreographer – not because he was now found innocent, but because few cared that he was guilty. General de Gaulle, who had rejected a petition signed by fifty-nine artists and intellectuals to spare Robert Brasillach from the firing squad, held a friendly meeting with Lifar in 1956 and on the occasion of the dancer's retirement in that year wrote him a cordial letter.

Cortot, Lubin, Lifar and Fournier were practitioners of hard collaboration. To their number must be added other notables, among them the composers Max d'Ollone, Florent Schmitt and Gustave Samazeuilh, as well as the dancer Solange Schwartz. The three composers were members of a French delegation to a Mozart Week – a.k.a. a Nazi propaganda vacation – in Vienna from 27 November to 6 December 1941. As with the writers and painters, the aim was to flatter the French guests while showing them how marvellous life was for artists in the Nazi Reich. Again, the evil genius behind the trip was Dr Goebbels. The event was camouflaged as a commemoration of the 150th anniversary of Mozart's death, but even Rebatet was frank enough to admit that it was 'more a Nazi than a Mozart pilgrimage'. The distinguished delegation included the head of the Beaux-Arts, the head of French theatres, the director of the Paris Opera, the composers Schmitt, Samazeuilh and Arthur Honegger, critics such as Rebatet and the director of Pathé-Marconi, the large recording company, Jean Bérard. The visitors met Lehár and Strauss and attended a gala dinner at the Hofburg hosted by Baldur von Schirach, the music-loving, poetry-writing governor of Vienna. For whatever reason, the junket did not provoke the same angry reaction at home as had those for writers and painters. Even so, many eyebrows were raised as a result of the gratuitous attendance of Honegger and Rouché. If it did not cause a commotion at the time, the trip was considered a serious blemish at the Liberation.

There was also soft collaboration. Popular as they were, the Opera and the Opéra-Comique did not draw crowds as large as those that swarmed to the nightclubs and music halls night after night. The French wanted to forget the Occupation, the Occupiers wanted to enjoy it. So for popular singers the dark years were anything but dark. Suzy Solidor made a fortune singing on Radio-Paris and at her nightclub, La Vie Parisienne, where she won the heart of many a Wehrmacht officer with her French version of 'Lili Marlene'. More acclaimed still was Édith Piaf. 'The Little Sparrow' was just becoming famous on the eve of the war. When the nightclubs reopened a few weeks after the armistice she was an instant hit. In no time she could demand as much for one performance as an average office worker earned in a full year. She had a number of German admirers and maintained an intimate, if apparently platonic, relationship with Colonel Waechter, head of the operational section of the Wehrmacht's Propaganda Department. Piaf used the Germans. 'She came sometimes to the hotel to check whether there were any chances of work for her colleagues or for herself', according to an official in the department. And the Germans used Piaf. 'Waechter persistently asked her to sing to the [Wehrmacht] troops, which she did on two or three occasions', according to the same official. Of this you would know nothing from the snippets of erroneous biographical data in various books and on internet sites where she is proclaimed a Resistance heroine who saved the lives of resisters and Jews and helped French war prisoners to escape. The various escape stories were a myth arising from her trip to Germany in 1943 with Charles Trenet and Maurice Chevalier, when the three of them sang to French prisoners and workers in German factories.

Chevalier was so blatantly pro-Vichy that he made a point of advertising his loyalty by being ostentatiously photographed drinking a bottle of Vichy mineral water. That along with his fraternizing with *collabo* low-life and his lucrative performances on Radio-Paris led, in the usual parlance, to 'quelques ennuis' at the time of the Liberation. Briefly locked up, he came out singing one of the great songs of the period, 'Fleur de Paris', without missing a beat or batting an eye. Charles Trenet had the nerve to claim that he had been a resister. His act of resistance? Although fluent in German, he had refused to speak the language for the duration of the Occupation. Not only that, he had suffered the humiliation of being accused of being the grandson of a rabbi – his name allegedly being an anagram of the Jewish Netter. An incensed Trenet had produced documents going back four generations to disprove the slur. Another prominent crooner, much loved by those who did not know him personally, was the Corsican Tino Rossi. His voice had entertained millions every day on Radio-Paris. Jean Guéhenno described that voice. 'It is Tino Rossi from morning to night. He vocalizes on Work, Family, the Nation, Collaboration. He says "The Marshal" the way he would say "*mon amour*".' Rossi was interned at the time of the Liberation but quickly released. Crooners and nightclub singers were too popular to be punished.

But there is another story about musical life during the Occupation, one of resistance. Some French artists there were in June 1940 who refused to accept that the war between Germany and France was over. They believed it could be continued on the cultural front with music as the principal weapon. You could say something by means of a concert or opera that you could not say in a journal, book, play or film. Music was therefore seen as a way for France to retain her self-respect and stand up to the Invader. As a member of the Resistance said after the war, 'We tried to save the essential values of French music which were being submerged under the magnificent torrent of German Romanticism. We wanted to show that we ourselves were capable of glorifying our great musicians, such as Berlioz who was taken over by the Germans and turned into a collaborator, despite himself.'

'The magnificent torrent of German Romanticism' – that was the threat. The defence was to hold fast and preserve the place of French music in the programmes of concert halls and opera houses. That is why it had been vital to keep key institutions in safe hands – Rouché at the Opera, Henri Busser at the Opéra-Comique, Delvincourt at the Conservatory and Charles Munch at the head of the Conservatory orchestra. It is also why both Paris opera houses reopened with performances of French works. So if it became necessary to exclude a few composers from programmes, to add a few German operas to the repertoire, to permit the Wehrmacht to vet programmes and take the best seats for themselves, and if Jewish instrumentalists had to be let go, all such accommodations were regrettable but necessary tactical retreats to hold the main battle line intact. To refuse these concessions would be to invite the Germans to intervene and hand over the institutions to creeps like Lifar, who would do in opera what Laval did in politics. This was what eventually happened at the Opéra-Comique, which under d'Ollone became infested with *collabo* singers and dancers.

And so, musical life went along essentially as it had before 1940. 'In the domain of music, the men in green were less terrible than they were for writers; relatively speaking, you could do what you wanted', Poulenc wrote to Milhaud shortly after the war. There was no 'Otto List' of composers and the Germans did not need to ban Berg, Bartók, Hindemith and other Modernists since their works were almost never performed in France. The Russians – Borodin, Glazunov, Moussorgsky, Tchaikovsky and Rimsky-Korsakov – were popular and continued to be played even after the German invasion of the Soviet Union, when their works were proscribed in the Third Reich. And since German classics had always been a dominant feature of French musical life, it was unnecessary for Occupation authorities to interfere with the orchestral repertoire. To be sure, they forbad works by Jewish composers. But since Mahler and Schoenberg were rarely if ever performed, the policy amounted in practice to a prohibition of Mendelssohn, Offenbach and the lesser-known Paul Dukas. Even so, the ban of Offenbach was violated every night at Paris nightspots where German patrons would have been completely disoriented had they not been entertained throughout the evening with his *French Cancan*.

What about the provinces? They were not the wasteland that has sometimes been imagined. But the story has never been told and is now lost in the mist of time. Nonetheless, it is clear that certain cities maintained a reasonable level of musical activity, in part thanks to the Germans, who established cultural centres and imported German artists to perform there. Bordeaux, for example, built on a strong local tradition of popular interest in music to offer a decent level of performances of opera, chamber music, and choral and organ works. Wehrmacht authorities contributed in their way by insisting on lengthening the musical season by two months and arranging for the Berlin Philharmonic, the pianist Wilhelm Kempf and other noted artists to perform. While no works by Modernist or Jewish composers were scheduled during those years, Occupation officials apparently did not interfere in programming. Nor was there much of an institutional purge, the sole casualty being the co-director of the Grand-Théâtre, who was deposed for being a Freemason.

At the opposite corner of the country, Strasbourg enjoyed an almost frenetic artistic life. As the capital of Alsace, which was de facto annexed to the German Reich in 1940, the city was subjected to a massive programme of Germanification – or, as the Germans thought, of re-Germanification – in which culture played the central role. Part of France until 1871, then annexed to Germany until 1919, the province now again became part of Germany. Hitler took a personal interest in the city, which he intended to turn into a beacon of German culture on the western border of the Third Reich. Significantly it was the Propaganda Ministry that was in charge of cultural indoctrination. Neither money nor resources were spared in replacing French influences. As in the days before 1918, opera enjoyed primacy. Hans Rosbaud was imported from Munster to conduct and leading stage designers were brought in to do the sets. In the theatre not only French but also American and British plays were banned, except for Shakespeare and Shaw. In the rush to get the cultural programme going – in the first season alone there were twenty-seven opera and operetta performances, a dozen plays and two ballet evenings – quality was sacrificed, with results that dismayed German critics.

In comparing the prewar repertoire of musical life in Paris with what was performed during the Occupation, what stands out is the continuity. This is evident in the programming of the Conservatory concerts that Charles Munch had begun conducting in 1939 and that had given Simone de Beauvoir so much pleasure during the phoney war. There was a bit more Bach, which needed relatively few musicians, and somewhat less Wagner, which needed a large number. There was a lot of Beethoven, but there were also plenty of contemporary French composers – even including Jacques Ibert, who had been prohibited by Vichy for a time after 1940. Surprisingly few performances reflected Vichy's predilection for the religious and traditional. Of the four symphony orchestras in Paris, it was Munch's alone that continued regularly to include Stravinsky in its repertoire. It is said that Munch took wicked pleasure in performing works that expressed subtle opposition. When the German censor forbad Mendelssohn's *A Midsummer Night's Dream*, Munch replaced it with Bizet's *Patrie*. In January 1942 he conducted the Conservatory orchestra in a programme entitled 'Composers of the Stalag'. This included a composition by Messiaen as well as works by two other prisoners. 'Musical life is very active and offers a way of forgetting the sadness of the moment', Poulenc wrote to Milhaud in July 1941. 'Charles [Munch] has had the success of Toscanini. He deserves it, because he is so stylish.'

Munch is a somewhat enigmatic figure, certainly no *collabo* but hardly a Resistance hero. When you have grown up in a province that was French, then German, then French and then German again, you are instinctively cautious and it was this Alsatian background that coloured his career. During the first quarter of his life he was German and it was in the German army that he fought in the Great War. In 1919 he automatically became French and in 1940 German again. During the Occupation he was an early member of the anti-collaborationist National Front without being active in it. He included works in his programmes by composers who were not in good odour with Vichy and did very well by Poulenc. Several of his concerts were devoted to music composed by war prisoners. But then in October 1942, for whatever reason, he conducted a concert at Vichy in 'Homage to Marshal Pétain'. While this was not collaboration with the Germans, it was highly visible collaboration with the collaborators.

The most ardent manifestation of cultural resistance in the face of the Invader occurred when the Opéra-Comique revived *Pelléas et Mélisande* shortly after the armistice on 12 September. Since its premiere in 1902 the opera had never been popular even in France and by 1940 had almost entirely disappeared from the repertoire everywhere. The prospects for the revival were hardly promising. The cast was not especially distinguished or experienced and the background of the conductor, Roger Désormière, lay in ballet music. Irène Joachim, though an intelligent soprano, was new to the role of Mélisande. That the performance became the most remarkable of the Occupation years was due to circumstances that were simultaneously emotional and political. Joachim herself explained how this came about. Walking onto the stage,

[I fell] into a panic on seeing that three-quarters of the audience were grey-green – German officers and soldiers. It was horrifying! I had to prove through Debussy's music that we were here, still capable of living for the greatest music, and to do my best for Debussy. And when Mélisande is pummelled, dragged on the ground by Golaud who seizes her by the hair and when Arkel finally says, 'If I were God, I should have pity on the hearts of men', I can say that the emotion was such that all [the French] in the audience, all the musicians and all us singers on stage – we were all in tears.

Two composers in the audience testified to the emotional impact. 'The shiver that one always feels at that point in the opera', Henri Dutilleux recalled, 'was never so intense as on that September evening in 1940 in an occupied Paris.' Georges Auric commented, 'We all listened with an emotion I cannot exactly define. Similarly, the whole audience listened with an attentiveness and a fervour that were difficult to analyse and which concluded in a thrill of grateful enthusiasm.' The opera's text – with Mélisande's first words, 'Don't touch me' – the symbolism of her imprisonment in a dark, forbidding castle and the location of the action in Allemonde – Allemagne – must have spoken to the French with a deeper meaning than ever before.

Pelléas offered throughout the Occupation years a powerful metaphor – the Verdun of the cultural war. *Ils ne passeront pas.* It was Pelléas v. Tristan, Mélisande v. Isolde. Soon thereafter a recording was made – the first of several during those years – and the twenty discs became the great operatic hit of the time. The logical next step was to induct Debussy himself into the Resistance. To celebrate the anniversary of his eightieth birthday – and the fortieth of the first performance of his opera – there was another performance of *Pelléas* in May 1942 with the same cast and conductor as in the recording. Once again it had a tremendous emotional resonance. Then, to commemorate the twenty-fifth anniversary of the composer's death the following year, the opera was yet again performed, this time with the Orchestre National, which had returned to Paris after the Wehrmacht moved into the Unoccupied Zone.

Another composer turned into a national cultural hero was Hector Berlioz. During the Occupation there were fully twenty-three performances of his *Damnation of Faust*. The work was also recorded and issued in a deluxe edition in 1942. In the same year *La Symphonie fantastique*, a film version of his life starring Jean-Louis Barrault, was released. Goebbels was furious that a movie so obviously appealing to French nationalistic feeling should have been produced and screened. The following year the composer occasioned one of the grandest musical events of the Occupation years – almost as though the intention was to blast the Wehrmacht out of Paris by sound – when his *Requiem* was performed at the Opera for the first time since its composition with the full complement the composer intended – an orchestra of 240 musicians and a chorus of 344 plus various soloists. It was conducted by Munch and, scooping the *collabo* Radio-Paris, was broadcast on Radio-Vichy.

Performing Berlioz was more of a battleground than might appear. The Germans also claimed him. Not only did his musical inspiration come from the German masters, but he had also lived and conducted in Germany for periods. And the Faust story was theirs, after all. The competition extended into performance – the aesthetic contrast within Western music between the German and the French camps, between solidity, profundity and structure on the one hand and delicacy, colour and transparency on the other. However unspoken, such were the underlying elements of the Battle of Berlioz.

All along a significant 'music of resistance' was developing, initially around the works of two communist poets, Paul Éluard and Louis Aragon. Some of these pieces were set to music by Poulenc. One such – Éluard's 'Liberté' – had its 'premiere' in December 1943 in a small private concert at which Poulenc sang, alone with piano accompaniment, a work composed for 240 singers. The text was later printed in leaflet form and dropped from the air by the RAF. A short time after that Poulenc and the baritone Pierre Bernac gave a public recital of two poems by Aragon which, in the words of the composer Charles Koechlin, 'expressed the soul of the wounded homeland'. Meanwhile Georges Auric wrote *Four Songs of France*, setting poems by both Aragon and Éluard. Musically it is often considered one of Auric's most deeply felt works. Of the text, de Gaulle himself commented in a speech in 1943, 'How can one not feel the heart-rending sentiment of these poems that are being recited secretly today all over France?' Music honouring the Resistance continued to be produced after the Liberation. The thirty-three sonnets written by Jean Cassou in prison in 1943 and published in the underground press in May 1944 inspired several composers. Milhaud was so moved by them – 'Of all the poems of the Resistance, these sonnets touched me the most profoundly' – that he composed his *Six Sonnets Written in Secret* for an *a cappella* choir. In subsequent years there was a veritable flood of commemorative works – for deportees, 'patriots who were executed', 'combatants for liberty', 'for all the innocent victims of the war', an oratorio entitled *Song of Mourning and Hope, France on the Road to Calvary* and the like.

Artistic resistance was paralleled by institutional resistance. Although Rouché managed to hold on at the Paris Opera, the Opéra-Comique was lost to the arch-*collabo* Max d'Ollone in 1941. That left the Conservatory, the distinguished but somnolent musical college that dated back to 1793. As the Wehrmacht approached Paris in June 1940 most of the instructors and students fled, leaving the building unoccupied except for the person in charge of financial accounts. Learning that the Germans intended to requisition the building, he immediately telephoned several of the faculty members still in Paris. To cut a long story short, seven professors formed a governing body, divided among themselves the twenty-five students remaining in Paris and resumed classes. The ruse worked.

But the institution still had to contend with the fact that nothing in the field of music escaped the attention of the Propaganda Department, which jealously vetted nominations to musical establishments. In this case German officials tried to impose the organist Marcel Dupré as the new director and only after months of hassle did they lift their veto on the composer Claude Delvincourt. For Vichy, Delvincourt appeared to have an ideal background. He had lost an eye in the Great War, was politically from the traditional hard right and appeared to share Vichy's cultural objectives.

On taking office in April 1942 he immediately confronted the problem of implementing race laws that required dismissing Jewish professors and students. Of the teaching staff of 75, only two were Jews and one of these was at retirement age; of the 580 students, around 20 were considered 'Jews' and some 15 others, 'half-Jews'. The latter were allowed to remain while eleven of the former category were expelled. A few lay low and stayed. Students whose surname did not indicate that they were Jewish remained and in at least one case a Jewish applicant was admitted to classes. According to some accounts, Delvincourt found various subterfuges to let the expelled students continue their studies by arranging for them to have private instruction.

Another problem came to a head not long afterwards. As the struggle to survive became more and more difficult for his students, Delvincourt had to balance their hardships against the Conservatory's traditional prohibition against outside employment. 'These young people represent our elite – that is to say, the way we can maintain our artistic prestige and influence', he wrote to a friend. 'They must undertake long and difficult study, which requires their being in good mental and physical health. But they must manage somehow to live, to earn some outside income. How could I humanly refuse to allow this? How would they live?' And so he permitted them to ignore the regulations and play in jazz clubs and dance bands. As Poulenc later commented, 'Delvincourt was an admirable director of the Conservatory. He showed his students solicitude and affection; he supported them with fairness and courage, finding them scholarships and positions.'

By September 1942, if not before, Delvincourt had entered the Resistance. He joined the National Front and permitted secret meetings to be held in his office. It was around this time that all the male students in the Conservatory became eligible for compulsory labour service in Germany. Delvincourt went to the Wehrmacht commandant in Paris and persuaded him to let them continue their studies. By 1944, however, the Germans were in such desperate need of manpower for their factories that his students faced imminent deportation. According to one story, Delvincourt ordered all sixty of them to appear at dawn at his office, provided them with false papers and told them to get lost. Another account has it that he persuaded Cortot to intervene with the minister of education on their behalf. Whatever the truth, as Poulenc reported to Milhaud, 'Delvincourt was *admirable* at the Conservatory; not a single student went to Germany.'

Germany itself was the site not just of forced labourers – more than half a million of them – but also of a million-and-a-half war prisoners. Little in life can be as degrading as to be a prisoner of war in a defeated army. And to be one in conditions of near-starvation, bone-breaking winter cold and psychological degradation is almost impossible to imagine. Yet in an amazing twist of irony it was in just such a camp that one of the most remarkable musical events of the war took place. On 15 January 1941 four ragged, starving, freezing French prisoners came together in a barracks in a godforsaken camp in Silesia and in the presence of hundreds of other ragged, starving, freezing inmates performed a quartet that one of them had just composed. In a reference to the cry of the angel of the Apocalypse, 'there shall be time no longer', the composition was entitled *Quatuor pour la fin du temps* (*Quartet for the End of Time*) and has come to be regarded as one of the century's outstanding chamber works. Within the concluding movement, entitled 'Praise to the Immortality of Jesus', was a slow and poignant passage dominated by the violin that must have wrenched the hearts of the miserable prisoners.

The composer, Olivier Messiaen, grew up in a literary family. But, reflective of his independence of mind, it was music that became his passion. Though an autodidact, he was already composing by the age of seven. He attended the Paris Conservatory, in 1931 became organist at the Trinité church in Paris and five years later was appointed professor at the École Normale Supérieure in Paris. It was then that he and a number of other composers formed a group called La Jeune France with the intention of guiding French music away from its anti-German stance and towards Romanticism and religious sentiment. While his first important composition, *Préludes* (1929), was in the tradition of Debussy, it already showed signs of originality. Originality and religious intent became the outstanding traits of Messiaen's works. Open to all sorts of traditions and sources – notably bird song – he introduced a variety of innovations in harmony, melody, rhythm and orchestration. By 1937 he was even experimenting with electronic music.

Conscripted into the army as a medical orderly in 1939, at the debacle he was taken captive near Nancy and there fortuitously met a few other prisoners – a Jewish clarinettist, Henri Akoka, the noted cellist Étienne Pasquier and, later, the violinist Jean Le Boulaire. Akoka, inseparable from his instrument, encouraged Messiaen to write something for him. The result was a work for unaccompanied clarinet, which later became the third movement of the *Quartet*. After that, Akoka found that Messiaen 'lost the will to compose' and only through prodding could he be motivated to go on. But how to go on and with what materials? In the answer to that lay the most amazing part of the story – a fascinating one, fascinatingly told by Rebecca Rischin.

On arriving at the camp, Messiaen found that his music-loving captors singled him out for special treatment. 'A German officer gave me, as a gift, an edition of Beethoven's piano sonatas. When I was young I had very carefully examined the treatise of Vincent d'Indy and his commentary on Beethoven and the sonata form. So I was quite prepared to read the sonatas very closely, and I could see that they were marvels of construction. That is how musical analysis entered my life.' But it was his chamber works that camp officials wanted to encourage, giving him privacy as well as paper, ink and so on and even procuring a cello and a piano. While studying scores and composing, Messiaen experienced bouts of synaesthesia, which he attributed to hunger. 'When I was a prisoner, the lack of food caused me to dream in colour. I saw the rainbow of the Angel and strange whirling colours . . . as well as strange, rotating colours . . . chords in violet-red, blue-orange, gold and green.' In the second movement of the quartet, the piano part was defined by its composer as 'soft cascades of chords in blue and mauve, gold and green, violet-red, blue-orange – all of it dominated by steel-grey'. As he said, 'Certain sonorities were linked in my mind to certain colour complexes, and I use them like colours, juxtaposing them.' These ideas were developed in his book *Technique de mon langage musical*, which he was working on at the time and published in 1944 – to hilarity in some circles and admiration in others.

Once the Quartet was completed and rehearsed, the camp commandant had programmes printed and arranged a grand premiere. Interest was enormous and the 'theatre barrack' was jammed. In the front were the camp officers and wounded prisoners on stretchers. The thermometer that night measured −10 degrees and only the body heat of the audience made the interior temperature even approach the bearable. The keys on the out-of-tune piano stuck. The performers, like the audience, were dressed in garb close to rags. Messiaen introduced the event with a speech explaining the work in quasi-religious terms – remarks that offended the other performers and apparently much of the audience. The Quartet itself was heard in total silence and there was little applause at the end. The work was as cold as the hall, conveying tragedy and suffering. To some in the audience it may have been so moving that silence was the fitting response, but to others the music seemed incomprehensible. Also incomprehensible was Messiaen's later behaviour. Distorting some of the conditions of the performance, he vastly exaggerated the size of the audience and the poor state of the instruments. Worse, when Karl-Albert Brüll, the German officer who had made it all possible, went to Paris many years later to meet Messiaen, the God-loving composer refused to see him.

A few weeks after the premiere, with the connivance of Brüll, Pasquier forged papers that qualified him and Messiaen for release. On returning to France, Messiaen went directly to Vichy where he spent six weeks working for Jeune France, the respectable government organization that promoted the arts in the Occupied Zone. His real intention, however, was to earn a little money and to lobby Vichy officials for an appointment to the Conservatory. He succeeded, and at the age of thirty-two became the institution's youngest professor. 'One day,' his star piano student and later wife, Yvonne Loriod, recalled,

> we saw Claude Delvincourt come into the classroom to introduce Messiaen to the students, saying, 'Here is your new teacher.' And then appeared a man with blond hair, around thirty-three, wearing a grey overcoat; very amiable, very modest. We were all immediately struck by his hands, swollen with chilblains, since he had for such a long time had nothing to eat except soup with a bit of whale blubber that was given to prisoners at noon to keep them from dying. . . . And so the new professor sat down at the piano and took out a pocket-score of Debussy's *Prélude à l'après-midi d'un faune.* Our admiration knew no bounds.

Although he was a devoted teacher with enormous influence on postwar music through such protégés as Pierre Boulez and Karlheinz Stockhausen, his works were only slowly received. The public premiere of the Quartet took place in Paris in June 1941 and was followed by a few more performances, some public and some private. In January 1942 Munch included *Les Offrandes,* composed in 1930, in one of his Conservatory concerts. But that was it. Messiaen should have suited Vichy well – an ex-war prisoner, a devout Catholic, the organist at Trinité in Paris and the pre-eminent composer of religious works. The only possible conclusion is that his type of Modernism was unacceptable to the authorities. Although *Les Offrandes* was recorded in 1942, his name was notoriously absent from the list of those who received commissions from the state. So while never banned, he was marginalized.

The composer who hit the jackpot during the Occupation years was Arthur Honegger. Born in Switzerland, he lived virtually all his life in France and was considered a French composer. After studying at the Conservatory, he joined the so-called Group of Six – composers who rebelled against the Wagnerian and Impressionist traditions of French music. From an early age he was a prolific composer, writing songs, concertos, chamber music, operas, sonatas, oratorios and symphonies, as well as music for the theatre, radio and cinema.

His fiftieth birthday fell in 1942 with a cascade of events in his honour at which his major compositions were performed. *Comoedia* published a special issue. There were two Honegger Festivals that year, at one of which Munch conducted the premiere of the *Second Symphony for Strings*, a dark, even tragic work befitting the times. Although Poulenc was normally far from generous in his estimation of Honegger, on this occasion he wrote to Milhaud describing it as 'an amazing work'. Throughout the Occupation his music was played so often – more than that of any other contemporary French composer – that he almost became the country's official musician.

Then after the war he suddenly fell into opprobrium. During the Occupation his behaviour had verged on collaboration. He had been the music critic of *Comoedia* from the time it was relaunched after the armistice and he was one of the group that went to Vienna for the Mozart Week. In July 1942 Lifar brought to the stage Egk's ballet *Joan von Zarissa*, which the Germans had forced on the Paris Opera. The work inspired Honegger to write an article of effusive praise, which under the circumstances caused a scandal. Poulenc reported the result in a letter to Milhaud. 'Arthur is no longer being played. . . . At the radio there has been a hostility that in my opinion is far too extreme and which I deplore.' Three months later: 'Arthur continues to live very much alone, in a sort of quarantine as a result of his foolishness, which was *not serious*. The radio is broadcasting him as a *Swiss* composer.' But the final cut went far deeper. Honegger represented the past in French music, Messiaen the future.

CHAPTER 9

FAIBLESSE OBLIGE

At the very moment German troops were entering Paris on 14 June, Count Thierry de Martel de Jonville injected himself with a fatal dose of strychnine. Dr Martel was France's leading neurosurgeon. During the Great War he had been badly wounded and his seventeen-year-old son killed. The fall of Paris was now more than he could bear. Throughout France the news of his suicide was greeted with horror. But not by Jean Cocteau. 'I find these days exciting. Too bad Martel was so lacking in curiosity', he wrote to a friend. Appalling, to say the least, but then the remark came from a man whose immediate reaction on hearing that war had been declared in 1939 was to ask, 'How will I get my opium?' And on the day Hitler launched his great blitzkrieg on Western Europe, what plunged Cocteau into near-hysteria was not the monumental battle and the fleeing millions but an article in the *Nouvelle Revue Française*. It was by Claude Mauriac and made Cocteau out to be a bumptious buffoon. The victim had no recourse but to appeal to the heavens. 'Mauriac must be arrested!'

Cocteau revelled in the role of *enfant terrible*, and here were instances of how he could be both infantile and terrible. There was always something of the court jester about him. He was like a water beetle, gliding across the water's face. If he asked how he did it, he would sink. He never asked and never sank. He thrived on wit and improvisation. Gide cut to the heart of the matter in commenting on an encounter with Cocteau: 'Although he made himself extremely agreeable, he simply cannot be serious, and to me all his aphorisms, his witticisms, his reactions, and the extraordinary brio of his customary ways of talking were as shocking as a luxury article on display in a period of famine and mourning.' That was said in August 1914 but could have been said – and in varying ways was – by many others in the course of Cocteau's life. While the charge was not entirely fair, certainly a lack of seriousness was both his *faiblesse* and his redeeming trait. It was why he was usually forgiven his sins.

Given Cocteau's carapace of egocentricity, frivolousness and so on, it is easy to see why many found him irritating. Even his undeniable wit, charm and elegance, not to mention his precocious social and artistic successes, evoked derision. In his novel *Les Faux-Monnayeurs*, Gide mocked him as the dilettantish prig, the Comte de Passavent. Many years later Camus commented, 'I continue to prefer [Gide] to every other writer and by inverse reaction, I detest Cocteau.' In a letter to Tristan Tzara, Breton once denounced him with typical violence as 'the most hateful being of our time'. Chanel dismissed him as 'a snobbish little pederast who did nothing all his life but steal from people'. Picasso was almost obsessed with his elegance of dress and enjoyed making fun of the sharp pleat of his trousers – 'like a razor blade', he would say in mock admiration. The painter could never resist a dig, even at the expense of someone he liked. 'Cocteau was born with a crease in his trousers. He is becoming terribly famous. You will find his works at every hairdresser's.'

Still, an annoying personal manner hardly explains why he aroused such reactions. After all, he was naturally gifted, highly intelligent, irrepressibly creative and ever ready with an amiable wit. No doubt some disliked him because he was openly homosexual, others out of jealousy for his achievements, still others in a belief that these accomplishments were much overrated. Cocteau displayed a seemingly effortless talent in an astonishing variety of fields – plays, novels, poems, ballets, essays, painting, drawing and sculpture. He wrote and directed films and plays. He designed posters, pottery, tapestries and even costume jewellery and neckties. But to the grave there followed him the charge of having scattered and dissipated his talents. Richard Strauss's remark that he himself was not a first-rate composer but a first-rate second-rate composer could be applied with greater justice to Cocteau as an artist and writer.

The child was father to the man. His early teachers found him intelligent and talented but 'inégal, distrait, agité'. The usual story among artists. By the age of twenty, however, he had co-founded *Schéhérazade*, a cultural review, brought out a volume of poems and had been published in the prestigious *Comoedia*. A few years later he choreographed a ballet and published a second volume of poems. The ballet failed and the poems were badly received but he was nonetheless making his way in artistic circles. Proust, Gide, Picasso, Diaghilev, Stravinsky and Satie could be counted among his friends and acquaintances. It was with the *grandes dames* of le Tout-Paris, however, that he was especially popular. 'God knows Jean was irresistible at twenty', said Misia Sert, a connoisseur of irresistible men. In a society where to be amusing was all-in-all, Cocteau amused. For him and the beautiful people around him, life was a party and he was the life of it.

He even managed to make the best of the Great War. While on military service in an ambulance unit, he found occasion to engage Satie and Picasso to work with him on the avant-garde ballet *Parade*. In 1917 Diaghilev took it for the Ballets Russes and assigned Léonide Massine to do the choreography. The work was artistically innovative and in its way Surrealist. Some considered it the first truly modern ballet. But though the performances created a stir, they did not produce the scandal required for a successful Paris premiere. The arty set loved it; critics and most others did not.

It was during the interwar period that Cocteau really glittered. He brought out a volume of memoirs, nine collections of poems, eight novels, reams of critical commentary, the chronicle of a trip around the world in eighty days serialized in *Paris-Soir*, plus a series of plays and ballets that made his international reputation. The theatrical outpouring began in 1920 with *Le Bœuf sur le toit*, a pantomime-ballet. Milhaud wrote the score, Dufy did the sets and the famous clowns the Fratellini brothers performed it. Somewhat to Cocteau's disdain, it was a notable success. There followed a succession of works with décors by Picasso, Braque and Dufy and music by the leading young composers of the day – Milhaud, Poulenc, Honegger, Auric and the Group of Six collectively. In 1928 he collaborated with Stravinsky to produce the opera-oratorio *Oedipus Rex*. A series of plays followed, of which *Les Parents terribles* of 1938 received the most notice. It was a psychological drama around the theme of a mother–son relationship that some chose to see as an apology for incest. After being closed by the Paris police, it reopened in another theatre and ran successfully until the war.

In the course of the Thirties Cocteau's popularity went up as the quality of his works went down. He was entering what his biographer Francis Steegmuller gently referred to as 'his period of least genial productivity'. This fact and his troubled personal life left him beset by what in contemporary jargon is known as issues of self-esteem. Behind the surface glitter there was suffering. Ernst Jünger perceived this when they met in November 1941. He described him in one concise phrase – 'likeable but at the same time in pain, like someone staying in a special but comfortable hell.' Although Cocteau had tried to find solace in the arms of the church, it was opium and cocaine, an indulgence begun in 1924 following the death of an intimate friend, that sustained him. He was hooked several times and had periodically to be detoxified. At the time war was declared, he was heavily doped.

Like Céline, he was always looking for novelty. Occupied Paris certainly offered that. And like Céline, he could hardly wait to return. 'As for me,' he wrote to a friend from his exile in Perpignan, 'you know I relish these great climaxes.' With German encouragement theatres were reopening, and having heard that *Les Parents terribles* was to be revived, he hurried back, taking his lover Jean

Marais with him. His life after that can be followed in detail thanks to a diary he began keeping in March 1942. When published in 1989, the 645 pages of the *Journal, 1942–1945* revealed to what an astonishing extent Cocteau went on living the same sort of life, professionally and socially, that he had had before the defeat. Out of the diary emerges a man totally self-absorbed, a solipsist who filtered everything through narrow personal interests. In the world of Jean Cocteau there was no war worth noticing, no Occupation, no cold, hunger or suffering, no disappearances or arrests, much less reprisal executions. The deportation of Jews in September 1942 was recorded in three pitiless words, '*Les juifs partent*'. His record of the times gives the impression that the Germans he knew were visiting tourists rather than officers of the invading army of a cruel enemy. 'Long live the shameful peace!' he once said. And that, *grosso modo*, summed up his state of mind throughout the Occupation.

In exalting the doctrine that poets should be indifferent to the follies of war and politics, Cocteau practised what he preached. Nonetheless, in early December 1940 he wrote an 'Address to Young Writers' that was published, oddly enough, in the collaborationist *La Gerbe*. It appealed to young people to stand up to the bullying of the far-right critics who were already beginning to dominate cultural life. 'What do you risk? The anger of those who attack Gide? If so, you owe it to him.' The cynic might say this was merely stirring up a butterfly's nest and that in defending Gide he was only defending himself. For all that, it was a still, small voice of protest when there were few to be heard. Thereafter, however, nothing.

In his diary Cocteau did record a few vague comments about political figures. His recollection of Churchill was that of a drunk at dinner weeping over the abdication of Edward VII. As for de Gaulle, his name was not even mentioned until February 1944 and then merely to note that he had given a radio address. The general's arrival in Paris on 25 August was recorded at length, though mostly in terms of his appearance. Pétain, in Cocteau's judgement, was a laughable figurehead. 'Marshal P. has not the slightest sense of grand theatre.' When Hitler – in one of those dramatic gestures he so loved – ordered the ashes of Napoleon's son to be transferred from Vienna to Paris in December 1940, Pétain refused to attend the interment ceremony, causing Cocteau to comment, 'One does not respond to high theatre with the reactions of an usherette.' Cocteau was also tremendously impressed by an imaginative proposal he attributed to Hitler to bury the bodies of all the French and Germans soldiers killed in all the wars between the two countries along the Maginot Line. At a great ceremony Hitler and Pétain would then declare an end for ever to hostility between the two countries.

Cocteau's high opinion of Hitler is the biggest surprise to emerge from the diary. Yet perhaps it should not surprise, since both were men of the theatre.

In his entry of 2 July 1942 Cocteau records a dinner conversation with the new head of the Paris municipal police, whom he found to be 'a charming young man':

> He speaks of Hitler with great esteem and without any pomposity and without any narrow-mindedness. Like me, he thinks that it would be disastrous to prevent someone like him from achieving his objectives, to limit him en route. Maps of the 'new Europe' are ready at the prefecture. [A sample address:] 'Mr So-and-So, European (District France).' No more customs. No more frontiers. Hitler wants Europe and Africa for food. He is aware of every mistake Napoleon made and avoids them one after the other.

The notion of a wise and benevolent Hitler so impressed Cocteau that three weeks later he mentioned it again. 'Hitler has studied Napoleon's mistakes and wants to combine his genius as a soldier with the [diplomatic] methods of Talleyrand. This is the reason the public fails to understand his greatness and his shifts of policy.' Cocteau even fantasized a meeting between Premier Daladier and Hitler following the 1938 Munich Conference at which the two leaders agreed that French and German soldiers should throw all their weapons into the Rhine. They themselves would then board a plane and vanish for two months. 'Imagine Daladier and Herriot [Speaker of the Chamber of Deputies] confronted with such grandiose ideas!' Cocteau commented, 'The false caution of parliamentarians! Out of fear of being duped, they ruin us. With Hitler we have a poet who rises above the mentality of these little men. Even if Hitler were later to change his mind and give his soldiers new weapons, this would not make any difference. An act of greatness remains an act of greatness.' Six months later he contrasted Hitler, the civilian, with Napoleon, the military man, and commented, 'Hitler the man of war is a spent force. Hitler the man of peace is hated. He was dragged into a war he detests. His pacifism was doomed from the start.'

For the political leaders of the Third Republic Cocteau felt only contempt. When in March 1942 Vichy authorities subjected Daladier, Blum and other figures of the Third Republic to a notorious show trial, he blithely commented that both accused and accusers were no better than 'microbes that attack other microbes in a typhoid epidemic'.

All the while Cocteau's social life went on pretty much as before the war. He frequently dined at the Grand Véfour, the Tour d'Argent, Maxim's and with Picasso at Le Catalan. The vicomtesse de Noailles – herself compromised as the bedmate of a Wehrmacht officer – remained one of his favourites. Such a comfort it was to visit her! 'Sunday lunch with the Noailles', a diary entry reads. 'I find at Marie-Laure's residence the old atmosphere, made up of mementos and paintings and marvellous objets d'art.' In addition to the ornaments of le Tout-Paris, he knew some of the Vichy big shots. François Darlan, commander of the navy and premier from February 1941 to April 1942, was his cousin. Ambassador de Brinon – executed for treason after the Liberation – was a regular lunch partner. He also seems to have been a good friend of the head of the metropolitan police, Maurice Toesca. Many of the leading *collabos* in the theatre world – Guitry, Arletty, Danielle Darrieux, Edwige Feuillère – were dining companions, and other leading personalities of intellectual collaborationism – Châteaubriant, Drieu, Jouhandeau among them – were social friends. Not Fabre-Luce, though, who considered him a clown – *jongleur, escamoteur, mime* were his epithets. Occasionally Cocteau attended receptions given by the Groupe Collaboration and once put in an appearance at Florence Gould's Nazi coterie. But his friendships were by no means limited to *collabos*. He was also close to Picasso, a man whom he admired above all others, and shared some of the painter's Left Bank friends.

Thoroughly untroubled by the presence of the Germans, Cocteau never recorded an unpleasant word about them. In fact, he much enjoyed the company of those he knew, such as Jünger and Heller, and admired them for their familiarity with French culture. In turn they comforted him by making fun of the press attacks he suffered. And they all laughed together at what they considered Epting's absurd literary infatuation with Céline. Several times he attended functions at the German Institute and was also an occasional guest of Abetz. When a visiting Munich theatre group performed Goethe's *Iphigenia* at the Comédie-Française, he sat with Abetz in the ambassador's box. So much did he feel at home with Germans he knew that he was moved to remark, 'A homeland is where people immediately find themselves on the same intellectual level.'

Whatever relative discretion Cocteau had maintained in his initial contacts with the Germans was completely undone when the Breker exhibition opened in May 1942. His effusive 'Salute to Breker', prominently published on the front page of *Comoedia*, was a blunder he never lived down. It was seen as a gratuitous act of osculation with a hated Invader. A furious Paul Éluard fired off a stinker of a letter: 'Freud, Kafka, Chaplin have been banned by the same people who honour Breker. You were considered one of the banned. How wrong you are suddenly to show yourself among the censors! Those who admire and like you most have been painfully surprised.' Paradoxically, in his diary Cocteau derided the show as ridiculous and jested that it 'had taken on proportions similar to those of the statues'. He went on to complain, 'Breker was received like a sovereign. Official dinner after official dinner. Article upon article. Poster upon poster. Speech after speech. In the face of such a spectacle, it would have been preferable to be humiliated, insulted, thrashed.' But he admitted that with his 'Salute' he had howled with the wolves. 'And what wolves!'

Throughout the Occupation years, Cocteau was professionally as active as ever. He arranged an important exhibition of his drawings at the Galerie Louis Carré. He regularly contributed articles to *Comoedia* and finished *La Fin du Potomak*, the sequel to an earlier novel. But his principal interests now lay in theatre and film. He did the décors and costumes for Feydeau's *La Main passe* and in early 1943 produced a version of *Antigone*, with music by Milhaud, that was a great success at the Opera. The year before, *Les Parents terribles* had been revived and caused a terrific critical rumpus. Laubreaux and Rebatet attacked it so ferociously that, as in 1938, the police closed it. However, again as in 1938, it was later authorized and once again enjoyed a good run. In the meantime Cocteau had written *La Machine à écrire*. Although completed in five days, it had cost him an unusual amount of effort and the result left him dissatisfied. On the simplest level it was a detective story about a writer of anonymous letters. Not far below the surface it was about vice and hypocrisy. The play opened on 29 April 1941 and Laubreaux damned it with such violence that the police closed it. Even the normally unshockable Céline was shocked. He had met Cocteau a short time before at a reception given by the Groupe Collaboration and on the strength of this acquaintance volunteered to mediate. But then, learning that Cocteau had before the war given moral support to the head of the International League against Anti-Semitism, he sent him a vile letter withdrawing his offer. 'You don't deserve to be defended from Laubreaux. Therefore the author of *La Machine à écrire* will be sacrificed "on the altar of racism".'

So exasperated was Cocteau by such continuous, gross harassment that he thought of appealing to various officials, Darlan and Abetz among them. What he actually did is unclear both from biographies and his diary. What *is* clear is that Laubreaux – like Rebatet and the hard-right press – showed again that he could prevent or at least disturb the performance of a work he disliked either by writing critical diatribes or by encouraging thugs to disrupt performances. Laubreaux's provocations eventually led to a notorious incident when Jean Marais set about him on the street one night – an incident re-enacted in Truffaut's famous film *Le Dernier Métro* (*The Last Metro*).

Although ostensibly a theatre critic of both *Je suis partout* and the equally right-wing daily *Le Petit Parisien*, Laubreaux was in reality a political journalist. He used theatrical criticism as a vehicle for spreading proto-fascist views and is generally considered to have been highly influential. In 1944 he published a sketchy diary, *Écrit pendant la guerre*, covering the first nine months of the war. On theatre it is silent. On political affairs it is vociferous. The first entry, dated 25 August 1939, sets the tone. Speaking of the military mobilization, he wrote, 'The Republic is summoning people to fight its Jewish war.' He went on to say that the German-Soviet pact would open the way for Hitler to take Poland, 'and it would be criminal to go to war to stop him'. Just after war had been declared, he ran into Darquier de Pellepoix, another wildly anti-Semitic journalist, who remarked, 'It is all over, mon ami. The Jews have won.' A later entry referred to an advertisement in a Toulouse newspaper for military uniforms made by 'A. Cohn'. About this he observed, 'They are always right on the spot, our good Jews. French soldiers risk their asses in war. They clothe them.' When Daladier declared in a speech that 'we are at war because it was forced on us', Laubreaux commented, 'Who imposed this war on the French that Daladier was addressing? The Jew. The English.' Later on he was more specific. It was the 'habitually hypocritical' British who were responsible; Daladier was nothing more than 'the henchman of London'. Even after Daladier had been imprisoned by the Germans following the defeat, he was without pity. 'My heart is filled with hate for Daladier.'

On the day the war began, Laubreaux said to his friend Rebatet, 'I can hope for only one thing for France – a war that will be short and disastrous.' Here he went too far even for the hard right. Challenged to defend himself, he explained that since France was destined to be defeated, it was best to have a brief war with a collapse that would wipe out the political elements that had led to the catastrophe. However, as things worked out, Vichy failed to wipe out these objectionable elements. So Laubreaux had a new set of enemies. 'Now it will be necessary to settle accounts with those who failed to do so.' Such is the gist of the diary. Though brief, it highlights the main elements in the hate litany of Laubreaux and his fellow right-wing critics – the Third Republic and its leaders, democracy, the British, the Jews and even Vichy.

In 1942 Laubreaux incorporated his views in a play, *Les Pirates de Paris*, about the Stavisky affair. Alexandre Stavisky was a Jewish con man of East European origin who had organized a huge bond swindle that was covered up by judicial officials. Its exposure in 1934 caused one of the most notable scandals of the interwar period, resulting not only in the suicide of the perpetrator but also the fall of the government of the day. To Laubreaux the affair epitomized the corruption leading to the debacle of 1940. He wrote the play under the pseudonym Michel Daxiat and once it got to the stage brazenly gave it a laudatory review under his real name.

Despite the warm praise of *Le Petit Parisien* and one or two other *collabo* papers, the play was a huge flop with both critics and audiences – a failure that says much about popular attitudes at the height of the Occupation. But how does all this explain his hatred of Cocteau and Marais? It doesn't. What it does show is that his hostility was not political – the two were not known to have political views. Nor was it aesthetic – Laubreaux had apparently not even attended the plays he condemned. As Sherlock Holmes said, when you eliminate all other factors, the one that remains must be the truth. And the truth must be that he hated them as gays.

For all his lightness of being, Cocteau was tough enough to go on with his theatrical work. In August 1941 he finished a beguiling love story in dramatic verse, *Renaud et Armide*, which was enthusiastically accepted by the Comédie-Française. Just as enthusiastically was it forbidden by Jerome Carcopino, the minister with oversight of cultural affairs. He pronounced the play 'inopportune' and the author 'undesirable at the Comédie-Française'. Not long afterwards Carcopino's son happened upon the manuscript in his father's office, read it, admired it and persuaded his father to lift the ban. At its premiere in April 1942 the play was a great success, though not of course in the judgement of Laubreaux and the other usual suspects.

Partly to sustain his relationship with Jean Marais and partly to explore the medium, Cocteau next turned to the cinema. His initial venture was to write the dialogue for an unpromising film, *Le Baron fantôme*. He made it as amusing as possible and even appeared in the film as the Baron, who in the end dissolves into dust, as any well-mannered phantom should do. A far more formidable proposition followed – turning the Tristan and Isolde legend into a contemporary story. *L'Éternel Retour* was written during the winter and filmed in Nice in the spring of 1943. When released in the autumn, it became the greatest movie success of the period.

Not until mid-1943 did the real world begin to intrude into Cocteau's poetic fantasy world. It was now evident that the Germans would lose their war and his comfortable life would be disturbed. A deep sense of self-pity set in. 'We will all be considered criminals for having stayed in France and continued our work', he and friends agreed at dinner one evening. 'Our suffering will not count.' After three years of living without complaint under the Germans, he was now worried. 'Times are changing. We shall see the worst. All the better. We must piously wait as destiny runs its course.' In early October he heard a rumour that Hitler and Stalin were trying to negotiate a peace settlement. 'But whatever happens, we shall be the victims.' Closer to home he was furious with Mauriac, 'who dreams only of vengeance against those of us who have worked during the past four years. What an odd sense of justice! Not to work meant that you had the income to live. Mauriac had it. Gide had it. Unfortunately I did not have it.'

He was even more incensed on learning that the BBC had accused him of being a collaborator. But then since the pro-collaborationist press considered him a Gaullist, he felt the one cancelled out the other. Nonetheless, he was indignant. 'That is what happens to free spirits who refuse to get mixed up in politics and don't know anything about them. After having just spent four years in Paris being insulted, I find it curious to say the least that the British radio should come out against me.'

By the time of the D-Day landings, Cocteau was thoroughly dejected. 'Did not the very calm of Paris suggest a blind fear of changing long-held habits, a fear of peace', he wondered. A month later he began to sense that France was descending into the chaos of the Liberation. 'The calm of the Germans stands in curious contrast to the panic of the French.' After four years without raising his voice or pen – even in the privacy of his diary – against the horrors of the Occupation, he now railed against the 'anarchy' that followed the Liberation and the 'ignoble excess of hatred' towards collaborators. 'I do not have the fortitude to record the horrible things that I have witnessed' – by this he had in mind the actions of the Resistance no less than the Milice. Three weeks after Paris was liberated he raised a general lamentation. 'I am frightened of this overwhelming uncertainty in which my countrymen are living, of theatres that have been divided up, of newspapers which are calling for justice, of the artists whom they imprison, of this Germany that is besieged.'

A sub-theme of Cocteau's disgust with the Liberation was his condescending, almost hostile attitude towards British and American soldiers – sentiments he never expressed about the Wehrmacht. Within a few days of the freeing of Paris he was offended by the sight of Americans swanning around with women in little jeeps, which put him in mind of merry-go-round carts. 'At the liberated Ritz American officers have lunch with whores off the street. The great joy that one should feel has been negated by a feeling of malaise and sadness. . . . The organized disorder of the Americans contrasts with the style of German discipline; it is disturbing, it is disorienting.' There was some truth to his complaint. Let loose in Paris, high-spirited young American soldiers reckoned they had a licence to do pretty much what they pleased, and what a few of them pleased included black-marketeering, mass whoring and even a bit of armed robbery. 'Winter will be terrible,' Cocteau predicted, 'because France under the German Occupation had the right and duty to be openly insolent, to eat, to glitter, to defy the oppressor, to say, "You are taking everything from me and leaving me everything." The Americans will not understand this process.'

Even worse was the *épuration sauvage* – the uncontrolled public settling of accounts – that swept across the country in the wake of the Wehrmacht's retreat. In his diary Cocteau filled page upon page with outraged comment. 'One must learn to live inside a nightmare that is more and more incredible. It is like some terrible epidemic. The hatred of the early days was but a cruel child's game beside what is now taking place', he wrote in mid-October. Throughout France people were being executed without the semblance of a trial. No one was immune from the caprice of the crowd. It was all too reminiscent of the Gestapo. The guilty went unpunished while artists were being arrested and subjected to spectacular trials. The country was afflicted by a moral plague. Here, too, Cocteau's grievances were not without validity. But again, they read oddly after his silence about the infinitely worse things that went on during the Occupation. It is not surprising that the public accolades paid to the Resistance disgusted him. 'The Free French want everything. They have everything, but they want more. Books about the Resistance. Poems on the Resistance. Plays about the Resistance. A flow of blood and ink.' Fortunately he found that it proved unnecessary to put up with such foolishness for long. 'In Paris everything passes fast.' At the end of the year Marie-Laure de Noailles gave a party at which guests made fun of songs of the Liberation by caricaturing them. This sort of banter would have been unthinkable, he noted, just two months earlier.

Lack of nourishment affects the mind, and that may explain Cocteau's frivolous behaviour. He was not a true *collabo* like Fabre-Luce, who looked forward to a united Europe under German direction. Nor was he an opportunist like Céline, who collaborated for personal advantage. Like Lifar, he was a self-absorbed artist without moral or political standards. In 1945 Cocteau was summoned to appear before two *épuration* committees and found innocent. The shallowness that Gide had observed and the fact that anyone who had regularly been reviled by Laubreaux and Rebatet could not be all bad were probably what saved him.

For some who knew him, however, that was not good enough. On returning to France late in 1944, his friend Jacques Maritain reproached him for not having joined the Resistance. 'I respond that it was impossible for me to belong to an official organization, even if clandestine. Clandestinity is for poets. My destiny is to avoid fads while appearing to be a dupe.' Cocteau mouthed similar nonsense to Harold Nicolson, who mildly dismissed his excuse as 'not very dignified'. He had a better alibi, but he did not know it. The Resistance would not have had him. It turned down his lover, Jean Marais, on the ground that he would be a security risk – not only did he like boys too much, but more to the point he blabbed too much.

With not a little hypocrisy, Cocteau had the cheek to write a poem – '25 août 1944' – to celebrate the Liberation of Paris. But he knew he had not behaved heroically and if he was in any doubt, he could have consulted Claude Mauriac's newly published portrait, *Jean Cocteau ou la verité du mensonge* (Jean Cocteau or the Truth of Lies). In January 1945 he was asked, presumably with Franco's authority, whether the Spanish government might propose him to be French ambassador to Spain. He wisely declined, declaring it was not the sort of position he would like and in any case he wished to have nothing to do with 'a Spain governed by Franco'. By now the tension of the post-Occupation period had taken its toll. Nicolson described him as 'looking like an aged cockatoo'. He began suffering from a psychosomatic skin ailment, which prompted Picasso to warn friends, 'Don't shake hands with Cocteau. He's suffering from a nasty skin disease – something he caught from the Germans during the war.'

Had skin disease been the consequence of social contact with the Germans, untold thousands would have suffered acute dermatophytosis. In the theatrical world no one would have been worse afflicted than Sacha Guitry. He dined with them, they dined with him; he entertained them, they entertained him; he attended their receptions, they attended his receptions; he introduced them to his colleagues in the theatre and film worlds, they introduced him to their colleagues in the Wehrmacht. Throughout the Occupation he remained just what he had always been – brilliant, unprincipled, selfish, bumptious, carefree. Having swashbuckled his way through life, he was not about to allow the presence of a German army to spoil his fun. A hundred years ago Guitry would have been known as a swell. And it was this arrogant grand posturing, this sense of being above it all, that eventually brought him down.

Perhaps his showmanship was genetic. Guitry was born into showbiz. His father was one of the most noted actor-comedians of his time, his mother a comedienne. At the age of five he appeared in a pantomime before Czar Alexander III in St Petersburg, where his parents were then performing. Back home in Paris, he distinguished himself at no fewer than eleven educational establishments as a prime dunce. This said as much about the schools as the scholar, who was indolent but in his way quite clever. At the age of fourteen he made his stage debut and at the ripe old age of seventeen wrote and performed in a one-act verse play in a Paris theatre. Two years later, performing in a drama directed by his father, he forgot his wig and missed his entry cue. His father refused to speak to him for the next thirteen years.

In 1906, at the age of twenty, Sacha Guitry the professional playwright was born. *Nono*, which he wrote and in which he acted, was a remarkable popular success. Next came *Chez les Zoaques* which was an even greater hit. There followed a few years of ups and downs but by the time of the Great War – which he managed to avoid – his reputation was secure and he went on to become famous primarily as a playwright but also as a comedian, stage director, film scriptwriter and filmmaker, not to mention prominent man about town. Priapically precocious as well, he took up a lifelong hobby of collecting and de-accessioning wives and girlfriends. Arletti once turned him down on the grounds that he was already married – to himself.

As he lived life there was remarkably little difference between the actor and the person. 'He acted all the time, even at breakfast. It was awful.' That was the comment of one of his five wives. Wherever he was, he immediately transformed the space into a theatre: a room became a stage and those around him an audience. His residence, near the Eiffel Tower, was as showy as a grand stage-set, its centrepiece a magnificent sweeping staircase leading to a long marble gallery suggestive of the Hall of Mirrors at Versailles. At night he kept the interior brightly lit so passers-by could look in and observe him as though he were on stage. Sometimes he would even dress up at home in one of his stage costumes so that visitors might be disconcerted to come upon what appeared to be Louis XIV on the telephone or Talleyrand at a typewriter. None of this diminished his obsession with playwriting. Following a performance, he would return home. Then, as his biographer, James Harding, has written, 'After dinner, at one in the morning, he would vanish into his study. With the applause of the evening's audience in his ears and the glow of the theater still warm upon him, he would start to write yet another play.' The man would have been a psychiatrist's delight.

Guitry's plays were *pièces de boulevard* – light comedies – which suited the mood of interwar Paris as perfectly as did Noël Coward's popular hits in London. The storyline was always much the same. The plot centred on the time-honoured triangle – husband, wife and lover – and dealt humorously with their romantic intrigues. The characters were talented, witty and worldly. The humour was flippant, impertinent and epigrammatic. Dialogue was paramount – a vehicle for Guitry's speciality of flaunting his wit. The stage directions for a typical character read, 'happy to be alive, pleased with other people, delighted with himself'. That was Guitry to a tee. The characters in his plays, as his biographer observes, 'rarely have an unselfish thought or do a good deed. Their behaviour is dictated by self-interest and they have no conception of what a social conscience is.' Guitry again.

In 1915 he had turned his hand to the cinema with a documentary, *Ceux de chez nous*, which filmed noted artists at work – Rodin sculpting, Renoir in front of an easel, Rostand writing, Saint-Saëns conducting, Monet painting water lilies, Sarah Bernhardt acting. Like many another playwright and actor, he disdained the cinema, however, and did not take it up again for another fifteen years. When he did so, as in the theatre, he wrote, directed and acted, usually taking for himself the role of the central character. Seventeen of his plays were turned into movies and were so close to the stage originals that they were criticized as *théâtre filmé*. Reflecting his fascination with great figures of the past, such as Louis XIV and Talleyrand, Guitry also produced great historical costume extravaganzas. In 1930 he adapted his popular novel *Les Mémoires d'un tricheur* (Memoirs of a Con Man) into a film that has been considered his best and a significant contribution to cinematic development.

Intellectually peripatetic, Guitry also wrote, painted, sketched and sculpted, with mostly undistinguished results. In a half-century of artistic activity he wrote 124 plays, which he also directed and starred in, produced 36 films, wrote 32 books and almost 900 articles for newspapers and journals, participated in 268 radio and TV broadcasts, and made some 30 recordings. He turned out several dozen paintings, drew caricatures and sculpted three busts.

Writing scripts was such a compulsion that it continued during his final months in 1957, when he was in bed, dying from the morphine used in his pain-killing injections. The tragedy of that life was the last dozen years, which passed in disgrace.

It was probably only natural that someone who wrote his sort of comedies for his sort of audience would be ideologically to the right. And while he was not known to be pro-Nazi or anti-Semitic, Guitry was certainly not anti-Nazi. For reasons never explained, he had always refused to permit his plays and films to be performed in Germany. There was nothing anti-Nazi about this since he had denied them equally to the liberal democratic Weimar Republic. His ideological stance was clear from an episode on the eve of the war when he became involved in a right-wing plot to take over the Académie Goncourt, the most prestigious French literary institution after the Académie Française. In 1938 René Benjamin – an outright fascist, biographer of Mussolini and later Pétain, for whom he wrote speeches – was elected to the body. The following year he proposed Guitry for membership. The nomination was supported by Léon Daudet, an active member of Action Française and ardent anti-Semite, who commented revealingly of Guitry, 'After all, at least he has never said he likes the Republic.' Amid considerable controversy, Guitry was duly elected. Shortly thereafter Laubreaux sought him out and appealed to him to vote for Brasillach's new book, *Les Sept Couleurs*, for the Académie's 1939 prize. 'How it will dismay the Sons of Abraham if the award goes to the editor of *Je suis partout*!' the critic remarked. The novel had a political message, and that message was out-and-out fascistic. Only Guitry and Benjamin supported Brasillach. What all this proves is that Guitry was associated with the pro-Nazi hard right even before 1939.

With the declaration of war the theatres were closed but reopened a month later. Even this brief fallow period was too much for Guitry, who stayed at home, took out his costumes and spent his days dressed as Louis XIV, Richelieu and some of his other heroes. Untroubled by the war, he spent the early months of 1940 touring the south of France. In Nice he gave a public lecture studded with his usual misogynous pleasantries. 'If I take the liberty of saying that I don't like women, it is of course because I adore them.' And, 'It is no very serious matter to love a woman for her qualities but when you love her for her defects, then it is the real thing.' The military collapse found Guitry in Dax in southwestern France. Little more than a week after the armistice was signed, he was back in Paris. There he directly sought out Wehrmacht authorities for permission to revive the Paris theatre and, as Hans Speidel affirmed in his memoirs, 'immediately made himself available'. In their desire to get things back to normal, the Germans found him exactly the sort of person they were looking for.

To his credit Guitry began with a piece of openly nationalistic defiance by reviving his 1919 play *Pasteur*, a work celebrating French scientific genius. The action took place during the Franco-Prussian War and at one point the actors shouted 'Vive la France!' The German censor objected, Guitry insisted and the play was allowed to go on. After that the Wehrmacht authorities were less tolerant. In 1943 they objected to his projected operetta *Le Dernier Troubadour* which took place in early fifteenth-century, English-occupied Paris before its liberation by Joan of Arc. The parallels were too glaring. In the words of an internal Propaganda Department memorandum, 'Sacha Guitry's play would be a veritable delight for the Gaullists. We would be seen as the occupiers.'

In the meantime a serious personal problem arose. Shortly after his return to Paris, several newspapers alleged he was Jewish. It was claimed that his father's real surname was, among other suggestions, Wolff. His mother, they claimed, was in reality a Russian Jew. The accusation occasioned such heated disagreement among German authorities – the German Institute discounting the claim and the Wehrmacht's Propaganda Department believing it – that the matter had to be referred to Berlin. Rudolf Rahn was instructed to get to the bottom of it. Twice he summoned Guitry to his home and asked for assurances. At their first meeting, Guitry laughed the whole thing off. At their second – very chilly – interview Rahn insisted on seeing documentary proof. Guitry later gave varying comic accounts of the sensationally exculpatory results of his genealogical investigation. According to one of his stories, he referred the question of whether he was Jewish to the chief rabbi of Paris, who supposedly replied, 'Hélas, non.' In any event he convinced the Occupation authorities of his racial purity and resumed his career.

Some historians speak of the Occupation years as a 'golden age' of the theatre. They point to the large number of plays put on – more than four hundred – and the size of the audiences – unprecedented. Yet how much gilt was there? Theatrical life was certainly lively, but a high proportion of the plays were revivals. Audiences were large partly because of the limited alternatives. Misery was also a factor. Statistics show that attendance rose as food supplies declined. An amazed Vichy official once remarked, 'You can put on anything, by anyone, anywhere and at any time and the public will flock to it.' To be sure, there were such outstanding productions as Montherlant's *La Reine morte*, Sartre's *Les Mouches*, Giraudoux's *Sodome et Gomorrhe*, Anouilh's *Antigone* and Cocteau's *Renaud et Armide*. For some, the theatrical highlight of the Occupation years was the Comédie-Française's lavish premiere of Claudel's eleven-hour *Soulier de satin* (*The Satin Slipper*), a work of such ineffable tedium that Guitry was merely the first of many over the decades to give thanks that there was only one slipper. Looking back on those years, de Beauvoir remarked, 'We read, but the bookshop windows offered nothing of interest. The theatre promised nothing more enticing.'

It is not that Occupation officials tried to use the theatre for pro-German propaganda. They did not. But they were determined that it should not be the opposite. More than any of the other arts, theatre made them nervous. Film, painting, art exhibitions, concert performances, writing for publication, whether in newspapers or journals, were all easy to control. But theatre was a live art. It was not just text but innuendo, not just acting but intonation of the spoken line, and these could drastically change the effect of the written text.

Text alone left the censors fretting. New scripts poured into the Propaganda Department at the rate of fifty or sixty a month. Ten per cent were rejected outright. Those by foreign or Jewish playwrights or translations by Jews were automatically chucked. The others were scrutinized for references to the Third Reich, the Occupation, French war prisoners, countries at war with Germany and a seemingly endless list of other taboo topics. Even certain words – 'jazz', for example – were forbidden. Above all they were on guard against anything that might arouse patriotic feeling or bring the Wehrmacht into disrepute. In the search for subversive ideas, many censors showed greater imagination than the author of the work. Their paranoia brings to mind the famous tale of a censor during the days of k. und k. Austria. When asked by a writer what was objectionable in his latest work, the official had a ready reply: 'Nothing at all. But then I thought to myself, you just never know.'

The cavilling began with the title. In 1941 Guitry wanted to revive his prewar comedy Le Soir d'Austerlitz. Austerlitz being the site of Napoleon's most famous victory, the allusion had undesirable connotations for Germans – even though the play had nothing to do with the battle itself. So he obligingly chose the evidently less provocative Vive l'empereur!

What especially worried the censors was double entendre. This was of course almost impossible to detect – as often by the audience as by the authorities. An example is Sartre's famous aphorism in Huis clos, 'l'enfer, c'est les autres' – hell is other people. In approving the play, were the censors unaware that 'les autres' was a phrase the French used in the early days of the Occupation to refer to Germans, or were they too preoccupied in the spring of 1944 with thinking about an exit for themselves? But then did audiences get it either? If they did, it was not what the author intended. Sartre later made it clear that he had not meant the words to be anti-German.

Following the initial vetting of a play, there was a second. This was on site, to make certain that the spoken lines conformed to the approved text and were not delivered in an unacceptable way. Even that was not the end of it. Censors were also on the lookout for inappropriate audience reaction. In a play at the Académie Française, for example, one bit of dialogue ran:

Whom do you see there in the vestibule?
M. Adolphe, the obnoxious Adolphe.

The exchange set off such an outbreak of sniggers in the audience that Adolphe had to be changed to Alfred in later performances. Occasionally plays were closed for such reasons. As a consequence playwrights felt inhibited in their writing and impresarios found it easier to mount revivals than to risk headaches by staging new works. Two-thirds of the offerings during the Occupation years were therefore reruns. Old stand-bys, including plays by Shaw, Synge, Ibsen, Shakespeare, Euripides and even apparently Noël Coward, continued to be staged, although restrictions tightened in late 1943.

The theatre world was subjected to a third type of censorship from the same moral-correctness brigade that had been the bane of Jean Cocteau. This comprised not just far-right critics such as Laubreaux and Rebatet and publications such as *La Gerbe* and *Le Petit Parisien* and the almost respectable *Comoedia* but also, as time passed, the Milice. It was Milice thugs who disrupted – or prevented – performances considered undesirable by letting loose mice and setting off stink bombs or threatening violence. Theatre in the interwar period had reflected the debauchery of the Third Republic, they said, and must now be cleaned up. Family values should replace love triangles. But here they came into conflict with the German authorities, who wanted the public to be entertained with light comedies, not confronted with boring 'moral' issues. So Guitry's romantic comedies slipped through the interstices and were performed without interference.

During the Occupation, as in the interwar years, Guitry was very much the boulevardier. Quite literally he had no sooner arrived back in Paris in July 1940 than he started cultivating German officials. With his social panache and ready humour he was everything they were not and became immensely popular in Wehrmacht circles. He was part of a coterie of social *collabos* from the theatre world – Cocteau, Arletty and Alice Cocéa among them – who could be counted on to radiate glamour on any important social event. They were frequent guests at the German embassy and the German Institute and never missed one of the famously sumptuous social affairs given by Göring's personal representative in Paris, General Hanesse. They were prominently in evidence at the Breker exhibition and graced Pétain's reception for Göring. It is not surprising that the Reich Marshal, himself a showboat who loved to dress up in gaudy uniforms, took a shine to Guitry and, on a visit to Paris, made a point of summoning the actor-playwright for a private meeting.

By no means did Guitry neglect Vichy. In 1942 he initiated a grand literary-artistic tribute to Pétain. The work, entitled *De Jeanne d'Arc à Philippe Pétain, 1492 à 1942*, was a handsome album of four hundred pages of text and

illustrations printed on fine paper in 650 copies. It was a celebration of a classic
Vichy theme – that Joan of Arc and the Marshal were the great saviours of
France – and the notion that modern French history culminated in Pétain. The
revisionist intent of the production was unmistakable from Guitry's selection
of contributors. Almost all of them – Cocteau, Cortot, Colette, Giraudoux,
Morand, Abel Hermant and the duc de Broglie, to mention a few – were to
some extent Vichyites and pro-German *collabos*. Pétain was duly impressed
and sent Guitry a note of thanks.

For all his popularity with the Invader – indeed, because of it – Guitry was
by the time of the Liberation probably the most disliked artistic figure in
France. Even in the United States he had a bad reputation, thanks in part to a
scathing interview with the American press by Françoise Rosay, a movie
actress in exile. 'Of all the actors who remained and collaborated the worst is
Sacha Guitry', was among her remarks. His name was one of those in the *Life*
magazine list of collaborators. By the latter days of the Occupation he was not
only receiving death threats but, according to some accounts, was also being
spat at and heckled in the street.

So intense was the animosity that several young members of the Resistance
did not even wait until the Germans had fully cleared out of Paris before
picking him up early on 23 August and bundling him off to the local
police headquarters. Ever the wit, Guitry later quipped, 'When was I arrested?
On the day of Liberation.' Initially he was taken to the prison at Drancy,
where he ran into his first wife, Lysès. A joker off stage as much as on, he
remarked, 'Misfortunes never come one at a time.' Two months later he was
released for health reasons and placed in a medical institution until January. In
one of the first public opinion polls ever taken in France, his arrest was considered 'deserved' by 56 per cent of those asked and 'unfair' by a mere 12 per cent.

Logically enough, those who were troubled least by the Occupation were
troubled most by the Liberation. The public antipathy caused Guitry acute
acid indignation. If Cocteau conjures up a water beetle and Lifar a reptile,
Guitry brings to mind a hippopotamus. He was so thick-skinned that nothing
could penetrate his consciousness, but when attacked he responded ferociously. He did so in 1947 in *Quatre ans d'occupations*, a 556-page paranoid
lamentation of the way 'they' – never identified – had victimized him. 'For the
four years of the Occupation . . . I was accused of being the perfect model of
a "collaborator". Everyone knows this is false, but that is not the issue. I was
chosen to be the scapegoat – I was to pay, to pay for everyone else and right
away because it was then or never. It was the opportunity that for fifteen or
twenty years they had been waiting for.'

The criticism that he had rushed back to Paris in 1940 to revive theatrical
life and thereby played into the Germans' hands? In serving the Germans, he

was serving France by exposing them to the greatness of French culture. The accusation that he was an anti-Semite? For four years he had been accused of being a Jew. The charge that he was pro-German? All his life he had hated Germany and never allowed any of his plays to be performed in that country. The fact that he had enjoyed special privileges during the Occupation? Who would have turned them down if offered? A Vichyite? He could never have supported a regime that bowdlerized Molière and outlawed divorce. The *Life* list of *collabos*? 'I found it in bad taste, nothing more.' The charge that in the foyer of his theatre stood a statue of Hitler? It was in reality a statue of his father, who looked like Mussolini. The Breker show? It was actually a case of German art paying homage to French art. That he had entertained Germans? 'I never had a German seated at my table – needless to say.'

The last assertion was a lie – needless to say. The main reason for the popular hostility towards Guitry was that he had shamelessly consorted with the enemy and had as a consequence blatantly benefited. True, social etiquette during the Occupation was ambiguous. For some – Galtier-Boissière and Guéhenno, for example – it was wrong so much as to speak to a German in the street. Guéhenno even tried to avoid looking at them. While few went so far, it was generally considered compromising to be seen in public with a German, especially one in uniform. To invite him home or go to his residence was excessive. Guitry was guilty of all of the above. In his diary Paul Léautaud recounts what a friend had found when he went to Maxim's for lunch only a few days after the Germans had marched into Paris. 'Outside a private dining room were hanging fourteen German officers' hats and one civilian hat. Intrigued, he asked the maître d'hôtel, "What's that?" The maître d'hôtel whispered in his ear, "It is Monsieur Sacha Guitry, who is giving lunch to German officers." '

In his diary Jünger recorded an occasion in October 1941 when he and Colonel Speidel were asked to lunch at Guitry's house.

On arrival Guitry handed me a folder with three holograph letters, by Octave Mirbeau, Léon Bloy and Debussy – three persons whom we had talked about at our first meeting – and invited me to include these in my collection. . . . He showed me a book by Bergson with the dedication, 'To Sacha Guitry – an admirer' – not *his* admirer but the much more delicate *an*, he pointed out. Among many other things there was also Molière's travel case containing the first editions of all his plays. Also there was a miniature bronze cast of Napoleon with all his marshals. . . .

At table, the salad was served on silver plates and the ice cream on gold dishes that had once belonged to Sarah Bernhardt. I was again astonished by the anecdotes in which meetings with royalty played a prominent role. He would mimic the people whose names arose in the conversation. It was blatant showing-off.

In her memoir, Alice Epting remembered him fondly as a guest, host and liar.

He came several times to the German Institute. On these occasions he entertained all the other guests with his sparkling wit. Once he invited us to his house. He worshipped success and lived on it. He always had to have a public around him, even if it was small. One of his last books was *Quatre ans d'occupations* in which he defended himself from accusations by the Resistance and sought to show in great detail that he had never been a 'collaborator', that during the German Occupation he had had absolutely nothing to do with the Germans and that no German had ever crossed the threshold of his house. He provided a long list of friends who could prove it. In this way the very imaginative actor succeeded in finding his way back to his theatre and to his audience. We Germans who know better are willing to forgive this man of the theatre, whom we admire, for his little lies.

In his 1977 memoirs General Speidel said the same but phrased it rather more gently. 'He was all in favour of close cooperation [with German authorities] but in the postwar period understandably did not wish to admit to this.'

Guitry had always fancied himself France's cultural ambassador and regarded his fraternizing as an act of high patriotism. When, for example, a friend rejected his offer of an introduction to Abetz with a view to getting a job, his reply was, 'So you do not want to do anything for France!' Promoting French culture was how he justified publishing articles in such compromised organs as *La Gerbe* and *Le Petit Parisien* as well as the *Cahiers franco-allemands*. And it is how he explained taking Breker around Paris to introduce him to the French theatrical world. So well connected with German officials was he that a Vichy official once turned to him for an introduction to an official of the Propaganda Department.

It was as a result of these connections and friendships that Guitry enjoyed quite exceptional privileges. No other figure from the cultural world had the right to keep and drive a car and even to have a special permit, otherwise restricted to German officers, to drive on Sundays. He also received a gas ration and coal to heat his house. His villas at Cap d'Ail and St Tropez and a country house near Versailles were de-requisitioned from the Wehrmacht. Far from being embarrassed about this special treatment, he proudly reproduced copies of the relevant documents in his book. The benefits he enjoyed during the Occupation made him a war profiteer in his way just as much as they did certain businessmen in theirs.

In April 1946 Guitry went on trial before a purge tribunal. He produced reams of testimony – all sounding much like publishers' book puffs – about what a fine fellow he was and how outstanding as an actor-playwright he had been. The core of his defence was the standard claim of *collabos* – he had saved lives thanks to his interventions with his German contacts. He did not deny his privileges and insisted that anyone who criticized him was simply jealous. Above all he had acted for France. 'From 1940 on it seemed to me right that the Germans should be confronted with the intellectual and cultural greatness of the French nation. . . . The only reproach which can truthfully be made against me is that I remained civilized.'

The case against Guitry was not well prepared, in part no doubt because compromising documents in the files of the Wehrmacht and German civilian agencies had been destroyed or hauled back to Berlin in 1944. No one seems to have read Jünger or Léautaud and Alice Epting's book had not yet been published. Concluding that nothing was culpable about his German contacts and that nothing was compromising in his professional life, the court decided in August 1947 that he had no case to answer. Legal punishment he escaped. But not that of society. Paul Valéry, Colette and other old friends had dropped him even before the end of the war and now others did so. His films, plays and books were for a time banned and his bank accounts frozen. Although he soon took up his theatre work again, his reputation never recovered.

Guitry was far from the only actor to disgrace himself for being friendly with the Germans. Of all the arts, the theatre was the most compromised. 'It is clear', Galtier-Boissière remarked after the Liberation, 'that the majority of our stars are more or less tainted.' Writing of her own appearances at German functions, Alice Cocéa observed, 'There I met le Tout-Paris of theatre and film.' Indeed she had, and they all met again in August 1944 – in prison. Cocéa, one of the earliest French film stars, had distinguished herself in 1940 by taking over the Théâtre des Ambassadeurs after its Jewish proprietor was forced to flee. She was personally a great hit with Wehrmacht officers. Arletty – Léonie Bathiat was her real name – was another camp follower. In no time she had found a bedmate among the officers of the invading army and was a veritable fixture at their social events. After the Liberation she, like many of her female colleagues, was interned for a time and prohibited from acting, in her case for three years.

Sacha Guitry's father could not keep his son away from the theatre. Jean Gabin's could not entice his son into it. Gabin was born into a family he himself labelled bohemian. Not until the birth of their third child could his parents be bothered to get married. His father was a successful actor-singer in popular operettas; his mother was also a singer, though to her lasting regret had to retire as the family grew. Jean was the youngest of seven children, four of whom survived. He saw little of his father, who spent his time on the stage and his money on the horses. It was largely an elder sister who raised him, with the result that he never needed to rebel since he was almost always on his own. Although he later looked back on his early years as not unhappy, he told his friend and biographer André Brunelin that there had been no warmth in family life. He could not recall his parents ever taking him in their arms, much less kissing him.

There were other lasting early influences. Trains have a fascination for some boys, and Gabin was one of them. A railway ran by the small town where he grew up and – for reasons Freud could have explained to him – he was fascinated by the pulsating energy of the locomotives with their camshafts and piston rods. He never entirely escaped the feeling that driving one of these engines was what he most wanted to do in life. That was not his father's intention, however. He was determined that his son should go on the stage. 'I hated my father's profession', Gabin later said. 'I could not understand it.' As a youth he had observed his father practising lines and gained the impression that the theatre was a hard and joyless master. In later years, when a star, he never forgot the difficulties his father and others like him had endured and ever after retained a respect for minor actors who never became famous.

To arouse his interest in the profession, Jean's father would take him along to the theatre. But these visits put him off all the more. Everything seemed like children's make-believe. He was shocked on first seeing make-up being applied and in later years always felt queasy about being made up himself. Props also added to the fakeness. Nothing was real. There was a certain charm about Gabin's naïveté. It went so far that he even found it inappropriate that an actor should be applauded at the end of a performance while an engine driver who hauled people safely from place to place was not. These were some of the psychological barriers his father could not break through. So he tried subterfuge. One day he inveigled his son to accompany him to the Folies Bergère. On arrival, as previously arranged, the manager took one look at him and hired him on the spot before Jean could open his mouth to say no.

Although he showed no great talent and felt no great commitment, Gabin gradually made his way. The louche morals of the theatre shocked him, but he came to like actors as people. And they liked him, with his Parisian argot and proletarian looks, his lack of pretension and good humour. 'I would never have had the courage to follow my father's path because I never loved the acting profession so much that I wanted to struggle to make it. I said to myself early on, either I have quick success or I give it up.' The first opportunity to shine arrived when he was asked to take on a star role at the last minute. When his big moment came, the result was something out of slapstick comedy. He opened his mouth but no sound came out; he took a step forward and fell flat, not just on his own face but also on the faces of any number of members of the revue. The audience howled in delight. The management howled in fury and sacked him. Now was his chance to quit the theatre for good. But he needed money and found another job.

Not long afterwards – in 1925 – he completed his two-year compulsory military service in the navy on the Breton coast. 'Following orders was never my strength', he commented on this unhappy time. But there was also a happy moment when he met, fell in love with and married an actress, Gaby Basset. Five years later they had an amicable divorce – marriage was not an institution either of them regarded highly – and ever after Basset spoke of Gabin with great affection. A second marriage was unhappy and ended in divorce in 1943.

On being discharged from the navy Gabin went back to the theatre. Unable to find a regular acting job, he turned to the music hall. To his great surprise he discovered he had an excellent voice and one similar to that of Maurice Chevalier, who was just becoming all the rage. It was now 1926, he was twenty-two and a success. He even began enjoying theatrical life. A few years later he was picked up by one of the most popular music-hall actress-singers of the time, Mistinguett. After that he sang in several operettas where his voice and humour made him highly popular. At least one review compared him with Guitry, though it is hard to think that the association would have pleased the stuck-up boulevardier. By now he was earning enough to dream of another life. That was to buy a farm in Normandy and leave the theatre for good.

And in 1930 he in fact did quit the theatre, though not to breed cows but to act in films. At the invitation of Pathé-Nathan, he appeared in an operetta which was such a success that he was given a three-year contract. Between 1931 and 1935 he starred in no fewer than eighteen films, six in 1932 alone. The French film industry was entering a brilliant period and by the time of the war he was in some of its very best productions. Though he was now the number one star in France, he continued to feel uneasy. In later years, when in a bad mood, he would grumble that acting was a profession for women. So it is not surprising that he felt comfortable only in roles he believed in and felt part of. One good example was a film produced by Jean Renoir, *La Belle Équipe*, taken from the famous novel by Zola. If Gabin could not be the engine driver of his dreams, here he could at least play one. Thanks to roles such as this, and his simple personal appearance, he became a working-class hero at the very time France was going through a period of exceptional social turmoil.

The outbreak of the war found Gabin in Brittany with Michèle Morgan making a film entitled *Remorque*. He was immediately called up into the navy, but in the absence of any military action during the phoney war was given leave to finish the movie. When the French defensive line collapsed in June 1940 Morgan made her way to Cannes while Gabin made his to Paris and eventually Nice. Like everyone else, he was staggered by the defeat. Renoir proposed their doing another film together but then saw it would be impossible and took off for the United States. Gabin refused to return to Paris and rejected the offer of a contract with the new German film company, Continental, to do a film in Nice. 'There had been a war; the Germans were the victors and we were the defeated', he later told his biographer. 'At that time everyone did what he thought was best for himself, and when I returned [in 1944] I never criticized anyone for what he decided. In my case I did not refuse out of any exaggerated patriotism; no, it was just that something in me revolted. Or, more simply, it just made me sick.' Stranded in Nice and at a loose end, he sailed in the Baie des Anges, cycled and played football. His romance with Morgan was a complication. For her the relationship was over and, with a Hollywood contract in hand, she planned to start a life and a new career in America. He still felt an attachment and, after seeing her off, suddenly felt impelled to follow and went to Vichy to apply for exit papers.

One of the few famous actors who refused to return to Paris, he knew his situation was precarious. The Wehrmacht threatened to requisition his country house – which in fact it later did and still later burned down. By the end of the year it was less a case of pursuing Morgan than of escaping from a France where he had no professional or personal future. With the help of a Spanish footballer in Nice, he made his way in February 1941 to Barcelona, where he received a visa from the American consulate. All he had with him were his accordion and his bicycle. He arrived in New York without money, job, friends or a word of English. He felt lost and homesick. When he reached Hollywood things improved. Darryl Zanuck offered him a contract. He found French friends – Jean Renoir, Jean-Pierre Aumont, René Clair, Charles Boyer and, of course, Michèle Morgan. He also came to know someone whom he had admired from afar, Ginger Rogers. Tinseltown itself he found so deserving of its nickname that he fled whenever possible to New York.

Enter Marlene Dietrich. She and Gabin had met briefly in Paris ten years earlier at dinner with Galtier-Boissière. With her European background and ways and fluent French, she made him feel less alien. They became companions as well as lovers. Although known in the film world as a 'commercial catastrophe' because of a series of movies that had bombed, Dietrich was socially popular and took Gabin in tow. He liked neither the beautiful people of Hollywood nor their way of life. His idea of an enjoyable day was to stay at home; hers was to go out. When she told him to read the novels of her friend Ernest Hemingway, he replied that he knew as much about life as any novelist. But it helped that she had a library of French cookbooks and was a reasonable cook.

It was not until a year after his arrival in America that Gabin resumed acting. He learned American English remarkably fast but was dissatisfied with his acting in English. 'When I act in French I do not hear myself, but in English I heard myself and got the impression that an entirely different person was speaking. It seemed like an echo and I felt myself completely asynchron. My movements, my body, everything I felt physically and also what I thought did not seem right, did not seem to fit with what I said. It was an extremely painful experience.' His first Hollywood film was called *Moontide* and had a cast that included Claude Rains, Thomas Mitchell and Ida Lupino. While not a flop, it was not the hoped-for success either; when it reached France after the war, it was snubbed by critics.

In her memoirs, written after his death, Dietrich expressed her deep affection for Gabin, though not in terms that he is likely to have found pleasing.

> Completely helpless, he clung to me as an orphan to an adoptive mother and I was delighted to mother him day and night. The world knows his acting talent; no point dwelling on that. But his soft side is largely unknown. The façade of a tough guy and his manly demeanour. He was the most sensitive man I have ever known – a little baby who was happiest crawling into his mother's lap, to be cradled and petted. . . . I was his mother, sister, girlfriend and much more. I loved him dearly.

Gabin never felt at home in America. 'I was bored to death and felt left out of what was going on in the world,' he told André Brunelin.

> Of course I went to demonstrations in support of the war effort and attended dinners. But I just could not stand it any longer. They told us that everyone in France was in the Resistance and fighting the Germans. We heard about the Maquis, sabotage and shootings. I was really sick at the thought that the Germans might win the war and I would have to end my days in the USA. I could not have returned to Paris and looked people in the face without shame if I had not done my bit for the Liberation.

And so at the end of 1942 he left Hollywood and went to New York to volunteer for the Free French.

On arriving, he was told he could do something far more useful than going into battle by making a propaganda film. So, rather than being sent out to Africa to fight against Rommel, as he had hoped, he was sent back to Hollywood. In this way came about *L'Imposteur*, a movie about a con man who dies a heroic death for France. When that was finished, he returned to New York and again volunteered to go into combat. This time he found they wanted to turn him into a walking advertisement. He was not asked to parade the streets wearing a sandwich board, but almost. He was to go around decked

out in a splendid uniform with the Gaullist Cross of Lorraine prominently
displayed, attend parties in New York and Hollywood and tell the French
guests to join the Free French. He refused. Later he said he was driven not by
a sense of gallantry but by the knowledge that he could never have lived with
himself had he not taken an active part in the war. Although the prospect of
physical danger frightened him, he was undeterred. And there was another
consideration. 'I felt that had I spent the rest of my life in the United States, I
would have died of boredom.'

Given his earlier naval training, he was assigned to a French escort convoy
that protected oil tankers en route to North Africa, a favourite target of
German submarines. Dietrich saw him off. On their last day together they
went to a film, *Our Russian Front*, in which Humphrey Bogart played the role
of a captain of an escort ship on the same sort of mission as Gabin's own.
When his ship was attacked by U-boats, Bogart responded with cool and
unshakeable courage and barked out orders with calm determination. Gabin
was greatly impressed. His own crossing was uneventful – only one tanker was
hit in the Atlantic – but once his ship passed Gibraltar the Luftwaffe struck
with ferocity.

The funny thing, if I may say so, is that when I think back on this mission
into hell, in the midst of all the carnage, where all around ships were sinking
or going up in flames, young sailors were firing away or being mowed
down, I could not help thinking of Bogart in his film in a situation exactly
the same as I was now going through. He was absolutely marvellous in his
calm assurance and without a shadow of fear when under fire. On the other
hand I was trembling. My helmet was bouncing around on my head and my
teeth were chattering. Of course I tried to conceal this from my comrades
who must have been in the same state. But I could not help thinking, what
an idiot this Bogart was. I would like to see him here and see what the hell
he would do in my place. I have often asked myself whether the example of
Bogart, which I could not get out of my head in the midst of all this horror,
may have saved my life. Perhaps I owe him a small thank-you.

On arriving in Algiers, Gabin was summoned by the Gaullist de facto navy
minister who had just the job for him – at a Centre Artistique de Propagande.
When he visibly cringed at the offer, the minister remarked, 'But tell me, Gabin,
at your age do you really want to play the hero?' To which Gabin replied that
he had no desire to play any role, least of all that of a hero. 'I did not cross the
Atlantic for that.' And so saying, he walked out. Shortly thereafter he was made
an instructor in a navy gunnery school and enlisted for the duration of the war.
Then Dietrich arrived. She was now in the Women's Auxiliary Corps, touring

American army bases to entertain the troops. Somehow she usually managed to be entertaining where Gabin was soldiering. When apart, he wrote to her every day. After a period of training he was made a tank commander in General Leclerc's regiment. It was not an ideal assignment since he was somewhat claustrophobic and had an overwhelming horror of being burned alive – the prime risk in tank warfare. Finally, in autumn 1944 he was sent into action, to participate in driving the Germans out of Lorraine. At one point he was given leave and returned to Paris to see his family. On the street and on the Métro people recognized him and commented – within his earshot – about how he had aged and how white his blond hair had turned. Even more was he offended by rumours that he had run off to Hollywood and made a fortune.

His return to Paris left him so disillusioned that he was happy to return to his unit and the rough company of his men, who had always regarded him as a tank commander, not a movie star, and knew him not by the name Jean Gabin but by his real surname, Moncorgé. When the surrender was signed on 8 May, Gabin found himself at Berchtesgaden and was given leave to spend several hours touring Hitler's Berghof.

At the moment Gabin was clambering around the ruins on the Obersalzburg, one of the leading French film producers was just starting work on *Naïs*, a movie based on a story by Zola. Marcel Pagnol, himself a Provençal whose studio was in Marseille, was known for his sentimental comedies set in Provence. His famous trilogy of *Marius, Fanny* and *César* tells popular stories about life around the port in Marseille. Adapted from his earlier plays, the films were not especially well made but enjoyed wide popularity for their dialogue and acting, especially by the remarkable Raimu. The theme of most of these movies was similar – a hero who suddenly goes away, a heroine pregnant with his illegitimate child, a loving family and everyday people doing everyday things.

Pagnol's previous film had the distinction of being the only one made during the disastrous days of 1940 when all the other film studios had closed. It was another sentimental comedy, *La Fille du puisatier* (*The Well-Digger's Daughter*) and was completed very shortly after the armistice. Criticized by Pauline Kael as an 'unjustifiably popular pastoral romp', the movie conveyed the notion that people close to the soil are the salt of the earth. Leaving aside the naughty daughter – great with illegitimate child – the film fitted in beautifully with the philosophy of the new government in Vichy. The impression was strengthened by Pagnol's insertion at the last minute of a concluding scene in which the main characters – played by his famous team of Raimu, Fernandel and Josette Day – are seen listening on a radio to Pétain's speech announcing the armistice. France was now at peace; the characters in the story were now at peace. In a way it was a typical Pagnol happy ending. But after the war he was called to account for that final scene, which appeared to endorse Pétain and collaboration. Lamely and anti-historically, Pagnol explained that he had intended to contest the notion that the public had enthusiastically welcomed the armistice – though it unquestionably had done so.

For all the sentimental nostalgia of his films, Pagnol had solid credentials as an intellectual. He had been an outstanding student, received a degree in philosophy and gone on to study English literature at the University of Aix-en-Provence. It was then that he helped to found *Fortunio*, a literary publication that was an ancestor of the *Cahiers du sud*. After teaching for a time in various lycées, he decided to make his way as a writer. In the course of the following years he wrote thirteen plays, several novels, numerous essays, any number of film scenarios and dialogues, translations of *Hamlet* and *A Midsummer Night's Dream* as well as Virgil's *Bucolics* and one work of history, *Le Masque de fer* (The Secret of the Iron Mask), about Louis XIV's twin brother. He also produced, directed or wrote scripts for twenty-eight films, and it is for these that he is known best.

Pagnol had begun his movie career in 1931 when he set up his own studio in Marseille and, in collaboration with Alexander Korda, made his first film, *Marius*. By the time the war began, eighteen more had followed. Neither the war nor the defeat immediately interfered with his work. After completing *La Fille du puisatier*, he began planning new films and the revival of some of his old plays. He bought a site outside Marseille where he hoped to fulfil his dream of establishing a French Hollywood that would make him rich and internationally famous. There was talk of his being elected to the Académie Française. His personal life was equally promising. Over the years Pagnol had frequently fallen in and out of love, occasionally marrying but more often merely having children on the wrong side of the sheets – possibly why his movies were populated with so many unmarried mothers. That changed in 1940 when he met Josette Day, who became so central a part of his life that Raymond Castans, a biographer, entitled his chapter on the Occupation years as 'The Years of Josette'.

Then suddenly everything turned sour. In the summer of 1941 Pagnol began work on *La Prière aux étoiles* (Prayer to the Stars), planned as the first in a new trilogy. Almost immediately he ran into the problems that were typical of independent filmmaking during those years. It proved difficult to find materials for sets and costumes and even film for the cameras. Electricity was rationed and sometimes cut off while scenes were being shot. Morale suffered from rumours that German censors were freely banning movies or demanding huge cuts. The final blow came when he failed to get German permission for the actors and crew to cross into the Occupied Zone to film scenes in Paris. Pagnol cancelled the project and destroyed what had so far been shot. That was not the end of his problems. Despite its success in both zones, *La Fille du puisatier* had not gone over well with Vichy officials. They liked neither the embarrassing out-of-wedlock pregnancy nor the story's failure to promote the sense of repentance that was to be the tone of the new France. On top of that, the Germans were pressing him to enter into a cooperative arrangement with Continental. Not willing to be under the control of anyone else and unable to keep going on his own, Pagnol sold his studio to the French concern Gaumont. And so it was that the country's most popular filmmaker produced no films during the Occupation.

Even minus Pagnol, some Marseille studios continued for a time to bring out films. Many of these starred Fernandel, Marseille's best-known personality and France's best-paid actor. 'It was in Marseille that I was born, it is Marseille that made me, and that is why I refuse to act in any other studio than that of my friend Pagnol,' he had said. But after Pagnol closed his studio, Fernandel continued acting. 'Me, I am only a comic. What can I do except to entertain, to cheer up my compatriots a little and to help them forget – at least for a few moments?' And he was right. Though he had a few questions to answer when the war was over – such as why he had worked with Continental – he had made people too happy to suffer any unfavourable consequences.

'Forget – at least for a few moments.' At a minimum the Seventh Art had always offered a diversion from the real world. For the French during the Occupation it promised, more than any of the other arts, a brief escape from prison or at least a glimpse outside the prison window. In the vast majority of towns and villages, with dancing forbidden, it was the only form of entertainment available. Not surprisingly, cinema receipts in those years doubled and in Paris trebled.

The industry soon transformed itself from dead duck into risen phoenix. No other branch of art or industry had been so battered by the Occupation. On arriving in Paris, the Wehrmacht had immediately outlawed British and American films and a little later those by producers or with actors who had gone into exile. In November 1940 an additional two hundred were removed from distribution. Six months later all those that had been shown in France before October 1937 were also banned. Apparently this was not so much an act of censorship as a means of forcing the French to see German movies.

In the meantime the industry itself went through a uniquely brutal personnel purge – of Jews, foreign nationals and political objectionables. Since one of the loudest complaints of the rightist press in the Thirties had been the bogus claim that Jews dominated the French film industry, it is not surprising that in the big 1941 exhibition *The Jew and France* there was a prominent display under the rubric 'Jews, Masters of the French Cinema'. There followed a purge that exempted no one – not even projectionists. The Propaganda Department further drew up a blacklist with the names of actors and directors who, though not Jews, were considered enemies of the Third Reich and whose films must therefore not be shown. Among the names were Marlene Dietrich, Conrad Veidt, Michèle Morgan, Erich von Stroheim and Charles Boyer.

The paradoxical result of the purge was that the French film industry was reborn. A fresh young generation of producers, directors and scriptwriters now stepped forward. And they had virtually a free run. For the first time in their history, French filmmakers did not face American competition. Hollywood's domination of French screens is evident in a few numbers. In 1938 French cinemas showed 169 American films as compared with 135 French ones; the figures for 1939 were 144 and 83. By 1942, when the domestic industry was back on its feet, cinemas in the Occupied Zone showed 74 French films as compared with 39 German ones and in the following year the figures were 81 and 28.

Censorship was rigorous. Those films made in the Unoccupied Zone, where controls were relatively lax, faced strict German scrutiny before they could be shown in the Occupied Zone and sometimes reached the screen only after months of delay. The same general rules applied to the cinema as to the theatre – nothing controversial, nothing about the war or political affairs. To this extent the public and the censors saw eye to eye. Apart from one or two openly anti-Semitic films, there was little propaganda. Interestingly enough, even though anti-Semitism and Anglophobia were now government policy, the caricatural Jews and British who had peopled some prewar films were no longer to be seen. Vichy imposed several standards, however, that gave rise to hilarity. Adultery, it was decreed, should not account for more than 49 per cent of a plot. And one of the most notable movies of the era, *Goupi mains rouges* (*It Happened at the Inn*), was licensed only after 'quelques éléments gais' – several happy episodes – had been introduced to lighten the mood.

Knowing that audiences wanted straightforward entertainment, film producers gave the public mostly comedies and stories that sought refuge in the past, in allegory or in a timeless world. Documentaries were a different matter. More often than not they were flagrant propaganda, predictably dilating on the nefarious influence of Jews, Freemasons, communists and, with the passage of time, the Resistance. The Germans also made it compulsory to show newsreels from Germans sources, only to find these were greeted with catcalls and other rude noises to such a degree that it was necessary to screen them in a lit auditorium to quell the commotion. Audiences frequently responded by waiting until the feature film began before taking their seats.

Of the 220 feature films made during the Occupation, all but thirty-five were produced in the Occupied Zone. Sixty of the total were made by German companies. The figure is not as odd as it might seem. Throughout the Thirties there had been considerable collaboration between France and Germany in terms of production, financing and acting, to the extent that the German film industry was a major producer of French movies. Taking advantage of this, Goebbels dreamed of making Berlin the great competitor to Hollywood. The Continental Film Company, formed in Paris in October 1940, was his Trojan horse. Its head was Alfred Greven, a staunch Nazi but one who did not mix film business with propaganda. Profits and popularity were the overriding interest. In fact, given the extent of technical collaboration before the war, it was sometimes difficult to know what counted as political collaboration during the Occupation.

But there could be no doubt about professional collaboration. Simone Signoret summed it up with Bruller-like simplicity, 'If there was a division among actors, it could only have been between those who agreed to work with the Germans at Continental and those who refused.' That was the fault line that ran through the entire profession. Few in the film world were on the right side of it.

One of the most conspicuous on the wrong side was none other than Georges Simenon, best known as a mystery writer and novelist but who since 1931 was also a purveyor of works for screen adaptation. Within a few months of the armistice he was contacted by Greven and happily accepted an invitation to work for him. Continental soon came to regard him as one of its stars; he regarded Continental as a source of money and a vehicle for wheedling favours out of the German authorities. For what his biographer, Pierre Assouline, termed 'a princely sum', he sold exclusive rights to his Inspector Maigret character and an option on three books – an arrangement he was careful to keep secret. In 1941 what Simenon made from Continental amounted to half his ample income. During the Occupation he was the writer whose works were most often brought to the screen – nine of them as compared to seven adaptations of Balzac.

All the while he was also submitting articles to a variety of *collabo* publications, including *Je suis partout*. Occasionally he entertained Wehrmacht officers and became friends with some of the most notorious Vichy bigwigs. Speculating on his motivations, Assouline concluded that it was a combination of opportunism, cowardice and greed. After the Liberation Simenon tried to exculpate himself by arguing that none of his writing was of a political nature. Be that as it may, privately he had laid his cards on the table very early, writing to his mother in March 1941, 'I hope the English will not hold out much longer.' They did hold out, however. The Germans eventually withdrew. And a compromised Simenon did a bunk, settling in the United States.

The two most important facts about the theatre – that it was highly popular and shunned propaganda – generally applied to the cinema as well. But what was propaganda? Pagnol's French were amusing, lovable Marseillais and good-hearted, wise and earthy Provençaux. Henri-Georges Clouzot's French were depraved and corrupt, with no redeeming traits. Such was the picture that emerged from his *Le Corbeau* (*The Raven*), the most controversial film to appear during the Occupation. Clouzot had begun as a journalist and then in the 1930s became head of the dubbing unit in a German company in Berlin. After the armistice he became increasingly involved with Continental, first writing dialogue, then constructing scenarios, after that writing entire scripts, and finally becoming head of Continental's script unit. Impressed by his talents, Greven commissioned him to make three films for Continental. The first, *L'Assassin habite au 21* (The Murderer Lives at Number 21), with the popular stars Pierre Fresnay and Suzy Delair, was such a success that Clouzot felt encouraged to go on.

It was at this point that he met Louis Chavance, a scriptwriter and actor who in 1936–37 had written a film script based on the true story of a town that had been torn apart by a series of poison-pen letters. The town was Tulle in south central France, where between 1917 and 1922 a wave of anonymous letters – around a thousand – had circulated, revealing family secrets, marital infidelities, illegitimate births and other disreputable secrets. The letters envenomed the atmosphere in the town to such an extent that some inhabitants were driven to crime and suicide. When Clouzot learned of the story in 1943, denunciatory letters had become an important feature of life in Occupied France. Written by *corbeaux* – literally 'crows' but slang for the writers of poison-pen letters – they were pouring into Wehrmacht headquarters at a rate of 1,500 a day. What could be a more relevant issue to tackle in a film? But it was also clearly a dangerous one. There was the ominous precedent of Cocteau's *Machine à écrire*. Clouzot went ahead despite the admonition of Greven, who considered the subject too delicate and contrary to the policy of avoiding social controversy. As filming progressed, so Continental's nervousness grew. The Wehrmacht authorities were uneasy, too. Even the Gestapo got involved. Denunciatory letters were an invaluable source of information in tracking down Jews, resisters and others they wanted. Nothing should dissuade the public from sending them. Tensions all round were such that by the time filming was finished, so was Clouzot.

Continental cancelled its contract with him. Greven was in trouble with Berlin. And the film was no doubt the sole occasion when Vichy, the Catholic church, the Resistance and the communists were all in agreement. It was condemned as a defamation of village life and of the French people, and a service to the Nazis – indeed, it had been paid for by them. The most vociferous attack appeared in *Lettres françaises*. In his article 'The Crow Is Deplumed', Georges Sadoul, a historian of the cinema and long-time Stalinist, accused

Clouzot not only of being in effect a traitor for working with Continental but also of producing a film that was being shown in Germany to anti-French effect.

These were charges brought up by a purge tribunal a few weeks after the Liberation. Clouzot responded that he had neither created the facts nor written the film script, that denunciatory letters were a highly pertinent issue at the time, that he had made the film over German objections and that it was never shown in Germany or even dubbed for screening there. In his *Le Cinéma français sous l'Occupation*, Jean-Pierre Bertin-Maghit refers to Clouzot's critics as a 'cabal' and maintains that the trial was orchestrated by Sadoul and the Communist party.

Given the mood of the time, the film could not be separated from its producer. The one condemned the other. In the end the communists had their way. Clouzot was barred from making films for evermore and *Le Corbeau* was banned from the screen. It was the harshest punishment meted out to a film-maker by a purge tribunal. Fresnay, an important actor in the film, was also banned, while the other performers as well as the crew members received lesser sanctions. Outraged, de Beauvoir, Sartre and Henri Jeanson, among others, circulated a petition defending Clouzot, as did a group of film producers. Eventually the prohibition on his professional activity was reduced to two years. Clouzot was luckier than his film, which continued to be prohibited until 1969. Pagnol exculpated himself by falsifying history. Clouzot was punished for telling the truth.

CHAPTER 10

HUMAN, ALL TOO HUMAN

A history of the Occupation is the story of how forty million French along with a million or so Germans lived together as prisoners in a nightmare world created by one man – an evil genius headquartered in Berlin. Like the characters in Sartre's *Huis clos*, they were all *personae* in a drama from which there was no escape. The artists and intellectuals among them behaved as all human beings always behave in dark times. In ways honourable and dishonourable, they sought to survive. Survival meant different things, of course. For some, it was a matter of staying alive in the most primitive sense of simply scrounging enough to eat or escaping arrest, deportation and execution. For others, it was to be able to ignore the world around them and to practise their art without interference. For still others, it was finding some way to endure spiritually in an unbearable environment. Of those who wanted to do more than survive, most were either opportunists motivated by greed and ambition or sincere believers in a united fascist Europe under German direction that would put an end for ever to war in Europe.

The Occupation was merciless in exposing character. So come the Liberation, survival gained a new meaning. There had been so much suffering, humiliation and shame, so many victims of betrayal, torture and deportation that, as in 1940, feelings of hatred and revenge permeated society. 'After such knowledge, what forgiveness?' to quote a line from T.S. Eliot. The consequent rush to judgement was all too human. In some cases the decisions were ferocious, in others lenient. Ferocious? Lenient? What were the standards? What was guilt? Was it moral or political? Was there a difference? Were deeds alone to be judged or also opinions? But how could guilt flow from a pen, paintbrush, voice or musical instrument? How could it result from a social occasion, attendance at a lecture by a German speaker or a visit to Weimar? Were artists and intellectuals to be weighed in the same legal scales as political figures, businessmen and Vichy bureaucrats? In any case, was there a more firmly established legal basis for the *épuration* in France than there was for the *épuration* at Nuremberg? Who was to judge? A magistrate who had loyally served Vichy for four years and in some cases had sentenced a member of the Resistance to death? And who was to defend? A lawyer who had practised his profession after swearing allegiance to Marshal Pétain? Easy to ask, not always easy to answer

Throughout the Occupation thousands of Madame Defarges had been knitting away. Charges of collaboration began to circulate in early 1941 and miniature coffins started arriving in mailboxes not long after that. The French service of the BBC occasionally broadcast the names of dangerous collaborators and called for their assassination – which sometimes followed. Next the clandestine press issued blacklists and in 1943 *Life* magazine published its own catalogue of 'persons to be investigated or sentenced to death as soon as France is freed'. When *collabos* learned that word had spread as far as America, they knew they were in trouble. After the Liberation, writers' groups drew up their own lists, with ninety-four names on one and 160 on another. Some names were strangely absent, some were strangely present. For the unscrupulous Aragon and other Stalinists, the *épuration* was not only a way of calling collaborators to account but also a long-awaited opportunity to get revenge on anti-communists – Gide, for example, because of his 1936 book criticizing the Soviet Union. Eventually most prominent Resistance figures became so appalled by the irresponsibility of various purge committees that they washed their hands of it all. 'Look at me well because you will never see me again', and, so saying, Jean Guéhenno stomped out of a meeting dominated by eleventh-hour converts to the Resistance who were out for blood. With scorching sarcasm Galtier-Boissière referred to them as 'the ultra-pure who just returned from spending the war in Honolulu'.

Even leaving aside the stigma of the Vichy past of most judges and prosecutors, purge trials raised troublesome moral and legal issues. In practice outcomes depended not just on the facts but also on chance. As in the case of Germaine Lubin, chance included the location of the court – some were far harsher than others – the competence of the prosecutor and the defence attorney, the mood of the judge and jury, and the timing of the trial – later was better. Chance could be tamed if you had connections or money for a bribe; it could be disastrous if it threw up a witness willing to lie because of some personal grudge.

Some important figures managed to escape trial – Drieu la Rochelle by committing suicide, the novelist Ramon Fernandez by a fatal heart attack, the publisher Robert Denoël by being gunned down in the street and Maurice Bunau-Varilla, proprietor of *Le Matin* and an open admirer of Hitler, by dying

just as Paris was liberated. Various other cultural celebrities such as Paul
Morand, Alfred Cortot, Horace de Carbuccia, Georges Simenon and Céline
were savvy enough to lie low outside France until things cooled down.

It was probably only to be expected that Céline's fate would be appropriately
picaresque. Thanks to Bickler, he was finally granted permission to travel to
Denmark and in March 1945 with his wife and Bébert made his way from
Sigmaringen through a Germany in smoking ruins to Copenhagen. With an
apartment and country house available to him and royalty monies in a Danish
bank, he anticipated living a safe, quiet and comfortable exile. It was not to be.
Even before the end of the war a Paris court had issued a warrant for his arrest
and not long afterwards the French government applied for his extradition to
stand trial for treason. Danish authorities rejected the request but imprisoned
him and his wife. Though she was released after four months, Céline remained
incarcerated for another six and was then confined for a long period to various
medical establishments.

Plagued as much as ever by what are known in some circles as anger-
management issues, Céline discharged a stream of bilious, churlish, self-pitying
letters pouring scorn on one and all and dismissing the ridiculous charges
against him – he who had never failed to use his credentials as a doctor to help
a Jew, a Resistance fighter or a person facing forced labour in Germany; he who
had never taken a sou from the Germans, who hated Abetz (and vice versa) and
who had never denounced anyone. Guilty of 'intelligence with the enemy'? Did
anyone fancy he had sold the Germans plans of the Maginot Line? It is never
easy to know whether Céline believed anything he said. But by piling up red
herrings, he must have hoped he could put his critics off the scent of the most
serious charge – that he was in some sense a German agent.

Artists and intellectuals posed a unique challenge to the courts. In a country
where ideas have always been more important than facts, the question was
whether the accused should be judged for their opinions as well as their deeds.
That led to the further question whether opinions could become deeds when
they called for action – such as arrest, assassination or deportation. And
behind this lay the still broader issue of the responsibility of artists and intellectuals to society. It was those on the extremes who were most deeply
conscious of a responsibility – the Gides, Brullers and Guéhennos on the one
hand, and the Brasillachs, Rebatets and Fabre-Luces on the other. Each had a
sense of unbending adherence to his principles. 'I can regret nothing of what
I have been', Brasillach insisted at his trial, even though he knew he faced the
death penalty for what he had been.

On this soggy legal terrain, the purge trials lurched forward. In the ancient
world an animal was sacrificed to atone for the sins of the nation. Now humans
were to have that honour. The most serious charge was 'intelligence with a

foreign power or its agents' – 'intelligence' meaning contact of some sort – thus even anyone who ever set foot in the German Institute. The first to go before judge and jury were not the Vichy officials who had ordered the arrest and deportation of Jews, communists and resisters, or the police who had carried out the orders. Nor were they the manufacturers who had supplied the Wehrmacht and Luftwaffe with equipment, or the contractors who had built the U-boat pens and defence installations on the Atlantic coast. Nor were they the gangsters who had tortured and killed members of the Resistance. Instead they were writers, journalists and newspaper editors. They were the most vulnerable. They had no political protection. There was no need to search archives and examine files for incriminating evidence: their words were there in cold print for anyone to read. And the words could be damning – defending deportations, soliciting denunciations, justifying the Wehrmacht's reprisal executions, vilifying the Jews, British, Gaullists and members of the Resistance. But could words alone amount to treason and, if so, should they be punished by death?

The trials began shortly after the Liberation of Paris. On 20 October Albert Lejeune, publisher of *L'Auto* and a number of regional dailies, was accused of having effectively been in the employ of the Germans and making a fortune by publishing their propaganda. The evidence was overwhelming. He was the first to stand in front of a firing squad. Next to be executed were George Suarez, editor of *Aujourd'hui*, Jean Luchaire, editor of *Les Nouveaux Temps*, the journalist Paul Chack and Brasillach. Henri Béraud, editorialist for *Gringoire*, André Algarron, editor of *Le Petit Parisien*, Martin de Briey of *Écho de Nancy*, Pierre Brummel of *Le Petit Ardennais*, Delion de Launois of *La Gerbe*, Lucien Rebatet and Benoist-Méchin also received death sentences, though Béraud was pardoned by de Gaulle and the sentences of the others were eventually reduced to prison terms. For the youngest of the newspaper editors, thirty-one-year-old Lucien Combelle, the prosecutor asked for the death penalty; thanks to testimonials from Gide and others, he was given fifteen years of hard labour instead. Alain Laubreaux and Abel Bonnard, who had fled to Spain, were condemned to death in absentia.

Sentenced to longer or shorter terms of imprisonment were Robert de Beauplan of *L'Illustration*, Benedetti of *L'Oeuvre*, Camille Fégy, editor of *La Gerbe*, Charles Tardieu, director of the *Grand Écho du nord*, Guy Crouset and Guy Zucarelli of *Les Nouveaux Temps*, Pierre Fau of *L'Union catholique*, Jean Lousteau and Claude Maubourguet of *Je suis partout*. *Je suis partout* – like similar publications – was liquidated; its assets were confiscated and warrants were issued for the arrest of its writers and staff. Those who had not fled to Latin America or somewhere in Europe were tried and sentenced to death or to life imprisonment, though the sentences were eventually commuted. Today these names mean little or nothing, but taken together they illustrate the extent to which writers and journalists were subjected to the full brunt of the purge or, as some said, made scapegoats for a nation.

And it was not just the written but also the spoken word that was murderously punished – again, not in the persons of Vichy officials who had broadcast speeches exhorting the French to collaborate with the Enemy, or of officials of the notorious Radio-Paris who worked under German direction and were responsible for what was broadcast, but the individuals who stood before the microphones. Paul Ferdonnet, 'the traitor of Stuttgart', had beamed propaganda from a German station in Stuttgart into France before the war. He was rewarded with the death penalty. Jean Hérold-Paquis, the young buffoon whose broadcast signature was the idiotic 'Like Carthage, England will be destroyed', fled from Sigmaringen to Switzerland. He was turned over to the French authorities and was also tried, sentenced to death and executed. For his pro-German and anti-Semitic broadcasts on Radio-Paris, Robert Le Vigan was condemned to ten years of hard labour, though later paroled.

It was Brasillach's case that excited the most unease. 'The treason of Brasillach is above all the treason of the intellectual', the prosecutor had told the court. The writer had used his talents to denounce people and call for their death. To this Brasillach had naturally responded, 'I believed that my writing served my country above all.' In essence the defence argued that since it could not be proved that anyone had been executed as a result of his writings, it was his opinions for which he was being tried and these did not amount to treason. The jury needed but twenty minutes to agree with the prosecutor. The conduct of the trial was hardly edifying for prosecutor, defence or jury and the outcome left many artists and intellectuals so troubled that they drafted a petition to de Gaulle, as head of the Provisional Government, appealing for clemency. Among the fifty-nine signatories were Anouilh, Claudel, Cocteau, Colette, Derain, Honegger, Mauriac, Valéry, Vlaminck and a very reluctant Camus. De Beauvoir, Gide, Picasso and Sartre were among those who refused to sign. The appeal was rejected. 'Vive la France, quand même' – 'Well, anyway, long live France' – Brasillach shouted at the end.

Even today the case remains controversial. There is no reason to doubt that Brasillach sincerely wanted the death of those he hated. De Beauvoir, among others, argued that through his writings 'he had directly collaborated with the Gestapo'. But had he really? Is there not a crucial gulf between wanting – and even publicly calling for – murder and committing it or causing it to be committed? The question enjoys a certain topicality in the early years of the twenty-first century, when expressing certain views about 'the terrorist menace' risks imprisonment.

The inequity of treatment is another problem. Fabre-Luce worked directly with the Germans by writing material explicitly intended as pro-German propaganda both on the home front and in French prison camps. After a brief internment, he was permitted to exile himself to Geneva. There for the next thirty-seven years he contributed to the neo-fascist weekly *Rivarol* and wrote no fewer than twenty-two books, not a few of which betrayed unrepentant fascist views. Far worse is the example of René Bousquet. As head of the Vichy police, he it was who, among other accomplishments, organized the infamous round-up in 1942 of thirteen thousand Jews in Paris and ten thousand in the Unoccupied Zone – the only case anywhere in Europe where Jews were deported from an unoccupied area. But government officials were understandably not keen to prosecute other government officials and, since what he did was not considered 'intelligence with the enemy', he was not tried – for nearly fifty years anyway, until in 1991 he was finally indicted for crimes against humanity. Even so, judgement came not from the court but from an assassin's bullet in 1993 while he was awaiting trial. His and other cases were frequently derailed by claims that the accused had once been arrested by the Gestapo or had late in the day helped the Resistance – as though a murderer should be let off because he had subsequently given money to a worthy charity. By far the most shocking of all was de Gaulle's pardoning of Helmut Knochen and his direct superior, General Karl Oberg, head of the Gestapo in France, for whom Bousquet had worked.

Within five years of the Liberation bygones were rapidly being treated as bygones. With the outbreak of the cold war, not so ex-*collabos* – like not so ex-Nazis in Germany – felt vindicated. The great menace to the West was, as they had always said and as had now come to be generally recognized, an aggressive Soviet Union. And so Rebatet was released from prison in July 1952 and resumed a writing career that was professionally more successful than ever. Paul Morand, Vichy's ambassador first to Bucharest and then to Bern, had remained in Switzerland until it was clear he would not be prosecuted. He returned to France in 1954; in 1968 the Académie Française disgraced itself by electing him a member. In February 1950 a Paris court reduced Céline's sentence to a year in prison and then later dropped even that with a formal amnesty. Tired and ill, he returned to France in July 1951. With the publication of *D'un Château l'autre* in 1957 his professional rehabilitation began. Through it all, two friends at least had remained loyal. Karl and Alice Epting visited twice and found him, despite his broken health, as animated as ever, drenching them in a never-ending torrent of verbiage in the fidgety style of his writing. His novels, having been banned for a time after the Liberation, gradually became popular again. He himself did not. 'Very few', Alice Epting commented, 'accompanied him to the grave.'

All in all 'de-collaboration' in France was as much a failure as 'de-Nazification' in Germany, and for essentially the same reasons. There were too many who were guilty and too many at the top – not least de Gaulle and Adenauer – who did not want them to be held to account in the interest of social harmony. The injustice of singling out authors while taking no action against the publishers of their words offended many Resistance figures, none more than Bruller. Yet at dinner with de Gaulle a few weeks after the Liberation he realized that the general had no intention of allowing a purge of publishers. And so, while *collabo* newspapers had the good taste at least to go out of business or change their names, publishing houses went on as nonchalantly in 1944 as they had in 1940. Not only that. During the early post-Liberation months when they were reporting the execution of writers, newspapers were at same time running ads – sometimes even on the same page – by the publishers who had brought out their works during the Occupation.

The 'cultural Occupation' vanished from one day to the next. The dark years had been so miserable it was only human that people tried to forget them. Apart from a smattering of German that a few earnest students may have picked up in language classes, pleasant recollections that some may have retained of German musical performances and translations of a few German classics that gathered dust in bookstalls, the German cultural presence disappeared on the heels of the retreating Wehrmacht and its agents.

And what of those agents who had played a central role in the enslavement of a nation? Abetz went into hiding in the Black Forest but was eventually tracked down and turned over to the French authorities. Epting was also taken into custody – to his enraged incredulity at the injustice of it all – and released a few years later. Some of the other alumni of the embassy and Institute were also interned for a short time but otherwise escaped punishment. When Abetz was brought to trial in a Paris court in July 1949 many of the older figures in the Quai d'Orsay and le Tout-Paris worried – unnecessarily as it turned out – that the former ambassador's testimony would expose them as willing *collabos* and beneficiaries of his black funds and other favours. The discreet Abetz was sentenced to twenty years of hard labour, primarily for his role in the deportation of Jews and the theft of art works. Immediately his ex-colleagues Achenbach, Rahn, Grimm – supported by such characters as Ernst Jünger and General Speidel, among many others – launched a relentless campaign for his pardon, which resulted in his release in 1954. While in prison he had written an apologia that was smuggled out and published by a firm whose director was none other than Karl Epting. In these pages, Abetz argued that the war was the fault of Churchill, Blum, Daladier and Reynaud. During the Occupation he had tried to protect the poor Jews but it was the French themselves who deported them, so what could he do? As for himself, he had tried his very best to make the Occupation pleasant. Instead of being grateful, the French had thrown him in jail. 'Unglaublich!'

Incredible, indeed. Abetz's feelings of resentment were shared by his ex-colleagues. They had also forgotten everything and learned nothing. Their cynicism, hypocrisy and arrogance were sublime. Even after the war they could not recognize the self-deception of considering themselves sincere Francophiles while planning to turn France into a state that would joyously – or by compulsion – accept a submissive position in a Nazi empire and devote her resources, material and otherwise, to serving the interests of the Third Reich. None of them ever repented. Quite the contrary. In their view they and French *collabos* were ahead of their time. The dark years were for them a sunny period which they for evermore looked back on nostalgically.

In this spirit the old embassy/German Institute crowd reassembled and in the early 1950s formed a Franco-German Circle, a Lazarus-type resurrection of the old France-Germany Committee set up by Abetz in 1935. 'Circle' was certainly the correct name because that described exactly the state of affairs – *corsi e ricorsi*. Although even they did not have the face to say so explicitly in public, they regarded the postwar European integration movement simply as a different brand name for the united Europe their Führer had in mind. Not only that, they used the postwar European ideal for their personal rehabilitation. Ernst Achenbach was not only elected to the Bundestag and the European Parliament, but even managed to have himself nominated to be a European community commissioner, withdrawing only after the exposure of his involvement, albeit minimal, in the deportation of Jews. Hans Speidel was slickest of all in cloaking his role in the Occupation. In 1957 he returned to Paris, not to stand trial as an important officer in a harsh military government but as grand military commander of all the NATO land forces. Heller was engaged by a publication established in 1946 called *Merkur*, which had the suggestive subtitle of 'German Journal for European Thought'. In 1981 he brazenly returned to Paris and presented himself to a French TV audience – which innocently swallowed his humbug – as the benevolent promoter of French letters during the Occupation. As for Abetz, after being sprung from prison he became European editor of the right-wing weekly *Der Fortschritt*, an odd name for a publication dedicated to the opposite of progress. As he returned home one night in May 1958 from giving a speech on his favourite topic – 'Frankreich und Deutschland' – his car spun out of control and he was killed. The circumstances of the accident raised suspicions. Was it an act of revenge by a victim of the Occupation? Or was it to forestall – or put a stop to – his blackmailing of French political figures with information gleaned during the Occupation?

In his *The Silence of the Sea* Bruller contrasted a cultured German officer, in civilian life a musician who admired French culture, with a brutal German officer who wanted to see France destroyed, body and soul. The real-life characters in *this* story – Abetz, Epting, Bremer, Heller, Grimm and the others – could have stepped off Bruller's pages, but with the crucial difference that each of them incorporated in himself both officers in the book. Here, again, is that remarkable and baffling trait of the Third Reich and its officials – the combination of culture and barbarism.

By the end of its second catastrophic civil war, Europe had come close to destroying itself for good. Yet somehow it pulled itself back together. Two developments in particular helped to restore the old continent to a semblance of well-being. As if to prove the sacred teaching that all things work together for the good of them that love gold, the Germans produced an economic miracle that became the motor for unprecedented European material prosperity. In the meantime the French were demonstrating the historic truism that all's well that ends badly. France had won the First World War but lost the peace; she lost the Second but won the peace. During the Occupation, it was the products of culture more than anything else that helped people to get through the hard times and the nation to preserve some sense of self-respect. Following the Liberation, it was again the products of culture that helped overcome the trauma of Occupation. 'I repeated to myself – it is over, it is over. It is over – now everything can begin.' With those words Simone de Beauvoir greeted the sight of retreating German soldiers. 'To be twenty or twenty-five in September '44 seemed a tremendous stroke of luck', she went on to say. 'Everything was possible. Journalists, writers, up-and-coming filmmakers argued, planned and excitedly reached decisions as though the future depended only on them.'

Out of this *état d'esprit* erupted a burst of artistic energy that briefly lit a darkened continent. Oddly – or not – the vitality and creativity of those early postwar years flourished in a mood of intellectual fatalism and pessimism. 'Existentialism' was the great buzzword in Paris in those days. As a philosophy it had its origins in the writings of Sartre and Camus. The titles of their books are a giveaway – Sartre's philosophical work, *L'Être et le néant* (*Being and Nothingness*), his novel *La Nausée* and his plays *Les Mouches* and *Huis clos* along with Camus's novel *L'Étranger* and *Le Mythe de Sisyphe*. But none expressed the mood more clearly than the title of a work by Sartre's disciple Colette Audry – *On joue perdant* (You're Bound to Lose).

At a time of anxiety and self-questioning, after established values had suffered a staggering blow, the existentialists were advising people to make the best of their predicament. The human race, they said, finds itself in the same situation as Sisyphus – constantly having to push the rock up the hill only to have it roll down again *e poi da capo*. Is life worth living, then, or is it too absurd, too aleatory, too pointless? 'There is only one really serious philosophical question,' are the opening words of *Le Mythe de Sisyphe*, 'and that is suicide.' The existentialist response was simple. Play the impossible game of life with as much courage and dignity as possible. Pascal Pia, editor of the famous leftist daily *Combat*, translated this into practical terms when he once told his staff, 'We shall try to make this a reasonable newspaper but because the world is absurd, we shall fail.'

In the face of a pessimism that would have left Schopenhauer smiling with approval, artistic and intellectual life thrived and to some extent reflected the existentialist ethic. The theatre boasted playwrights Arthur Adamov, Samuel Beckett, Jean Genet and Eugène Ionesco and the *théâtre de l'absurde*. 'Absurdism' also touched French music through John Cage. Among the large number of noted composers – Messiaen, Poulenc, Milhaud, Koechlin and Boulez – none was more inventive than Boulez. Rejecting Cage's technique of blind chance as well as total serialism, he developed a method he called 'aleatoric' which involved the break-up of the traditional concept of form. Painting was still dominated by Matisse, Léger and Braque, who went on until nearly the mid-Fifties, and Picasso who went on longer still. That art must begin again from zero was an understandable attitude in 1944 and this notion was the starting point of two new notable figures of the early postwar period, Jean Dubuffet and Alberto Giacometti. In literature the influence of Sartre and Camus was overpowering. The older generation, such as Gide, Mauriac and Aragon, were passing into history. A remarkable new development came from the writings of Marguerite Duras, Marguerite Yourcenar and even Françoise Sagan, which challenged bourgeois convention and in particular the place of women in society. De Beauvoir's *Le Deuxième Sexe* (*The Second Sex*) and *Mémoires d'une jeune fille rangée* (*Memoirs of a Dutiful Daughter*) can be said to have launched the postwar feminist movement. But film – the *nouvelle vague* – was perhaps the most dynamic of the arts during this period. Claude Chabrol, Jean-Luc Godard, Alain Resnais, Eric Rohmer and François Truffaut – all children of existentialism – were among the best known of the new filmmakers.

For all its effervescence, the cultural climate of Paris was now vastly different from before the war. Intellectual and cultural life had become deeply politicized. *L'art pour l'art* was supplanted by *littérature engagée*, social indifference by social responsibility, the *Nouvelle Revue Française* by Sartre's *Les Temps modernes*. The dominant intellectual tone of the prewar years had been leftist but not overtly committed – many cultural figures were communist but few were Communist. After the Liberation a great number were not merely committed to the left, they were militant Communists, even Stalinists. The party exploited its role in the Occupation for all it was worth – and more. 'We are the party of the 75,000' – the number of members it claimed had been executed. Galtier-Boissière could not resist poking fun at this: 'Of the 29,000 French people executed during the Occupation, 75,000 were Communists.' But there was no denying that Communists had formed the backbone of the Resistance, and it was also a widespread view in France that Hitler had been defeated not by Britain and the United States but by the Red Army. In short, being a member or open sympathizer of the Communist party became a badge of moral and political righteousness. Picasso is an example of the phenomenon.

It had been the disgrace of many prewar intellectuals and artists that they failed to distinguish between the Germany of Weimar and the Germany of Hitler. Following the Liberation many did not wish to see the difference between democratic socialism and Stalinism. This partly explains another important change in French cultural life. With the growing rivalry between America and the Soviet Union, most intellectuals and artists sided with the Russians. The far left now took over from the far right leadership of anti-Americanism in culture as much as in politics. From that time on – and, to be sure, for reasons of simple national pride as well – American culture was viewed as a menace. It was synthetic, lowbrow, vulgar, crass, violent, shallow, anti-intellectual. Worst of all it was extremely popular, offering something domestic cultural life did not. Hence the dread that, having survived the German Occupation, France's civilizing mission was being undermined by imperialist, lowbrow American un-culture.

But there was another change, the most significant and permanent of all. By 1945 something had been lost to Europe that could never be recovered. In destroying the international role of Paris in the arts, the war had undermined Europe's sense of cultural supremacy. No longer was Paris the Mecca of Western culture. For the first time the École de Paris was purely French. And for the first time the centre of the visual arts had shifted to America. Paris as the centre of an Arts International had vanished for good. By the mid-Sixties it had settled down to being a museum of museums. And the Judgement of Paris? Destroyed by the war, it no longer cut any ice. Like the culprit in Christie's mystery story, most people by the twenty-first century had no idea even what it meant.

SOURCES

Chapters 1 and 2

Dwarfs on the shoulders of giants and all that. It was standing on the shoulders of various scholars, writers and first-hand observers that I first surveyed the bizarre situation of France during the Occupation. The quality of scholarship and writing is outstanding – intelligent, reliable and readable – and deficient only on the cultural side. Among the works in English that were most helpful for general background were Ian Ousby, *Occupation: The Ordeal of France 1940–1944*; H.R. Kedward, *Occupied France: Collaboration and Resistance*; Julian Jackson, *France: The Dark Years*; and David Pryce-Jones, *Paris in the Third Reich*.

Of unique interest was *Decline or Renewal: France since the 1930s* by Stanley Hoffmann, who not only lived through the Occupation but lived through it as a young man in danger of his life. His essays 'The Vichy Circle of French Conservatives', 'Self-Ensnared: Collaboration with Nazi Germany' and 'In the Looking Glass: Sorrow and Pity?', in particular, have a rare authenticity. I also benefited from a variety of essays in *Collaboration in France*, edited by Gerhard Hirschfeld and Patrick Marsh. Robert Paxton's ground-breaking *Vichy France* provided general guidance; Robert Gildea, *Marianne in Chains*, elucidated political life on the local level. Richard Vinen, *France, 1934–1970*, placed the Occupation in a broader historical context.

Among works in French, Philippe Burrin's rightly praised *La France à l'heure allemande* was an outstanding guide, with several valuable chapters on cultural affairs. Helpful also was Hervé Le Boterf, *La Vie parisienne sous l'Occupation*, a detailed but at times erroneous account of cultural life in Paris. Other works worth mentioning are Robert Aron, *Histoire de Vichy*; Henri Amouroux, *La Vie des Français sous l'Occupation* (2 vols); and *La Grande Histoire de l'Occupation* (7 vols); Henri Michel, *Paris allemand* (an invaluable account of life in Paris in the dark years) and *Histoire de la France libre*; and Pascal Ory, *La France allemande*. Jean-Pierre Azéma and François Bédarida (eds), *Le Régime de Vichy et les Français,* is a useful political-social history. Jacques Varin (ed.), *Été 40,* reproduces newspaper articles published during the summer of 1940.

I also found helpful both in these chapters and throughout the book a number of general works on cultural topics. These include *La Vie quotidienne des écrivains et des artistes sous l'Occupation* by Gilles and Jean Robert Ragache; *L'Art de la défaite* by Laurence Bertrand Dorléac; *La Vie culturelle sous l'Occupation* by Stéphanie Corcy; and *La Vie culturelle sous Vichy* by Jean-Pierre Rioux (ed.).

Information on the whereabouts of artists and intellectuals at the time of the debacle was compiled from a variety of memoirs and histories. Titles referred to but not mentioned in the text include Simone de Beauvoir, *La Force de l'âge* and *La Force des choses*; Victor Serge, *Memoirs of a Revolutionary*; Andy Marino, *American Pimpernel* (about Varian Fry); Sylvia Beach, *Shakespeare and Company*; Myriam Chimènes (ed.), *Francis Poulenc: Correspondance 1910–1963*; Paul Léautaud, *Journal littéraire*; and Mark Polizzotti, *Revolution of the Mind: The Life of André Breton*. Véronique Rebatet's effusions were quoted in David Pryce-Jones, *Paris in the Third Reich*. Simenon's anti-hate movement is mentioned in Pierre Assouline's biography, *Simenon*. Guéhenno and Galtier-Boissière are cited in the sources for chapter 6. Other books worth mentioning are Suzanne Blum, *Vivre sans la Patrie* and André Breton, *La Clé des champs*.

Particularly helpful for the early post-Liberation period were Antony Beevor and Artemis Cooper, *Paris after the Liberation,* and Paul Webster and Nicholas Powell, *Saint-Germain-des-Prés*.

Chapters 3 and 4

Descriptions of the jolly life – for the Germans and le Tout-Paris – were found in Pryce-Jones and any number of diaries and memoirs. Fugitive comments by the Invaders themselves came from German sources, notably Ernst Jünger, *Das Erste Pariser Tagebuch* and *Das Zweite Pariser Tagebuch*; Albert Speer, *Inside the Third Reich*; Arno Breker, *Paris, Hitler et moi*; and many of the books cited immediately below. The Breker exhibition is widely mentioned, most fully in Ragache and Pryce-Jones. Cocteau's comments come from his diary (see chapter 9). The remarks of von Collenberg and Molden are quoted in Pryce-Jones, those of Lifar in his autobiography (see chapter 8), those of Corinne Luchaire in her memoir, *Ma Drôle de vie* and Fabienne Jamet's in her book, *One Two Two*.

German cultural policy is nowhere better described than in Eckard Michels's scholarly work *Das Deutsche Institut in Paris 1940–1944*, which I found indispensable. I am also indebted to Barbara Lambauer, whose *Otto Abetz et les Français* offers the fullest picture of the ambassador's activities. Useful for background were Rudolf Rahn, *Ruhelos Leben*; Hans Speidel, *Aus unserer Zeit*; Lucien Steinberg, *Les Allemands en France*; Otto Abetz, *Das Offene Problem*; Hermann Eich, *Die unheimlichen Deutschen*; Friedrich Grimm, *Frankreich-Berichte* as well as his *Mit offenem Visier*. Karl Epting left three books: *Frankreich im Widerspruch*, *Aus dem Cherchemidi* and *Frankreichs goldene Jahre*. More interesting are his wife's deathbed reminiscences, *Pariser Begegnungen*. Wolfgang Benz, Gerhard Otto and Anabella Weismann (eds), *Kultur, Propaganda, Öffentlichkeit*, compares German cultural policy in a variety of Occupied countries. Gérard Loiseaux's *La Littérature de la défaite et de la collaboration* is a highly useful survey of the German role in French intellectual life during the Occupation. Brasillach's trenchant comment on the Institute's importance as a centre of cultural collaboration is in Alice Kaplan, *The Collaborator: The Trial and Execution of Robert Brasillach*, and Pierre Assouline, *L'Épuration des intellectuels*. In his *Journal sous l'Occupation*, Marcel Jouhandeau gives a first-hand account of the writers' trip to Weimar.

The collaboration of publishers is described in Pascal Fouché, *L'Édition française sous l'occupation* and Pierre Assouline's biography *Gaston Gallimard*. Also worthwhile are Assouline's *Le Fleuve Combelle* and his biography *Simenon*. The Otto List (*Liste Otto*) is a facsimile of the 'Harvard Copy', published by the Harvard College Library. For subsequent editions of the modified list, I am indebted to the Hoover Institution archives.

The genius for survival of Parisian hostesses is mentioned in passing in any number of books and memoirs. An adoring account of the life, though not the loves or collaboration, of Florence Gould is given by Gilles Cornut-Gentile and Philippe Michel-Thiriet, *Florence Gould*.

Chapter 5

In writing about the *cité phocéenne*, I am much indebted to Jean-Michel Guiraud's *La Vie intellectuelle et artistique à Marseille à l'époque de Vichy et sous l'Occupation 1940–1944* and his 'Marseille, cité-refuge des écrivains' in Jean-Pierre Rioux (ed.), *La Vie culturelle sous Vichy*. Another work on Marseille is Paul Jankowski, *Communism and Collaboration*. Many of the quotations of exiled painters come from Michèle C. Cone, *Artists under Vichy*. I also benefited from her discussion of *l'art Maréchal*. Information about Provençal regionalism came from Guiraud. Lévi-Strauss told his story in *Tristes Tropiques*, Consuelo de Saint-Exupéry told hers in *Oppède* and Peggy Guggenhim recounted hers in *Confessions of an Art Addict*. Dorgelès's nice figure of speech is in his *La Drôle de guerre*, André Roussin's from his *Rideau gris et habit vert* and Maurice Chevalier's from *Ma Route et mes chansons*.

Chapter 6

Gisèle Sapiro, *La Guerre des écrivains* is a veritable encyclopaedia of the literary scene. Albrecht Betz and Stefan Martens (eds), *Les Intellectuels et l'Occupation, 1940–1944,* is a compilation of scholarly essays primarily on writing and radio. Jean Bruller (Vercors) tells his story in *La Bataille du Silence*). James W. Brown and Lawrence D. Stokes provide a historical and literary commentary about the novel in their *The Silence of the Sea*. In *Gaston Gallimard*, Pierre Assouline also comments on the novel and its historical context. Combelle's remark about ideological commitment was made in an interview in Pryce-Jones. For Camus I have relied on Olivier Todd's biography, *Albert Camus*.

The primary source for Gide's life during the Occupation is his diary, *Journal 1889–1949*. Also helpful were Claude Mauriac's *Conversations avec André Gide* as well as a number of biographies, in particular Justin O'Brien's *Portrait of André Gide*. George D. Painter, *Gide*, Claude Martin, *Gide*, Marc Beigbeder, *André Gide,* and Albert J. Guerard, *André Gide,* were also consulted.

The titles of the published editions of the diaries of Jeanson, Guéhenno, Fabre-Luce and Drieu la Rochelle are all cited in the text. Galtier-Boissière published four volumes of diaries (*Mon Journal pendant l'Occupation, Mon Journal depuis la Libération, Mon Journal dans la drôle de paix* and *Mon Journal dans la grande pagaïe*) as well as *Mémoires d'un Parisien*. F.J. Grover's *Drieu la Rochelle* and Huguette Bouchardeau's *Elsa Triolet* were among many helpful biographies. Out of the enormous bibliography on Céline, I have principally relied on François Gibault's biography, *Céline 1932–1944*, and Nicholas Hewitt, *The Life of Céline*. Rebatet's comment on the novelist's arrival at Sigmaringen is quoted in the latter. I am grateful to the Hoover Institution archives for a copy of Hermann Bickler's report about his meetings with Céline.

Chapter 7

For general background information on painters, I have relied on Corcy, *La Vie culturelle sous Vichy*; Dorléac, *L'Art de la défaite*; Cone, *Artists Under Vichy*; John Russell, *The Meanings of Modern Art*; and Gaston Diehl, *La Peinture en France dans les années noires*.

I am much indebted to Steven A. Nash (ed.) for *Picasso and the War Years* and Gertje Utley, *Picasso: The Communist Years*. I also found helpful Roland Penrose, *Picasso: His Life and Work*; Brassaï, *Conversations avec Picasso*; Jaime

Sabartés, *Picasso: An Intimate Portrait*; Françoise Gilot and Carlton Lake, *Life with Picasso*; and Françoise Gilot, *Matisse et Picasso*. The figures for Picasso's wartime output came from Mary-Margaret Goggin, 'Picasso and his Art during the German Occupation' (Stanford University doctoral dissertation). The rejection of Picasso's request for naturalization was published in 'En 1940, Picasso n'était pas digne de devenir Français' in *Le Monde*, 21 April 2004. The letter from Christian Zervos to Alfred Barr is held by the Museum of Modern Art in New York.

For Matisse I relied principally on Hilary Spurling, *Matisse the Master*. Jean Clair and Antoine Terrasse, *Bonnard–Matisse Correspondance*, as well as Gilot, *Matisse et Picasso*, were helpful. I found virtually no information about André Fougeron during the Occupation. There are a few relevant illustrations in *André Fougeron 1913–1998*, an exhibition catalogue from the Musée National d'Histoire et d'Art de Luxembourg.

Jean Cassou tells his story in *Une Vie pour la liberté*. His activities are also widely mentioned in other books about the Occupation.

For the story of art dealing, I am grateful to Pierre Assouline, *An Artful Life: A Biography of D.H. Kahnweiler*. Kahnweiler's own words are recorded in Daniel-Henry Kahnweiler with Francis Crémieux, *My Galleries and Painters*. Maurice Laffaille tells his story in *Chronique d'une galerie de tableaux sous l'Occupation*. Martin Fabiani does *not* tell his story in *Quand j'étais marchand de tableaux*. I have pieced together this account of his activities primarily from Galtier-Boissière, *Mon Journal dans la drôle de paix* and *Mémoires d'un Parisien*, and Jean-Paul Morel, *C'était Ambroise Vollard*. Additional detail on the 'Aryanization' of art galleries was found in Hector Feliciano, *The Lost Museum*, and Laurence Bertrand Dorléac, *L'Art de la défaite*.

The text of Vlaminck's attack on Picasso appeared in *Comoedia*, 6 June 1942. André Lhote's reply was published in the same paper a week later. Information about the artists' trip to Germany came largely from Dorléac and Corcy.

In the formidable literature about Surrealists and other painters in exile, Martica Sawin's *Surrealism in Exile* provided an incomparable overview. The photograph of the fourteen artists at the *Artists in Exile* exhibition can be found there. The principal sources for Fernand Léger were Gaston Diehl, *F. Léger*; Haus der Kunst (Munich) exhibition catalogue, *F. Léger*. Léger's own *Correspondance de guerre* is about his life in the Great War. Information and quotations by and about Peggy Guggenheim came from Peggy Guggenheim, *Confessions of an Art Addict*, and Anton Gill, *Art Lover*. Marc Chagall's exile is related in Ingo F. Walther and Rainer Metzger, *Chagall*. Jean Hélion, *They Shall Have Me*, tells his story as a war prisoner. Calvin Tomkins, *Duchamp*; Stephanie Terenzio, *The Collected Writings of Robert Motherwell*; Steven Naifeh and Gregory White Smith, *Pollock: An American Saga*; Deborah Solomon, *Pollock:*

A Biography; Mark Stevens and Annalyn Swan, *De Kooning: An American Master*; and William Rubin and Carolyn Lanchner, *André Masson*, were all indispensable. Solomon's article 'Surrealism in Exile' appeared in the *New York Times* on 8 October 1995.

Chapter 8

At more than one point in this chapter, I benefited from the volume of essays *La Vie musicale sous Vichy*, compiled and edited by Myriam Chimènes, based on papers presented at a conference on the subject in Paris in 1999. Among these contributions, I might invidiously single out the following as of particular help: Myriam Chimènes, 'Alfred Cortot et la politique musicale du gouvernement de Vichy'; Manuela Schwartz, 'La musique, outil majeur de la propagande culturelle des Nazis'; Sandrine Gransgambe, 'Le Réunion des théâtres lyriques nationaux'; Agnès Callu, 'Le Conservatoire de Paris: les réformes structurelles'; Jean Gribenski, 'L'Exclusion des juifs du Conservatoire'; Leslie Sprout, 'Les commandes de Vichy, aube d'une ère nouvelle'; Marie-Claire Mussat, 'Rennes, capitale musicale de la France'; Françoise Taliano-des Garets, 'La musique, enjeu politique dans Bordeaux occupé'; and Jean-Marie Jacono, 'Marseille en liberté surveillée'. I am also indebted to François Porcile, *Les Conflits de la musique française 1940–1965*; Chimènes (ed.), *Francis Poulenc: Correspondance 1910–1963*; Stéphanie Corcy, *La Vie culturelle sous Vichy*; and Laurence Bertrand Dorléac, *L'Art de la défaite*.

   For Alfred Cortot I have drawn both on Chimènes's chapter mentioned above and, *faute de mieux*, on Bernard Gavoty's biography, *Alfred Cortot*. Nicole Casanova's biography, *Isolde 39 – Germaine Lubin*, though brief, was an essential source. Also helpful were Lanfranco Rasponi's chapter on Lubin in *The Last of the Prima Donnas* as well as Max de Schauensee, 'Lubin Revisited', in *Opera News*, 22 January 1966. Articles in the German press (*Frankfurter Zeitung* and *Dresdner Nachrichten*) as well as Goebbels's diary entry for 27 July 1939 on the critical reception of her Bayreuth performances in 1938 and 1939 added useful detail. For Rouché, Lifar and the Paris Opera, various chapters in Chimènes and Porcile's books were helpful. Lifar's fantasy that Hitler caressed his arm is mentioned in Arthur Gold and Robert Fizdale, *Misia: The Life of Misia Sert*. In assessing the trends in Conservatory performances, D.K. Holoman's complete list of its concerts was indispensable.

   I am indebted to Rebecca Rischin, *For the End of Time,* for its account of Messiaen's famous Quartet. Nigel Simeone's review article, 'Messiaen and Concerts of Pléiade', in *Music and Letters*, November 2000, was a helpful commentary.

Chapter 9

The main source for Cocteau is, appropriately, Cocteau – his *Journal 1942–1945* and, to a much lesser extent, his *Journal d'un inconnu*. Francis Steegmuller's highly polished biography, *Cocteau*, was written before the publication of the *Journal 1942–1945* and is of no help for the Occupation period. Biographies by Jean Touzot and Claude Arnaud, while defensive, contain interesting detail, as does John Richardson, *The Sorcerer's Apprentice*. Neal Oxenhandler, *Scandal and Parade*, was helpful in elucidating the plays.

Sacha Guitry, *Quatre ans d'occupations* was essential reading for his self-exculpation. James Harding's uncritical biography, *Sacha Guitry*, was useful. Jacques Siclier, *Guitry* also discusses the films. Hans Speidel's comment about Guitry comes from his autobiography, *Aus unserer Zeit*. Testimony of Guitry's eager fraternization with German officials came from Paul Léautaud, *Journal littéraire*, volume 13, Jünger's diary and Alice Epting's *Pariser Begegnungen*.

For background about the theatre, Serge Added, *Le Théâtre dans les années Vichy* and his 'L'euphorie théâtrale dans Paris occupé' in Rioux, ed., *La Vie culturelle sous Vichy*, were a help.

For film I am indebted to François Garçon's essay 'Ce curieux âge d'or des cinéastes français', in Rioux, ed., *La Vie culturelle sous Vichy*, and Jean-Pierre Bertin-Maghit, *Le Cinéma français sous l'Occupation*. The figures showing Hollywood's domination of the French screen come from Garçon. I have relied largely on André Brunelin, *Jean Gabin*, for biographical information on the actor. Jürgen Reitz, *Jean Gabin*, and Claude Gauteur and André Bernard, *Jean Gabin*, were also consulted. For information about Marcel Pagnol I am much indebted to Ramond Castans's biography, *Marcel Pagnol*. Pierre Billard's essay on Clouzot and *Le Corbeau* was especially helpful. The information about Georges Simenon, along with Simone Signoret's comment on collaboration, come from Pierre Assouline, *Simenon*.

Chapter 10

Helpful in this chapter was Pierre Assouline, *L'Épuration des intellectuels* and Jean-Paul Cointet, *Expier Vichy: L'épuration en France 1943–1958*. The issue of intellectual collaboration, a central issue in the trial of Robert Brasillach, is discussed in Alice Kaplan's *The Collaborator*, already cited. I have also benefited from Pascal Ory's *Les Collaborateurs*. The Eptings' visit to Céline is described in Alice Epting, *Pariser Begegnungen*. Much of the information about the postwar adventures of German Occupation officials comes from Barbara Lambauer, *Otto Abetz et les Français* and Otto Abetz, *Das Offene Problem*. Simone de Beauvoir words are in *La Force des choses*.

INDEX

ACKNOWLEDGEMENTS

For information relating to the chapter on painters, I am grateful to Sylvie Fresnault of the Picasso Museum in Paris, Molly Shea of the Museum of Modern Art in New York and Florence Monnier of the Fondation Maeght in St Paul de Vence. For the chapter on music, it is my pleasure to thank Myriam Chimènes and Philippe Olivier for reading the draft chapter as well as Henri-Louis de la Grange and Frère Thierry-Jean de Brunhoff for recollections of Cortot and his 1947 performances. Thanks are also due Didier Bonnet and Robert Tuggle for comments on Germaine Lubin. For responding to a number of general questions, I am grateful to Pierre Assouline.

The resources of the Paris Opera library, the Centre de Documentation Musicale in Paris, the Fondation Maeght library in St Paul de Vence, the Metropolitan Opera archive and the Hoover Institution archives in Stanford were of great assistance in my research.

My greatest debt is to the intellectuals and artists who lived through the Occupation and told their stories in the diaries, memoirs and autobiographies that form the foundation of this book.

That said, the book would not have been published – or even written – without the encouragement of my agent, Anthea Morton-Saner, and Robert Baldock at Yale University Press.

Hearty thanks are due James Leonard for reading the entire text and catching factual and conceptual blunders, to Ina Cooper for her warm support in reading an early draft, and to Sally Ciampa for prompt research assistance.

PHOTOGRAPH ACKNOWLEDGEMENTS

Illustrations nos 1 and 13 are reproduced by permission of Art Media/HIP/TopFoto; no. 2 (from the Peggy Guggenheim Collection, Venice) by permission of the Solomon R. Guggenheim Foundation, New York; nos 3 and 19 by permission of TopFoto; nos 4, 5, 6, 11 and 14 by permission of LAPI/Roger-Viollet; nos 7, 9 (photo by Boris Lipnitzki) and 15 (photo by Pierre Jahan) by permission of Roger-Viollet/Getty Images; no. 8 by permission of the Pierpont Morgan Library, New York (MA5020); nos 10 (photo by Brassaï, Simone de Beauvoir in the Café de Flore, 1945, from a private collection), 12 (photo by Brassaï, Picasso with *Women at their Toilette*, 1939, from the Musée Picasso, Paris) and 20 (photo by Brassaï, taken after a performance of *Le Désir attrapé par la queue*, 1944, from the Musée Picasso, Paris) © Estate Brassaï/RMN; no. 16 (photo by Serge de Sazo) by permission of RAPHO/Camera Press, London; no 17 by permission of the Imperial War Museum, London; no 18 by permission of Henri Cartier-Bresson/Magnum Photos.